MASSIVELY PARALLEL
GLOBALIZATION

SUNY series, James N. Rosenau series in Global Politics
———————
David C. Earnest, editor

MASSIVELY PARALLEL GLOBALIZATION

Explorations in Self-Organization and World Politics

DAVID C. EARNEST

STATE UNIVERSITY OF NEW YORK PRESS

Published by
STATE UNIVERSITY OF NEW YORK PRESS, ALBANY

© 2015 State University of New York

All rights reserved

Printed in the United States of America

No part of this book may be used or reproduced in any manner whatsoever without written permission. No part of this book may be stored in a retrieval system or transmitted in any form or by any means including electronic, electrostatic, magnetic tape, mechanical, photocopying, recording, or otherwise without the prior permission in writing of the publisher.

For information, contact
State University of New York Press, Albany, NY
www.sunypress.edu

Production, Laurie D. Searl
Marketing, Anne M. Valentine

Library of Congress Cataloging-in-Publication Data

Earnest, David C.
 Massively parallel globalization : explorations in self-organization and world politics / David C. Earnest.
   pages cm. — (SUNY series, James N. Rosenau series in global politics)
 Includes bibliographical references and index.
 ISBN 978-1-4384-5661-4 (hardcover : alk. paper)
 ISBN 978-1-4384-5660-7 (pbk. : alk. paper)
 ISBN 978-1-4384-5662-1 (e-book)
 1. Political sociology. 2. Social networks—Political aspects.
 3. Globalization—Political aspects. 4. World politics—21st century. I. Title.

JA76.E28 2015
306.2—dc23   2014027595

10 9 8 7 6 5 4 3 2 1

To Jim, Simon, Marty, and Bill

We have to look for power sources here, and distribution networks we were never taught, routes of power our teachers never imagined, or were encouraged to avoid . . . we have to find meters whose scales are unknown in the world, draw our own schematics, getting feedback, making connections, reducing the error, trying to learn the real function . . .

—Thomas Pynchon, *Gravity's Rainbow*

CONTENTS

LIST OF ILLUSTRATIONS ix

ACKNOWLEDGMENTS xi

CHAPTER ONE
The Gyre: Rethinking Systems in World Politics 1

CHAPTER TWO
Agents and Networks: Complex Social Systems and Theories of
World Politics 29

CHAPTER THREE
The Advantage of Size: Why Large Groups Solve Coordination
Problems Better than Small Ones 57

CHAPTER FOUR
Dividing the Pie: How Complex Networks Learn to Solve
Distributive Conflicts 77

CHAPTER FIVE
Cows Grow Trees, Nets Grow Fish: How Social Networks Manage
the Commons 101

CHAPTER SIX
Too Big to Compromise: Did Eleven Banks Block Reform
during the Great Recession? 141

CHAPTER SEVEN
Nets of Insecurity: Trade Networks, Cascading Failures, and
Economic Vulnerability 171

CHAPTER EIGHT
Conclusions: Self-Organization in World Politics   191

NOTES   201

REFERENCES   237

INDEX   259

ILLUSTRATIONS

FIGURES

3.1.	Active nonlinear test's maximization of periods of discord, over 40 generations of the test	69
3.2.	An example of a failure to coordinate the social choice	70
3.3.	An example of a coordinated social choice at $t = 24$	71
4.1.	Normal-form representation of the four two-person games	84
4.2.	Effect of memory on average player score, twelve-player rules of the road game	93
5.1.	Mean appropriator scores for each information rule, by technology and memory	126
5.2.	Average survival time for each information rule, by technology and memory	127
5.3.	Mean appropriator score standardized per time step and percentage of simulations in which the ecosystem collapsed, by information rule	129
6.1.	Battle of the sexes game and extensions for the Basel simulation	156
7.1.	Log-log plot of the distribution of out degrees	179
7.2.	Box plot of strategy fitness by GA generation	183

TABLES

3.1.	A Condorcet decision problem among three nominal alternatives	62
3.2.	Parameters of theoretic interest as operationalized in the model	64

3.3.	Pseudo code for the Condorcet model	66
3.4.	Summary statistics for the simulations	68
3.5.	Final parameter sets as annealed by the Active Nonlinear Test	71
4.1.	Pseudo code for the distribution of gains model	86
4.2.	Distribution of strategies in 1,500 tournaments of two-player iterated prisoner's dilemma	89
4.3.	OLS regression estimates of effect on average player score	91
4.4.	Probit estimated effects on the likelihood of coordination	94
4.5.	Probit estimated effects on the likelihood of pure cheating strategy	96
5.1.	Model parameters and expectations	114
5.2.	Pseudo code for the fisheries model	117
5.3.	Experimental results	121
5.4.	Estimated partial effect of parameters, interactions terms, and controls on player payoffs	130
5.5.	Estimated partial effects of model parameters, interaction terms, and controls on measures of social network structure	132
5.6.	Estimated partial effects of model parameters, interaction terms, and controls on likelihood of collapse	135
6.1.	Actors' orders of preferences	157
6.2.	Measures of the actual and simulated interbank networks	158
6.3.	Pseudo code for the Basel III model	160
6.4.	Experimental results with comparisons to baseline simulations	162
6.5.	Multinomial logit estimates of effect of simulation parameters on Basel game outcomes	166
7.1.	Summary statistics of the U.S. air route network	178
7.2.	Pseudo code for the air transportation network model	181
7.3.	Results of the GA experiments	185
7.4.	Most frequently selected strategy sets	187

ACKNOWLEDGMENTS

This book seeks to explain self-organization in world politics. Regrettably, book projects do not self-organize, yet one could argue that authors receive too much of the credit for what is, in the end, the enterprise of a community of scholars. Research itself is a complex adaptive social system, in which innumerable actors contribute in small yet important ways that defy easy measurement or attribution. Nevertheless, I wish to acknowledge the many colleagues and friends—a massively parallel community, if you will—to whom I have incurred numerous intellectual and practical debts.

The earliest thoughts about this project originated at the 2009 annual convention of the American Political Science Association. My good friend Matthew J. Hoffmann of the University of Toronto invited me to contribute a paper to a panel tasked with "Understanding a Complex World: Complexity Theory and Political Science." As chair of the panel, Matt helped me formulate my thinking about the relationship between complex systems theory and network theory. Thomas F. Homer-Dixon, Ian S. Lustick, and Kenneth W. Kollman, the panel's other participants, provided useful comments and suggestions—Ken Kollman in particular encouraged me to develop my argument about the relationship between game theory and agent-based modeling. Subsequent revisions of what became the first two chapters of this book benefited from the criticism and attention to detail of colleagues at the George Washington University. In particular, I thank Professor Susan Sell, Professor James Lebovic, and doctoral candidate Miles Townes.

At my home institution of Old Dominion University, several of my colleagues in the Department of Political Science & Geography and the Graduate Program in International Studies read and commented on different portions of the manuscript. Simon Serfaty in particular carefully read and reread my introductory chapter, and offered words of patient support as the manuscript worked its way through a lengthy gestation. Kurt Taylor Gaubatz read early versions of chapters 3 and 5. At various times Francis Adams, Jennifer Fish, Regina Karp, Aaron Karp, and Steve Yetiv also provided helpful suggestions and encouragement. Professors Maura Hametz, Austin Jersild,

Michael Carhart, and Jane Merritt, all of ODU's Department of History, graciously welcomed me to join a faculty writing group. The group's monthly meetings taught me a great deal about communicating effectively across disciplines. As prolific scholars, my colleagues in the Department of History also helped me rid my introductory chapter (more or less) of excessive jargon. Beyond critical evaluation, various individuals at ODU provided me with the material support to complete this book. I am indebted to the College of Arts & Letters for a Faculty Summer Research Fellowship in 2010 and research leave during the fall semester of 2011, both of which provided me with the time to perform the simulation experiments reported in chapters 4 through 7. Dr. John Sokolowski, the director of the Virginia Modeling, Analysis & Simulation Center (VMASC), graciously made available to me the center's computational resources, an invaluable access that permitted me to complete in hours those experiments that otherwise would have taken weeks. Research Associate Professor Joshua Behr of VMASC was among my earliest advocates and supporters, and facilitated my access to the center's resources. David Ralph, VMASC's director of information technology, developed a distributed computation architecture that allowed me to run experiments seamlessly across many workstations. I also thank Jessica Jones and Aaron Sander, graduate research assistants who helped me with the experiments reported in chapters 5 and 6 respectively. The innate curiosity of Christopher Ray, an MA student who volunteered to read my first chapters and who provided trenchant commentary, motivated me to write and argue with the passion of my younger days. Erika Frydenlund, a doctoral candidate at ODU, possesses a natural understanding of complex systems that through the years she has generously shared to correct my misunderstandings.

Associate Professor Emilian Kavalski, then of the University of Western Sydney and now of Australian Catholic University, introduced me to a vibrant community of complexity researchers when he invited me to present a paper to a workshop sponsored by the Academy of the Social Sciences in Australia. The spirited debate among the workshop's participants informed much of the analysis that now appears in chapter 5. Emilian's workshop also introduced me to Professors Ian Wilkinson of the University of Sydney and Louise Young of the University of Western Sydney, who in July 2011 hosted me as a visiting faculty member in the University of Sydney Business School. My five weeks in Australia introduced me to scholars and audiences who humbled me with their mastery of the concepts and methods of computational social science. In particular, Professor Emeritus Robert Marks, a distinguished economist at the University of New South Wales, invited me to deliver a paper that became chapter 6. His students at the Australian School of Business proved to be a demanding and skeptical audience, yet an unfailingly courteous and encouraging one. In general, Sydney's community of innovative complexity scholars provided me with the opportunities for creative exchange and mutual support that any book project requires.

My wife Carla and my son Zach endured this manuscript's long incubation with patience and good humor. I am grateful for their unqualified encouragement particularly when I feared the manuscript would never be published.

An earlier version of chapter 3 was originally published in *International Studies Quarterly* 52, 2 (June 2008). I thank John Wiley and Sons, the publishers of *ISQ*, for permission to adapt portions of this article for this book. I also thank three anonymous referees for their careful evaluation of the manuscript. I am solely responsible for any errors in the manuscript.

Finally, the editorial staff at the State University of New York Press has provided superb support throughout the production of this manuscript. Michael Rinella is an exceptional acquisition editor who has assembled a compelling list of complexity-related titles, to which I am honored to contribute. Rafael Chaiken answers my tedious queries with patience and good humor. Laurie Searl has adroitly supervised the production process; I thank her as well for creating the beautiful cover art. Finally, I thank Anne Valentine for her thoughtful promotion and marketing of the book. To the entire SUNY Press staff I offer my thanks for their patience whenever I have been tardy in responding to e-mails.

As I argue in the next chapter, in complex adaptive social systems actors often replicate the successful strategies of others. So it is in academia, though I am a poor mimic of the four scholars whom I am privileged to call my mentors. The late Professor James N. Rosenau of the George Washington University profoundly shaped my scholarship. Not only did he introduce me to both globalization theory and complex systems theory, but he also encouraged me to eschew disciplinary conventions and become an intellectual explorer and integrator as much as a discoverer. Professor Martha Finnemore, also of GWU, demonstrated to me the inseparable connection between graduate instruction and creative research. Eminent Scholar Simon Serfaty, my colleague at ODU, has suffered through my excessive enthusiasms and has patiently taught me how to contribute to the intellectual vibrancy of a department and university. He also has taught me how opportunities outside of the walls of academia contribute to one's intellectual rejuvenation. Finally, Dr. William J. Taylor Jr., formerly the vice president of the Center for Strategic & International Studies in Washington, D.C., was my first mentor. When I was a young researcher in the mid-1990s, Bill taught me not only how to be a professional but how to make mistakes—how to learn and grow from them, and to find in them the kernel of opportunity. In the terms of complex systems theory, in my scholarship and teaching I seek to conserve the strategies that my mentors have taught me. In human terms, with a gratitude that defies words I thank them for their investment in and care for me. My dedication of this book to Jim, Simon, Marty, and Bill is, I believe, the highest expression of thanks one friend can offer another.

ONE

THE GYRE

Rethinking Systems in World Politics

The North Pacific Gyre offers an odd yet important lesson for scholars of world politics. Consisting of four ocean currents, the gyre swirls clockwise in the North Pacific Ocean, touching the United States in the east, Japan in the west, the equator to the south, and the Aleutian Islands of Alaska to the north, while sheltering Hawaii in its central "convergence zone." While much of the gyre's approximately twenty million square kilometers are geographically remote from humans, it nevertheless harbors one of humanity's largest unintended creations: the Great Pacific Garbage Patch, "an area of widely dispersed trash that doubles in size every decade that is now believed to be roughly twice the size of Texas."[1] Others estimate the size of the patch as one-and-one-half times the size of the United States, extending to a depth of one hundred feet below the surface of the Pacific.[2] A "plastic soup" that includes degraded small particles of waste plastics, massive driftnets, and other refuse, the patch includes enough plastic to outweigh the zooplankton in the gyre by a factor of six to one, according to some estimates.[3] Because marine wildlife mistakes fine plastic particles for food, researchers have found increasing amounts of toxic chemicals in birds and fish. One concern is that these toxins will travel up the food chain with possible health consequences for the 20 percent of humanity that relies on fish for protein. This ecological nightmare arguably is a product of the global organization of production and consumption:

[T]oday plastics have invaded the most distant places, from the Bering Sea to the South Pole. Indeed, when I was exploring a remote beach past the South Point of Hawaii, I found pill bottles from India and mashed pieces of various products—oil containers, detergent jugs, plastic cups—with Russian, Korean, and Chinese writing on them. It's hard to get your brain around these connections.[4]

The Great Pacific Garbage Patch clearly fits Hardin's definition of a tragedy of the commons.[5] The world's oceans are common property, untouched by state regulation and subject to overuse by self-interested actors who spread the costs of their overconsumption across vast distances. Yet the patch also is a *system* that exhibits coherence but is not static: It grows and evolves with the currents and winds. It is, furthermore, a "system of systems," a product of the interaction of social systems with a biophysical system. The interdependent, uncoordinated decisions of billions of human beings produce unintended consequences and create positive feedbacks that make state-based regulation increasingly difficult. The patch, in other words, is self-organizing. Governments did not create it, consumers did not intend it, yet consumption choices interact with wind, water, and rain to produce a thick plastic soup covering one-quarter of the Pacific Ocean.

This book is about such self-organized systems in global politics. It examines how individuals, civil society groups, firms, nation-states, and others organize to solve—or equally importantly, fail to solve—collective action problems characterized by "complexity." Although researchers have yet to agree on a definition of complexity,[6] they appear to share a sense that complexity suggests nonlinear and/or recursive relationships between causes and effects, and consequently "limits [to] the ability of individuals to identify the full set of possible outcomes or assign probabilities to particular outcomes of specific actions."[7] How do individuals, groups, and governments make decisions when faced with an inability to assess the likelihood of the outcomes of their actions? Answers to this question may shed light on some of the most vexing problems of world politics, in which the patterns of interactions among actors are as important to solutions as are the nature of the problems themselves. Such interactions characterize the simplest of social choice problems—how do groups make decisions when choosing among three or more options?—to the far-reaching global systems that touch everyone on the planet: the climate, finance, and public health, among others.

Complexity and self-organization are defining features of world politics today. This book makes three claims of interest to observers of world politics. First, self-organization is an important but nevertheless largely ignored reality of world politics. Although several scholars in the 1990s suggested complexity theory promised to make contributions to the study of world politics, the recent scholarship has failed to build on the foundation of these works.[8] Second, the interactions that create complexity and self-organization are not random. Rather, the networked structure of interactions crucially shapes the success or failure of collective action. To illustrate the ubiquity of these networks of interaction, the book explores broadly similar patterns and dynamics across economic, ecological, and political domains of world affairs. Finally, the book illustrates that computational methods—specifically the synthesis of agent-based models, social network analysis, and genetic algorithms—are invaluable tools for studying self-organization and complexity in world politics. The emerging field of computational social science seeks to investigate complex social phenomena. By definition, complex systems have a high degree of interaction effects; instability in cause-effect relationships over time and across scales, particularly due to feedback effects; and infrequent but sudden and theoretically and politically important changes. All of these attributes make it difficult for researchers to study complexity with empirical and statistical methods. For many important events, from state failure and secession to ecological catastrophes, researchers face additional difficulties gathering relevant data.[9] Computational methods have matured rapidly in the last decade, providing most researchers with an accessible if underutilized tool for understanding self-organization and complexity in world affairs.

The imagery of world politics as a complex gyre is not new. "Things fall apart; the centre cannot hold," William Butler Yeats wrote in his famous 1920 poem *The Second Coming*. The "widening gyre" that concerned him was the apocalypse, a metaphor for the destruction and political conflict Europe suffered during and immediately after World War I.[10] Yeats wrote about an event that has profoundly influenced theories of international conflict. Scholars argue that World War I occurred because of statesmen who possessed a cult-like faith in the superiority of offensive military doctrines;[11] inflexible bureaucratic routines that spread the conflict from the Balkans to the rest of Europe;[12] and the mismanagement by statesmen of the July crisis.[13] The war was inadvertent as events in obscure places and seemingly innocuous decisions contributed to a spiral of events over which statesmen quickly lost control. In this respect, the spiral theory of inadvertent war provides one of the most compelling arguments about emergent phenomena in world politics: microdecisions produced macrobehaviors that none of the political actors desired. One cannot simply reduce the war to the preferences of the tsar, kaiser, emperor, or king. Thirty-seven million people died.

The gyre also offers a useful metaphor for the seemingly uncontrollable and unpredictable nature of world politics today. Whether it is the sudden crisis in global finance capitalism, the civil conflict in Ukraine, or climate change, like Yeats's gyre global politics seem structured and coherent and yet, in the details, are unpredictable. Rosenau has characterized contemporary world politics as "the turbulence puzzle": "It consists of complex pieces that do not fit readily together and thus serves as an endless provocation to the intellect, to our capacity to grasp those individual, organizational, and international dynamics in which actions are negations of values and outcomes are discrepant from intentions."[14] Whichever metaphor one prefers—turbulence, spirals, or the gyre—together they suggest a conceptual focus on dynamics in world politics, and on the divergence between actors, preferences, and interests at one level and structures and outcomes at another.

World politics today feature many self-organized actors that one might characterize as "complex global social systems." One may generally define a complex global social system as a massively parallel organization of social actors who transcend the constraints imposed by sovereign boundaries and physical geography. Some of these systems help nation-states and others may oppose governments. Like the Occupy Movement, skilled individuals everywhere organize themselves into coordinated groups that produce collective goods on a local, transnational, and global scale. They do so often without the direction or involvement of governments, yet these social systems have profound consequences for what might be called traditional international politics, that is, among sovereign nation-states. These systems share some common features. Social actors organize themselves. They use information technology to coordinate their efforts. By using a massively parallel architecture, they not only multiply their scarce resources but also incentivize others to join the system. These complex global social systems may reflect national allegiances, as in the case of so-called patriotic hackers, but in all cases their efforts transcend territorial constraints and national borders. Their efforts have profound consequences for states, in some cases empowering them to improve social services while in others undermining their security and legitimacy.

The study of world politics is poorly equipped to conceptualize and theorize about such complex social systems. One example is "e-medicine." In South Africa, Project Masiluleke uses text messaging to direct people to HIV clinics outside their immediate communities, helping them avoid the stigma of the disease. A similar program in Uganda has helped authorities increase testing for the disease by about 40 percent. These efforts all take advantage of the power of networks to multiply modest efforts of individuals. The two-way communication of text messaging "forces you to take a moment to think and maybe act" in a way that passive media such as newsprint, leaflets, or billboards do not.[15] Even small efforts—such as providing people a map to the nearest clinic—can quickly mobilize large numbers.[16] Text messaging reminds tuberculosis patients in Thailand to take their medicines, improving their compliance with doctor-ordered care. Similar use of cell phones allows public health officials to provide basic care to remote villages in Mexico. The use of cell phones thus allows public health authorities to partner with private providers and extend scarce resources in places lacking adequate public health infrastructure.[17]

"Rumor registries" and crisis maps are other forms of self-organized social action. The Ushaihidi project empowered Kenyans to use cell phones to report postelection violence in 2007 and plotted these reports on an online map for others to read and to which to contribute new reports. Similar self-organized maps allowed humanitarian organizations to prioritize their efforts after the Haitian (2010) and Japanese earthquakes (2011) and the Pakistani floods of 2010. Such tools are not merely for societies lacking resources and infrastructure. The *Washington Post* used an online user-generated crisis map to monitor snow removal efforts during the "snowpocalypse" storm of February 2010 that dumped twenty inches on Washington.[18] Remarkably, these efforts become more valuable and effective as more individuals participate—a self-organizing virtuous circle of positive feedback—all without centralized direction or a hierarchy of authority. The *New York Times*, for one, suggests this may be the future of humanitarian relief: "The new paradigm is many-to-many-to-many: victims supply on-the-ground data; a self-organized mob of global volunteers translates text messages and helps to orchestrate relief; journalists and aid workers use the data to target the response."[19]

Complex global social systems may produce social ills as well as social benefits. The global interrelationship among banks holding credit default swaps helps explain how the failure of a relatively small portion of the American financial services industry reverberated in credit markets around the world: "What happens deep inside one national financial system can wreck another halfway around the world."[20] While presumably banks did not intend to cause harm, other social systems may have explicitly political agendas that seek to affect others adversely. Consider the phenomenon of patriotic hackers, or self-organized communities of like-minded individuals with computer skills. Russian nationalists staged a distributed denial-of-service attack on Georgian government agency Web sites during the August 2008 Russian-Georgian war. A similar cyberattack occurred on Estonian government information systems in 2007.[21] Other patriotic hackers seek to spy rather than disrupt. Chinese hackers have infiltrated the Pentagon, White House, and even the 2008 presidential campaigns of Barack Obama and John McCain.[22] During the protests following the contested 2009 election in Iran, an Iranian group of patriotic hackers attacked Twitter. Democracy advocates following the protests—indeed, any Twitter user—found their feeds redirected to an English-language page stating "This page has been hacked by the Iranian cyberarmy."[23] Responding to a request from the Dalai Lama to check his offices' information systems for malware, a team at the University of Toronto uncovered a vast cyberspy network they labeled "GhostNet." The researchers identified more than 1,200 computers in 103 countries that GhostNet had infiltrated, including computers at the Indian Embassy in Washington and at a NATO facility.[24] One advantage of patriotic hacking is that it blurs the relationship between governments and the hackers themselves; in none of the above cases could investigators prove conclusively that governments supported the patriotic hackers. This "attribution problem" protects hackers and governments alike from retribution; in general, anonymity may afford actors opportunities to pursue their interests unfettered from the state's ability to enforce the law. Interestingly, the hackers themselves appear to recognize the power of complex global social systems to amplify their modest efforts: in one instance, hackers broke into the information systems that control the United States' power grid and reportedly installed software that could disable the grid.[25] Some commentators suggest the United States is vulnerable to a "digital Pearl Harbor," in which a social network of patriotic hackers uses access to the computers that govern transportation and utility networks to wreak havoc on the American economy.[26]

Epidemics and pandemics also illustrate how interactions between social networks and individual behavior challenge the ability of states to govern effectively. One need only look at the public discussion a few years ago about the H1N1 virus, or "swine flu." A *Washington Post*-ABC News poll in 2009 found that more than 60 percent of Americans were unconcerned with the virus, suggesting that public health officials had yet to persuade people to get a vaccine shot.[27] Epstein reports an interesting counterexample from 1994, when citizens of Surat, India, fled the city to escape an outbreak of pneumonic plague even though the World Health Organization found no cases of the disease there.[28] This interaction between social networks and behavior makes it difficult to model the prevalence and speed of propagation of a disease. Classic epidemiological models "are ill-suited to capture complex social networks and the direct contacts between individuals, who adapt their behavior—perhaps irrationally—based on disease prevalence."[29] Indeed, similar interactions of networks and behaviors explain how computer viruses such as self-replicating "worms" propagate over computer networks: because computer users do not perceive the presence of such a computer virus, they unwittingly take risks by sharing disks and memory sticks or e-mailing attachments that infect other computers. Researchers tend to miss these interactions when focusing only on network structure on the one hand or behavioral modeling on the other. Scholars of world politics need to understand these interactions between patterns of communication and behavioral factors that they previously took for granted.

One reason for this is that the study of world politics suffers from a levels-of-analysis problem. The economic, technological, demographic, communications and ideational processes of "globalization" have fundamentally reconfigured the nature of social space, such that relations among individuals, organizations, and states increasingly assume forms that transcend territorial limitations, occur across the spaces of the planet, and defy the conventional hierarchy of the individual, the state, and the interstate system.[30] Scholars of globalization and civil society have made considerable progress in recognizing and explaining a domain of world politics outside of relations among sovereign states, but these efforts so far have failed to identify some common organizational features and processes of this "polycentric" world.[31] Rather than proffering an alternative theory of world politics, however, this book argues that such grand theory is unnecessary. Nor does the book argue for (or against) midrange theories. What our scholarship needs instead is a break with the orthodoxy of levels of analysis, which is a legacy of a specific subfield of political science (international relations) that is poorly suited to the ecumenical field of world politics. The traditional typology of the individual, state, and the system is both hierarchical and incomplete. Instead, to understand world politics today we need an analytical framework that emphasizes units of analysis, their interrelations, and the processes of self-organization these units produce either intentionally or by accident. In other words, we need to complement Waltz's classic formulation of *Man, The State, and War* with relational methods of analysis.[32] Fortunately, such a shift in our thinking about world politics requires very little methodological innovation. As the book shows, three separate traditions loosely united under the umbrella of "computational social science" provide scholars with the means to formalize the relational study of global politics. In the following chapters, the book discusses complex systems theory, evolutionary game theory, and social network analysis as useful tools for formalizing our thinking about how skilled individuals in world politics organize themselves outside the domain of interstate relations; how they adapt and learn; and how they produce the collective goods—whether socially beneficial or not—that are an enduring feature of world politics today.

WHAT ARE COMPLEX GLOBAL SOCIAL SYSTEMS?

A complex system is one "in which large networks of components with no central control and simple rules of operation give rise to complex collective behavior, sophisticated information processing, and adaptation via learning or evolution."[33] A complex *social* system is a complex system in which the components are social actors. A complex *global* social system is one in which the actors organize their interactions across the sovereign boundaries of two or more nation-states. As such, the networked topography of complex global social systems transcends the spatial topography of many forms of social behavior. Foremost, we think of people as the actors in complex global social systems, but a system may also consist of human-directed organizations: nation-states, multinational corporations, banks, and insurgent groups, to name just a few. Jervis offers a useful two-part definition of a "system" that helps us understand how we may conceive of relations among social actors as a complex social system. First, a system is a set of units that have some form of interdependency—that is, "changes in some elements of their relations produce changes in other parts of the system."[34] These interdependencies give rise to a second feature of a system, what some theorists call "emergent behavior" of the system, or simply "emergence": the system as a whole "exhibits properties or behaviors that are different from those of the parts."[35] Emergence is an important concept because it highlights the fallacy of composition in thinking about systems: one cannot infer properties or behaviors of a system simply by studying the units. Conversely, we cannot infer the behaviors or—importantly for social scientists—the preferences of units simply by observing the system.[36] This is the ecological fallacy. To avoid these inferential errors, we must study patterns of interactions as well as actors, interests, and structures. Social systems are "complex" not only because they produce emergent behavior, but also because this behavior allows the system to evolve, learn, adapt, and change over time even if actors in the system do not learn. Such change and adaptation in the system may emerge suddenly and chaotically—that is, complex social systems exhibit nonlinear change, in which small perturbations among social actors may produce large changes in the behavior of the system. Cause-effect relationships in complex adaptive social systems may break down, furthermore, across scales of aggregation or over time. Because social relations by definition involve social actors creating interdependencies, Miller and Page argue that "the innate features of many social systems tend to produce complexity."[37] To study complex social systems, then, one must study not only the social actors in the system but must also understand the nature and patterns of interdependencies among actors and the rules that govern their interactions over time. As a unit of analysis, then, the complex social system is fundamentally an aggregate, relational, and process-oriented unit.

One useful way to think about a complex global social system is as a network. As the next chapter explores, the metaphor of a network has broad appeal among scholars of world politics. Beyond the metaphor, however, social network analysis and its related field of graph theory offer a set of tools for formalizing the representation of relations among social actors, and for studying properties of social systems. Network analysis represents each unit as a "node" (which the literature sometimes calls a "vertex") and interdependent relations among actors as "links" (or "edges"). The distinction between nodes and links does not imply, however, that the nodes or links themselves are units of analysis. Rather, network theory finds that the pattern of interdependencies—that is, the structure of the network—has greater influence on the behavior of nodes than do individual-level attributes.[38] For this reason, network theorists formally map and measure the interdependencies among units; one cannot simply assert some general but unspecified relations among units and call it a "network." The mathematical field of graph theory is devoted to the representation of relations among nodes and the measurement of network properties, both at the macro level (for example, how "connected" is the network as a percentage of the total possible number of connections) and at the level of individual nodes (if one were to remove a particular node from a network, how would it affect the overall structure of the network?). With the tools of network theory and graph theory, one can represent almost any system characterized by discrete units with defined relations. *Social* network analysis is concerned, of course, with networks of social actors. Typically, social network analysis focuses on people as nodes; an epidemiologist might use social network analysis to study the spread of sexually transmitted diseases in a community, for example, by mapping relations among sexual partners.[39] But social network analysis also can also treat collectivities as nodes. For example, Davis et al. map ties among corporations by measuring the number of shared directors.[40] Similar studies have examined how networks of financial institutions affect market entry;[41] how innovator networks consisting of researchers, firms, and public laboratories formed in Jena, Germany;[42] and how network relations among nongovernmental organizations affected flood relief efforts in Mozambique in 2000.[43] Benson uses methods of social network analysis to estimate the effect of trading and security relationships on the incidence of interstate disputes.[44] In each of these studies, a "node" in the network represents a social group rather than an individual: a corporation, a bank, a laboratory, an NGO, or a nation-state.

Of course, one can use the methods of network analysis to study physical networks that facilitate global exchanges of goods, money, people, images, and ideas. Transportation grids (roads, rail, ports, and hub airports) are extraordinarily large networks. Likewise, utility networks consist of defined nodes (water treatment plants or power generation facilities) and links (pipes or transmission lines). While information systems such as cell phone networks or the Internet also have physical characteristics—fixed cell towers and servers, for example—they begin to blur the distinction between physical networks and social networks. While the power lines to my home are always connected, I am not always on the phone or always checking my e-mail. Thus, information networks exhibit some of the dynamism that characterizes social networks. This anticipates two important differences between social networks and physical networks. Systems such as transportation grids and utility networks change their structures in the long run, but with high degrees of asset specificity and high fixed costs they are not nearly as dynamic as social networks. Social networks by contrast "are continually changing through interactions among their constituent people, groups, or organizations."[45] The second important distinction is that actors in social networks learn and adapt. Social actors perceive their relations with others, they are endowed with beliefs, and they can act strategically. Importantly, social networks can affect the information that social actors receive, and hence shape their perceptions, knowledge, and behavior. In physical networks, nodes may have some limited capacity for adaptation—power stations can help equilibrate supply and demand for electricity across the grid, for example. Social actors are, however, much more adaptive and more idiosyncratic. While "networks help to create interests and shared identities and . . . promote shared norms and values,"[46] they may also provide nodes with resources to change the network. As the chapters that follow illustrate, communication among social actors has surprising effects on collective action: too much information in certain network structures can actually harm a group's social welfare. To understand complex social systems in world politics, then, we must study the organization or pattern of their interdependencies, whether we call these patterns "networks" or "systems."

An added layer of self-organized complexity in world politics arises from the interaction of social and physical systems. Actors as varied as terrorists, nongovernmental organizations, transnational advocacy groups, corporations, and others use physical networks, from communications to transportation, to provide collective goods. They do so without the hierarchical organization that characterizes both nation-states and traditional Fordist modes of production, and without recourse to the state's power to coerce. Admittedly, this is somewhat of a strong claim: traditional collective action theory asserts that smaller groups, and those with powerful actors willing to bear the costs of provision, are more likely to succeed in producing collective goods.[47] Yet numerous scholars of globalization and global civil society have noted that nonstate actors today are quite adept at producing collective goods both for their own organizations and for society as a whole.[48] So how do such massively parallel, loosely organized systems succeed, often in the face of opposition from nation-states? Traditional levels of analysis do not help us answer this question. Networks of action do not reside at the individual level, the state level, or the systemic level as traditionally conceived. Much of the literature on transnational activism, civil society, and nonstate actors offers some insights, but by and large this literature tends to ignore the specific patterns of interrelationships among actors. That is, while it posits "networks of knowledge and action"[49] and "transnational advocacy networks,"[50] the literature uses the word *network* metaphorically rather than formally. To formalize our thinking about these relationships, this book proposes that we focus on how specific systematized interdependencies help actors learn, adapt, and produce collective emergent behavior that is greater than the sum of their intentions.

From this discussion of the properties of a complex social system, one can see that the Great Pacific Garbage Patch is not a complex global social system. Its constituent parts are pieces of garbage, not social actors. It may be that, thanks to the ecology of Pacific Ocean currents, these pieces of garbage do indeed have some interdependencies that would allow us to characterize the patch as a *system*. But it is not a social system. Rather, it is the emergent property of a set of complex social systems involving production and consumption choices of individuals (that is, the global market) and their interactions with the ecosystem. To begin to understand social emergence on such a geographically vast scale, one must first consider the processes through which complex social systems evolve and adapt. Three such processes are integral to all complex social systems: conservation, selection, and innovation.

Conservation of Information and Strategies

All complex social systems conserve information in two ways. Today, networks may physically store information, a fact that allows rumor registries such as the Ushaihidi project or online traffic maps to inform the decisions of individuals, leaders, and organizations. The Program for the Monitoring of Emerging Diseases, or ProMED, allows physicians from around the world to e-mail reports of outbreaks of infectious diseases and toxins. A similar organization is the Computer Emergency Response Team, or CERT. This organization based at Carnegie Mellon University receives reports of computer viruses and Internet security vulnerabilities, reports them, and distributes recommendations and solutions. Each of these social systems takes advantage of the Internet's ability to receive, store, and distribute information with little or no centralized control. Yet complex social systems have existed since before the rise of digital media, and have used other, simpler ways to store information that do not require a physical repository. Indeed, an important feature of complex social systems is what one might call "collective memory," an idea that is somewhat counterintuitive but nevertheless is important. Collective memory persists in systems because actors pass along knowledge to their neighbors in the system. This phenomenon is well known in biology. Researchers have demonstrated that slime mold bacteria—primitive organisms with no brains—pass along information to nearby bacteria using pheromones. Such "pheromone tagging" allows the mold to communicate about the location of resources such as food. Using this mechanism, researchers were able to train a colony of slime mold to "solve" a maze; because they resided along the shortest path between two food sources, the bacteria more efficiently shared information and food than organisms off the shortest path.[51] Consider also the curious case of red deer residing in Germany and the Czech Republic which, two decades after the fall of the Berlin Wall, still do not cross the former East-West frontier: the "deer have traditional trails, passed on through the generations, with a collective memory that their grounds end at the erstwhile barrier."[52] Researchers have observed that deer that are only two years old will never venture across what once were dangerous grounds, clear evidence that deer pass knowledge of their trails to future generations. Just as in biological systems, complex social systems develop collective memory when actors learn from others, imitate successful actors, follow habitual routines, and combine all these behaviors over time.[53] There is some emerging evidence, furthermore, that social behaviors may in fact be "heritable," or passed genetically from parents to children.[54] Because complex social systems have many thousands, millions, or even billions of actors, furthermore, any given actor's departure from the network is unlikely to lead to the loss of knowledge that, in effect, resides in the collectivity as well as in individuals.

Selection of the Best Strategies

Complex social systems not only preserve information but also have mechanisms to identify or select the "best" performers. In ecosystems, natural selection identifies species and animals that are fittest through a couple of mechanisms. Herbert Spencer's oft-cited phrase "survival of the fittest" captures Darwin's idea of competition among species for scarce resources arising from environmental constraints. Thus, although antibiotics kill most bacteria, the population of bacteria has sufficient variation in resistance that the microbes that survive are highly resistant to antibiotics. This competition explains why tuberculosis has reoccurred in drug-resistant forms in New York City, for example.[55] Another mechanism of natural selection is sexual selection, or competition among individuals for mates. Interestingly, ecological competition and sexual selection may work at cross purposes: the peacock's feathers may give him a reproductive advantage, but he is notably conspicuous to predators. Complex social systems may exhibit some analogies to ecological competition and sexual selection. Clearly, in microeconomics, competition among firms for scarce customers is one form of selection; Jensen's study of commercial banks entering the investment banking market illustrates that the banks' ties to each other can facilitate advantageous access to consumers.[56] Likewise, sexual selection may play a role in the spread of sexually transmitted diseases.[57] Complex social systems may also create, however, selection mechanisms that are not found in complex biological systems. One example is the process of community enforcement. Though a very old example, the commercial laws of medieval Champagne fairs depended upon community enforcement to punish merchants who cheated. This allowed trade to flourish even though merchants in these traveling markets had strong incentives to cheat customers.[58] Information technologies today greatly facilitate community-based mechanisms of selection. Just as the World Wide Web empowers patriotic hackers to launch disruptions of government information systems, so too does it empower groups that monitor such abuses of the internet. After U.S. authorities arrested Colleen R. LaRose, known as "JihadJane" for her alleged involvement in a terrorist plot, her neighbors apparently were unaware of her political views. Yet My Pet Jawa and YouTube Smackdown Corps—both online communities of "anti-Jihadi Internet activists"—reported they each had tracked Ms. Rose's online postings for several years.[59] Wikipedia uses a similar form of community enforcement. Because anyone can create entries and edit the online encyclopedia, some have questioned its accuracy in the absence of editorial control. In one notable incident, someone edited the Wikipedia biographical entry of veteran journalist John Siegenthaler, accusing him of involvement in the assassinations of John F. and Robert F. Kennedy. "For four months, Wikipedia depicted me as a suspected assassin before [Wikipedia founder Jimmy] Wales erased it from his website's history. . . . The falsehoods remained on Answers.com and Reference.com for three more weeks."[60] Yet the Siegenthaler entry appears to be the exception. With millions of readers, Wikipedia's community of users is quick to correct errors—the accuracy of its entries today is comparable to that of *Encyclopedia Britannica*.[61] Wikipedia's community model has additional advantages over traditional print encyclopedias, furthermore. Not only does it have far more entries—more than four million English-language articles alone, compared to *Britannica*'s 65,000 articles—but the community corrects errors more quickly than any print encyclopedia possibly can.[62] Indeed, John Siegenthaler's biographical entry on Wikipedia now includes a link to another entry dedicated to the controversy over his biography.[63] These examples illustrate how selection processes such as community enforcement help complex social systems learn and adapt.

Innovation, Learning, and Adaptation

While competition and selection in complex social systems empower actors, these systems also encourage learning and innovation. Complex social systems are surprisingly adept at solving some challenging problems, in part because they recruit new ideas through one form of self-organized positive feedback: the more these systems attract knowledgeable and skillful individuals, the more useful they become to future users who may bring new ideas to the system. This is one form of "preferential attachment"—that is, the probability of an individual joining a system grows as other individuals join. Social systems also reward those individuals or organizations that learn the quickest or outperform others. One simple example is the Netflix Prize, established by the eponymous company that streams films online to subscribers. In 2006, the company offered a $1 million reward to anyone who could devise a way to improve by 10 percent the service's movie recommendations. Three years later, a team of seven mathematicians, computer scientists, and engineers from the United States, Canada, Israel, and Austria known as Pragmatic Chaos won the prize. In the intervening three years, Netflix received submissions from more than one hundred countries. Pragmatic Chaos itself emerged during the competition when three separate teams joined their efforts. Remarkably, another team of thirty volunteers had achieved an identical 10 percent improvement in Netflix's recommendations but submitted their solution twenty minutes after Pragmatic Chaos. Had Netflix tried to engineer a solution using traditional software research and development methods, it would have been much more costly. "The company would have had to shell out more than $3 million for just one year of the top performers' time, and that's assuming it could've sussed out who the top performers were going to be."[64] Yet the prize not only encouraged unlikely individuals to coordinate their efforts—it turns out Pragmatic Chaos's members worked for firms that are competitors—but it also encouraged innovation and a process of self-selection in which the community of competitors themselves identified the top performers. It saved the company both money and time.

Clearly, mechanisms of innovation work closely with those of conservation and selection. The rise of e-medicine shows how social systems can use technology to spread not only information but also innovations. Information networks may "allow the most promising ideas to spread easily, quickly and widely. 'If the internet is humanity's planetary nervous system, we are now building our planetary immune system,'" argued Nathan Wolfe of the Global Viral Forecasting Initiative.[65] Complex social systems have remarkable abilities to adapt, learn, and even predict political events with an accuracy even the most expert observers could only hope to achieve. For example, researchers have used search engine query data from Google to predict influenza outbreaks. If I am concerned that I have the flu, I may conduct a Google search to learn about the symptoms, treatment options, medicines, and perhaps nearby doctors. Even if I am well but know someone who has the flu, I may wish to get inoculated and ask Google to direct me to the nearest public clinic. Through my search engine queries, I have unwittingly identified myself as a susceptible individual. In this way, those in whom public officials are most interested identify themselves, an important form of self-organizing complex social systems. By using records of such searches on Google, researchers found they can identify outbreaks with a time lag of about one day, compared to the Centers for Disease Control and Prevention's reporting lag of one to two weeks.[66] Just as mechanisms of conservation, selection, and innovation help civil society solve problems, however, criminals may also use these mechanisms to achieve their objectives. After discovering GhostNet, one set of researchers noted problems of cyberespionage are likely to worsen: "What Chinese spooks did in 2008, Russian crooks will do in 2010 and even low-budget criminals from less developed countries will follow in due course."[67]

Similarly, prediction markets use mechanisms of competition and selection to learn about and predict social and political trends. In a prediction market, individuals buy and sell contracts for a particular future event such as whether a candidate wins an election. If the event occurs, holders of the contract receive payment, but if the event fails to occur the holder receives nothing. Because participants can trade contracts continuously, the current price of a contract reflects the trading community's estimation of the probability of the event occurring. In this respect, prediction markets institutionalize selection mechanisms: those who routinely guess poorly lose money, go broke, and exit the market, while those whose guesses tend to be more accurate will make money and continue to play. Speculators may play iteratively and continuously as long as they have money to purchase contracts. Without any centralized direction or leadership, then, prediction markets draw forth the latent expertise of the most knowledgeable members of a social group. In other words, prediction markets are one mechanism for aggregating social beliefs. They are surprisingly good at predicting social and political events. In one well-known example similar to the Google influenza prediction, a prediction market in Iowa identified flu epidemics two to four weeks before the state's public health reporting system identified them.[68] Another online prediction market, Intrade.com, allowed trading in contracts on the 2004, 2008, and 2012 presidential elections in the United States. Rather than polling a random sample of the electorate, Intrade's market allows anyone who is willing to risk money to buy future contracts. While one might expect problems with sample bias—perhaps only the wealthy and compulsive gamblers participate in the prediction market—in fact, the participants have strong incentives to make accurate predictions. Rather than asking themselves, "Whom am I going to vote for?" traders instead ask (1) whom is everyone else going to vote for? And (2) are other traders over- or underestimating the likelihood of a given outcome, because I can make money by buying and selling contracts before market movements? Those who answer these questions most accurately make money, while those who are less knowledgeable drop out of the market. Thus, Intrade's selection mechanism (the market) attracts and identifies expertise. In all three elections, the markets not only accurately predicted the eventual winner but also outperformed predictions based on traditional opinion polls. The 2008 presidential election in particular showed the prescience of the prediction market. Although most pollsters predicted Obama's victory in the weeks before the November 2008 election, none provided a prediction as accurate as Intrade's markets did. On November 3, 2008—the night before Barack Obama was elected president—the *Washington Post's* online election map, based on data from Real Clear Politics, predicted Obama would win 338 electoral votes to John McCain's 200 electoral votes.[69] National Public Radio's pollster Kenneth Rudin predicted a 291-247 split in Obama's favor.[70] The *New York Times*, *Wall Street Journal*, Fox News, *Los Angeles Times*, and others identified several states as too close to call.[71] By contrast, Intrade.com's markets correctly identified the winners in forty-eight of the fifty states and predicted the exact ultimate electoral split of 365-173.[72] Intrade's markets also correctly predicted all fifty state contests in the 2004 presidential election.[73] What is more, Intrade forecast an electoral split that was larger than most pollsters had predicted, yet its outlier proved to be the actual Electoral College split. Although recent scholarship has identified deficiencies with "big data" analysis,[74] these examples illustrate how complex social systems use conservation, selection, and innovation to harness "the wisdom of crowds"[75] to solve difficult problems and provide collective goods, from encouraging citizens to seek health care to monitoring the spread of computer viruses.

SELF-ORGANIZATION AND ADAPTATION IN COMPLEX GLOBAL SOCIAL SYSTEMS

How do complex global social systems unleash the processes of conservation, selection, and innovation? Four features in particular explain the surprising ability of complex social systems to survive, adapt, and thrive in world politics: the skill revolution, massive parallelism, nonlinearity, and creative errors.

The Skill Revolution

Rosenau, for one, has argued that individuals have become increasingly skillful players in world politics.[76] Individuals have the knowledge to use information technology to inform their leaders, international organizations, and other states of human rights injustices, humanitarian crises, and other issues that concern them. Yet Rosenau argues that of greater importance is the ability of political actors to recognize how distant events affect their daily lives, and conversely how their local actions can affect distant happenings.[77] That is, actors today better understand "micro-macro" linkages between individuals on the one hand and national, transnational and global processes and structures on the other. This is an important difference between social systems and physical ones: in the former, "nodes" not only receive information from the network but try to change both the network itself and the behavior of distant nodes. For example, Iranian protestors during the summer of 2009 used a Persian-language social networking site based in the United States to mobilize both protestors residing in Iran and those Iranians living overseas.[78] Recognizing that social media empowered the protestors, the U.S. State Department quietly asked Twitter to delay routine maintenance that would have denied protestors an important source of information.[79] Similarly, patriotic hackers employ their skills in the service of their shared goals. Social systems not only help skillful individuals collaborate, they also empower actors to directly influence governments.

Massive Parallelism

Crisis maps, e-medicine, and community enforcement all are massive social systems characterized not by hierarchy but instead by parallelism. This "many-to-many-to-many" network structure helps social networks conserve information; avoid detection and circumvent state power; quickly identify and solve problems; and innovate.[80] Massively parallel systems conserve information; as noted above, even if someone leaves the social network, that person's departure is unlikely to cause a loss of information or expertise in the system. Such systems also protect members in a web of anonymity. This is one reason states find "cyberwar" so difficult to combat. The best that computer experts can do is identify the location of the servers from which cyberattacks originate, but they cannot identify the individuals who orchestrated the attacks:

> Leaving the attacks to informal cybergangs (the extent of the Russian state's involvement remains unclear), rather than trying to organize a formal cyberarmy, is cheaper, for one thing. The most talented attackers, with the best tools, might not want to work for the state directly. Best of all, from the state's point of view, is that it can deny responsibility for the attacks.[81]

Conversely, massive parallelism facilitates community problem solving. With so many participants in a social system, members can weed out bad information (as in Wikipedia) and identify those who violate social norms (as occurred with JihadJane). Open-sourced software takes advantage of a large community of volunteer programmers to identify problems and security vulnerabilities, and to engineer solutions. The popular Web browser Firefox illustrates an interesting paradox of massively parallel system. Firefox typically has more security vulnerabilities than other Web browsers: one report identified 169 vulnerabilities in Firefox compared to ninety-four in Apple's Safari browser and forty-five in Microsoft's Internet Explorer, both of which are proprietary or "closed-source" software. But Firefox has one of the smallest "windows of vulnerability," or time between when a security fault is identified and developer Mozilla pushes out a security patch. Indeed, Firefox had the smallest window of vulnerability of any browser in 2008, bested Safari in vulnerability times in 2009, and had a quicker time to patching vulnerabilities than Internet Explorer in 2011.[82] Along with Wikipedia, this example illustrates that although massively parallel systems may have more errors, they also may solve those errors and adapt more quickly than hierarchical systems. Finally, the sheer number of people in massively parallel social systems allows innovation to percolate from unlikely sources. The Netflix prize succeeded precisely because the company could not affordably and reliably identify engineers who could solve their business problem; the prize merely incentivized individuals to join into problem-solving networks. One researcher has suggested that individuals participating in massively parallel online role-playing games, or MMORPGs, would provide the U.S. armed forces with more realistic counterinsurgency experience than conventional training does.[83] A neuropsychologist who contributes to Wikipedia noted that the online encyclopedia's process of resolving disagreements about entries can encourage innovation. "Even people who are a pain in the arse can stimulate new thinking."[84]

Nonlinearity

Complex social systems exhibit increasing returns—that is, the system's output grows by a factor greater than one for each unit of input.[85] Increasing returns thus facilitate both growth and self-organization in complex social systems. Network effects are an important source of increasing returns. The idea of network effects is simple: to take a dated example, the first fax machine was useless because it fundamentally derives its utility from the fact that others use the technology as well. But with each additional purchase of a fax machine, the technology became more valuable. Systems with such network effects are characterized by *s*-shaped growth—that is, an initial period of slow growth followed by explosively rapid growth and then tailing off as the system is saturated. This explains why complex global social systems self-organize suddenly and surprisingly. These systems exhibit similar patterns of growth as they become more valuable both to their users and to those outside the system. While a crisis map with two users might be marginally useful, for example, each additional user makes the crisis map more informative, attracting new users who then contribute new information, and so on. Walt, for one, notes that as transnational connectivity grows, the likelihood of such "political contagion," or the spread of political ideas and methods, rapidly increases.[86] One consequence of such nonlinear growth is that complex systems are not decomposable—one cannot simply explain the properties of the system by examining the behavior of the components. Few recent episodes illustrate the nonlinearity of complex social systems and the fallacy of composition better than the financial crisis meltdown that began in 2007 but accelerated in October 2008. Interbank lending assured that the failure of a small portion of the U.S. credit market—subprime mortgages—quickly spread not only to the broader U.S. credit market but to overseas credit markets as well. In retrospect, national banking regulators were guilty of assuming the composability of finance: "The assumption was that if each institution was safe, then the system as a whole would be too."[87] Regulators today still struggle with the interdependent relationships among financial institutions. Although President Obama announced in January 2010 that "[n]ever again will the American taxpayer be held hostage to a bank that is too big to fail," one assessment noted that if implemented, this would require splitting the United States' four largest banks into forty-eight separate companies.[88] Such proposals ignored, furthermore, the systematic quality of finance:

> The proposals also betray a desire to ring-fence deposit-taking firms and let everything else fry. However understandable, the reality is that investment banks, credit-card operators, insurers and even carmakers' finance arms had to be bailed out. The system was too interconnected.[89]

While the liberalization of finance unleashed the power of positive returns in banking, it simultaneously created risks of cascading failures.

To capture the dynamism and nonlinearity of complex global social systems today, a number of scholars have offered neologisms. Two portmanteaus seem particularly insightful. Dee Hock, the founder of the Visa credit card company, proposed describing these social systems as "chaordic," or organizations that simultaneously exhibit properties of chaos and order.[90] Similarly, Rosenau suggests "fragmegration," or the "simultaneity and interaction of the fragmenting and integrating dynamics" that characterize new actors in world politics.[91] Such nonlinear dynamics in complex systems help explain their rapid constitution, evolution, and dissolution. So-called flash mobs take advantage of these multiplying effects to organize quickly, protest, and disperse before state authorities can react. The first presidential campaign of Barack Obama in 2008 provides another piquant example: it released an app for Apple's popular and then-revolutionary iPhone. Not only did the free app deliver to the user's phone information about the campaign's position on a range of issues, but it also included "a great volunteering tool that lets you make a difference any time you want by talking to people you already know. Your contacts are prioritized by key battleground states, and you can make calls and organize results all in one place."[92] Given the nature of iPhones—at once status symbols for elites and costly devices—the campaign tapped into the social networks of well-educated, motivated, and wealthy voters who in turn contact their well-educated, wealthy and motivated friends.[93] In effect, the phone does the campaigning for the candidate. These examples illustrate how skillful political actors can use network effects to multiply their efforts, communicate with others, and rapidly organize and mobilize supporters for their cause.

Creative Errors

Schumpeter's observation that "gales of creative destruction" characterize innovation in capitalist economies anticipates an important feature of contemporary complex global social systems.[94] They may be sloppy, inefficient, noisy, and error-prone, but such slack in complex global social systems serves three important purposes. First, it helps such systems escape what a game theorist might call suboptima. People can manage known errors but not unknown ones; deliberate errors and inefficiencies actually can help solve problems. Before seafarers had solved the navigational challenge of determining their longitude, they often would deliberately sail to either the east or west of their destination. Once they had reached the proper latitude, they would then know which direction to turn toward their destination. Such "off-course navigation" featured prominently in early aviation as navigators learned to find small islands in the Pacific Ocean. Ernest K. Gann, an aviator and author, memorably recalled the dangers of attempting to navigate precisely toward one's destination as he recounted flying across the rainforests of the Amazon to Corumbá, Brazil, in the 1940s. To find this city near the border with Bolivia, he and his captain sought a river to guide them:

> It is an axiom of flying that he who starts wandering around when in doubt never discovers his true whereabouts until it is too late. . . . Somehow, because of the unknown winds or the inaccuracies of the chart, we had come upon the wrong section of the river. Which way, then was Corumbá? To the north or to

the south? There was no one to ask except the flamingos and we were in poor shape for exploration. We did not have enough fuel to fly north beyond the horizon and then, if Corumbá did not appear, retrace our flight southward until it did. The same would be true if we started off to the south. We could only allow a few moments to consider the decision which must now be made. It was not really a decision. It was pure black and white gamble and we recognized it as such. If Corumbá was to the north and we turned that way, we would make it. If not, we would not. At least not in an airplane.[95]

Deliberate error also can help prevent problems of mutual interference, furthermore, a point that radio and signal engineers have long recognized. Conversely, too much efficiency and precision in a system can be catastrophic. As Perrow noted in his seminal study, tightly coupled systems characterized by interactive complexity—that is, systems with components so interdependent that a failure of one may interact with other failures—are susceptible to failures that are "normal" in the sense that they are intrinsic to the nature of systems of interrelated components, and hence are to be expected.[96] For example, in September 2006 a commercial airliner and an executive jet collided over the Amazon rain forests, about one thousand kilometers north of where Ernest Gann had made his fortunate decision. Through inattentiveness by controllers and pilots and some bad luck, the two aircraft were flying at the same altitude on precisely opposite courses. Normally, "head-on airplanes mistakenly assigned the same altitude and route by Air Traffic Control would almost certainly have passed some distance apart, due to the navigation slop inherent in their systems."[97] Yet in these two modern aircraft, their precise global positioning system (GPS) navigation systems placed them on a course offset by a mere thirty feet laterally and two feet vertically. One hundred and fifty-four people died in the resulting collision.[98] Systems that have some "inherent slop," however, are less susceptible to such catastrophes.

Complex social systems may exhibit a similar vulnerability to excess precision. Jervis noted that excess efficiency, while desirable in a system, may spread problems "as air travelers discover when they sit in a plane that is awaiting passengers from a delayed connecting flight and wonder if their own connecting flight will be held for them."[99] Similarly, too much accurate information can keep social systems from working well. Some research suggests, for example, that providing extensive traffic information to drivers may lead them to contribute to rather than lessen congestion.[100] This phenomenon arises in part because drivers exhibit "alert fatigue"—that is, they tend to discount repeated and regular traffic warnings about the congestion in the same locations—but also because some drivers are contrarians. They behave strategically, calculating that if all other drivers follow traffic advice, their preferred original route likely will have less congestion.[101] In this respect, traffic route choice is similar to Schelling's Beach Problem and the well-known El Farol Bar Problem articulated by W. Brian Arthur. In all three problems, people seek to use a resource—a preferred highway, the bar, or the beach—but only if it is not too crowded. In game theoretic terms, the solution to these problems is a mixed strategy—that is, people do not make the same choice every time they face the same dilemma. "Noise" or inefficiency is one way players achieve optimal mixing strategies and avoid the suboptima of mutual interference.[102] Rather than deliberating going to the beach some days but not others, people who lack information naturally vary their behavior in a manner that creates a de facto mixing strategy and helps solve dilemmas of collective action. Another simple example illustrates the importance of error: imagine if weather forecasters could predict perfectly rainfall six months in advance. Everyone would plan their beach vacations for the same sunny weeks to avoid the rain, making the beaches unbearably crowded.

Thanks to positive returns, furthermore, inefficiency and noise at one level of analysis can give rise to emergent behavior or structures at another level of analysis. Far from being a source of chaos or something that is detrimental to order, randomness may in fact be necessary for order to emerge. "Phantom" traffic jams, while undeniably costly and annoying, nevertheless represent a coherent, ordered emergent behavior. These jams emerge not because of an accident or road construction, but instead because of "nothing more sinister than sharp banking, unnecessary lane changes, and lorries overtaking one another."[103] Cosmologists theorize that microscopic random movements and electrostatic forces of dust particles triggered a process of accretion that produced planets—"Here is one of nature's more dramatic examples of great things arising from humble beginnings."[104] Indeed, physicists predicate the Big Bang Theory, the explanation for the entire universe, on an initial random quantum flux, "the smallest phenomenon in nature."[105] The creative role of noise is ubiquitous in world politics, from Schumpeter's gales of creative destruction to modern economic theories such as endogenous growth theory and the new economic geography.[106] Interestingly, however, the very nature of randomness at one level—that is, accidents without cause—leads people to overlook its fundamental constitutive role at higher levels; we are too quick to dismiss it as meaningless. Observers of complex systems regularly exhibit such "level confusion."[107]

Finally, creative errors and inefficiencies do not merely help players avoid bad outcomes or create emergent behaviors and structures. They also indirectly encourage innovation either by recruiting new expertise or by drawing forth the latent knowledge already in the social system. The Netflix Prize worked similarly, drawing disparate individuals to work on a noisy problem. Likewise, the controversy over the science of climate change illustrates how uncertainty can play a constructive role. In 2005, Wikipedia experienced a "revert war"—where volunteer editors iteratively undo each other's changes to an entry—as climate change scientists and skeptics leveled charges at each other. In this particular case, the editors referred their dispute to Wikipedia's administrators.[108] Irrespective of one's view of climate change, however, it is undeniable that the recent controversy has expanded the debate not only among politicians and voters but among scientists as well.[109] In each of these examples, noisy problems attract individuals who volunteer their time and talents to a process of competition and selection.

Nonlinearity, massive parallelism, increasingly skilled individuals, and creative error are all important mechanisms of conservation, selection, and innovation in world politics today. Each of them helps self-organized systems balance the needs of exploiting resources versus the exploration of perhaps better alternatives. That is, complex global social systems attempt to strike a balance between collective specialization and generalization. Just like species in an ecosystem, human organizations that specialize in a particular environment may have particular advantages but are susceptible to environmental changes, whereas organizations that are generalists can survive radical environmental shifts but only at the cost of short-term inefficiencies and disadvantages in a particular environment. These ecological analogies are no accident. The study of complexity owes much to the natural sciences, and complex global social systems exhibit ecological characteristics. These conceptual and methodological tools allow scholars to analyze and understand complex social systems in world politics. These tools require, however, a break from the foundational ontology on which most scholars of world politics rely. While man, the state, and war will remain necessary for international relations theory, they are hardly sufficient. We need to begin thinking about nodes, nets, and gyres—people, their networks, and the dynamics produced by their interactions. The Pacific Gyre thus not only reminds us of the range of issues in world politics that do not fit neatly in traditional levels of analysis, but also that insights from the natural sciences can help us understand the swirling dynamism in world politics that nevertheless is coherent and comprehensible. Nodes and nets produce the social gyres that characterize global politics today.

ORGANIZATION OF THE BOOK

This study illustrates how self-organized networks are a new reality of world politics. These networks shape outcomes of actors' coordination and collaboration, and help explain the paradox of punctuated equilibrium—periods of stability in the structures and institutions of world politics interrupted by sudden and often dramatic changes.[110] The book examines broadly similar patterns and dynamics across domains of world politics, from ecological conservation to trade networks, rather than examining a single issue, puzzle, or theoretical question in depth. This organization of the manuscript diverges considerably from a "traditional" academic study that sustains a cumulative analysis of a research question across chapters. For example, chapter 6 of this manuscript examines a puzzle that deserves a book-length analysis: Why did German banks fail to support increased capital adequacy standards after the 2007–08 financial crisis? To answer such a question, one can envision a book in which each chapter is an individual building block in developing a sustained argument. By contrast, this manuscript seeks to answer a more general question: What does the example of German banks teach us about overfishing, disagreement in the UN Security Council, or other areas of world politics? Of necessity, the latter question requires a book whose chapters explore very different empirical puzzles to elucidate connections, similarities, and generalizations. Each question emphasizes different objectives of a research design: the former question seeks to understand contingent and unique features of a particular social phenomenon, while the latter attempts to identify general concepts, explanations, or laws that may obtain across issues, domains, or academic fields. The two questions emphasize, furthermore, the different purposes of research designs. "Idiographic" or particularistic questions seek to test theory and emphasize depth and richness of explanation. "Nomothetic" approaches, by contrast, sacrifice some depth of analysis to build general theories. Inevitably, all scholarly studies must balance these competing objectives, and often combine elements of both research traditions. To the degree that scholarly books tend to study a particular issue in depth, they reflect research programs and traditions that may be common in academic disciplines. That does not mean, however, that exploratory, theory-building studies have no place in research.

Bernard K. Forscher memorably captured the essence of the tension between these research paradigms.[111] Forscher argued that scientific progress requires both "builders"—researchers who assemble edifices of facts into theories that may or may not withstand the bracing forces of empirical testing and peer criticism—and "brick makers," or researchers who produce new and more facts with little concern for the edifices into which we place facts to build theories. Forscher argued that academic disciplines have increasingly cultivated many brick makers but too few builders. The problem with the profusion of bricks is that they do not assemble themselves, explore interrelationships, draw strength from each other, or compose theoretical edifices. Perhaps it is inevitable that the architect and the mason have disagreements over the quality of bricks, or over the design of the creations they erect. Yet the progress of science requires both types of scholars, provided they complement each other. In Forscher's terms, this manuscript is an edifice that seeks to draw together the strengths of several different theories and disciplines. The word *explorations* in the book's subtitle indicates that, like the builder, it examines how many different bricks—both theoretical and real world, from banking to fisheries—fit together to produce the self-organized dynamism that characterizes many domains of global life today. A brick maker might argue (not unreasonably) that strong structures require sound bricks. Reasonable scholars inevitably will disagree about the level of detail required to understand bricks; the following chapters attempt to provide the reader with sufficient detail to understand how the models work without excessive and tedious details that detract from the book's objective of theoretical generality.

Each of the chapters is a pillar in this edifice. Chapter 2 illustrates that three areas of research, together known as computational social science, address three debates that are central to understanding world politics today: the agent-structure debate, the level of analysis problem, and understanding "change." The chapter makes an important point that is worth anticipating here: the book does not purport to offer a "theory" of world politics. Indeed, complex social science is not a theory but instead is a method of social science. Grand theoretical claims for complexity theory in the social sciences are more likely to create disappointment and disillusionment than theoretical progress.[112] So, while complex social science offers some insights into theoretical debates, it is not an alternative theory. To illustrate these new insights, the book then examines coordination games that characterize, for example, negotiations over international standards; cooperation games with distribution, such as state efforts to construct a global finance regime; common pool resources that characterize global environmental sustainability; and complex physical networks that characterize global communications, finance, transportation, and energy.

Chapter 3 revisits one of the simplest collective action problems, a coordination game. While game theory has studied coordination games extensively, it is not clear that the findings for a two-player game hold for more realistic games with a large number of players—so-called large-n games—or for games with more than two choices. The chapter examines how large social systems communicate information through their social networks to solve a difficult coordination problem. Chapter 4 extends this analysis to look at more demanding cooperation games in which players must not only solve a collective choice problem but must also agree to the distribution of gains from cooperation. Again, game theory offers considerable insight in cooperation games with distributive conflict that nevertheless may not be extensible to social systems with many players. Chapter 5 examines how people deal with the depletion of natural resources. It seeks to explain how actors can construct a regime to manage such resources without resort to coercion or centralization. Given that these resources characterize not only environmental problems in world politics but, potentially, other collective goods such as financial regulation, the chapter offers some insight into how both governments and global civil society may self-organize to solve these problems. Chapter 6 examines how the global organization of the financial services industry not only creates risks of financial crises, but also prevents governments from making the reforms needed to protect the global economy from financial meltdowns such as the one that almost occurred in 2008. In chapter 7, the book examines how complex social systems interact with the infrastructure networks that allow people to exchange goods, money, images, and ideas globally. How likely to occur is a "digital Pearl Harbor" that massively disrupts communications, utility, or transportation networks? This question is more than just a policy concern: fundamentally, it asks how physical networks may distribute costs among social actors, much as the financial crisis has shifted the costs of adjustment to surprising locations.[113] To answer this question, the chapter examines disruptions to a global network and assesses how different actors bear a disproportionate share of the costs. The final chapter draws together insights from the five analytical chapters and articulates a research agenda for computational models of globalization.

The fields of globalization theory and computational social science share a number of attributes. Both are relatively new fields—globalization theory is no more than three decades old, while computational social science's origins date to the early 1990s—they both draw from multiple academic fields, and they explicitly seek to transcend traditional disciplinary boundaries.[114] Because this book uses computational social science to explore global dynamics, its arguments speak to a broad audience of scholars from both fields. These include sociologists, political scientists, economists, communications theorists, anthropologists, and others who think about globalization, and the computer scientists, game theorists, mathematicians, and network theorists who have developed a computational paradigm for the analysis of social phenomena. With such a wide audience, the book inevitably must make some choices about the necessary degree of specificity or generality in its examples and analysis. Advanced readers in a particular field may find examples in the book too obvious, while scholars who are new either to globalization theory or to computational social science may find the text provides too little detail about models or lacks sufficient explanation of some concepts. Such compromises are, in my view, necessary if one is to build an intellectual edifice such as Forscher proposed. My intent is not to minimize the conceptual challenges in either field or the problems that global dynamics present to societies—as noted above, chapter 6's concern with the global financial crisis merits a book-length treatment on its own rather than the brief exploration provided here. Nevertheless, the book's intent is to promote and advance a dialogue among scholars who, because of their interests in globalization and computational social science, already understand both the challenges and promises of working across disciplines.

I should add one additional note about terminology. Unless the text refers specifically to political science's subfield of international relations (in which I received my training) the book refers to its subject matter as "world politics." This is consistent with the book's thesis about levels and units of analysis in the study of world politics. Traditional levels of analysis—the individual, the state, and the system—are not only analytic devices but also disciplinary ones that separate spheres of global activity into separate scholarly fields. I choose to focus on an ecumenical, if admittedly imprecise, conception of world politics. Such language implies, furthermore, that we rethink the boundaries not only between subfields but also between social sciences and the natural sciences. This is hardly a novel position: as chapter 2 mentions, social scientists have borrowed from other disciplines for decades. The goal is not merely to exercise interdisciplinary skills, but also "to rethink the content of the disciplines that are being connected."[115]

Finally, our call on the natural sciences reminds us that scientific inquiry arguably is itself a global complex system. In the generation of knowledge, there is no statis or equilibrium, and our learning about world politics is ongoing. For this reason, our language to capture these relationships inevitably will be imprecise. The expansive dynamism of the North Pacific Gyre offers one final metaphor, then. As we gaze across the oceans of the natural, physical, and social sciences, our efforts to comprehend complex social systems will require a humility that acknowledges the challenges of understanding the vast gyre we call world politics.

TWO

AGENTS AND NETWORKS

Complex Social Systems and Theories of World Politics

> [T]he widespread growth of the Internet, the World Wide Web, and the other electronic technologies that are shrinking the world offers considerable potential as a source of democracy. More accurately, by facilitating the continued proliferation of networks that know no boundaries, these technologies have introduced a horizontal dimension to the politics of the [domestic-foreign] Frontier. They enable like-minded people in distant places to converge, share perspectives, protest abuses, provide information, and mobilize resources—dynamics that seem bound to constrain the vertical structures that sustain governments, corporations, and any other hierarchical organizations.
>
> —James N. Rosenau, *Along the Domestic-Foreign Frontier*

The metaphor of "networks" appeals broadly today to a wide variety of scholars of world politics. As a heuristic device, the imagery of a "horizontal dimension" of politics contrasts sharply with the vertical imagery of Waltz's seminal *Man, the State and War*, a statement of the levels of analysis problem that has influenced the training of generations of scholars.[1] At the same time, the image of "flat" social systems effortlessly crossing sovereign borders corresponds to criticisms of the state-centric ontology of the most influential international relations theories. Scholars from critical theory,[2] Gramscian Marxism,[3] and globalization theory[4] (among others) share this criticism; unsurprisingly, the heuristic of social networks finds its way into their ontological discussions. For example, "transnational advocacy networks" disarticulate traditional relations between citizens and sovereign states by "building new links among multiple actors in civil societies, states, and international organizations," thus "multiply[ing] channels of access to the international system."[5] Global civil society itself assumes a networked quality that "reconstructs world politics," according to Lipschutz. Civil society is a "parallel arrangement of political interaction: one that does not take anarchy or self-help as central organizing principles, but is focused on the self-conscious constructions of networks of knowledge and action, by decentered, local actors, that cross the reified boundaries of space as though they were not there."[6] The metaphor of social networks in world politics simultaneously questions our use of the state as unit-of-analysis, and suggests a respatialization of world politics that may transform the Westphalian state system itself. Our focus on interstate relations is inadequate for understanding these emergent social systems, and for this reason we cannot yet anticipate the fundamental ways in which the international system itself is changing.

Despite the extensive appeal of complex social systems as a *metaphor*, curiously the formalized study of patterns of interdependencies has yet to find broad application in the scholarship on globalization. This may change soon for two reasons. First, three theories—network theory, complex systems theory, and evolutionary game theory—offer scholars of world politics new insights into three central theoretical debates: the agent-structure debate, the level-of-analysis problem, and how to understand "change" in the global system. This chapter illustrates how these theories address questions about recursive relations between agents and structures in world politics; how we can understand confounding phenomena that cross the traditional boundaries between the individual, the state, and the global system; and how we can understand dynamics in world politics. The second reason is methodological: social network analysis, complex systems theory, and evolutionary game theory not only offer theoretical purchase but also require scholars to formalize their arguments about the organization of interdependencies in social systems. Although scholars undoubtedly will continue use the word *network* as a heuristic, increasingly, the formalized study of social systems introduces a methodological consistency that is necessary for conducting empirical investigations, reproducing experimental results, transmitting findings throughout the community of world politics scholars, and generalizing findings across empirical domains. That is, this methodological rigor greatly aids the social scientific enterprise of studying global politics. Perhaps most importantly from a social scientific perspective, even scholars without extensive training in quantitative methodology increasingly find these methods accessible. Network theory, complex systems theory, and evolutionary game theory thus lie at the crossroads of core theoretical debates in world politics and innovative but accessible methodologies. Along with new methods of collecting and analyzing vast quantities of social data, these theories provide the foundation for a new computational social science that offers a much-needed formalism to theorizing about agents and structures, interactions between levels of analysis, and the dynamics of world politics.[7]

First, however, a caveat: the argument that complex social systems are important in world politics entails an ontological commitment that such systems, though not tangible in the way that physical systems are, do in fact exist. As Walker notes, one cannot separate discussions of units of analysis from such philosophical commitments: "It is not a matter of arguing about ontological or epistemological issues in the abstract. Philosophical commitments are already embedded in concepts like state or state-system, utilitarian accounts of rational action, and . . . typologies like the so-called levels of analysis schema that has played such an important role" in studying world politics.[8] For this reason, to propose complex social systems as a unit of analysis quickly verges on some fundamental debates in contemporary social theory about ontology and epistemology. Due in part to the "constructivist turn," these discussions from social theory have reinvigorated theory in political science.[9] These debates include positivists versus scientific realists;[10] differences between "units" and "levels" of analysis;[11] structure versus agency;[12] the levels of analysis problem versus the agent-structure debate;[13] micro- versus macrolevel explanations;[14] structural versus reductionist explanations;[15] causal versus interpretive explanations;[16] universalism versus historicism;[17] and cognitive versus behavioral explanations,[18] to name just a few. Such a brief recounting of these debates obviously trivializes what are important disagreements among social theorists. Yet given Walker's point that *any* ontological position entails epistemological commitments, debates about ontology risk a futile circularity—that is, scholars end up debating epistemological commitments rather than units of analysis. For this reason, these divides paradoxically are important and yet ultimately irresolvable. Sawyer offers one way forward, noting that ontological individualism does not logically entail methodological individualism.[19] Likewise, Wendt notes, "one can take a systemic level of analysis with respect to behavior and be an individualist with respect to the constitution of unit properties."[20] Together, these arguments suggest one can separate ontological from methodological commitments. This is particularly useful for this book: rather than assert the ontological status of complex social systems, it seeks to demonstrate how globalization theory and computational social science increasingly share concerns with process, change, learning, recursion, and contingency in world politics.

"SYSTEM OF SYSTEMS" IN WORLD POLITICS

It is hardly controversial to claim that networks play a consequential role in world politics. Yet as scholars we do not understand well how complex social systems interact with each other, the "system of systems" problem that calls attention to the challenge of drawing boundaries around units of analysis that, in reality, interact with and depend upon other complex social systems. Whether physical networks such as utilities or telecommunications, financial relationships among banks, or social ties among individuals, networks have profound effects on nation-states that are readily apparent, for example, in information technologies. Chapter 1 noted several examples, from disrupted government information systems in Estonia and Georgia to the Dalai Lama's hacked computers and GhostNet. In each case, these patriotic hackers represent a loosely organized social network, suggesting that social systems and physical systems such as information networks are interrelated in complex ways: are people embedded in physical networks, or are communications networks themselves embedded in larger social networks? This anticipates the challenges of drawing analytical boundaries around social networks that, in reality, are deeply enmeshed in broader social and physical structures that may be global in scope.[21]

One compelling example of this analytical challenge is the global financial crisis. In addition to the interrelationships among banks holding securitized debt, one must consider the relationships among homeowners, insurers, and regulators. By bundling debt and repackaging it as "tranches" of new securities, financial instruments such as credit-default swaps and collateralized obligations seek to reduce risk to lenders by diversifying their portfolios. Because banks increasingly sold securities in global markets, however, securitization created interrelationships among international banks holding each other's debt obligations as well as the insurers that sold policies to guard against default losses—in effect, coupling the network of banks to a network of insurers. The resulting financial meltdown in September 2008 illustrates how difficult it is even for professional financiers to understand such interdependencies, who focused on regulating the banks instead of the system as a whole.[22] Regulators suffered from the fallacy of composition and the confounding intricacies of modern global social networks. This faulty reasoning helps explains why

> what happens deep inside one national financial system can wreck another halfway across the world. In the United States subprime lending was a relatively small bit of the mortgage market—itself just a part of America's financial markets. And yet the cascade of failing credit and risk aversion that began there,

partly as a result of inadequate supervision, has spread not just to the overstretched banking systems of Europe, but also now to untroubled banks in emerging markets.[23]

While faulty regulation may be partly to blame, the networks of shared debt among banks are also important. Hypothetically, other network structures of shared risk might have mitigated the crisis. Also important, apparently, are social ties among financiers themselves. One journalist argues that financiers largely misunderstood their risk in part because of their pack mentality: they simply mimicked their successful colleagues. For this reason, financiers broadly adopted the same risk assessment practices even though they did not fully understand them. One such technique was the "Gaussian copula model," a model to assess risk developed by economist David X. Li. However, because this model relied on historical data on credit default swaps from the housing boom of the 1990s, it tended to understate true risk in securitized debt during periods of declining housing prices. Salmon notes:

> "Li can't be blamed," says [Kai] Gilkes of CreditSights. After all, he just invented the model. Instead, we should blame the bankers who misinterpreted it. And even then, the real danger was created not because *any given* trader adopted it but because *every* trader did. In financial markets, everybody doing the same thing is a recipe for a bubble and an inevitable bust.[24]

Indeed, Nobel laureate Robert Lucas argues that for this reason, economists will never be able to forecast bubbles and busts: "If an economist had a formula that could reliably forecast crises a week in advance, say, then that formula would become part of generally available information and prices would fall a week earlier."[25] In this respect, social networks transmit knowledge and practices that help social actors internalize expert predictions, rendering such forecasts moot. Giddens noted that this "double hermeneutic" distinguishes the social from physical sciences.[26] As these examples show, although social networks may coordinate beneficial behaviors, they may also produce socially harmful choices.[27] Indeed, social actors with full information may find it harder to coordinate their behavior and produce collective goods.[28] Only by considering these relationships among bankers, insurers, homeowners, and regulators can one begin to understand how an initial small drop in housing prices in the United States could threaten financial markets around the world.

This brief overview suggests that one needs to specify what a "system" is, a point to which the chapter turns shortly. This discussion illustrates that systems are consequential in world politics for three reasons. First, they *distribute costs and benefits among states and other actors* in the global system. For example, after one simple but malicious computer worm found its way around the World Wide Web in 2008, "at least one bank has dealt with [it] by blocking all its computers' USB ports with glue. Every bit of portable memory in the sprawling American military establishment now needs to be scrubbed clean before it can be used again."[29] Likewise, externalities arising from networks may benefit some actors and deprive others: for example, the United States has benefited from establishing protocols for the Internet. Such increasing returns from network externalities may cause long-term disparities in the economic growth rates of nation-states, an insight of endogenous growth theory.[30]

Second, complex social systems matter because *their networked topology defies systems of regulation predicated on territorial jurisdictions*. This is why "one national financial system can wreck another halfway across the world,"[31] and patriotic hackers sitting at home can attack the computers of distant countries. Another compelling example is a recent study of the global intermodal shipping network (i.e., container shipping) that illustrated that a smart terrorist could wreak havoc on the American economy not by attacking ports in the United States, but instead by attacking Singapore. It estimated that a four-week closure of the port of Singapore would cost the American economy $23 billion in direct costs.[32] In this respect, complex social systems challenge traditional understandings of the "distant" and the "proximate"—geographically distant others may nevertheless be nearby in a social network:

> Organizational networks offer opportunities for people in both the local and global worlds to pursue their interests, serve their values, and become engaged in one or another aspect of public affairs . . . thereby rendering the tasks of states and other hierarchical organizations ever more difficult. Viewed from a micro perspective, moreover, the vast network of networks facilitates movement among the local, global and private worlds through which people cope with distant proximities.[33]

In this way, the processes of globalization undermine the "territorialist" ontology of traditional international relations theory.[34]

Third, complex social systems are consequential because policymakers *do not quite know how to manage their risks*. States have yet to agree whether cyberattacks constitute an act of war, an act of terrorism, or crime. Political leaders disagree whether to modify existing laws to prosecute offenders or to create new laws to strengthen enforcement.[35] Likewise, policymakers debate how best to prevent cyberattacks: one analyst has even proposed a deterrent strategy whereby a "botnet" of friendly computers would "carpet-bomb in cyberspace" to overwhelm the would-be attacker's computers.[36] Because complex systems have exponential effects, policymakers face stark choices when trying to control them. For example, when 2,500 turkeys in Britain developed the bird flu, public health officials culled an additional 160,000 birds to prevent the virus from spreading. Similarly, during an outbreak of foot-and-mouth disease, the government of Britain slaughtered four million livestock to manage the disease's propagation.[37] In a world of complex social systems with fuzzy, shifting, or nonexistent borders, policy instruments are blunt.

Until recently, theorists have shared the puzzlement of policymakers: although we recognize the importance of complex social systems, we do not know quite how to treat them theoretically. Part of this confusion arises from our adherence to the levels of analysis proposed by Waltz in *Man, the State, and War*: transnational networks do not fit neatly into the individual, state or systemic levels of analysis.[38] Likewise, do such systems constitute an "agent" or a "structure" in world politics (or perhaps both)? Our theoretical confusion also arises from debates about "change" in the international system, and yet theoretical treatments of change that focus on concepts such as path dependence, lock-in, and nonlinearity relate closely to the study of complex social systems. Computational social science helps us formalize such concepts. Increasingly, network theory, complex systems theory, and evolutionary game theory empower researchers of world politics to study difficult concepts such as "turbulence"[39] by problematizing interest formation, explicating agent-structure dynamics, and explaining how processes at lower levels of analysis "emerge" as important political phenomena.

Jackson and Nexon offer one of the more cogent explanations of how transnational and global social systems challenge our traditional methods of inquiry. Globalization, they argue, is a set of processes that "cordon[s] off subsets of social relations and bundle[s] them together to produce relatively coherent units."[40] This continual "mapping and remapping" of social relations undermines, however, the core ontological assumption of comparative analysis: that objects of comparison (whether states, institutions, classes, or other units of analysis) are "distinct, symmetrical and stable." For this reason, Jackson and Nexon call for the comparative study of "processes" as units of analysis, based on the insights of sociological relationalism.[41] Importantly, such processes relate closely to this book's definition of a complex social system:

> Social ties are created and maintained by processes of transaction. A social tie is a relation between two actors (or "sites"), such as domination, economic exchange, or communication.

> When taken together, social ties form networks of social transaction—such as hierarchies, organizational networks, scholarly communities, and so on.
>
> Units are particular kinds of configurations of social ties or networks of social relations. While the comparative method treats units as essentially stable entities, comparative process analysis assumes that units, categories, and corporate actors are constituted by dynamic networks of social and political ties. The discreteness and symmetry of units are properties of their underlying network form.[42]

Jackson and Nexon's comparative process ontology in essence calls for the study of systems over time: "underlying network form" provides the symmetry and discreteness necessary for units of analysis, while the focus on dynamics allows scholars to understand the ongoing mapping and remapping of social ties. These processes are, furthermore, independent of levels of analysis: such processes may occur at any level and may operate across levels.[43] Although such a process ontology is not necessarily equivalent to social network analysis, the language Jackson and Nexon use—for "ties" and "sites" one could easily substitute the words "vertices" and "nodes"—suggests parallels to the concerns of social network analysis and complex systems theory.

Jackson and Nexon's interest in exchange, transaction, and communication recalls, furthermore, earlier attention among political scientists to cybernetics. Karl Deutsch's *The Nerves of Government: Models of Political Communication and Control* was an early attempt to apply cybernetics and communication theory to political science questions.[44] Deutsch is only one of a number of political scientists who have expressed an interest in understanding problems of learning, adaptation, and change in politics. Thomas Schelling explored the irreducibility of social phenomena in *Micromotives and Macrobehavior*;[45] polymath Herbert Simon was an early critic of rational choice theory who introduced ideas such as "satisficing" and bounded rationality that have influenced the study of political adaptation;[46] and Barry Hughes has followed Deutsch's lead in applying system dynamics modeling to explain change in international politics.[47] This brief survey suggests that the ideas of network theory, complex systems, and evolutionary game theory are not entirely novel: for several decades they have been central concerns of observers of world politics. This is not a criticism. Quite the contrary: computational social science represents a continuity of thought that is the hallmark of progressive social science.

None of the three theories under consideration in this chapter is a theory of world politics—comparable, for example, to structural realism or neoliberal institutionalism, to take two of the more influential theories. Of course, neither is rational choice a theory of world politics, but it nevertheless has influenced both structural realism and neoliberal institutionalism. Likewise, organizational process models apply to both firms and governments, while bureaucratic politics models offer hypotheses of decision making in the Pentagon, the Supreme Court, and in corporate board rooms. To criticize complex social science for its silence on the questions of world politics misses the point: Theories can offer hypotheses that apply to various units and levels of analysis. In this respect, criticisms of computational social science are symptomatic of broader problems in globalization theory. Walker has argued that structural theories of international relations derived from rational choice have marginalized the subdiscipline from broader insights of social theory.[48] Whether or not one agrees with the sociological turn in theories of world politics, critical theorists such as Walker, Gramscians such as Gill, and constructivists such as Wendt have reintroduced ideas from social theory into debates about how we theorize about global dynamics.[49] Likewise, network, complex systems, and evolutionary game theories all address core concerns of social theory. To the degree that scholars of world politics have re-embedded theories in broader insights from social theory, then, they may draw insights about complexity, dynamism, and adaptation in world politics from the theories and methods of computational social science.[50]

Network Theory and Social Network Analysis

In world politics, some properties of interaction among actors "are not reducible either to individual properties or structural characteristics."[51] That is, the organization of relations among social actors may shape their behavior independent of their preferences (an individual-level trait) and social structural factors (such as constitutive and regulative norms). As Sawyer notes, such irreducible properties may include patterns of communications and control, issues with which cybernetics and communications have long been concerned.[52] Network theory seeks to understand and model formally these relationships between interacting and interdependent units; rather than simply assuming interdependencies, network theory formalizes and explicitly represents the structure and nature of these relationships using graphs.[53] As a methodological subfield, social network analysis seeks to "measure and represent these structural relations accurately, and to explain both why they occur and what are their consequences."[54] Social network analysis represents social actors as "nodes" or "vertices" and maps relations among actors as "edges." Edges may be directed (the relationship is one way—a student may consider me his friend, though I think otherwise) or undirected (such as a mutual relationship—my wife and I presumably think of each other as friends). Importantly, relations captured by edges are a "joint dyadic property that exists only so long as both actors maintain their association."[55] Thus, one cannot attribute edges in a network to the behavior or preferences of a single social actor: "Relations reflect emergent dimensions of complex social systems that cannot be captured by simply summing or averaging its members' attitudes."[56]

Because social networks shape perceptions, beliefs, and interests of actors, they may facilitate social cooperation through a variety of mechanisms: control over information, the promotion of shared values and norms, and the construction of shared identities.[57] Social networks are dynamic, furthermore:

> Networks are not static structures, but are continually changing through interactions among their constituent people, groups, or organizations. In applying their knowledge about networks to leverage advantages, these entities also transform the relational structures within which they are embedded, both intentionally and unintentionally.[58]

Thus, network theory is one approach to thinking about the interrelationship between social agents and social structures. Indeed, it is explicitly concerned with understanding social phenomena across levels of analysis: "Because network analysis simultaneously encompasses both structures and entities, it provides conceptual and methodological tools for linking changes in microlevel choices to macrolevel structural alterations."[59]

Methods for analyzing network dynamics include formal representations of networks (graph theory) and an array of statistical measures of network properties, including the density of ties; the identification of "subgraphs" or social cliques; "distance" or path lengths between social actors; actor centrality and prestige; and others.[60] A "network" simply consists of a number n of nodes (vertices), each of which has k connections (edges) to some of the other nodes; these edges may be directed or undirected. The number of edges a given node has is its "degree." One can characterize a network by its density D, the ratio of the number of edges to the total number of possible edges, or $D = \Sigma k / [n (n - 1)]$; the distribution of k; and many other measures. Two important measures are a network's clustering coefficient and its average path length. To recall, a "path length" between two nodes is the number of edges along the shortest route between them. The average path length thus measures the mean distance between nodes in a network. The clustering coefficient of a network is the probability that two nodes are connected given that both are connected to a common third node. The clustering coefficient measures the tendency of nodes to cluster together.[61]

By measuring the attributes of networks, researchers have identified several common types. A random network is one in which a random process creates edges among vertices. In random networks, the degree distribution approximates the Poisson distribution. The random attachment rule generally creates a network with very low clustering and relatively short path lengths. A "scale-free" network is one for which the degree follows a power law distribution. This distribution arises because such networks grow through a process of preferential attachment, whereby the probability of new edges incident to a node increases as the node's degree increases.[62] Scale-free networks are characterized by a few large "hubs," or vertices with a large number of incident edges, but most vertices have just a few edges.[63] For this reason, they tend to have lower clustering but higher average path lengths. By contrast, "small world" networks have higher clustering coefficients but shorter average path lengths.[64]

In principle, these methodological tools allow researchers to study any social network provided they have sufficient empirical data. Of course, data collection is always a challenge, but it is particularly so for the study of networks in world politics. For example, suppose one wanted to study transnational class allegiances. A number of researchers recently have argued that elites have increasingly dense transnational ties that weaken their sense of loyalty to their home states. Sklair and others argue these ties reflect class relations;[65] Huntington similarly asserts American elites increasingly are "denationalized" as their social ties with fellow citizens weaken.[66] Elites are "more likely to spend their time chatting with their peers around the world—via phone or email—than talking with their neighbors in the projects around the corner."[67] These arguments suggest a reconfiguration of the social ties of elites: from local networks of national elites to transnational networks of global elites. One can envision a research project that identifies a community of global elites and maps their domestic and international social networks, but the research costs would be considerable. In additional to the usual challenges of boundary specification—both of identifying who are elites and of establishing a boundary on their relations—a researcher likely would face language barriers as well. Similar research obstacles would face a scholar studying transnational advocacy networks.[68] The challenge of social network analysis then is not theoretical or methodological: it is empirical, the lack of useable network data. Perhaps for this reason, political scientists and other social scientists have simply assumed that network structure does not matter: "Many models assume that agents are bunched together on the head of a pin, whereas the reality is that most agents exist within a topology of connections to other agents, and such connections may have an important influence on behavior."[69] In the argot of network theory, the "head of a pin" assumption is equivalent to assuming that social networks are "fully connected"—that is to say, that each actor has a symmetrical, undirected relationship with every other actor. While this may be a useful simplifying assumption driven by practical research considerations, it nevertheless is incommensurate with arguments that the organization of social ties affects the possibilities and forms of collective political action.

Complex Systems Theory and Agent-Based Modeling

The "new" network theory, a field in which researchers use computers to study very large and complex networks, relates closely to complex systems theory.[70] This theory's name begs the question of what political scientists mean by "complex." With origins in physics and economics, complex systems theory studies "complex adaptive systems" (or CAS) that share three characteristics. The first is massive parallelism: such systems consist of thousands, millions, or even billions of autonomous actors, with actors at one level of analysis aggregating into actors at a higher level. These actors are autonomous in the sense that they are free of centralized control or authority, but they may have interdependent interests and choices. Many physical, biological, and social phenomena exhibit these properties of massive parallelism, from "the connected lives of ants, brains, cities, and software" to "termites and traffic jams."[71] The metaphor of a traffic jam is illustrative and harkens to Schelling's discussion of interdependent decision making: drivers are independent in the sense that they take no direction from a single, central authority, yet their choices are interdependent and consequently may produce traffic jams.[72] Second, actors in a CAS typically follow local and often simple decision rules. Rather than being omniscient beings, actors have imperfect and incomplete information. They are not rational utility maximizers: rather, they may be satisficiers, cognitive misers, boundedly rational, and "prone to error, bias, fear and other foibles."[73] The characterization of agents as prone to foibles shares the goal of behavioral economists to understand how a relaxation of the assumption of rational utility maximization may affect our understanding of the behavior of social systems.[74] Third, as their name suggests, CAS grow, change, evolve, and adapt over time as agents in the system incorporate new information into their behavior through learning, mimicry of successful actors, and other strategies.[75] This focus on simple and local decision rules shares with constructivists a commitment to understanding processes of interest formation. As discussed below, complex systems theorists today model such agent adaptation using insights from evolutionary game theory.

Complex systems theorists seek to study "emergence," or "stable macroscopic patterns arising from the local interactions of agents."[76] Emergence is a paradoxical property of complex systems. While the interactions of a large number of interdependent actors may produce an emergent phenomenon, the phenomenon itself may assume an ontological importance of its own, shaping future decisions of actors. While emergent phenomena themselves may be unsurprising, Epstein and Axtell argue that it is nevertheless surprising that local (i.e., microlevel) and simple decision rules produce such stable macroscopic patterns.[77] There are numerous examples of emergence: drivers wish to avoid traffic jams but nevertheless produce them; fireflies synchronize their flashing;[78] slime can "learn" to solve a maze;[79] competitive firms cluster together in high-cost areas;[80] and people make runs on healthy banks,[81] to name just a few. All of these examples illustrate the fallacies of inferring properties of constituent parts from the system as a whole, or, conversely, of inferring systemic properties from those of its constituent parts. Miller and Page note, "Knowledge of the old system . . . does not directly help us model the new, higher-level system."[82] Thus, complex systems theory explains how behaviors at the individual level aggregate into higher-level structural features of a system. It explicitly investigates micro-macro linkages and the level-of-analysis problem by offering specific causal explanations. Complex systems theory is a general theory: its hypotheses are independent of empirical domains, offering a general set of tools and concepts—if not a theory—to understand social complexity.[83] Like biological and physical systems, social systems feature positive and negative feedback; multiple interactions over time; and learning and adaptation.

Evolutionary Game Theory

Two important sources of dynamics in complex systems are the adaptation and learning of social actors. Recent research suggests that statesmen and citizens alike exhibit greater levels of cognitive complexity today than they did a century ago.[84] Another study finds evidence that the spread of neoliberal market practices in part arises from policy "diffusion," or the process through which states learn of the benefits of a policy from their neighbors.[85] Terrorist groups likewise appear to learn and adopt innovations based on their relationships with other groups.[86] Policymakers exhibit learning in the field of national security as well; Adler finds, for example, that U.S. technical experts helped teach strategic concepts to Soviet leaders that made the 1972 Anti-Ballistic Missile Treaty possible.[87] The work of Adler and others on the role of epistemic communities in educating decision makers has generated a research agenda on international learning.[88] Together, this research suggests that learning and adaptation in world politics are both evolutionary and relational: states, terrorists, leaders, corporations, NGOs, individuals, and others adapt and learn not in isolation, but in relation to the learning and innovations of others. This coevolution of political actors is arguably a constitutive feature of world politics.

A branch of evolutionary game theory takes a similar approach to analyzing how players learn when facing dilemmas of social choice. Player learning arises from two forms of feedback from the structure of social interaction. One is changes in the distribution of strategies within the population of actors due to players dropping out, mimicking successful players, or the reproduction of "offspring." As players exit the game or ape the tactics of others, a player competes against an ever-changing "ecology" or set of strategies. The other form of feedback is the process of reinforcement, in which an individual player changes his or her portfolio of strategies in response to success or failure.[89] The coevolution of reinforcement with the ecology of strategies represents one way to model how actors in world politics learn and adapt. First developed in the field of behavioral ecology, evolutionary game theory has adopted insights from evolutionary biology to explain why some strategies, though suboptimal, are nevertheless "evolutionarily stable" in the sense that, if a population of players adopts the strategy, no other possible strategy will tip the population to a different configuration of strategies.[90] Much like genes in a species embedded in an ecosystem, then, player strategies are embedded in an ecology of other players with other strategies.

This approach to learning represents one solution to the analytic challenge of multiple equilibria in many social dilemmas from classical game theory. Social dilemmas with multiple equilibria are both an achievement and a problem of game theory. The parsimony of game theory's formalism allows researchers to deduce multiple possible outcomes in social dilemmas, but many find it unsatisfying that we have to resort to ad hoc explanations to understand which equilibrium players will achieve in real world social dilemmas. David Kreps, a prominent game theorist, used the example of the "ultimatum game" to discuss why multiple equilibria are so unsatisfying. In this game, if two players can agree to a division of some fixed pot of money, they will divide the spoils, but in the absence of agreement, neither player receives a payoff. This game is interesting because players may divide the money in many ways that one cannot predict a priori. Suppose two players in a one-round ultimatum game must divide $100. A shrewd player might insist on $99; if indeed the other player is rational, he or she will accept the $1 because, after all, he or she will be a dollar better off than before the game. Using this logic, a split of $90 to $10 is also an equilibrium as is 80/20 or 50/50. Kreps noted:

> There are, therefore, lots of Nash equilibria to this game. Which one is the "solution"? I have no idea and, more to the point, game

theory isn't much help. . . . *Some (important) sorts of games have many equilibria, and the theory is of no help in sorting out whether any one is the "solution" and, if one is, which one is.*[91]

Evolutionary game theory tries to solve the problem of multiple equilibria by exploring the probability distribution of the universe of possible outcomes. By experimentally varying factors that classical game theory takes as a given—including how players learn, noisy versus perfect communication, and social networks—we understand not which of many equilibria is "the" solution, but rather the likelihood that players will reach a particular equilibrium. Computer simulations are particularly useful for studying such problems because they can explore vast parameter spaces efficiently and inexpensively. Compared to human subject experiments, simulation is a much more efficient way of tackling the problem of multiple equilibria.

Related to the idea of multiple equilibria is the problem of multiple strategies. In an iterative game, how do players form expectations, learn, and change their strategies? Again, Kreps notes, "Formal mathematical game theory has said little or nothing about where these expectations come from, how or why they persist, or when and why we might expect them to arise."[92] Evolutionary game theory addresses these questions in part using three insights from natural selection discussed in chapter 1: conservation, innovation, and selection. Suppose one simulates a multiplayer game by creating a population of players with expectations and memories that initially are random. *Conservation mechanisms* in such a simulation allow the best strategies to persist in a multiplayer game. *Innovation mechanisms* give rise to new strategies to compete against current ones. *Selection mechanisms* allow better strategies to thrive and multiply in the long run. The analogy to natural selection is useful: players compete and innovate, while selection pressures allow only the fittest to continue to play. One important implication of evolutionary game theory is that multiple "best" strategies are theoretically possible: because one strategy competes against a population of strategies, the fittest strategy is the "best" one only in the sense that it is optimal for that particular and historically unique set of strategies. Other distributions of strategies and/or players might produce other "best" strategies. Indeed, some researchers have concluded that the variety of possible equilibrium strategies in social dilemma games is very large. The "folk theorem" captures this idea: given infinite time and iteration, any strategy is an equilibrium strategy.[93] Thus, an important insight of evolutionary game theory is that the population of strategies in the game itself changes over time. While classical game theory may be correct that "tit-for-tat" is the best strategy for an iterated prisoner's dilemma (that is, a strategy of reciprocating cooperation with cooperation, and defection with defection), this result only holds for particular configurations of strategies in a particular population of players. Indeed, Boyd and Lorberbaum find that many strategies perform as well as tit-for-tat and that no one strategy is evolutionarily stable.[94]

Among scholars of world politics, one of the more well-known applications of evolutionary game theory was Robert Axelrod's prisoner's dilemma tournament, which found that the tit-for-tat strategy performed the best.[95] Axelrod's tournament allowed several researchers to develop a variety of strategies that they implemented in computer code, but the strategies themselves did not change or evolve during the tournament. By contrast, simulations informed by evolutionary game theory increasingly allow player strategies to evolve endogenously.[96] In this respect, evolutionary game theory illustrates how actors form their preferences and how this preference formation itself reflects opportunities and constraints of an ever-changing social structure. This is a considerable advance from classic game theory's embrace of Morgenstern and von Neumann's rational utility theory. Nevertheless, Macy and Flache offer two cautions. One is that it "leaves to our imagination how successful rules might spread throughout the culture."[97] Of course, one mechanism of transmission may be social networks, suggesting fruitful interchange between social network analysis and evolutionary game theory, but the theory itself is silent on these mechanisms of transmission. The other concern is that "little is known about how fitness translates into the replication of cultural rules like reciprocity or altruistic norms. Analogs of genetic replication can be deceptive since social learning and sexual reproduction operate with very different logics."[98] These are important warnings to social scientists who borrow concepts from ecology. Nevertheless, as if in response to Macy and Flache's criticism, two studies recently have used simulations informed by evolutionary game theory to explore the emergence of altruism.[99] Other researchers also use insights from evolutionary game theory to explore constructivists' concerns with ideational and identity factors.[100]

It is worth reiterating that evolutionary game theory departs from classical game theory's interest in equilibria solutions. The evolutionary approach illustrates how multiple possible solutions to social choice problems are possible, and how these solutions themselves depend upon processes of interaction, communication, and learning among a population of players. This approach offers a method for studying the constitutive dynamics that recently have interested scholars of world politics. A substantial body of literature in the field is concerned with understanding the processes by which states adapt, from neofunctionalism to ideas about socialization of states and "world models."[101] Evolutionary game theory thus is consistent with theories that emphasize learning and change as a corrective for the static bias in structural theories.[102]

LINKING SOCIAL THEORY TO SIMULATION METHODS: FROM BEHAVIOR TO INTERESTS

Computational social science does not offer answers to an essential question of globalization theory: Who are the actors in world politics? Nevertheless, complex systems theory, social network analysis, and evolutionary game theory help formalize our thinking about three debates that are central to the study of world politics: How do actors relate to social structure? How do actors form and change their preferences? What does the process of interest formation imply for the prospects for change in the global system? To answer these questions, computational social science makes theoretically and empirically informed assumptions about actor behavior, and then simulates how their interests emerge from interactions with other actors.

Complex systems theory and network theory both implicitly seek to understand how agents and social structures are mutually constitutive. Miller and Page note, for example, that political scientists who use complex systems theory "would like to be able to develop a theory that helps us understand how states of the world (composed of lower-level entities and interaction rules) are transformed into higher-level entities."[103] This argument closely parallels Wight's discussion of the agent-structure debate: "What appears as a structure on one level becomes an agent on another. Hence . . . the international system plays the role of structure with the nation state as an agent."[104] The conception of social structure put forth by Wendt, Giddens, and other structuration theorists is very similar to complexity theorists' concept of emergence: while the actions and choices of actors produce the emergent behavior of complex systems, such emergent properties in turn constrain the actions and choices of actors. This recursion of agency and structure is readily apparent in Schelling's classic segregation model, which complex systems theorists often cite as an important example of emergence.[105] Schelling illustrated how even a society of tolerant individuals can produce patterns of stark residential segregation; thus, one cannot reduce the emergent property (segregation) to the preferences of social actors (tolerant citizens). The interdependent decision making of tolerant citizens produces, furthermore, a "locked in" social structure that is robust. Wendt makes a very similar argument about anarchy in the international system: though in an important way states have "made" anarchy, this social structure in turn is robust and conditions the preferences of states such that actors and structures reproduce each other.[106] Likewise, Miller and Page see mutual constitution in institutions and social structure: "Institutions do not sit in isolation from one another, but are linked to each other and the culture within which they exist. Cultural features like the level of trust, the set of common behavioral rules, and the density of social networks all provide an important context for an institution."[107] In this respect, mutual constitution is one emergent property of complex social systems.

While the levels of analysis problem in world politics relates to the agent-structure debate, several scholars argue it is a distinct epistemological concern.[108] Computational social science does not identify any fundamental levels of analysis in the study of world politics. There is nothing ontologically inherent about social individuals in complex systems, while social network analysis acknowledges that while analysts can draw a boundary around a social network for purposes of analysis, in reality they are deeply enmeshed in larger-scale networks. In this respect, computational social science calls attention to the levels of analysis problem even though none of these theories speak to the classic levels of the individual, state, and global system. Nevertheless, social network analysis and complex systems theory are powerful tools for analyzing the relationships between levels of analysis. Miller and Page argue that complex systems theory helps social scientists "explore a new realm that both acknowledges the microfoundations of macrobehavior while simultaneously recognizing the potential for seemingly magical transformations that link one level to another."[109] Similarly, Jackson and Nexon argue their proposed process ontology is useful precisely because political processes can occur at different levels of analysis.[110] Indeed, early theorists of complex systems and networks developed their ideas precisely as a critique of reductionist social science. Networks and systems possess causal properties that one cannot attribute to constituent parts: "There are fundamental properties and laws of interaction—based, for example, on semiotics, cybernetics, or communications theory—that are not reducible either to individual properties or structural characteristics."[111] In essence, network theory, complex systems theory, and game theory (both in its classic and evolutionary variants) address the fallacy of composition and the ecological fallacy. Just because social agents exhibit behaviors or interests does not logically mean the social system will possess those traits: rational self-interested farmers produces a socially sub-Pareto optimal outcome in the tragedy of the commons, while tolerant citizens may nevertheless produce segregated neighborhoods and cities. To take another example, individuals with stable, transitive, and ordered preferences may nevertheless produce intransitive swings in social choices, as the next chapter discusses. Even though the collective choice may change, it does not follow that individual citizens are changing their minds (rather, we simply may have changed the rules by which we aggregate individual choices into social choices).[112] Conversely, one cannot infer the voting behavior of subpopulations based on the population as a whole. Computational social science helps us think through these fallacies of inference across levels of analysis. It provides hypotheses to explain why the behavior and properties of social collectives may diverge from the preferences and properties of individuals.

The observable dynamism of complex systems in the natural and physical worlds suggests that computational social science has something useful to say about "change" in world politics. The literature on "change" in world politics is vast[113] but one recent theoretical debate seems apposite to evolutionary game theory and complex systems theory. Constructivists have criticized structural theories that rely on rational choice because they take the interests of social actors as a given. If so, theories such as neo-realism and neoliberal institutionalism fail to explain the origins of state preferences, and without a theory of preference formation, these theories cannot explain processes of learning among states.[114] The resulting structural explanation of "change" is rather modest: these theories can explain regular interstate processes such as cooperation, trade, and warfare that Gilpin characterizes as "interaction change," but they explain neither evolution in the nature of actors nor changes in the governance of the global system.[115] For this reason, Wendt calls for theories and models that endogenize processes of actor preference formation and learning: "The challenge for those who would be holists rather than individualists on the systemic level is to build a theory in which state identities and interests are endogenous rather than exogenous to interaction."[116] Interestingly, complex systems theory takes this very approach: it inverts the assumptions of rational choice theory that constructivists criticize. Rational choice theory takes interests as a given and then models behavior. Complex systems theory, by contrast, makes theoretically informed assumptions about simple agent behavior and then models processes of interest formation and learning. Rather than being omniscient utility maximizers, computational social scientists tend to model social agents as cognitive misers who follow simple decision rules—much as behavioral economists assume.[117] Actor preferences and interests coevolve, or respond both to the selection pressures of other actors in the social system and to their own internalized rule models of "success" and "failure."[118] Computational social scientists likewise study the contingency of social actors themselves. Tellingly, some constructivists use methods and concepts from complex systems theory. Hoffmann employs an agent-based model (ABM) to study the emergence of regulative and constitutive norms of environmental governance.[119] Lustick simulates social actors with repertoires of latent identities and uses insights from constructivist theory to explain the emergence of collective identities.[120] Miodownik similarly studies the emergence of regional autonomy movements.[121] These examples all exhibit a shared concern with endogenizing processes of identity and interest formation. As these works show, furthermore, complex systems theory and evolutionary game theory offer theoretical and methodological tools to "mediat[e] the social-scientific goal of causal generalization and the constructivist emphasis on contingency."[122] Miller and Page see the use of these simulation methods as a natural progression in social science: "[W]e have seen a movement toward behavioralism and learning models. At each point along this path, social scientists have struggled with what to assume about behavior. A complex adaptive systems approach allows the level of agent sophistication, and even the behavior itself, to adapt."[123]

Of course, the agent-structure debate, levels of analysis, and arguments about preference formation exist independently of the tools of computational social science. One does not *need* these tools to understand the relationship between agents and structures, logical fallacies arising from levels of analysis, and the relationship between preferences and behavior. Yet computational social science offers a methodological rigor that existing theories of agents and structures sorely lack. This rigor includes a commitment to three of the goals of social science: the reproducibility of findings, the transmission of knowledge to the community of scholars, and generalization across empirical domains. All three theories offer *general* arguments. Complex systems theory posits causal hypotheses that characterize massively parallel systems of all empirical fields from physics to chemistry, biology, anthropology, sociology, economics, and political science. Evolutionary game theory, with its origins in mathematical biology, is similarly ecumenical in its focus, while network theory offers statistical and mathematical tools for characterizing and studying physical and biological as well as social networks. All three theories assure transmissibility and reproducibility through a set of shared methodological tools. Perhaps the biggest challenge to the methods of computational social science is the reproducibility of findings, but practitioners have engaged in an ongoing and productive debate on protocols for model validation and replication.[124] Game theory in general has a long tradition of formal modeling that is an invaluable tool for rigorous inquiry, while network theory also has developed formal and statistical methods that permit replication of results. Given the difficulty that even professional researchers have disentangling cause-and-effect relationships in complex social systems, such methodological consistency is all the more important. Computational social science can help researchers understand these confounding social systems by providing rigorous analytical methods.

These theories also provide formal definitions for ideas and concepts that students of world politics have used in abundance, but often without providing operational definitions. The profligate use of "networks" as a heuristic is but one example. Complex systems theory offers formal definitions for ideas such as the coevolution of political actors and their environments, sensitivity to initial conditions, phase transitions, punctuated equilibria, and the "power of small events."[125] Ideas from political economy and historical institutionalism such as cumulative causation, path dependence, and historical lock-in also find operational definitions in complex systems theory.[126] By no means are these methods the only formal ways to study agents and structures, learning, emergence across levels, and change. However, scholars have developed extensively the tools of computational social science and practice them widely across disciplines. These methods force the student of world politics to think precisely about the processes and ontologies that Giddens, Wendt, Wight, Walker, Jackson and Nexon, and others identify as centrally important to understanding contemporary world politics.

SIMULATING COMPLEX GLOBAL SOCIAL SYSTEMS WITH AGENT-BASED MODELS

Chapters 3 through 7 explore various complex systems in world politics, from the most general social choice problems to practical challenges such as environmental conservation and banking regulation. Each chapter presents an agent-based model (ABM). As a method, ABM seeks to illustrate how simple decision rules at the micro level are sufficient to generate stable macrolevel structures. This is a computational method that represents each social actor as a discrete software miniprogram known as an "object," which a computer then aggregates into a "system" by keeping track of each actor's interests, decisions, and position over time either in a simulated physical space or in a network topology.[127] Thus, an ABM uses thousands or more objects to replicate the parallelism of complex social systems. ABMs require researchers to use algorithms—or statements of procedures written in a computer language—to formalize the details of social processes. This encoding process is similar to the process of formalization in traditional game theory, and introduces a rigor to the modeling process that can help researchers identify hidden assumptions in their theories:

> Appreciating the lack of process precision we employ in our modeling is difficult until one takes a standard model and implements it computationally. . . . Given both the flexibility and precision inherent in computational models, these methods can be a nice way to structure new problems. Computational implementations of problems often illuminate the key features and processes that must be modeled.[128]

Like deductive reasoning, ABM shares a commitment to explicit assumptions: whereas game theory does so with formulae, ABMs do so with algorithms. Yet ABM also allows for induction as well. By creating emergent social phenomena from the "bottom up,"[129] ABMs produce pseudo data that scholars then can analyze inductively to detect patterns and causal interactions of interest. Because ABMs are computer models, furthermore, they permit researchers to vary parameters experimentally and generate thousands of simulations "to build a robust statistical portrait" of the system of interest.[130] Axelrod argues that ABMs represent a "third way of doing science"[131] while Epstein and Axtell call agent-based modeling "generative social science," in which "Can you explain it?" is replaced with "Can you grow it?" in an ABM.[132]

Several of the models in this book use genetic algorithms to simulate processes of actor learning and adaptation. A genetic algorithm is a set of computer procedures that borrows insights from evolutionary biology to allow the program to change, adapt, and learn over time.[133] The language of genetic algorithms illustrates the intellectual debt it owes to biology. An ABM may endow actors with a "population" of randomly generated strategies. Through repeated runs of the models, actors will select those strategies that are most effective, and then will "cross over" these strategies to create new ones—fit parents should produce fit offspring. Finally, a genetic algorithm has actors "mutate" their strategies. That is, with some low probability actors will try a new strategy. Through repeated cycles of selection, crossover, and mutation, genetic algorithms help actors find fit strategies for solving difficult social choice problems. A genetic algorithm's use of selection, crossover, and mutation procedures allows it to identify and select good strategies, conserve information about effective strategies, and innovate—all elements of how real world actors learn. Researchers have found that genetic algorithms efficiently search vast parameter spaces and find high-performing solutions to problems for which there are multiple possible solutions. For example, Axelrod used a genetic algorithm to demonstrate that tit-for-tat (or related retaliation strategies such as tit-for-two-tats) optimizes players' payoffs in the iterated prisoner's dilemma.[134] The use of genetic algorithms in social simulation has become more commonplace.[135]

Although it is not the only method for studying complex social systems, ABM offers observers of world politics several advantages. First, ABM methods focus on nonlinear and interactive dynamics rather than on equilibrium solutions. By their very nature, complex social systems produce surprising outcomes: minor microlevel perturbations may produce considerable macrolevel changes—the well-known "butterfly effect."[136] Alternatively, large macrolevel fluctuations may dampen out over time, making systems resilient to perturbation. As Pepinsky notes, one cannot easily study these nonlinear dynamics empirically, since statistical techniques require either knowledge of the data generation process (in which case statistics is superfluous) or strong assumptions about structural equations (which may limit the generality of findings).[137] By modeling actors at the micro level, ABM does not require any assumptions about structural factors. Of course, mathematical techniques such as game theory explicitly seek to uncover such nonobvious systemic implications by proceeding deductively from axiom to outcome. By focusing on equilibrium solutions, however, formal theory may eschew precisely those dynamics across levels of analysis that are of most interest to the researcher. By contrast, ABM permits the researcher to induce systemic dynamics and to uncover surprising implications of simple individual-level decision rules. Likewise, ABM is useful for studying systems with a large number of confounding variables and with a large number of interaction effects.[138] Second, in many complex social systems, theoretically interesting events may be extraordinarily rare. This is one reason the researcher may face difficulties with and high costs to gathering data.[139] Global climate change is one such complex social system. While researchers may have a small number of observations of ecological collapse—of fisheries, for example—we have valid and reliable empirical data about only one human-induced global warming event. The rarity of such events makes problematic the statistical analysis of causal relationships. By contrast, an ABM allows scholars of world politics a method for exploring counterfactuals. Because researchers construct such models in a computer, they can easily explore how alternative specifications of the model affect outcomes of interest. This exploration of counterfactuals allows researchers to produce alternative "histories" of a nonlinear system that many empirical methods do not permit.[140] Finally, agent-based models permit the researcher to probe for internal inconsistencies in a model.[141] By exploring the parameter space, either through the iterative combination of parameter values or through artificially intelligent algorithms, a researcher may uncover particular values of factors that give rise to phenomena of interest. This can allow researchers to gain theoretic insights, but also to uncover hidden assumptions and causal factors that are not plausible. For example, Miller used a genetic algorithm to explore the parameter space of a well-known computer simulation of resource depletion and environmental degradation.[142]

Of course, ABM is not a true experimental method: the researcher experiments with a model rather than an actual social system. Nevertheless, ABM researchers can use quasi-true experimental designs both to validate the model's representation of the real world system, and to test hypotheses about the real world system. As in a true experimental design, in a quasi-true ABM experiment the researcher can repeat the application of experimental stimulus, determine the timing of the application of the stimulus, alter parameter values, and explore alternative specifications.[143] This is important not only for inference, but also because it shifts the scientific enterprise away from the habit of searching for "the" answer and toward the habit of evaluating competing, and inherently incomplete, explanations.[144] That is, with repeated ABM simulations, scholars of world politics can ask which models offer better explanations and which do not, rather than debating which theory or model is the "right" one.

ABM also is an intuitive method for understanding the turbulence of world politics. There is considerable research to suggest individuals have a difficult time understanding such nonlinear systems. Even highly educated scholars do not necessarily recognize positive and negative feedback in systems, temporal lags, and other dynamics typical of complex adaptive social systems. One study found no significant difference in the "systems thinking" skills of high school teachers and their students.[145] Another study presented asked researchers at MIT to explain observed dynamics in two simulations, one of a traffic jam and the other of the life cycle of slime mold. In the traffic jam simulation, the researchers confused the relationship between microlevel behavior (the cars) and macrolevel structures (the propagation of the jam from front to back).[146] In the other simulation, many of the researchers incorrectly predicted how a slight change in the behavior of slime bacteria would affect the emergent mold.[147] Unlike other areas of scientific inquiry in which individuals may possess natural or innate understandings,[148] individuals neither possess inherent systems thinking skills nor develop them naturally as they mature or receive more education. That is, individuals of all ages must be taught systems thinking skills.[149] ABM helps improve our systems thinking because simulations "are expressed in terms (e.g., agents, space, forces, growth, inhibition, attraction, and causation) that are close to natural psychological structures and processes."[150] For these reasons, ABM holds the promise of helping scholars of world politics better understand *processes*—the evolution, adaptation, aggregation, dissolution, learning, stretching, intensification, acceleration, and other dynamics of complex social systems—in ways that static or equilibrium methods such as game theory and statistics cannot.

Artificial Societies versus Evidence-Driven ABM

Two competing ABM paradigms have emerged in the last fifteen years. One tradition is what one might call the "artificial society" tradition, while the other is the "evidence-driven modeling" tradition.[151] As Moss notes, "The point of departure for the design and implementation of any formal model will be characterized by some balance of theory and evidence."[152] The different traditions place greater emphasis on one criterion or the other, but inevitably both must make assumptions and compromises between these two objectives. The models in chapters 3 through 6 reflect the artificial society tradition, while that in chapter 7 adopts an evidence-driven approach. Artificial society modelers prefer parsimonious models characterized by very few parameters; simple procedures; few types of social actors; and a simple representation of the spaces in which simulated actors interact.[153] These modelers do not claim that their models are "valid" representations of the real world system they seek to understand. Instead, they argue that simple, parsimonious models may nevertheless produce nontrivial and nonobvious explanations about emergent phenomena in the real world. For artificial society modelers, the purpose of a model—even one that is "wrong" in the sense that it omits many important features of reality—is to help us understand dynamics, and to direct our theorizing and empirical research toward causal relationships that otherwise we cannot identify. Models are meant to be explorations rather than explanations.

By contrast, the evidence-driven modeling tradition emphasizes building computational models that are valid representations of the real world. Unlike artificial society modelers for whom empirical research is the final step of modeling, evidence-driven modelers begin with careful empirical measurement of the real world system, its actors, and their preferences, behaviors, and decision-making procedures. Only with a considerable understanding of the real world system can an evidence-driven modeler begin to write computer code and then simulate the real world system. Evidence-driven models tend to have more parameters, a greater variety of actors, and more numerous and more complicated procedures than artificial life models.

The two types of models present some tradeoffs. Put simply, artificial society models are easier to understand, whereas evidence-driven models tend to be more "realistic" or valid. Because evidence-driven models have more parameters and more procedures, researchers have a harder time discerning the causal processes in such models. By contrast, although artificial life modelers have an easier time uncovering causal relationships in their models, the abstract nature of their models makes them hard to validate—that is, to demonstrate that they more or less accurately represent reality. It is important to note, furthermore, that researchers do not agree on the meaning of "validation," let alone protocols for validating models. To some, "validity" means that the model produces emergent or system behaviors that one observes in the real world system (macro validity), while for others "validity" means that agents in the model behave similarly to real world actors (micro validity).[154]

Limitations of ABM

Like all methods, agent-based modeling has some drawbacks. For one, the *sufficiency* of local rules to produce emergent behavior is not logically the same as the *necessity* of local rules. "Consider the converse of the generative claim," Diermeier cautions. "'If you grew it, you explained it.'"[155] Such strong claims are absurd, of course, and agent-based modelers argue researchers must complement computer models with empirical investigations, though here too computational social science affords vast new opportunities for collecting and analyzing empirical data.[156] Second, many agent-based models may treat as unproblematic a variety of ontological concerns that have infused scholarship on world politics in recent years.[157] As Pepinsky further notes, "Both the methodology and epistemology of simulation rely on thick ontological and epistemological presuppositions of what agents are relevant, how the environment appears to the agents, and how processes and parameters shape complex systems. . . . Unfortunately, these epistemological issues and ontological presumptions are obscured by the methodology."[158] Cederman likewise notes that ABMs tend to rely upon ad hoc rather than theoretically informed assumptions.[159] As with formal and statistical techniques, researchers need to avoid reification. Third, modelers have yet to agree on what constitutes a "valid" model or how to validate them.[160] To some, validation refers to the calibration of a model's initial parameters;[161] others discuss "validity" as the replication of results;[162] and still others use validity to refer to the relationship between theory, the model, simulation software, and operational and empirical measures.[163] However, Marks makes a useful distinction between model accuracy (the model's behavior matches known historical behavior in an actual social system) and completeness (the model may describe some but not all known behaviors, and may produce hitherto unknown results).[164] Only rarely is a model valid and complete. Moss and Edmonds use the term *macro validity* to describe what Marks calls "accuracy."[165] Without validation, ABMs may produce results that are fragile and that fail to produce unique predictions.[166] Finally, due to the difficulties of sharing computer code and the absence of best practices in constructing models, researchers cannot easily share models. These inherent barriers to the transmissibility of ABM findings suggest a lack of cumulation in the research program.[167] For all these reasons, scholars and policymakers have expressed concerns with ABM methods. *Nature* magazine, for example, recently questioned the use of agent-based models for economic forecasting and policymaking.[168]

Recognizing these challenges of ABM, this book facilitates replication of results and the sharing of computer code in three ways. I provide online versions of the model (at http://www.odu.edu/~dearnest/), where researchers can run the simulations and reproduce the findings of the following chapters. The Web site also provides downloadable source code for purposes of verification. Each chapter includes "pseudo code," or "an informal mixture of natural language and programming conventions that makes the structure and flow of a program clear."[169] While these conventions can aid in the transmission and replication of results, however, they do not make the models "better" or more "valid." To debate whether or not ABMs are valid, however, misses the point of simulation. As Box and Draper note, "Remember that all models are wrong; the practical question is how wrong do they have to be to not be useful."[170] One might best think of these as models that help researchers identify various emergent properties of complex systems. They are an invaluable complement to, but not substitutes for, formal and empirical methods.

Any research method has inherent strengths and weaknesses. As scholars of complex social systems have faced the bracing winds of peer criticism, they have tackled challenges of validation, generalization, and cumulation. Arguably, today computational social science shows some progress in contributing to our understanding of world politics. Scholars have built ABMs to study insurgencies;[171] secessionism;[172] power structures and networks in Afghanistan;[173] the emergence of new political actors;[174] and the size of interstate wars[175] among a variety of other subjects. From early models from the 1990s in which perhaps one thousand agents interacted, researchers today use models with billions of agents to study networks of disease transmission in global pandemics.[176] Advances in computational capacity have produced a new generation of ABMs that model systems on a scale equivalent to real world systems. Together, these studies share an interest in dynamics and change in social systems, emergent properties that shape the interests of social actors, and the patterns of interrelations among specific social actors. The relevance for understanding the dynamics of world politics is manifest.[177]

CONCLUSION

This chapter has argued that network theory, complex systems theory, and evolutionary game theory offer both hypotheses and methodological tools to tease out turbulent relationships in world politics. None of these is a theory of world politics per se: they are silent on the question of who the actors in world politics are, and consequently do not offer hypotheses specifically about states, governments, institutions, voters, terrorists, or myriad other actors in world politics. Yet together the three theories offer specific causal arguments to explain recursive relationships between agents and structures. They hypothesize about how interactions among units at one level produce important phenomena at higher levels. They contribute to theories of change in world politics by studying how political actors form preferences and learn over time. Together, the methods of computational social science provide a methodological rigor and consistency that not only formalize ubiquitous but poorly operationalized concepts such as networks, but also permit the replication and transmission of findings. While the imagery of man, the state, and war undoubtedly will continue to shape our thinking about world politics, the imagery of nodes, nets, and global dynamics provide us with new opportunities to understand contemporary world politics. The following five chapters illustrate this, starting with among the simplest questions in social theory: How do actors solve the three-choice problem?

THREE

THE ADVANTAGE OF SIZE

Why Large Groups Solve Coordination Problems Better than Small Ones

The three-choice problem is among the oldest questions social theorists have considered. Given three or more choices, can a group devise a social choice rule that is fair and prevents society from cycling among the choices? Rarely do social groups face simple yes-or-no decisions. Voters in parliamentary democracies typically have more than two candidates from which to choose. During the Arab Spring, Egyptians, Tunisians, Libyans, and others had to choose among more than two options: they could join the protests; provide aid to protestors even if they did not march; support the regime; or do nothing. Governments hoping to curtail Iran's nuclear research program face even more complicated choices: do nothing, impose sanctions, offer incentives, work unilaterally or within multilateral bodies, pursue covert operations, attack Iranian facilities, or some combination of all of these. In each of these examples, actors not only have multiple choices but face different gains and losses from the group's ultimate choice. In addition to the challenges posed by differing preferences and the unequal distribution of gains, actors facing such options need to learn about each other's preference rankings from among multiple choices. When actors have constituencies who must be satisfied—whether voters, shareholders, or volunteers—then leaders must consider how their supporters consider and prioritize their own goals. In world politics, then, actors must often not only evaluate the rewards and costs of many possible choices but also must build constituent support for their choices.

This process of learning and communication may have profound consequences for the prospects for cooperation, independent of the problems of cheating and the distribution of gains. Yet negotiators also need to sort through each other's preferences from among more than two options. Such n-choice problems can create problems for interest aggregation, as classic social choice theorists recognized. There is a rich literature in the rational choice tradition of social choice theory that addresses different pathologies.[1] This chapter explores the dynamics of preference cycles, first recognized by the Marquis de Condorcet. In brief, social groups may have intransitive preferences in n-choice decisions even if individual preferences are perfectly ordered and transitive. When people must decide from three or more choices, their efforts may produce preference cycles that frustrate the realization of collective goals.

In principle, actors at all levels of world politics may suffer from the same dilemmas of social choice in the n-choice problem. This chapter analyzes a three-choice coordination problem that has no unique equilibrium solution. Of theoretic interest, then, is the process through which actors solve the coordination problem—it is the path history of negotiation and learning that is as interesting as is the outcome of the coordination game. Traditional game theory is of little help in understanding these path histories, though evolutionary game theory recently has focused on the paths through which actors reach equilibria.[2] Conversely, empirical analysis may face nonlinearities that both violate classical statistical assumptions and obscure underlying causal mechanisms. For these reasons, this chapter's ABM explores the conditions under which the three-choice problem leads to coordinated behavior, and conversely the factors that may explain failure to coordinate through communication and learning. The simulation uses Putnam's well-known two-level games model to illustrate the complexities of negotiations in which actors have multifaceted preferences and changing constituency constraints.[3] Although Putnam focused on international negotiations, his two-level game is general. One can apply it to any social choice problem characterized by negotiators with constituencies who ratify agreements. Heads of governments must consider the wishes of their voters and bureaucrats; CEOs often must win approval from shareholders; judges must consider the preferences of their peers at the appellate level; leaders of transnational activist networks rely upon volunteers whose wishes strongly shape the choices of leaders. For this reason, the ABM captures a range of social choice problems across levels of analysis of world politics. While this chapter's ABM is simplified, the chapter illustrates how actors learn; how they evolve social networks of influence; and how individual preferences may aggregate into suboptimal social choices. In particular, the model speaks to three important ongoing debates among IR theorists.

First, the model explores the divide between international relations theories that treat state preferences axiomatically, and foreign policy analysis that problematizes the source of preferences. Structural theories have added considerably to our understanding of how states solve coordination problems such as the one presented here.[4] A number of scholars nevertheless have criticized the tendency of structural approaches to make assumptions about actor preferences that are both spare and may not hold up to empirical scrutiny. Scholars in the liberal tradition and those in foreign policy analysis seek to investigate how societal actors shape state preferences.[5] Although parsimonious, the model presented here reflects the heritage of this debate. It creates a coordination problem of interdependent payoffs at the structural level, but has subsystemic actors interact to constrain and shape state preferences.

Second, the model speaks to competing conceptions of global governance. Should we best think of governance in terms of interstate institutions, or in terms of networks of transnational actors? Neoliberal institutionalism primarily focuses on the role of institutions and regimes in the management of international and global public goods.[6] The burgeoning literature on transnationalism complements this tradition by highlighting the growing importance of transnational networks to global governance. In the absence of coordinated state behavior, such networks of activists may help states achieve their goals;[7] reshape state interests;[8] or both. The coordination problem this chapter explores obviates by construction the need for institutions to distribute the gains of cooperation or to monitor compliance. But this need not necessarily be so. As the chapter discusses later, conceptually one can extend the model to examine cooperation problems in which institutions serve an enforcement role. With these extensions a researcher may investigate differing modes of global governance.

Finally, the model assumes that state preferences come from the bottom up, but again there is nothing in the model that requires such an assumption. A considerable advantage of agent-based modeling is the ability of the modeler to vary experimentally his or her assumptions. With some thoughtful coding, a modeler can treat as variables precisely those arguments that define contemporary IR scholarship. For example, do states derive interests from structural factors or state-level actors? One can model this debate by varying the state's receptivity to societal influences: international negotiators may be perfectly insensitive to societal actors, analogous to the parsimonious assumption that structural factors are determinative of state preferences.

Because social choice problems are general in world politics, the particular model presented here is general by construction and, of necessity, makes only modest theoretical claims. It nevertheless produces some surprising findings about the optimum number of negotiating partners;[9] the role of transnational factors in coordinating state behavior;[10] and the consequences of "reverberation" for the prospects of agreement.[11] The chapter also suggests some extensions of the model that may improve its heuristic value and offer even richer insights into the complexities of international negotiations in an interdependent world.

SOCIAL PREFERENCES AS A COMPLEX ADAPTIVE SYSTEM

The process of aggregating social preferences exhibits the properties of a complex adaptive system, or CAS. As chapter 1 discussed, all CAS consist of multiple agents who act autonomously, free from the control or influence of central authority. The analogy to the notion of anarchy in international relations is readily apparent—irrespective of whether or not one adheres to the neorealist or neoliberal institutionalist conception of anarchy.[12] Because of this autonomy of agents, CAS exhibit massive parallelism and multiple levels of organization, with actors at one level aggregating into actors at another level.[13] Second, the actors in CAS follow local and often simple decision rules, and incorporate their local knowledge about the system into their decision routines. Actors in a CAS, like states in the international system, may have imperfect information, but nevertheless they learn and adapt as the system evolves over time. The adaptive behavior of agents produces the third property of complex adaptive social systems. The systems themselves grow, change, evolve, and adapt as agents in the system incorporate new information into their routines. These dynamics are more than simply the aggregation of local interactions alone, furthermore. As Holland has illustrated, agents who follow even conditioned and simple decision rules can produce systemic behavior that is complex and not repeatable.[14]

One could argue that international organizations exhibit the properties of a complex adaptive system because they serve to aggregate state preferences into collective social choices. Sovereign states pursue internal (local) decision rules; states' decisions are autonomous even if their payoffs may be interdependent; and states adapt in ways that change both the structure of interaction and their own expectations. States and nonstate actors produce structural phenomena that are greater than the sum of their localized interactions, from conflict to the anarchic structure of the international system.[15] A complex systems theorist who looks at IR theory no doubt will recognize much.[16]

SIMULATING SOCIAL CHOICE PROBLEMS

Traditionally, researchers have studied social choice problems using the formal methods of game theory. Recently, however, a number of researchers have used the method of agent-based modeling to simulate voting institutions.[17] To construct an ABM of how constituencies may shape decision making in negotiations, the model implements the two-level games framework first proposed by Putnam.[18] Every agent-based model makes theoretically informed assumptions about agents; the environment in which agents interact; and the rules that govern interactions between agents and the environment. As a demonstrated method of empirical analysis, the two-level games framework can help a modeler think explicitly about the nature of agents, the environment, rules of interaction, and outcomes of theoretic interest.

The Environment

In this simple model, the "environment" is a social choice problem with three options. The model assumes that actors will bargain in good faith with each other and will express their sincere preferences. This, of course, is a simplification: Putnam, for one, suggests that shrewd negotiators may misrepresent their preferences in order to gain a greater share of the gains from cooperation (though at increased risk of no agreement).[19] The following analysis assumes, however, that actors in coordination games—which by definition have no distributive consequences—have nothing to gain from insincere negotiations. To simulate the "noise" of bargaining, the model presents states with a coordination problem analogous to the "rules of the road": actors are indifferent as to which solution they adopt, but have differing initial preferences among choices.[20] In principle, a two-choice coordination decision should lead easily to a social choice: as actors express and reorder their preferences, the social choice eventually will tip toward one of two possible equilibria.[21] Once actors achieve an equilibrium, no one will have any incentive to deviate from the solution. Rather than having actors negotiate a simple two-choice problem, however, the chapter opts for a richer three-choice problem. As the Marquis de Condorcet first noted in the eighteenth century, such three-choice decisions create the possibility for intransitive and cycling social preferences.[22] Unlike the two-choice coordination problem, the three-choice problem does not necessarily lead to an equilibrium outcome. What matters is whether actors can learn and create institutions that allow them to solve three-choice problems that do not have a unique equilibrium solution.

Table 3.1 presents a Condorcet problem with three nominal choices: blue, green, and yellow. A quick glance at the table shows how intransitivities may arise. In any pairwise comparison of options, any option can defeat the other two. For example, suppose one proposed a simple decision rule: we would vote on the question of blue versus green first, and then the winner

Table 3.1. A Condorcet decision problem among three nominal alternatives

Voter	Order of preferences				
	1		2		3
A	Blue	>	Green	>	Yellow
B	Yellow	>	Blue	>	Green
C	Green	>	Yellow	>	Blue

of that choice versus yellow. If we followed this choice rule, blue would defeat green (since A and B both prefer blue to green) but would lose to yellow (since B and C both prefer yellow to blue). Yet if we changed the order of pairwise comparisons, we would get a different collective choice. If we compared yellow to blue first, yellow would win (thanks to B and C) but would lose out when compared to green (thanks to A and C). Hence, the social choice has changed with a different decision rule, even though the order of each individual's preferences has not changed. The Condorcet problem highlights two important concepts: the choice of decision rule can never be politically neutral; and groups can cycle through social choices even if individuals maintain constant and ordered preferences.

The model treats enforcement of agreements as unproblematic. Its focus is not on cheating once actors reach an agreement; rather, it explores the path history of negotiations among actors to reach the equilibrium point. Martin shows that coordination problems typically lead actors to emphasize norms of reciprocity of choices and indivisibility of benefits.[23] These norms help actors reduce the costs of achieving an equilibrium outcome. Such coordination problems typically do not require centralized monitoring and enforcement of agreements, since once states have achieved an agreement none has an incentive to defect.[24] For this reason, the model assumes that coordination problems do not require formal rules or institutions to enforce agreements.

Relevant Agents

There are two types of agents in the model. Borrowing from Putnam, the "agents" of interest in this model are negotiators at the international level (or level I) who bargain over the collective choice, and their constituencies (level II) who do not participate in bargaining but who ratify agreements or withhold consent. Each actor in the model has *ab initio* preferences for the nominal social choices; these initial preferences satisfy classic assumptions of ordering, transitivity, and independence from irrelevant alternatives.

The model randomizes agent preferences at the point of generation. Actors simply prefer one alternative to the others, for example, one prefers blue to green to yellow. Constituencies, by contrast, have weighted preferences among the alternatives. This weighting simulates constituencies as amalgamated actors, representing "groups [who] pursue their interests by pressuring the government to adopt their favored policies, and politicians [who] seek power by constructing coalitions among those groups."[25] Any given constituency will have a distribution of preferences for social choices that rarely if ever will be uniform. The assigned weights always total to one, so that each weight represents the proportion of a constituency that prefers a given choice. In the model's implementation, a constituency will have preferences such as 0.45 green (analogous to 45 percent of the society prefers the green choice), 0.32 blue (32 percent prefers blue), and 0.23 yellow. Admittedly, these modeling choices treat axiomatically many of the determinants of constituency preferences. The goal is, however, to focus on the emergence of social cooperation rather than the richness of bargaining factors (but see the discussion of extensions of the model below).

The model allows a researcher to vary the number of states in a negotiation. A "minilateral" implementation would consist of as few as three negotiators with their three constituencies, while a large multiparty negotiation could consist of as many as forty negotiators and constituencies.[26] The model thus allows the researcher to investigate whether fewer negotiators can reach a social choice more easily than a large number.[27] The model assumes each negotiator has only one constituency, while likewise each constituency has only one negotiator.

Rules and Parameters

At each step in "time" in the model, the social choice is the plurality winner of the negotiators' preferences. The model uses five variables (see Table 3.2). The first is the number of negotiators. Second, negotiators are "sensitive" to the preferences of other negotiators (variable N_n). The third variable is negotiators' sensitivity to the preferences of their constituencies (N_c). The fourth and fifth variables relate to transnational effects among constituencies. One of these is the "radius" within which transnational effects may occur (variable T); this variable models the idea that not all constituencies have transnational ties with every other constituency. To capture the spatial nature of transnational relations, the simulation positions constituencies in a circle within a 35 X 35 matrix: variable T simply determines the radius within which a given constituency polls its neighboring constituencies. Finally, the model allows the magnitude of transnational effects to vary. That is to say, a given constituency may give considerable weight to the

Table 3.2. Parameters of theoretic interest as operationalized in the model

Variable	Concept	Operationalized	Possible values
Number of negotiators (M)	Group size	Number of level I negotiators	3 to 40
Extent of transnational networks (T)	Transnational politics	Radius in which a given constituency can appeal to a neighboring constituency	10 to 30
Voter swings (D)	Domestic politics: changes in level II preferences	Weighted rate at which constituencies reorder their preferences; higher values indicate quicker reordering	1 to 5
Sensitivity of negotiators to constituents (N_c)	Strength of level II constraints on level I negotiations	Probability that a negotiator will adopt the position of its constituency	0.20 to 0.80
Sensitivity of negotiators to other negotiators (N_n)	Effectiveness of level I bargaining	Probability that a negotiator will change the position of another negotiator	0.20 to 0.80

preferences of a neighboring constituency, or may attribute relatively little importance to the preferences of neighbors (variable D).

Negotiators change their preferences in two ways. First, in direct negotiation a given negotiator can change the preferences of another negotiator (N_n). This simulated negotiation allows for actors at level I to change each other's minds with some probability less than one. One can simulate either accommodating or obstinate negotiations by experimentally varying the probability of a given negotiator persuading another negotiator. Second, a negotiator will change its preference to accord with their constituency's preference with some probability less than 1 (N_c). As Odell has shown, the strength of constituency preferences can affect both the probability of an agreement and the distribution of gains from any agreement.[28] However, a constituency will change its negotiator's preference with a probability less than one, to simulate the ability of negotiators to innovate in level I negotiations.

Constituencies change their preferences in two possible ways. First, reflecting processes of transnational interest articulation, constituencies respond to the preferences of other constituencies. At each step in the model, a constituency polls some subset of the neighboring constituencies, and will re-weight and reorder its preferences if its top choice is not the social winner. The researcher can vary both the magnitude of re-weighting and the number of other constituencies a given constituency will poll (from two neighbors to all other constituencies). This reflects the idea that transnational effects are greater between states that are proximate. Thus, the modeler can vary both the extent and intensity of transnational effects on preferences in a given state. Constituencies may change preferences in a second way. A negotiator may persuade its constituency to adopt the negotiator's preference (with probability $1- N_c$). This is analogous to research that has found a skillful negotiator can expand his or her level II win set by appealing to others' constituencies.[29] Table 3.3 provides the pseudo code for this model.

It is important to note that while negotiators may bargain with any other negotiator, constituencies may or may not be able to affect any other constituency. Because the model varies the density of transnational connections, the analysis here problematizes the extent of transnational networks. Conversely, the analysis assumes that networks among negotiators assume an "all-to-all" structure—in the terms of network theory, the social network of negotiators is fully connected. Because any negotiator can bargain with any other negotiator, network dynamics such as "small world" phenomena do not affect communications among negotiators.[30] Nevertheless, at any given step in "time" in the model, a negotiator bargains with only one other negotiator, and a constituency communicates with only one neighbor.

Outcomes of Interest

Under what conditions will actors reach a consensus? Alternatively, under what conditions will they bicker, equivocate, and fail to reach a consensus? Research on two-level games offer some answers.[31] A "win set" is the set of all possible agreements among negotiators at level I that constituents at level II would ratify. Several factors may influence the size of a given negotiator's win set. These include preferences and coalitions of constituencies; the rules of ratification of agreements; and negotiator's strategies. Using this framework, researchers have identified some ironies of two-level bargaining. Negotiators with accommodating constituencies would more often have to make

Table 3.3. Pseudo code for the Condorcet model

Initialization:
Create M *constituency agents* and distribute them in a circle
  endow them with a neighborhood of other constituencies in radius T
  endow them with a rate D at which constituency will reorder its preferences
  endow them with weighted preferences
Create M *negotiator agents* and distribute them in a circle
  endow them with a random preference order
  assign them a constituency agent
  endow them with sensitivity N_c to constituency preferences
  endow them with sensitivity N_n to other negotiator preferences

Execution:
Loop until a consensus emerges or for 200 ticks, whichever comes first:
  Each negotiator agent:
    Determines the preference of its constituency agent
    Determines the social choice of the other negotiator agents
    With $p \le N_n$, tells another negotiator agent to set its preference to the negotiator's preference
    With $p \le N_c$, sets its preference to that of its constituency
    With $p \le (1 - N_c)$, sets its constituency's preference to its preference
  Each constituency agent:
    Determines the preferences of its neighboring constituencies in radius T
    Reweights preferences to increase the weight for the option preferred by neighboring constituencies
    If reweighting changes preferences, reorders preferences
  The model:
    Measures the aggregate preferences of negotiators
    Measures the aggregate preferences of constituencies
  End Loop

Genetic Algorithm:
Initialization:
  Create 40 random strategies with:
    M randomly drawn from a uniform distribution bounded by 3 and 40
    T randomly drawn from a uniform distribution bounded by 10 and 30
    D randomly drawn from a uniform distribution bounded by 1 and 5
    N_n randomly drawn from a uniform distribution bounded by .2 and .8
    N_c randomly drawn from a uniform distribution bounded by .2 and .8
Loop for 40 generations:
  At the end of each generation:
    Use a pairwise tournament to select 40 strategies
    Repeat 20 times: randomly select two tournament winners and crossover the strategies
  Use each new strategy to initialize the model
End Loop

concessions to other negotiators. Conversely, negotiators with unyielding constituencies would gain a greater distribution of gains from agreements.[32] Hence, preferences of constituencies can shape the prospects for agreement. The model assumes level II ratification follows simple plurality rules.

The chapter first examines the emergence of stable level I agreements, then explores the emergence of instability and discord in level I negotiations. To simulate these outcomes, the model uses Miller's active nonlinear test or ANT, a genetic algorithm to explore the model's parameter space.[33] In brief, a genetic algorithm is a set of computer procedures that uses insights from natural selection to search for optimal solutions to a problem.[34] When simulating players, a "strategy" is simply either a set of digits or a "bit string" (a set of zeroes and ones) that represent discrete choices a player has (e.g., cooperate or defect). Players start with randomized strategies but learn through competition and selection. "Selection" simply is a procedure for identifying the best performing strategies and discarding others—a process modelers may call "tournaments."[35] Genetic algorithms also create new strategies in two ways. One form of innovation is to have two of the top strategies "mate"—that is, to crossover the digits in each strategy's set of numbers. Another is to allow a strategy to "mutate" (i.e., randomly rewrite one portion of the strategy) with some small probability. Finally, the algorithm may generate a random set of new strategies to introduce variety and novelty. By iterating the procedures of selection, crossover, and mutation, the algorithm allows agents continuously to learn about and adapt to each other, precisely the kind of coevolution we see in world politics.

This implementation of the active nonlinear test starts with a list of forty randomly generated parameter sets to run the model. At the end of the first generation of forty runs, the algorithm undertakes a tournament from among the forty parameter sets, selecting those that performed best according to specific fitness criteria—in this chapter, those parameter values that maximize or minimize problems of coordination. The algorithm also incorporates a genetic crossover routine, in which parameter sets selected by the tournament procedure swap parameter values with sets not selected. This crossover allows for the possibility of fit parameter sets to reproduce even better performing sets. It occurs with a probability that declines over generations, however, to allow the algorithm to converge on a small set of good performing parameters. The model's implementation of the active nonlinear test conducts the selection tournament and genetic crossover for forty generations, for a total of 1,600 runs of the model for each of two experiments.[36] The analysis specifically tests two fitness criteria: it maximizes negotiator discord in one test, and minimizes it in another. This provides 3,200 simulated negotiations. Table 3.4 presents the summary statistics for the simulations. It is important to note that this does not constitute a

Table 3.4. Summary statistics for the simulations

	N	Mean	St. Dev.	Min	Max
Overall	3,200 runs				
Simulation to maximize discord	1,600 runs				
Periods of discord (of 200 time periods per run)		42.51	18.64	0	88
Number of negotiators		8.79	5.32	3	38
Extent of transnational networks		15.00	2.80	10	29
Swings		1.21	0.58	1	4
Sensitivity of negotiators to constituents		0.46	0.07	0.26	0.77
Sensitivity of negotiators to other negotiators		0.65	0.09	0.21	0.78
Simulation to minimize discord	1,600 runs				
Periods of discord (of 200 time periods per run)		7.30	12.07	0	72
Number of negotiators		34.13	6.56	6	39
Extent of transnational networks		23.79	3.45	10	29
Swings		3.00	0.33	1	4
Sensitivity of negotiators to constituents		0.55	0.09	0.22	0.79
Sensitivity of negotiators to other negotiators		0.43	0.11	0.20	0.79

random sample of the parameter space: the genetic algorithm progressively samples the parameter space around the optimum until it converges on a single parameter set. Consequently, about half the simulations in the sample represent extreme values of cooperation or discord.

To assess cooperation and discord in two-level games, at each step in simulated time the model measures whether or not the level I choice of negotiators concurs with the global distribution of preferences among constituencies (measured as the weighted support for the winning choice averaged across all constituencies). This is analogous to negotiators concluding agreements that fail to win ratification from their constituencies. When the level I choice is not the level II winner, the model identifies that step as a period of discord. In one experiment, I used the ANT to maximize the number of steps of discord. In the other, the ANT minimizes the discord, analogous to negotiators concluding agreements that most often will win ratification from constituencies. Figure 3.1 illustrates how the ANT anneals the model over forty generations, by increasing the average number of time periods of discord. Similarly, the ANT anneals the model to maximize the periods of cooperation in the model (i.e., minimizes the number of periods of discord).

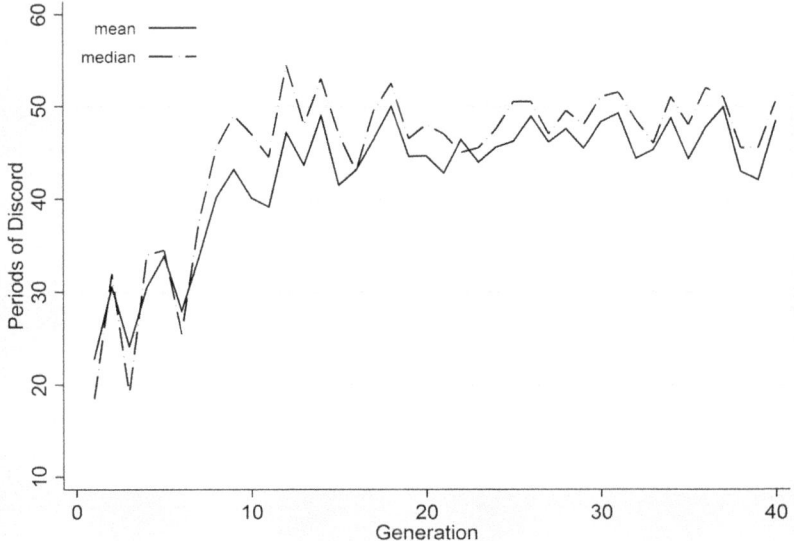

Figure 3.1. Active nonlinear test's maximization of periods of discord, over 40 generations of the test.

WHEN DO ACTORS COORDINATE?

Discord occurs when (1) the number of negotiating partners is relatively small; (2) transnational connections are sparse; (3) constituencies are relatively slow to re-weight their preferences in response to discord; (4) negotiators are relatively independent of constituent pressures (that is to say, their sensitivity to other negotiators N_n is greater than their sensitivity to their constituencies N_c); and (5) negotiators are relatively accommodating of other negotiators. Figure 3.2 shows a simulation in which negotiators fail to cooperate, cycling among the three possible choices in the coordination problem. Conversely, negotiations produce coordination at level I when (1) the number of negotiating partners is large; (2) transnational connections are dense; (3) constituencies re-weight and reorder their preferences quickly; (4) negotiators are relatively sensitive to constituencies' preferences (or $N_n < N_c$); and (5) negotiators are relatively insensitive to other negotiators. Table 3.5 presents the winning parameter sets produced by the ANT. Figure 3.3 exhibits a run of the simulation in which negotiators quickly produce a level I agreement.

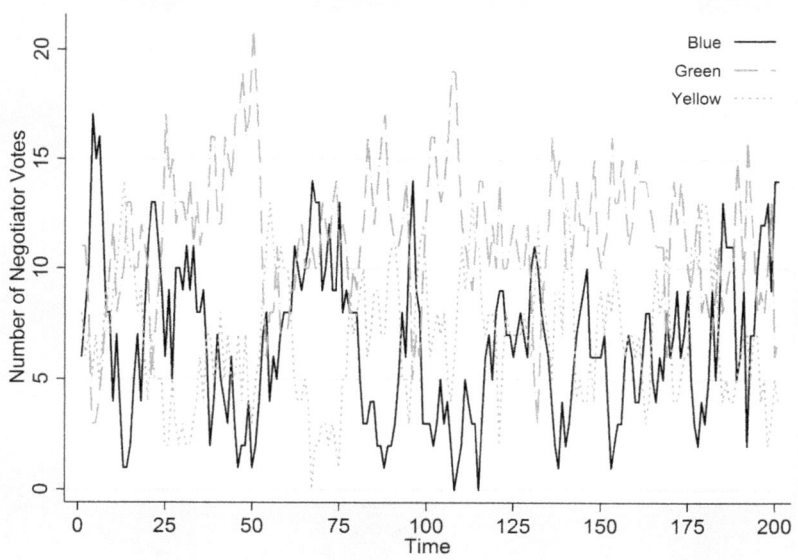

Figure 3.2. An example of a failure to coordinate the social choice.

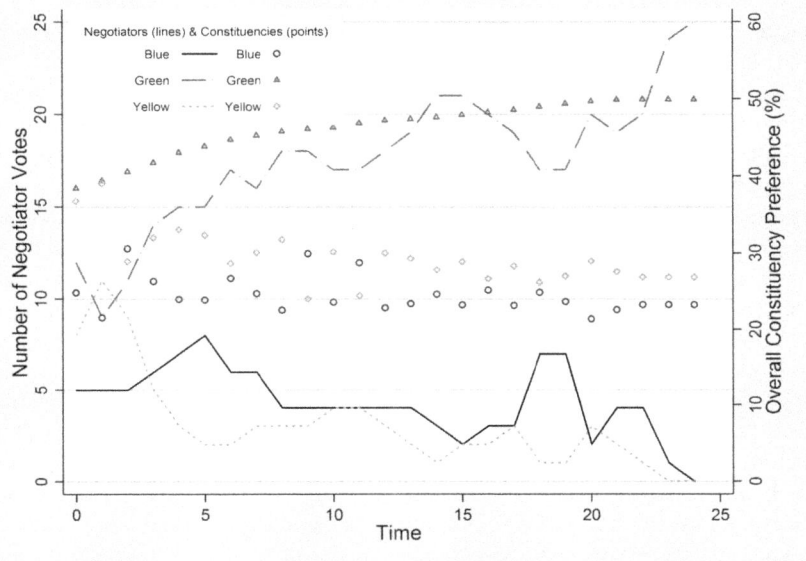

Figure 3.3. An example of a coordinated social choice at $t = 24$.

Contrary to expectations, the model finds that a larger number of negotiating partners leads to more agreements. This is contrary both to Olson's findings about collective action and the literature on interstate cooperation.[37] Kahler finds that states have solved large-n cooperation problems either through "minilateral" arrangements, in which a few great powers agree to a solution that other states then adopt, or through bilateral or regional

Table 3.5. Final parameter sets as annealed by the active nonlinear test (ANT)

Fitness criterion	Number of negotiators	Extent of transnational networks	Swings	Sensitivity of negotiators to constituents	Sensivitivty of negotiators to other negotiators
Maximize discord	7	14	1	0.47	0.67
Minimize discord	38	26	3	0.54	0.39

agreements.[38] In other words, actors solve coordination problems by negotiating in smaller groups. The model presented here illustrates, however, that larger groups offer certain informational advantages in multilateral negotiations. Snidal for one found that large-n negotiations attenuate pressures of concerns over the distribution of gains, making cooperation easier.[39] Independent of concerns for gains, however, this model shows that large-n groups may have denser connections that allow for the more efficient communication of preferences among actors. These informational dynamics in large-n negotiations can help actors solve coordination problems. This finding is somewhat qualified however. It may arise from the model's assumption that every negotiator can communicate with every other negotiator, an "all-to-all" network form. Alternative structures for negotiating networks may affect the prospects for coordination.

Transnational relationships among constituencies are another mechanism that facilitates the communications of constituency preferences. This finding is consistent with the interdependence and globalization literature. Keck and Sikkink find, for example, that dense transnational networks contribute to the convergence of norms supporting regional and international integration and instigate changes in the principles that regulate state behavior.[40] There are grounds to suspect, furthermore, that the information dynamics in the model may alleviate the concerns of states about the distribution of gains.[41] Not only do denser networks enable states to communicate preferences sincerely, but this sincerity may contribute substantially to trust among actors. Indeed, democratic peace theorists make precisely this argument: the transparency of domestic political institutions enables democracies to communicate preferences sincerely, to build trust, and to sustain credible commitments to each other.[42] Sociologists have also explored the relationship between the structure of social networks and the building of trust.[43] In comparative politics, researchers have illustrated how informational "cascades" can rapidly shift individuals from inaction to assertive collective action, even in the absence of central organization.[44] As in these studies, the ABM suggests that transnational relations may have a critical point or threshold beyond which societal-level preferences may dramatically reshape state behavior.[45]

Putnam focused on the strength of level II preferences to explain not only the probability of an agreement at level I, but also the distribution of gains among states from the agreement. While the simulation presented here does not create a cooperation problem with distributional consequences, it nevertheless affirms the importance of the strength of constituency preferences for the prospect of an agreement. As Putnam suggested, negotiators with flexible constituencies achieve stable accords, while inflexible constituencies lead to a greater likelihood of discord. This finding is somewhat qualified, however, both by the absence of distributional concerns in the model's negotiations, and by the model's unrealistic assumption that all constituencies have the same strength of preferences in a given simulation, whether strong or weak. By allowing this assumption to vary, an extended version of the model would enable a researcher to explore when the strength of constituency preferences matters.

Finally, the role of negotiators is particularly interesting. The model finds that discord occurs when negotiators are relatively free from constituency pressures, and when negotiators are relatively accommodating to other negotiators. These findings are somewhat contrary to the findings of the literature on two-level bargaining. Putnam noted that "the larger [the negotiator's] win set, the more easily he can conclude an agreement, but also the weaker his bargaining position vis-à-vis the other negotiator."[46] This simulation suggests a complement to Putnam's reasoning: while negotiators with greater freedom from constituent pressures may be more likely *ceteris paribus* to reach an agreement, such freedom detracts from the informational content of the negotiator's actions. Even a relatively independent negotiator needs to win ratification at the domestic level: by pursuing his or her own preferred objectives, a negotiator fails to communicate to other negotiators the preferences of his or her constituency. This lack of information makes coordination more difficult. This insight suggests one more reason constituencies try to tie the hands of their negotiators. The two-level games literature suggests such constraints help states gain a greater distribution of the gains from an agreement. The model suggests that such constraints help states coordinate in the first place by communicating the prospects for domestic ratification, even before negotiators can squabble over the gains.

Schultz finds that when democracies negotiate, opposition parties may facilitate cooperation by revealing the prospects for ratification to another state's negotiator.[47] The analysis here suggests an important complement: overly solicitous negotiators may, ironically, prevent the emergence of coordinated behavior. As the findings of the ANT show, negotiators who accommodate other negotiators—particularly when negotiators are insensitive to their constituencies—may perpetuate misinformation about the prospects for constituents' ratification. That is to say, a solicitous negotiator may pass along information about a level I win set to his or her constituents that a negotiating partner has communicated insincerely. Hence, misunderstandings about the coordination win set "reverberate" in the model, tipping the model away from a coordinated solution rather than toward one.[48] "Given the pervasive uncertainty that surrounds many international issues," Putnam noted, "messages from abroad can change minds, move the undecided, and hearten those in the domestic minority." True—but insincere messages can also harden positions, add to the ranks of the undecided, and discourage prospective supporters of an agreement. Reverberation can cut both ways, particularly when negotiators are insensitive to constituency preferences and highly sensitive to each other.

BEYOND COORDINATION PROBLEMS

The highly simplified model presented here offers some interesting insights into the informational dynamics of multilevel bargaining in world politics. To create a more realistic simulation, however, the model should incorporate a number of additional factors.

First, the simulation would benefit from adaptive, intelligent agents. As currently implemented, the decision algorithms for both constituencies and negotiators are "dumb" algorithms: constituencies and negotiators have no memory of past outcomes, and do not learn and adapt in a way that voters and diplomats realistically do. There are a couple of algorithmic ways to create adaptive, learning agents. One is to give agents a simple memory of past social choice outcomes that may shape their future preferences and actions. Agents who have even modest memories of past negotiations may produce surprises: Young notes that "high-rationality solution concepts in game theory can emerge in a world populated by low-rationality agents."[49] More ambitiously, one could use genetic algorithms to have agents learn not only about the social choice but to learn about which voting strategies might "succeed." Though more sophisticated, the use of such genetic algorithms in social simulation is fairly commonplace.[50]

A second extension is to create more realistic algorithms for the ways in which constituencies articulate their preferences. The current model implements a simple algorithm: a constituency's "strength" of preferences is simply the probability that another constituency or its negotiator may cause it to re-weight and reorder its preferences. Yet this probability remains the same for all agents in the model. As Putnam has shown, however, differences in the strengths of preferences among constituencies can have profound implications not only for the probability of a level I agreement, but also of the distribution of gains.[51] A more realistic simulation thus should include constituencies with varying strengths of preferences as well as distributional gains from level I negotiations.

Third, the model's simple coordination game ignores problems of distribution and commitment. For one, the model assumes that all three equilibria offer the same payoffs. The classic coordination game assumes, however, that players prefer one equilibrium to another because that equilibrium has a higher absolute payoff for each player. An extended model could rank the outcomes (e.g., blue win set > green win set > yellow win set > no agreement) and reward actors for achieving more desirable win sets. The basic coordination game treats axiomatically, furthermore, distributional games such as the "battle of the sexes," in which actors prefer cooperation, but the different equilibria offer a different reward to each state. For example, one actor will receive higher payoffs if blue is the win-set equilibrium while another actor will receive a greater share of the payoff if green is the social choice. By assuming that coordinated solutions are stable equilibria, furthermore, the model ignores the commitment problem—that is, whether laws or organizations may influence actors' behavior by raising the costs of reneging on an agreement.[52] The inclusion of commitment costs and distributional conflicts from social choice problems would make the model applicable to a wider domain of social choice problems in contemporary world politics. The next chapter turns to these problems with a social choice model that includes distributional games.

Finally, the institutions for constituency ratification may also affect the prospect for coordinated social choices. The current simulation has a simple rule for ratification (plurality) that is common to all constituencies in the model. To test the importance of domestic institutions of ratification, the model could allow for and test different ratification procedures, such as majority or supermajority requirements. Along with an added distributional component of a social choice problem, this extension will allow the researcher to investigate the consequences of ratification institutions for the prospects of level I cooperation. Chapter 6 explores this question in the context of global financial regulation. By examining how different economies organize their interbank lending networks, it illustrates how variations in constituency relations may affect the prospects for realizing Pareto-improving social choices.

CONCLUSIONS

While existing empirical and game theoretic studies have identified factors that contribute to solutions to social choice problems, the agent-based model here shows how researchers can study the path histories that are important to a range of problems in world politics. The model uses five simple variables: the number of negotiators, the sensitivity of negotiators to their constituencies, the sensitivity of negotiators to other states' negotiators, the magnitude of transnational effects, and the scope of transnational relations. With these five variables the model illustrates the conditions under which actors may solve coordination problems, and those factors that contribute to preference cycles and ineffective governance. By expanding the model to account for additional factors and by exploring counterfactual assumptions, future studies can enrich their explanations of different path histories of two-level games.

The model also calls attention to the value of using multiple levels of analysis. As Pepinsky notes, "Simulations of international phenomena have currently only included states as agents; theory thus pervades the model, and emergence and simulated data are correspondingly tied to theory."[53] This chapter attempts to move beyond a state-centric ontology by modeling the interactions between negotiators and constituencies, whether governments and voters, executives and shareholders, or NGOs and volunteers. Pepinsky has identified this "variety in ontological assumptions" as an important complement to existing simulations of international processes.[54] Likewise, the model illustrates how complex dynamics such as preference cycles can emerge from these decision-making processes, even if the model's simulation of these processes is relatively simplistic. Agents in the model do not remember past outcomes, learn, or adapt in ways that typify actors in complex adaptive systems. By endowing agents with memory, with adaptive voting strategies such as tactical voting (i.e., voting for a second-preferred option), and with varying preferences, the model may create greater complexity in state-level decision making. The next chapter turns to this challenge.

FOUR

DIVIDING THE PIE

*How Complex Networks Learn to
Solve Distributive Conflicts*

Though classic game theory has offered insights into how social actors solve collective action problems, its simplifying assumptions mean that it represents world politics only in the most general and abstract sense. Game theorists often represent social choice problems as a game played by two players only. This simplification means one does not need to think about how preferences among many actors interact, and whether the space in which actors play matters. Of course, in actual world politics, social space can affect people's preferences and the information that informs their choices. When the citizens of Cairo considered whether or not to join protests in Tahrir Square, their decision likely depended upon both the choices of those nearby—in a crowd, I am less likely to be arrested—as well as those in their social network—what would my neighbors and family think? This simple example suggests that the interplay between forms of social distance—the difference between "strong" and "weak" ties—is an important source of the dynamism of world politics. To better understand this, students of world politics need to study massively parallel forms of social interaction that occur in "real" spaces, whether a physical location or a social network. This chapter turns to this challenge.

Four common choice dilemmas typify a range of problems in world politics: battle of the sexes, rules of the road, the stag hunt, and the prisoner's dilemma. Although game theorists have long studied these choice dilemmas, they have also noted that cooperation among players is highly sensitive to a number of factors that traditional game theory treats as exogenous to choices. Simulation methods in general, and evolutionary game theory in particular, are one way game theorists have attempted to model and understand these other factors. This chapter seeks to demonstrate that agent-based modeling is another useful simulation methodology that can complement, and in many ways enhance, evolutionary game theory—indeed, the distinction between the two methods is increasingly blurred.

The chapter begins with a discussion of the current literature on multiplayer games and evolutionary game theory. This review demonstrates that current research seeks to understand how social structure may influence the likelihood of cooperation in choice dilemmas. Related to this is the literature on collective action and group size. As the last chapter illustrated, contrary to conventional collective action arguments, large groups have some advantages and may even be necessary for cooperation in some dilemmas.[1] The chapter then presents some findings from a bargaining model and illustrates how the model produces results that are consistent with existing game theory.

MULTIPLAYER GAMES AND SOCIAL STRUCTURE

The prisoner's dilemma is ubiquitous in modern textbooks on world politics, and continues to offer a useful metaphor for understanding the challenges to social cooperation when actors cannot enforce agreements and are concerned about the distribution of gains. But the very parsimony of prisoner's dilemma also limits its applicability. Although it is useful for thinking about security dilemmas, the two-player prisoner's dilemma and other two-player games are not very helpful when thinking about how large groups divide collective goods, whether civil society groups competing for scarce contributions from donors or multinational firms setting technical standards. With the growth of international organizations, not to mention the challenge of tragedy of the commons problems such as climate change, game theory required analytical techniques to understand multiplayer games. Schelling recognized this in his seminal work *The Strategy of Conflict*, noting that a range of factors that game theory treats exogenously (at least in 1960, it did) might affect the prospects for coordinated action.[2] These factors include the order of moves, "imperfect communication structures," "precedents," and "asymmetries."[3] Schelling also anticipated the importance of extending games beyond two players. The challenge of multiplayer games is that, once the researcher extends a two-player game to an *n*-player game, he or she requires some theoretically informed model of social structure. How do groups of three, four, or five communicate preferences? Do such groups play a game simultaneously or instead a series of sequential two-person games nested in a larger social context? As Skyrms and Pemantle note, "The dynamics of strategic interaction can be strikingly different if interaction is governed by some spatial structure, or more generally, some graph structure."[4] Power calls this the problem of "context preservation."[5] If iteration is necessary for cooperation to emerge in the prisoner's dilemma, then the game requires some mechanism to preserve the neighborhood or context (either physical or social) of the players.[6]

Contemporary game theorists have modeled social structure in two ways. The first is to model explicitly the spatial relationship between players in multiplayer games.[7] Early efforts in this line of research modeled players in cellular automata in which players would interact only with their Moore neighbors (that is, those other players above, below, left, or right of the player). Nowak and May used cellular automata to study the prisoner's dilemma and illustrated an important finding: in a multiplayer game with players using deterministic strategies (such as always cooperate or always defect), the spatial distribution of players alone may produce chaotic patterns of cooperation and defection.[8] This is a striking finding: even when players' strategies remain fixed in an iterated game, the level of cooperation changes chaotically due to the physical location of players and their neighbors. Akimov and Soutchanski also used cellular automata to study multiplayer social dilemma games.[9] More recently, researchers have explored how spatial relationships among players may influence the strategies that players use. Alonso et al. studied how different assumptions about spatial relationships may affect the likelihood of a player mimicking another who has garnered higher payoffs.[10] Power moves beyond abstract representations of space to couple geographic information science (GIS) technologies and ABM to simulate multiplayer choice games in an actual space (the town of Catalina, Newfoundland and Labrador, Canada).[11] More generally, Matsushima and Ikegami studied a three-player iterated prisoner's dilemma and found that "introducing spatial structure drastically changes the repertoire of strategies."[12] Skyrms and Pemantle note, however, that most treatments of spatial structure treat such spatial organization as fixed during the play of an iterated game. They adopt a different approach, allowing both players' strategies and the spatial organization of players to evolve over iterations of games.[13] This latter concern with the coevolution (or mutual constitution) of players' strategies and social structure is a central concern of evolutionary game theory.

Differences in network structure also may profoundly influence the prospects for communication and learning in social choice dilemmas. For this reason, the second approach to context preservation is to model social networks rather than physical spaces. This approach utilizes advances in network theory and graph theory to understand patterns of interaction in multiplayer games.[14] Though the formalism of graph theory can be daunting, the intuition is simple: in large social groups, it is rare for everyone to know everyone else (if they do, this is an all-to-all network in which the social network structure is trivial, as anyone can play a game with anyone else). More often, individuals may have a few close relations, who in turn have a circle of close friends, and so on. Watts and Strogatz have found that social networks have organizational characteristics similar to a range of physical and biological networks.[15] Granovetter has illustrated the importance of "weak ties" (that is, friends of friends) for the communication of credible information in groups.[16] Network theory thus suggests that social networks rarely are structured as all-to-all networks. Recently, game theorists have modeled social networks explicitly to understand how network structure may affect cooperation. One study finds that even in simple games without sophisticated strategies and reputation effects, cooperation will emerge if the average number of a player's neighbors exceeds the ratio of benefits to costs of action.[17] Santos and Pacheco illustrate that one particular network structure—scale-free networks—greatly enhances cooperation in multiplayer games.[18]

It is important to note that the number of players in a multiplayer game may affect the prospects for cooperation independent of social structure, however one chooses to model it. Olson's classic discussion of collective action problems suggests that small groups will solve collective action problems more frequently and easily than will large groups.[19] Kahler has made a similar argument about multilateral negotiations.[20] As the previous chapter showed, large groups may solve social dilemmas more readily than small groups. Pahre studied the iterated prisoner's dilemma and found that multilateral agreements not only are sufficient for cooperation to emerge but also are necessary in some conditions.[21] Snidal argues that large-n negotiations tend to attenuate the pressures of relative gains.[22] Liebrand used human subjects to study group decision making in a mixed-motive game to divide a finite resource. He found that large groups ($n = 20$ subjects) tended to produce more equitable and altruistic distribution of resources than small groups ($n = 7$).[23] This is because large groups provide more effective social sanctions of norms violators.

In multiplayer games, then, the prospects for cooperation depend on a variety of factors. These may include the type of cooperation problem: game theory suggests that cooperation is easier in coordination games than in collaborative games with distributional gains. Social structure and "context preservation" may influence the emergence of cooperation or defection in multiplayer iterated games. The number of players may also have an effect. To understand cooperation across the kaleidoscope of actors in world politics, then, one should examine the type of cooperation problem, the structure of social networks, and the number of players.

WHY USE COMPUTATIONAL SOCIAL SCIENCE?

Social dilemmas with multiple equilibria are, depending on your perspective, either a problem or an achievement of game theory. It is a testament to the parsimony of game theory's formalism that it can identify multiple possible outcomes in social dilemmas, though many find it unsatisfying that we have to resort to ad hoc theorizing to understand which equilibrium players will achieve in real world social dilemmas. Evolutionary game theory has tackled the problem of multiple equilibria by exploring the probability distribution of the universe of outcomes. By experimentally varying factors that classical game theory takes as a given (how players learn, noisy versus perfect communication, etc.) we can understand not which equilibrium is "the" solution, but rather what is the likelihood that players will reach a particular equilibrium. Computer simulation is particularly useful for studying such problems because it can efficiently explore problems with vast parameter spaces. Compared to human subject experiments, simulation is a much more efficient way of tackling the problem of multiple equilibria.

Related to the idea of multiple equilibria is the problem of multiple strategies. In an iterative game, how do players form expectations, learn, and change their strategies? Kreps notes that "formal mathematical game theory has said little or nothing about where these expectations come from, how or why they persist, or when and why we might expect them to arise."[24] Chapter 2 noted that evolutionary game theory addresses these questions in part using three insights from natural selection: conservation, innovation, and selection. Suppose one simulates a multiplayer game by creating a population of players with randomized expectations and memories. In these games, a conservation mechanism is one that allows the best-performing strategies to persist and continue playing. Mechanisms of innovation assure perpetual novelty by creating new strategies to compete against current ones. From this ever-changing population of strategies, a selection mechanism allows only the best strategies to thrive and multiply. Because the population of strategies changes over time, however, evolutionary game theory suggests that there may be many "best" strategies in a given game—that is, the best strategy is not optimal in an objective sense, but rather is the best performing given the population of strategies against which it competes. Because the evolution of these strategies occurred due to chance and path-dependent processes, alternative histories of a game may produce different best-performing strategies. Evolutionary game theory captures this with the concept of an "evolutionarily stable strategy." This is a strategy that, once it becomes dominant in a population, will defeat any other possible strategy by natural selection alone.[25] For any given iterated game, the set of evolutionarily stable strategies is potentially very large thanks to random chance events in the evolution of strategies. Although tit-for-tat may be an optimal solution to the iterated prisoner's dilemma, the game has other potentially evolutionarily stable strategies if the population of players learns and coevolves a different set of strategies. To understand how a large population of actors solves collective action problems, then, one must study explicitly the history of bargaining and learning.

Thus, both multiple equilibria and the heterogeneity of strategies suggest that multiplayer games will be at least partly path dependent. Solutions to any particular multiplayer social dilemma are probabilistic, following distributions we can observe only through experimentation. For this reason, researchers increasingly have relied upon computational social science to study collective action problems. In this context, a "simulation" refers to a research design that studies how actors produce collective behavior over time.[26] Two aspects of this definition are worth emphasizing. Simulation research designs are concerned, first, with how actors produce macrolevel social phenomena such as cooperation, collective action, deadlock, or conflict. To the degree that computational social science is interested in the attributes of actors, it is only to relate these attributes to the "emergent" macrophenomenon. Thus, simulation is a research design to think explicitly across levels of analysis in social problems. Second, simulation designs typically study and measure the history of the social system rather than its time-invariant features. To study such path dependence and emergence, researchers increasingly have used computer-based simulation primarily for its speed and low cost, but, in principal, role-playing exercises could also aid our understanding of the temporal dynamics of collective action. Among scholars of world politics, one of the more well-known simulations was Robert Axelrod's prisoner's dilemma tournament, which found that the "tit-for-tat" strategy performed the best.[27] By contrast, simulations informed by evolutionary game theory increasingly allow strategies to evolve endogenously in the simulation.[28]

THE SIMULATION

I constructed an ABM in which negotiators play one of four classic games: rules of the road, battle of the sexes, the stag hunt, and the prisoner's dilemma. I chose these four because they arguably are the most influential and most studied games in contemporary international relations theory.[29] The "rules of the road" (sometimes colorfully called "Chicken") refers to a coordination problem without distributive conflict. It characterizes social dilemmas in which actors are indifferent about what the collective choice is as long as everyone chooses the same option (there is no difference between driving on the left side of the road or the right side, as long as everyone drives on the same side). In world politics, the rules of the road game characterizes everything from international technical standards for internet protocol (IP) addresses to military forces monitoring each other but who wish to avoid misunderstandings and accidental conflicts. "Battle of the sexes" refers to a coordination game with distributional consequences: both players prefer cooperation to noncooperation but are no longer indifferent between the multiple cooperative equilibria. An example is a couple deciding on where to vacation: they prefer vacationing together to being alone, but one might prefer the mountains while the other prefers a beach vacation. Krasner, for one, discusses how state power and institutions may affect international cooperation in dilemmas typified by the rules of the road or the battle of the sexes (e.g., international telecommunications standards).[30] The "stag hunt" represents problems of assurance first described by Jean-Jacques Rousseau: two players will eat better (i.e., receive higher payoffs) if they hunt a stag, but to succeed they must cooperate. By contrast, either player will have a modest meal if he hunts a hare but does not have to rely on the cooperation of a partner. This game thus captures the tension between the higher payoffs of social cooperation and the safety of self-reliance. Martin argues that different types of assurance problems will affect the design of multilateral institutions.[31] Stein similarly discusses how coordination and collaboration games produce different types of international institutions.[32] Finally, the prisoner's dilemma is well known and hardly needs elaboration here. It suffices to note that it has received extensive theoretical attention from scholars of international studies precisely because it typifies a range of problems of international cooperation.[33] Figure 4.1 provides the normal form representation of all four games.

The model presented here can simulate two-player and multiplayer games for any one of these four social dilemmas. It allows the researcher to choose the number of players, from two to fifty. To explore the effect of social structure on the prospects for cooperation, the researcher can choose one of four network structures. The structure assumes that the players may play with any other player on a given turn of the game—that is, it assumes the network is fully connected. Researchers who study n-person games often implicitly make this assumption. However, most social networks are not fully connected—although all of my neighbors and I may share interests in efficient trash collection and good public schools, I probably will discuss these issues with only a select few neighbors. So it is in world politics: civil society groups tend to cluster into issue networks, banks tend to trade with a small subset of their potential lending partners, and very few nation-states have the resources to place diplomats in all the capitals of the world. For this reason, network structures other than the fully connected network are more restrictive, more realistic and general, and theoretically more

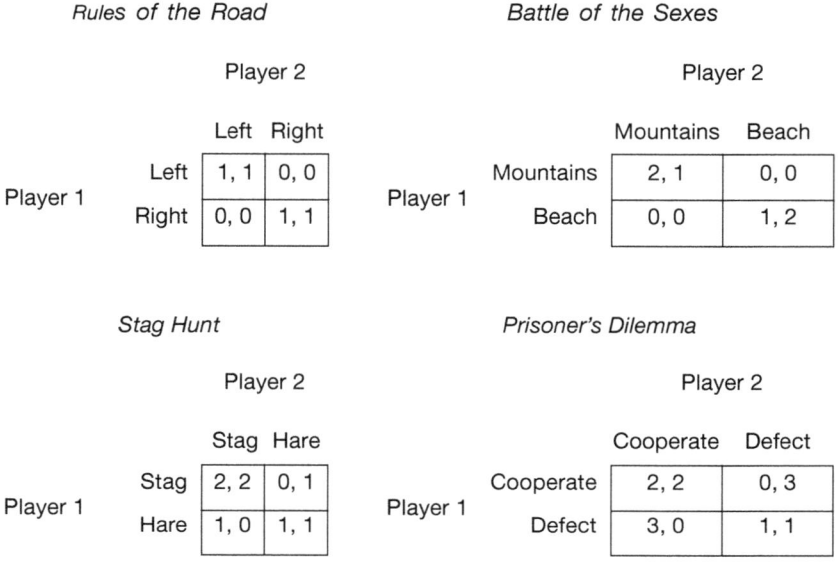

Figure 4.1. Normal form representation of the four two-person games

interesting. The "nearest-neighbor" structure assumes that each player has only two other potential players—all players in the simulation are arrayed in a circle, so nearest neighbors are always one player to the left and one to the right. By contrast, a "small world" structure reflects the small world network structure first noted by Watts and Strogatz.[34] A small world network is one characterized by relatively short path lengths—that is, most actors are just a few "degrees" away from every other actor—yet enjoy relatively high "clustering," or actors who are friends are very likely to share other friends. Small world networks not only are ubiquitous in nature but exhibit surprising adaptability to perturbations. One interesting feature of small world networks is that they seem remarkably efficient at coordinating the behavior of actors in the network; the short path lengths in small world networks provide "high-speed communication channels, enabling mutual influence to spread swiftly throughout the population."[35] Finally, the "scale-free" network structure represents a social network characterized by processes of preferential attachment.[36] Such social networks typically exhibit a hub-and-spoke structure, in which a small number of individuals have many connections to lots of other individuals, but most players have only one or two connections to other players.[37] Santos and Pacheco have found that scale-free networks greatly enhance cooperation in social dilemmas.[38] Matthew and Shambaugh argue that the terrorist networks assume a scale-free organization because they simultaneously improve coordination while the diffuse, decentralized structure limits the overall vulnerability of the network.[39]

The simulation makes two simplifying assumptions. First, it assumes that when negotiators play a game, the outcome of play is "noiseless"—that is, each player knows the other player's choice and the outcome of the game. In the language of game theory, each player has perfect information. This is not a trivial assumption: several simulations of social choice problems have found that "noise" or imperfect information may actually play a role in facilitating cooperation.[40] Second, I assume agents are homogenous in their utility functions: all seek to maximize an objective payoff for a given game, and their memory is uniform and fixed. By contrast, some researchers recently have studied choice problems with populations of "Pavlovian" agents whose learning and hence probability of cooperation evolves as they face selective pressures from the environment.[41] Both noise and player heterogeneity may influence cooperation in social choice models, so evolutionary game theory recently has explored both. These insights suggest future work for the simulation, as discussed below.

The simulation starts with a population of players, the size of which the researcher can set in advance. To capture the importance of iteration to the emergence of cooperation, negotiators in the model have memory and play an iterated game.[42] The simulation experimentally varies both: negotiators may play a game from ten to fifty iterations long, and may have memories ranging from the previous play only to five previous turns. The game proceeds as follows: a randomly chosen negotiator picks from his social network one partner with whom to play a game. Each of the pair plays a choice and receives a payoff for the appropriate game. After all negotiators have played this pairwise game once, the process starts again and repeats until the number of iterations is done. For example, if the researcher has ten negotiators play the prisoner's dilemma twenty times, all ten will have played a two-person prisoner's dilemma a total of twenty times. Because a negotiator picks a random playing partner at each step in the game, it is unlikely that a negotiator will play the game with the same partner every time unless the negotiator happens to have a very small social network (which is least likely in a fully connected all-to-all network and most likely in a scale-free social network). Table 4.1 presents the pseudo code for the model.

It is important to note that technically the model does not simulate a multiplayer game. Strictly speaking, it simulates a series of simultaneous and parallel two-person games. This is the approach that other researchers have

Table 4.1. Pseudo code for the distribution of gains model

Initialization:
Create N *negotiator agents* and distribute them in a circle
   Endow them with a memory of length M
   Seed initial memory set with random bit string of length M
   Endow with a network of other negotiators
     Network types: fully connected, nearest neighbor, small world, scale free

Execution:
Loop for 20 rounds of play:
   Each negotiator agent:
     Randomly select one neighbor to play
     Checks memory of game play
     Convert memory bit string m from binary to decimal format = history h
     Play choice x from position h in the strategy
     Record partner's choice y
     Receive payoff for outcome x, y for the game
     Add partner's choice y to the end of memory bit string
End Loop

Genetic Algorithm:
Initialization:
   Endow negotiator agents with a set of 40 strategies
     One strategy = bit string of length $2^{M^\wedge 2}$ with $p(i = 1) = 0.5$
   40 strategies = 1 generation
Loop for 40 generations:
   Record the mean Hamming distance of negotiators' strategies
   Record the percentage of cooperation plays in all negotiators' strategies
   Record the mean total payoffs of negotiators
   At the end of each generation:
     Select 20 strategies, using either pairwise or fitness proportionate rule
     With $p = .25$, crossover two selected strategies at a randomly selected bit
     With $p = .001$, flip each bit of a selected strategy
     Add 20 strategies of length $2^{M^\wedge 2}$ with $p(i = 1) = 0.5$
   Execute the game play
End Loop

adopted. By contrast, a true multiplayer game is one in which all players play against each other simultaneously and receive a payoff determined by a function of the choices of all players. I opt for the simultaneous two-person game structure, however, precisely because true multiplayer games make an assumption about social structure, one that I seek to problematize. By allowing players to receive payoffs based on all other players in the social system, a true multiplayer game assumes that the social network is fully connected—that the strategy and payoffs of each player depend on the choices of all other players. This may indeed be the case but need not be so. In a scale-free social network, for example, a "hub" player may be connected to every other player while one of the "spoke" players is connected to only one, the hub player. The simultaneous two-player iterated game allows for a more productive investigation of the effects of social structure on the prospects for cooperation than a true multiplayer game.

To model player learning in the simulation, I use a genetic algorithm described by Mitchell that she in turn attributes to Axelrod.[43] The model allows the researcher to choose the game; the number of players; the number of iterations ("rounds") of the game; the social network structure; and the length of each player's memory of past events. For simplicity, each game uses only cardinal payoffs as depicted in Figure 4.1: this differs from Axelrod's use of interval payoffs in the prisoner's dilemma tournament.[44] For computational reasons, negotiators have memories limited to no more than the last five plays of the game.[45] It also includes several controls to allow the researcher to fine-tune the genetic algorithm.

MODEL VALIDATION

Is the simulation accurately modeling the dynamics of real world multiplayer social dilemmas? One can validate the model using the two-person iterated prisoner's dilemma, about which there is both vast experimental data and specific theoretical predictions. I ran the simulation to see if it produces two well-known results of the prisoner's dilemma. First, Axelrod's tournaments and subsequent work suggests that players with longer memories should cooperate more than players with short memories.[46] Second, Axelrod's tournaments suggest that tit-for-tat is an optimal strategy. Thus, if the model is valid, one would expect that players with longer memories will cooperate more than players with short memories, and that players frequently should adopt tit-for-tat as their strategy. Toward this end, I used the model to simulate 1,500 tournaments of the two-person iterated prisoner's dilemma. In the simulation, one can measure cooperation in several ways. One is simply the probability that one or both players adopt a strategy other than pure defection (that is, any other strategy involves at least some cooperation). This approach is indifferent to the type of mixing strategy players adopt; rather, it seeks to understand the conditions under which players choose any strategy other than defection. Another is to measure the average score of the players in the final round of the tournament; for example, in a twenty-round iterated prisoner's dilemma with cardinal payoffs, the maximum possible payoff for a player is sixty (twenty rounds of defect-cooperate with three points per round). The maximum possible pure cooperation payoff is forty, whereas two players both retaliating with tit-for-tat would earn thirty points. One would expect higher scores from players with longer memories. A third way to assess the level of cooperation is to measure the similarities in player strategies: are both players adopting tit-for-tat or some other strategies? Since each strategy set is simply a bit string, one can measure similarity of strategies by calculating the average Hamming distance of the strategies of all players. The "Hamming distance" of any two bit strings is the number of positions in which the two strings disagree. For example, the Hamming distance between 0 1 0 and 0 1 1 is one because the third bit in the two strings differs; the distance between 1 0 1 1 1 and 0 1 1 1 0 is three. Finally, one can measure the distribution of winning strategies in the 1,500 simulations. If the genetic algorithm is simulating player adaptation and learning, we should observe the emergence of cooperation in general, and specifically tit-for-tat as a strategy.

Table 4.2 lists the frequency with which the two players in the simulation adopted various strategies. As predicted, at least one player chooses some cooperative strategy in about three-quarters of the simulations. In about 63 percent of the games, *both* players choose cooperation of some kind instead of pure defection. The table also gives some sense about the distribution of cooperative strategies. Surprisingly, in almost 12 percent of the simulations both players chose a strategy of pure cooperation. This finding is consistent with the finding of evolutionary game theorists that the equilibrium strategy depends in part upon the population of strategies adopted by other players; in a world of cooperators, negotiators learn to cooperate and hence get higher payoffs than tit-for-tat. In about 8 percent of simulations, at least one player chose tit-for-tat. Overall, in one of every four simulations, at least one player chooses all-cooperation or tit-for-tat as its strategy. Furthermore, in a number of simulations at least one player adopted variants of tit-for-tat. Axelrod once suggested a more forgiving strategy in which a player would cooperate an extra turn before retaliating for defection—the so-called tit-for-two-tats strategy. Indeed, in 4.1 percent of the simulations at least one player chose tit-for-two-tats. The table lists a few other exotic strategies: tit-for-three-tats and two-tits-for-two-tats. Not listed is the "grim trigger" strategy of cooperation until a player defects and then pure defection afterward; in 1,500 simulations, only once did a player choose the grim trigger. This distribution of winning strategies is consistent with theory in several respects. For one, players more often than not learn to choose some cooperative strategy over defection. For another, as evolutionary game theory suggests, a heterogeneity of cooperative strategies emerges as the population of strategies itself coevolves.[47] Third, as predicted by Axelrod's work,

Table 4.2. Distribution of strategies in 1,500 tournaments of two-player iterated prisoner's dilemma.

Strategy		Example	Freq. (Pct.)
Pure Defection (ALLD)	At least one player Both players	0 0 0 0 0 0	558 (37.2%) 389 (25.9%)
Any Cooperation	At least one player Both players		1,111 (74.1%) 942 (62.8%)
Pure Cooperation (ALLC)	At least one player Both players	1 1 1 1 1 1	260 (17.3%) 175 (11.7%)
Tit for Tat (TFT)	At least one player Both players	1 0 1 0 1 0	127 (8.5%) 50 (3.3%)
Two Tits for Tat (2TFT)	At least one player Both players	1 0 0 1 0 0	61 (4.1%) 11 (0.7%)
Tit for Two Tat (TF2T)	At least one player Both players	1 1 0 1 1 0	61 (4.1%) 23 (1.5%)
Three Tits for Tat (TF3T)	At least one player Both players	1 1 1 0 1 1 1 0	30 (2.0%) 7 (0.5%)
Two Tits for Two Tats (2TF2T)	At least one player Both players	1 1 0 0 1 1 0 0	33 (2.2%) 3 (0.2%)
Total:			1,500 (100%)

tit-for-tat is indeed one of the strategies that players adopt in a considerable number of cases.

To test the expectation that players with longer memory tend to be more cooperative, one can simply regress a number of measures of cooperation on the measure of the players' memory. Probit analysis of the likelihood of cooperation ($y = 1$ indicating any strategy other than pure defection) shows that an increase in player memory significantly increases the likelihood of cooperation. Memory also significantly predicts the number of cooperative plays in a game: a one-round increase in player memory results in a nearly 6 percent increase in the number of cooperative plays. A one-unit increase in player memory also significantly increases the players' average scores by about 2.2 points. All these findings are consistent with expectations from the literature on the two-person iterated prisoner's dilemma. The only surprising finding concerns the Hamming distance between players' strategy: longer memory significantly increases the Hamming distance. Yet this is an imprecise measure of cooperation because the genetic algorithm selects an increasingly lower proportion of agents' genes as coevolution and convergence of behaviors progress.[48]

Overall, the data suggest the players are learning to solve social dilemmas in a manner that is consistent with both traditional game theory findings about the iterated prisoner's dilemma and with evolutionary game theory's insights into selection pressures, coevolution and strategy heterogeneity. For this reason, we can proceed to use the simulation to study how social structure may influence the prospects for cooperation in four classic games.

SOME FINDINGS

I repeated the simulation 7,680 times, or 1,920 times for each of the four games.[49] The simulation systematically varied players' memories (ranging from 1 to 3); the number of players (using $n = 4, 8, 12,$ and 20); and the four network structures (all to all; nearest neighbor; scale free; and small world). I repeated the simulation forty times for each parameter set. Each simulation conducted 3,200 iterated games of the particular collective action problem. For any given simulation, each player played forty strategies before undertaking the genetic algorithm to optimize the strategy set, and then repeated this optimization algorithm eighty times (thus, forty strategies times eighty generations = 3,200 games). For each simulation, I measured the average score of all players in the final generation; the percentage of cooperative plays in the final round; and the average Hamming distance between players' final strategy sets. I also inspected two randomly selected players at the end of each simulation to identify whether or not players were coordinating strategies. Together these measures allow me to assess how players' memories, the number of players, and the network structure of social interaction influence the prospects for cooperation.

Table 4.3 presents the results of regressing players' average scores on their memory length, the number of players, and the network structure for each of the four games. Each regression controls for two different selection mechanisms in the genetic algorithm: 0 = fitness proportionate and 1 = pairwise. A "fitness proportionate" selection mechanism is one that weights the probability of selection by the strategy's relative fitness in the population, so that the selection tournament is more likely to select high-performing strategies. A "pairwise" rule simply selects two random strategies, compares their fitness, and selects the more fit of the two strategies. Each selection mechanism has strengths and weaknesses. Fitness-proportionate selection

Table 4.3. OLS regression estimates of effect on average player score.

Variable	Game			
	Rules of the Road	Battle of the Sexes	Stag Hunt	Prisoner's Dilemma
Tournament (1 = pairwise)	−0.04 (0.17)	−0.11 (0.25)	−1.73 (0.72)*	−0.10 (0.11)
Memory length	−4.29 (0.11)***	−6.56 (0.16)***	−5.20 (0.44)***	1.78 (0.07)***
Number of Players	−0.13 (0.01)***	−0.17 (0.02)***	−0.31 (0.06)***	0.00 (0.01)
Nearest neighbor dummy	−1.68 (0.24)***	−2.60 (0.36)***	3.35 (1.02)**	−1.65 (0.16)***
Scale free dummy	0.29 (0.24)	−0.22 (0.36)	11.35 (1.02)***	1.21 (0.16)**
Small world dummy	−0.54 (0.24)*	−1.11 (0.36)**	−1.51 (1.02)	−0.37 (0.16)*
Constant	32.25 (0.33)***	48.24 (0.48)***	61.69 (1.37)***	24.93 (0.21)***

Legend: b(se); *p < .05; **p < .01; ***p < .001

tends to converge quickly on a high-performing strategy but may settle on suboptimal ones. By contrast, pairwise selection introduces more heterogeneity and exploration of the fitness landscape, but may fail to converge on a single winning strategy. The estimates for network structure use the all-to-all structure as the baseline; the dummy is omitted because by construction it is perfectly collinear with the intercept term.

Several striking results emerge from this analysis. As predicted by collective action theory, larger numbers of players typically score lower than small numbers.[50] In the simulation, this probably arises because players take longer to learn about the population of strategies played by other players; the analogy in real world collective action dilemmas would be the challenges of monitoring and enforcement of cheating in large groups. Interestingly, the length of players' memory has a significant and positive effect on average scores in the prisoner's dilemma game, but a significant and *negative* effect in the other three games. Why would players with longer memories score lower on average in the rules of the road, battle of the sexes, and stag hunt games? One possible explanation is that players with longer memories take much longer to optimize against each other. Another explanation may be that one player's optimization may cancel out another player's efforts as players coevolve. Hence, individual players constantly optimize against strategies that themselves have changed, leading to no social learning and improvement. Figure 4.2 compares two simulations of the rules of the road game with twelve players who differ only in the length of their memory. It illustrates how "dumb" players with a memory of only one previous play coordinate their behavior by about the twentieth generation; by contrast, "smart" players with memories of four previous plays never improve their scores on rules of the road. This suggests that, in some collective action dilemmas, player learning and adaption may actually inhibit cooperation. This finding may be consistent, furthermore, with other research that illustrates how imperfect information in games may actually facilitate cooperation.[51] With more noise, very efficient optimizers may learn in a more probabilistic fashion so that they do not "overlearn" of others' strategies. This might help players avoid the trap of overcompensating in their future play. This illustrates formally an argument from chapter 1: in world politics, "noise" and inefficiency can play a constructive and perhaps necessary role in helping social actors escape dilemmas of collective choice, whether phantom traffic jams or gales of creative destruction in capitalist economies.

Table 4.3 also illustrates the effect of social structure on the prospects for cooperation. In the two coordination games (rules of the road and battle of the sexes), the nearest neighbor and small world network structures perform significantly worse than the all-to-all network structure. Interestingly, players in a scale-free network structure receive statistically

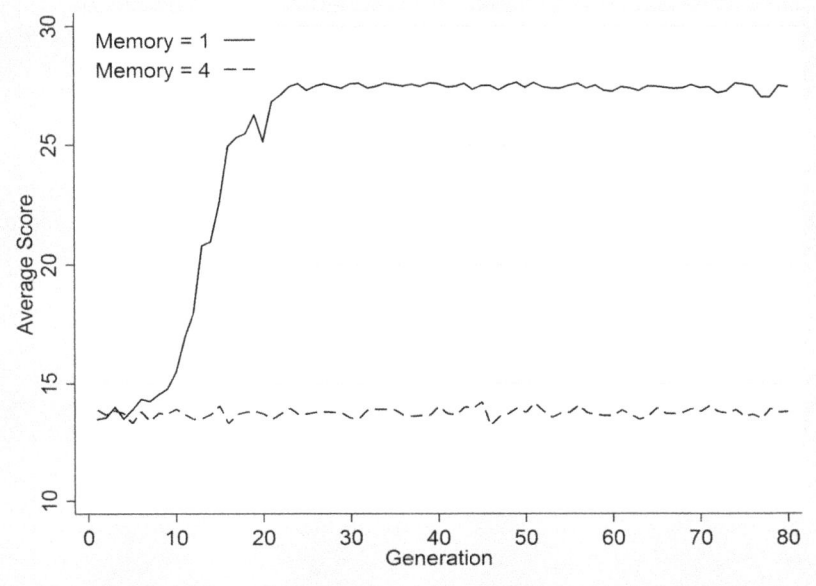

Figure 4.2. Effect of memory on average player score, twelve-player rules of the road game.

equivalent scores to those playing in an all-to-all structure. The effects of structure differ, however, for the two collaboration games (stag hunt and rules of the road). Players in scale-free networks score significantly higher than players in the all-to-all structure, as Santos and Pacheco predict.[52] The effect of scale-free networks is strongest on stag hunt games. It is interesting to note, furthermore, that the nearest neighbor structure has opposite effects in the two games: players in a nearest neighbor structure score significantly higher in the stag hunt but significantly lower on the prisoner's dilemma. Similarly, the small world structure produces lower average player scores on the prisoner's dilemma, but produces no differences on the stag hunt. Several observations emerge from this analysis. One is that the problem of "context preservation"—how to model multiplayer interaction—is not trivial. There appear to be important differences, furthermore, in the types of social networks: nearest neighbor networks score significantly different than all-to-all networks on all four games; small world networks score significantly worse on three of the four; and the effects of scale-free networks appear to be significant on collaboration problems but not coordination problems. More generally, researchers who assume an all-to-all social network among actors may significantly overstate the prospect for cooperation on coordination games and the prisoner's dilemma, but significantly understate the prospects for cooperation on the stag hunt. To understand cooperation in multiplayer games, then, researchers require some theoretically informed model of social interaction in groups.

Each simulation randomly drew two players at the end of the game and measured their optimized strategies. Two players is only a small subset of the entire group of players (which ranged in size from four to twenty), so their strategies may not be representative of the population of strategies. With that proviso in mind, it is interesting to see whether or not players coordinate their strategies on the two coordination games. In about 55 percent of these games, both players adopted identical strategies. Table 4.4 presents the results of probit analysis of the two coordination games, with the dependent variable whether or not the two sampled players adopted identical strategies. Interestingly, the effects of social network structure appear weaker on the rules of the road than on the battle of the sexes. In scale-free networks players are less likely to adopt identical strategies on rules of the road, but there is no difference between all-to-all, small world or nearest neighbor networks. By contrast, with the introduction of a distribution of gains in the battle of the sexes, social network structures appear to become more important. Players in all three networks are significantly less likely to coordinate their strategies. The probit analysis thus is consistent with the findings of the regression analysis of players' scores: social network structure has significant effects in the simulations. As the density of network connections increases, so does the probability of coordination. Whether the Occupy Movement's peaceful protests, the assertive demonstrations of the

Table 4.4. Probit estimated effects on the likelihood of coordination

	Game	
Variable	Rules of the Road	Battle of the Sexes
Tournament (1 = pairwise)	−0.11 (0.07)	−0.07 (0.07)
Memory length	−1.25 (0.05)**	−1.17 (0.05)**
Number of Players	−0.07 (0.01)**	−0.06 (0.01)**
Nearest neighbor dummy	−0.19 (0.10)	−0.43 (0.10)**
Scale free dummy	−0.25 (0.10)	−0.36 (0.10)**
Small world dummy	−0.11 (0.10)	−0.20 (0.10)
Constant	3.73 (0.16)**	−3.41 (0.15)**

Legend: b(se); *$p < .05$; **$p < .01$; ***$p < .001$

Arab Spring, the civil war in Syria, or insurgencies in Iraq and Afghanistan, social movements experience a positive feedback mechanism conducive to tipping points. As more actors join—as social networks become denser—the probability of coordinated group behavior increases dramatically.

For the two collaboration games, one can use the sampled players' strategies to test for the likelihood of cheating. I constructed two dummy variables: one measures whether at least one player adopted a pure cheating strategy (i.e., defecting on every move); the other measures whether both sampled players adopted pure cheating strategies. Table 4.5 presents the probit analysis of the likelihood of cheating for the stag hunt and the prisoner's dilemma simulations. As one would expect, as players' memories increase the probability of cheating appears to decrease significantly in both games as players learn to improve their payoffs. Network structure again appears to matter: in both games scale-free networks significantly reduce the likelihood of one or two players cheating. Nearest neighbor networks appear to reduce significantly the likelihood of cheating in the stag hunt, but not in the prisoner's dilemma. Small world networks appear to have no effect on either game, when compared to all-to-all network structures. Interestingly, the number of players appears to have weak to no effects on cheating. This suggests an intriguing possibility. In multiplayer games with distributive conflict such as the stag hunt or the prisoner's dilemma, the number of players is less important than how the players are organized into a social network. Scale-free networks in particular may help large groups detect and punish cheating more effectively than all-to-all networks, in which cheaters can hide in plain view as it were. Because the tests in tables 4.4 and 4.5 observed only two randomly chosen players in each simulation, however, their strategies may not be representative of the population of player strategies. One needs to measure the distribution of strategies for all players to better understand the likelihood of coordination in multiplayer coordination games, or of cheating in multiplayer collaboration games.

These findings are consistent with the expectation that the structure of players' relationships may profoundly affect the prospects for cooperation. The effects of network structure differ, furthermore, between the types of games. For example, scale-free networks matter on collaboration games but not coordination games. Nearest neighbor networks have negative effects on collaboration games and the prisoner's dilemma, but positive effects on the stag hunt. These observations suggest that the effect of social network structure is highly contingent on the collective action problem. One must study network effects in specific contexts rather than generally. This does not obviate, however, the observation that network effects matter. To ignore social structure leads game theory to misstate the prospects for collective action.

Table 4.5. Probit estimated effects on the likelihood of pure cheating strategy.

	Game			
	Stag Hunt		Prisoner's Dilemma	
Variable	One Cheats	Two Cheat	One Cheats	Two Cheat
Tournament (1 = pairwise)	0.17 (0.07)*	0.07 (0.08)	0.03 (0.10)	0.01 (0.08)
Memory length	−0.86 (0.05)***	−0.91 (0.07)***	−1.76 (0.13)***	−1.23 (0.06)***
Number of Players	0.02 (0.01)**	−0.01 (0.01)	0.01 (0.01)	−0.01 (0.01)
Nearest neighbor dummy	−0.20 (0.10)*	−0.60 (0.12)***	−0.12 (0.14)	−0.30 (0.11)**
Scale free dummy	−0.50 (0.10)***	−0.87 (0.13)***	−0.54 (0.13)***	−1.00 (0.11)***
Small world dummy	0.18 (0.10)	0.02 (0.11)	0.05 (0.14)	−0.11 (0.11)
Constant	0.59 (0.13)***	0.73 (0.16)***	5.76 (0.41)***	3.94 (0.19)***

Legend: b(se); *$p < .05$; **$p < .01$; ***$p < .001$

NEXT STEPS

So far, this discussion of coordination and collaboration problems is generic and not particularly unique to world politics. As noted in chapter 3, negotiators in multilateral discussions rarely consider the simple two-choice problems explored in this chapter. To reduce debates in Kyoto over carbon emissions or discussions in Oslo over Israeli-Palestinian peace to simple either/or choices seems unsatisfying. For almost any problem in world politics, actors face an array of choices that may prove satisfactory, and must bargain simultaneously with both other actors and their constituencies. Such n-choice problems with two-level bargaining may present a variety of interesting dynamics and social pathologies. Yet so far I have skirted what international relations theorists claim is the most important challenge to cooperation among nation-states: sensitivity to relative gains. Grieco provides a useful discussion of the differences between neorealists and neoliberal institutionalists on the issue of relative gains.[53] Helpfully, he proposes what he calls the "k factor." A state's payoff (or utility U) from an international transaction is:

$$U = V - k(W - V)$$

with V representing the state's payoff and W representing the partner's payoff. In this conception of payoffs, relative gains represent the difference between the player and his partner: $W - V$. If the k factor is zero, then actors are indifferent to relative gains and an actor's utility becomes strictly the absolute gain of the transaction, as neoliberal institutionalism suggests. If k is greater than zero, a player's payoff may be discounted (or augmented) by differences in the distribution of gains from the transaction, as neorealism argues. The k factor thus captures one of the central theoretical disagreements between neorealists and neoliberal institutionalists, and can help us think about the truculence of actors in world politics, whether persistent Israeli-Palestinian disagreement over territory or governments' unwillingness to participate in carbon-trading markets.

The k factor also helps one think, furthermore, about how to model payoffs in iterated games. The simulation I present here uses cardinal (i.e., rank-ordered) payoffs only. Thus, in simulations of the prisoner's dilemma a player who gives the sucker's payoff to another earns three points, while two players cooperating earn two points apiece. Yet Axelrod used different awards in his prisoner's dilemma tournament: a player who defected against a cheater received five points, not three.[54] Thus, Axelrod's tournament gave higher rewards to cheating than the simulations presented here. In a world of relative gains (i.e., one in which $k > 0$) the rewards of cheating become even more pronounced. If $k = 0$ and we use cardinal payoffs, then a defector against a cooperator in a prisoner's dilemma game receives $U = 3 - 0 (0 - 3) = 3$. But if $k = 1$, then the defector receives $U = 3 - 1 (0 - 3) = 6$. Thus, the k factor represents a way of weighting payoffs in the simulation. Such weighting would allow the simulation to model productively the differences in expectations between neorealism and neoliberal institutionalism. Because both theories make specific predictions about the prospects for cooperation as well as the design of institutions, one can validate the simulation by testing whether a world of relative gains concerns is less cooperative than one in which relative gains concerns are absent.

Two final extensions to the simulation are to use heterogeneous actors, and to introduce noise to the games. Currently, the simulation uses negotiators who differ only in their initial strategies: otherwise, they perceive and learn about the game in identical fashion. Other researchers have explored how heterogeneity in agent perception and learning may affect the evolution of cooperative strategies.[55] One interesting possibility is to populate a world of negotiators with different sensitivities to relative gains (i.e., each negotiator has its own value for k). How would a distribution of k affect the prospects for cooperation? Does social network structure interact in meaningful ways with relative gains sensitivity to enhance cooperation or to undermine it? A variety of perception styles among agents also begs the question of "noise." Currently the simulation makes simplifying assumptions analogous to perfect information in game theory: all players know a partner's choices and know payoffs of the game. What if players are uncertain about each other's payoffs? Interestingly, some scholars have noted that imperfect information may be essential to the emergence of cooperative behavior.[56] But does imperfect information interact with sensitivity to relative gains, perhaps enhancing concerns about taking the sucker's payoff? With a few simple extensions, one can explore how player heterogeneity and imperfect information affect the stability of players' strategies and the prospects for social cooperation.

SOME CONCLUDING THOUGHTS

The four games examined in this chapter are simple but powerful models for understanding a range of social choice problems. When one expands these classic two-player games to examine social networks, the analysis yields a number of interesting findings. For one, social networks matter. The scale-free network structure significantly improved players' payoffs in the two games with distributive conflicts, but not in the two coordination games. In all four games, the scale-free structure likewise significantly reduced the probability of players evolving cheating strategies. This suggests that social networks condition how actors learn and adapt in social choice problems. In social movements, transnational activist networks, and other forms of civil society, one would expect that the density of network ties would significantly affect the prospects for these actors to provide collective goods. By using evolutionary approaches, one can model not only social dilemmas of common aversions and common interests, but also the emergence of social structures that may lock in cooperation (or defection) as the distribution of strategies assumes evolutionarily stable properties. Evolutionary modeling thus reintroduces the importance of history in understanding world politics, and hence opens up intellectual space to explore prospects for change as actors coevolve, adapt, and learn not only about their dilemmas, but about each other as well.

The next two chapters move beyond these simple, abstract representations of social choice dilemmas to examine specific problems in contemporary world politics. How can governments manage the dynamism of the global gyre, if at all? Are they capable of adapting strategies that balance the competing objectives of providing public goods while managing the risks of sudden changes? To explore these questions, the next two chapters examine two of the more dynamic, chaotic, and vexing problems in global politics: environmental change and global finance.

FIVE

COWS GROW TREES, NETS GROW FISH

How Social Networks Manage the Commons

The sturgeon of the Caspian Sea, whose roe gourmands worldwide covet as caviar, offers a somewhat obscure but nonetheless interesting example of complexity in world politics. Social and ecological factors interact in ways that defy prediction and management, threatening the sturgeon with extinction. Because the sturgeon's Caspian Sea habitat encompasses territorial waters of five nation-states, the industry of harvesters is widely dispersed, small-scale, and poorly (if at all) regulated. That is to say, Caspian Sea fishers have no central authority to solve collective action problems; conservation efforts are weak and ineffective. Global demand for caviar creates incentives for harvesters to maximize short-term personal welfare at the expense of their own long-term economic interests. It also has prompted a growing black market, organized criminal fishing enterprises that operate transnationally, and corrupt officials who circumvent international agreements intended to protect sturgeon.[1] Interactions between social and ecosystems produce positive and negative feedbacks that complicate preservation efforts as well. Like many large fish, most of the twenty-four species of sturgeon grow slowly, live long, reach reproductive maturity late in life, and spawn rarely and irregularly.[2] Female sturgeons carry eggs for years. The demand for caviar thus produces perverse market incentives: like other luxury goods, scarcity of caviar drives up demand, which increases the incentives to harvest Caspian Sea female sturgeons. But with fewer females and slow maturation, both fish and caviar becomes scarcer, which in turn drives demand and triggers the vicious cycle. As Chivers notes, "The dynamic is perfectly counterproductive: the best money is in the eggs, the part of the fish needed to replenish stocks."[3] Unsurprisingly, the sturgeon is facing extinction, and not just in the Caspian: all twenty-four species worldwide reside on the endangered list of the Convention on International Trade in Endangered Species.[4] The plight of the sturgeon illustrates four features that characterize many important social systems in global politics today. Actors pursue their interests in parallel rather than under a centralized authority; chaotic and nonlinear dynamics may arise from positive and negative feedback; actors learn about and adapt to both their environment and other actors; and actors may "self-organize," or provide collective goods without any external guidance. To understand such self-organized governance, one must first understand the sources of complexity in world politics. Only then can we consider how actors adapt to solve collective action problems characterized as "complex" or "chaotic."

The previous two chapters examined general but abstract coordination and collaboration problems. This chapter turns to a more specific problem. How can social groups—whether communities, cities, or nation-states—conserve environmental resources? Although the Great Pacific Garbage Patch suggests we have some way to go, the scholarship on common pool resources has identified a variety of factors that affect the prospects for conservation. One important feature of these conservation challenges is that they are both a social and an ecological problem. Clearly, as the patch shows, dilemmas of collective action can deplete scarce resources. The properties of a resource itself—whether the resource is mobile or fixed and its rate of replenishment, among others—affect the likelihood of its conservation. Adding to the challenge, however, is that social and ecological systems are loosely coupled such that choices or happenings in one affect the other. Often these interactions exhibit nonlinear dynamics and temporal delays that make it difficult for actors to discern cause-effect relationships and whether their choices aid or harm the resource. Given the many factors affecting socioecological systems, an important question is whether actors can learn enough about the system's dynamics to manage the resource in a socially beneficial way. This chapter explores how actors can self-organize—that is, without the state's power to coerce—to preserve environmental resources.

Why do some actors successfully manage social-ecological complexity when others cannot? This chapter illustrates that three factors help explain self-organized governance of complexity: the efficiency with which technology transfers the externalities of individual action to the environment; the patterns in which actors share information about the socioeconomic system; and how actors learn, mimic each other, and build trust. The chapter presents the results of an ABM of social-ecological complexity, in which simulated appropriators harvest a common pool resource that is analogous to pelagic fish. It reviews recent research on common pool resources and derives hypotheses about self-organized governance of social-ecological complexity. To test these hypotheses, the chapter presents an ABM of a common pool resource that simulates how actors learn to manage and preserve the resource despite incomplete information and technological pressures. Though the ABM is an abstract artificial society type, the general nature of the model gives insights into a range of environmental problems in world politics. Fundamentally, it examines the central dilemma of any public good: actors must balance their short-term private gains with the long-term expected future welfare from a public good. Too much short-term free-riding creates future losses, while slavish concern for the "shadow of the future" reduces private gains and increases opportunity costs. After presenting the findings of the model, the chapter turns to its theoretical implications. It finds that actors manage dilemmas of common pool resources by building small world–type networks. The structure of these social networks helps actors balance the competing goals of private welfare and preservation of public goods.

ECOLOGICAL COMPLEXITY

The complexity of interactions between humans and ecosystems creates nonlinear dynamics and unpredictability that challenge effective governance. Although the term *ecology* suggests natural and biological systems, ecological complexity more generally characterizes any environment in which "local interactions affect the global composition and dynamics of whole communities."[5] Actors both consciously and unconsciously change the environment in which they are interacting, inducing changes in the rewards they receive from their structure of interaction. One interesting example of such ecological complexity comes from the introduction of the Nassau grouper to a Caribbean fish reserve. The grouper's primary diet is the parrotfish, which in turn grazes on algae growing on coral reefs. Ecologists were concerned that the grouper's predation on the parrotfish would lead to overgrowth of algae and the destruction of the reserve's coral reefs, but in fact the opposite happened. Grouper did indeed thin the parrotfish population, but the surviving parrotfish were larger and more capable grazers that doubled the grazing of algae and reduced algae coverage of the reefs by four times.[6] Ecologists recognize in general that predation improves the welfare of the population of prey, a paradox which ecological complexity helps us understand. Jervis quotes a Maasai proverb that captures this type of complexity: "Cows grow trees, elephants grow grass."[7]

Such complexity exists in the social as well as the natural world. In the global economy, for example, governments can alter markets to increase returns to their national firms and technological industrial bases. Government investment in research and development and in education produces positive externalities that spill over to the public as a whole. These spillovers in turn incentivize private investment, thus creating a virtuous cycle of technological growth.[8] Even in globally competitive markets, nation-states can deliberately change the environment in which firms compete and increase the rewards their firms receive.

Actors pursue two strategies to manage—but not eliminate—ecological complexity in world politics. First, they create small world–like social networks to manage uncertainty arising from complexity. Such a network structure helps balance two competing needs: it provides sufficient information about changes in the supply of natural resources to allow actors to learn and adapt, but attenuates the effects of chaos by muting the transmission of chaotic information. In this respect, small world–like networks help actors avoid the trap of overreacting and inducing chaotic dynamics. Second, actors adapt to complexity in several ways: they change their strategies over time in a process of trial-and-error learning; they mimic actors who perform well; and they learn to trust some neighbors and disregard others. Actors do not learn and adapt in isolation, but in relation to the learning and adaptation of others. Indeed, actors often adapt by imitating others.[9] In this view, the "best" solution for actors depends on the distribution of strategies among other players and on communication and interaction among actors.[10] Such adaptation of actors implies that we cannot consider solutions to complex collective action problems in isolation from the strategies, learning, and communication in the population of actors.

To support these arguments, the chapter presents an ABM of a "tragedy of the commons," or a collective action problem characterized by strong incentives for free-riding that tends to exhaust scarce resources.[11] The plight of the sturgeon is but one example of such socioecological resource problems: others include greenhouse gases, irrigation systems, forests, and other resources. Ostrom has noted that actors who manage such resources are boundedly rational, they experiment with policies in a decentralized manner without central direction from the state, and they learn from mistakes and adapt to changing conditions.[12] Such decentralized experimentation, learning, and adaptation characterize a wide variety of "polycentric" forms of governance in contemporary world politics.[13] Agrawal argues, furthermore, that the study of common pool resources can help us understand how social actors self-organize to create social movements and revolutions; how people vote and participate in collective decision making; how they may collude, cheat, and corrupt; and how actors form and maintain the rules and principles that become institutions.[14] Indeed, free-riding, rent-seeking behavior, and social-ecological complexity characterize some of the most pressing policy challenges of world politics today, from the prospective Basel III

Accords that would reform global regulation of banking (as the next chapter discusses) to air pollution, declining biodiversity, and rising sea levels.

PRESERVING COMMON POOL RESOURCES

Collective action theory hypothesizes that individuals have no incentive to provide common goods.[15] A common or public good is one that is non-excludable and non-rivalrous. "Non-excludability" simply means that all individuals can consume the good whether or not they pay for it because the nature of the good does not permit excluding individuals. A "non-rivalrous" good is one whose supply does not diminish as individuals consume it. For this reason, the resource does not exhibit scarcity that would allow markets to price the good efficiently. A classic example of a public good is national security: once the state provides it, it cannot exclude an individual citizen from consuming the good without denying it to everyone, and an individual's consumption of the good does not reduce the national security that others enjoy. Olson first formalized the problems of provision of public goods. He argued that because the state cannot exclude individuals from consuming a public good, the rational individual has no economic incentive to provide the good.[16] By contrast, a common pool resource (CPR) combines features of public and private goods. Like public goods, CPRs are non-excludable—the nature of the good prevents markets or governments from excluding anyone from consuming the good. Unlike public goods, however, common pool resources are "highly subtractable." That is, like private goods, the consumption of a CPR diminishes the supply available to other consumers.[17] One example of a CPR is fresh water: one farmer's use of water from an irrigation canal diminishes the supply available to farmers farther downstream. The properties of the non-excludability and scarcity of CPRs create incentives for their exploitation and destruction. Because no one is excluded from consuming them, individuals have strong incentives to consume the good without paying for it. Such free-riding diminishes the supply and eventually leads to exhaustion of the good—what Hardin characterized as the "tragedy of the commons."[18] CPRs thus give rise to two collective action problems. The first is an appropriation problem: How can society allocate rights to consume the good when society cannot exclude individuals from consumption? The second is a provision problem: How can society provide for the sustainment of the resource when its highly subtractable nature encourages individuals to consume before others exhaust the resource? The problems of appropriation and provision characterize a variety of CPRs including irrigation systems; forests; hunting and grazing land; and both inland and offshore fisheries.[19]

Researchers have found some examples of societies that have successfully provided for the long-term sustainment of CPRs despite these collective action problems. Agrawal provides a useful review of the hypothesized explanations for such success.[20] One set of explanations focuses on the nature of the community of resource appropriators. The number of appropriators matters. Although Olson hypothesized that small groups are better at providing public goods than large groups,[21] Agrawal and Goyal find that an intermediate-sized population of appropriators has more success than either small or large groups.[22] Independent of the number of appropriators, homogeneous groups—those with a high degree of shared interests and little socioeconomic differentiation—solve provision and appropriation problems more readily than heterogeneous groups.[23] Similarly, Ostrom identifies several important factors internal to a community of users: their shared trust, communication, sense of a common fate, the presence of interest groups, and their expected utility of future benefits.[24] Together, these hypotheses suggest that the social characteristics of the appropriators themselves may affect the provision of CPRs.

Researchers also have found that institutions may help actors preserve CPRs. To prevent free-riding and exhaustion of the resource, societies must develop principles and rules to monitor the health of the resource; guard the commons if feasible; punish individuals who violate appropriation rules; and adjudicate disputes between appropriators. While such factors undoubtedly influence the provision of CPRs, Ostrom finds that institutions to monitor and guard the resource are themselves public goods. Thus, the provision of institutions is a "second-order" or nested dilemma because rational egoists have no incentive to provide rules to monitor or guard the resource.[25] This raises two important questions: Can individuals organize to provide such institutions? And if not, can individuals design rules to preserve the CPR without centralized monitoring and sanctioning? Ostrom, for one, has found that appropriators may design self-governed systems of "a voluntary exchange of information and mutual monitoring" that both enhance everyone's knowledge of the resource and monitor it efficiently.[26] Indeed, Ostrom explicitly states that we should understand a self-organized community of appropriators as a complex adaptive system that has evolved to manage the nonlinearity and uncertainty of CPRs.[27]

A third set of hypotheses concerns factors external to the community of appropriators. Demographic changes clearly can stress CPRs: population growth in Brazil, for example, has accelerated the rent-seeking deforestation of the Amazon.[28] Technological change may have either positive or negative impacts on CPRs by changing the cost-benefit calculus of would-be appropriators. New technologies might make it easier and cheaper for appropriators to harvest the resource, but they may also affect knowledge about the nature and dynamics of resource flows. Pauly et al. note a paradoxical example of this. The fishing industry has progressively adopted more efficient harvesting technologies, from steam-powered ships to motorized winches and large trawling nets. Because these technologies have increased yields, however, they have masked the overall decline in fishing populations, making a collapse of the CPR even more likely.[29] Conversely, low-cost technologies for excluding appropriators may aid the preservation of CPRs. National and international markets can affect a CPR, above and beyond the stresses introduced by demographic and technological change, as the example of the sturgeon shows. Scholars disagree, however, on whether or not markets can help preserve CPRs. Agrawal's review of the literature finds that the integration of appropriation decisions into markets generally harms the management of CPRs.[30] Ostrom notes, however, that the introduction of property rights may help manage CPRs, depending upon the technical qualities of the CPR. In some areas, the privatization of rights of access to a resource has improved conservation efforts: Teitenberg finds that a market for air pollution permits has largely succeeded, but the externalities in markets for fishing and water access have undermined rights-based management of these CPRs.[31] While authorities can partition land to award title to it, for example, for irrigation systems and fisheries it is unclear what individual property rights would be.[32] A final external factor is the relationship of local appropriators to national authorities. Collective action theory suggests that centralized authority is necessary to prevent free-riding. Whether to prevent overharvesting or to impose market-based solutions, this position asserts that central authorities must help appropriators solve provision problems that they cannot address on their own.[33] By contrast, Ostrom finds that decentralized models of managing CPRs have several advantages because "the parallel efforts by a large number of local resource users to search out and design local rule configurations may find better rule combinations over the long term, whereas top-down design processes are more limited in their capacity to search and to find appropriate rules."[34] Similarly, decentralized systems allow efficient monitoring of the health of the CPR, collection of scientific information, and the provision of guards to prevent free-riding. Ostrom finds such polycentric governance characterizes efforts to manage Maine's lobster fisheries and the Pacific salmon fisheries in Washington State.

Finally, the technical properties of the CPR itself are an important source of complexity, which can affect the management of the resource. Resources such as forests and grazing lands have well-defined boundaries that may make the flow of benefits regular and predictable. Such regularity may aid sustainable management. By contrast, other resources such as fisheries have poorly defined and constantly shifting boundaries.[35] While this may create an unpredictable flow of benefits, Agrawal notes that "fuzzy resource boundaries may better accommodate variations in group needs and resource flows."[36] Related to the question of resource boundaries is the mobility of the boundary itself. Stationary resources such as grazing lands and forests facilitate management because the flow of the resource is fairly predictable. By contrast, the very nature of mobile resources introduces considerable volatility and unpredictability in the expected future benefits of a resource. Because appropriators and resource managers must learn about the ecological characteristics and health of the resource, mobile resources create a considerable informational problem. CPRs such as wildlife and breathable air make it extraordinarily difficult for appropriators to anticipate the likely costs and benefits of their harvesting. Such uncertainty tends to induce overharvesting. Finally, although managers can store some CPRs, others defy storage. Irrigation systems manage the unpredictable natural supply of water by using reservoirs, for example. Together, these natural properties explain the likelihood of successfully managing CPRs. Managers of resources with well-defined boundaries that are stationary and may be stored tend to have greater success. Conversely, systems characterized by mobile and non-storable resources with boundaries that constantly change are difficult to manage.

For all these reasons, the habitat of the Caspian Sea sturgeon is nearly impossible to manage. A large number of appropriators are politically, culturally, and economically heterogeneous, divided between five riparian countries. International institutions for monitoring and punishing violators are weak. They are subject to corruption, furthermore, because the market for caviar creates strong incentives for cheating. The sturgeon themselves are highly mobile, have a habitat whose boundary spans not only a million square miles but also the brackish waters of the rivers that feed the Caspian Sea.

In general, pelagic fisheries worldwide are a particularly challenging collective action problem. Fuzzy resource boundaries, mobile resources, difficulties of storage, and market demands create three problems for the design of institutions. First, the design of property rights is difficult. Tradable permit programs only give rights of access to appropriators but cannot guarantee a fixed amount of resource to the permit holder. A second problem is information. Appropriators and managers find it costly (if not prohibitive) to collect reliable information about the health and expected yield of the resource. Third, this information problem creates tradeoffs in the design of regimes to manage a CPR. Regimes that limit the number of harvesters are more likely to preserve the resource, but at the loss of information about the CPR. Ostrom notes appropriators often are the only source of information, however unreliable it may be, about a mobile resource. But if appropriators are too numerous, they stress the system and increase the likelihood of the collapse of the natural replenishment of the CPR. For these reasons, one would expect actors to have a particularly difficult time designing rules and institutions to manage these tradeoffs.[37]

These informational problems have prompted Wilson to propose using complex systems theory to understand the management of CPRs.[38] He notes that conventional approaches to managing resources have tended to focus on a single species, in effect ignoring interactions among species (or other systems) within an ecosystem. Such conventional views of the management of ecosystems assume that scientific investigations can reduce uncertainty arising from exogenous disturbances and improve our knowledge of how cause-and-effect operates in such systems. In essence, conventional management has adopted a reductionist scientific method that assumes causal relationships remain stable. Wilson identifies, however, several factors in ecosystems that make problematic the assumption of stable causal relationships. One is the nonlinear interaction among species that may produce "regime shifts," or sudden movements of an ecosystem from one stable equilibrium state to another. A second is the problem of multiple scales. Wilson notes that CPRs fit Herbert Simon's definition of a "nearly decomposable" system, or one with multiple interacting subsystems such as different species. Interactions within subsystems tend to be numerous, but interactions between subsystems are fewer. For this reason, nearly decomposable systems tend to be efficient and resilient, but also create feedback mechanisms that induce instability in causal relationships over time and across scales. Finally, because ecosystems are so complex—due to "their size, spatial distributions, multiple scales, large number of components, continuous change, and other factors"[39]—no individual or group is likely to understand completely the relationships governing the provision of the resource. For this reason, management of a CPR becomes a question of collective learning under conditions of extreme uncertainty. Ostrom makes this very point:

> A better foundation for public policy is to assume that humans may not be able to analyze all situations fully but that they will make an effort to solve complex problems through the design of regularized procedures and will be able to draw on inherited capabilities to learn norms of behavior.[40]

Wilson similarly concludes "This is much a social problem as a scientific problem. In fact, it is the difficulty of the collective learning in a complex environment that weaves the social and scientific problems into an inseparable matrix."[41]

HYPOTHESES AND METHODS

I propose three hypotheses about how actors preserve CPRs. First, I hypothesize that actors who have past experiences of cooperation are more likely to cooperate to preserve CPRs. In part, this reflects the finding from chapter 4 that iteration increases the likelihood of cooperation in complex social choice problems.[42] Baland and Platteau also find that a history of cooperation improves the current prospects for managing CPRs.[43] Second, I hypothesize that appropriators with more efficient harvesting technology are less likely to preserve a CPR. Pauly et al. find that fishing efficiencies gained from power winches, diesel engines, precise navigation, sea bottom cartography, and echolocation have had both direct and indirect effects on efforts to sustain fisheries. Direct effects include a speed of harvesting that outpaces both natural replenishment of fish stocks as well as human efforts to regulate overharvesting. Just as important, however, are indirect effects: efficient harvesting both leads to overestimates in the fish population, and induces extreme short-term population fluctuations that mask long-term trends.[44] In this respect, technology affects the information that appropriators receive about the health of the ecosystem. To test the role of information, the third hypothesis proposes that appropriators who share information will better manage the long-term sustainment of the CPR. Ostrom finds that communication between appropriators enhances CPR management in three ways: it allows appropriators to internalize norms governing harvesting, it empowers them to create enforceable covenants, and it helps them identify and punish violators.[45] Beyond rule construction, furthermore, information may help appropriators understand characteristics of the resource itself. Agrawal notes the importance of actors' understanding of the boundaries of mobile resources and the risks and variations in resource flows.[46] Ostrom also finds this information problem is central to understanding successful collaboration:

> We can think of appropriators trying to . . . explore and discover the biophysical structure of a particular resource that will differ in key parameters from similar resources in the same region. Further, appropriators have to cope with considerable uncertainty related to the weather [and] complicated growth patterns of biological systems that may be chaotic in nature.[47]

For these reasons, one expects that as appropriators share more and better information about resource flows, they will have more success preserving the resource over the long term. Tests of these hypotheses should, in turn, give us insights into how actors manage social-ecological complexity.

Agent-based models are a valuable method for investigating systems characterized by: autonomous agents who interact repeatedly over time; nonlinear cause-effect relationships; a large number of variables that exhibit interaction complexity; difficulties with gathering empirical data; and a scarcity of events.[48] Arguably, all five conditions characterize the study of CPRs. Ostrom notes that nonlinear effects are pervasive in CPRs: "Given the nonlinearity and complexity of action situations, it is rarely easy to predict what effect a change in a particular rule will produce."[49] Researchers who study CPRs also have identified a large number of hypothesized factors affecting sustainability. One review of the three studies on CPRs found twenty-four conditions common to all three, which "makes it almost impossible to be sure that the observed differences in [real world] outcomes are indeed a result of hypothesized causes."[50] Another study evaluated seven dimensions of institutions, each of which had five different values, implying 75,000 possible configurations of institutions to manage CPRs.[51] Interaction effects among these many variables in CPRs suggests that Newtonian predictability is not possible

> because the relative intensity of causal relationships in the system changes from time to time. Extreme examples are the regime shifts such as have occurred in response to fishing and environmental changes in many places around the world. . . . Under these circumstances, similar species may be present, but in such radically altered proportions that predictions based on past relationships would be far off the mark. Certainly, if one were in a position to compare the entirety of the two systems (before and after the shift) as if they were stable systems, one probably would find strong dissimilarities in the intensity and relative importance of the interactions among components.[52]

For all these reasons, several researchers who study CPRs have advocated using simulation methods such as ABMs that allow for the study of nonlinear relationships, resource flows over time, a diversity of actor strategies and attributes, and the messy processes through which actors learn to manage such collective action problems.[53]

THE FISHERIES MODEL

The following ABM of social-ecological complexity has boundedly rational agents learn to develop appropriation rules. The model creates an ecosystem populated by resource agents that are mobile. Each resource agent has an initial energy endowment and an age that limit its mobility and lifespan. The resource agents in turn consume "food" produced by patches (i.e., fixed units of space) in the ecosystem. Patches have finite food and replenish their food stocks at a rate of 0.4 units per period of simulated time, or "timestep." Resource agents expend one unit of energy to move toward the patch with the highest concentration of food, but can consume up to five units of energy from a patch in a given timestep. If resource agents amass a sufficient store of energy, they can produce offspring with a probability of 25 percent if another resource agent with sufficient energy to reproduce is within a radius of one. Resource agents age one unit per timestep, and die (i.e., the simulation removes them) if their age exceeds a random value drawn from a normal distributed variable with a mean of 75 and a standard deviation of 5. Resource agents also will die if their energy budget reaches zero. Two factors keep the population of resource agents in homeostasis: the limit on the amount of food produced per time period gives the simulated ecosystem a carrying capacity, and the age and energy budgets of resource agents simulate a natural death rate. The simulation typically reaches a condition of homeostasis after about one hundred timesteps.

The ABM creates a population of twenty appropriator agents who seek to harvest the simulated resource agents. Each appropriator has six endowed properties: a harvesting strategy (S); a harvesting technology (call this parameter C); a memory of the past actions of its social network (M); a rule to share information about the state of the population of resource agents (I, for information); a social network neighborhood (N); and an initial endowment of wealth (W). To model the efficiency of technology, the ABM encodes parameter C as the radius between 1 and 5 in which an appropriator harvests resources, which the model tests experimentally. A larger value of C means the appropriator on average will harvest more resources in a given timestep. An appropriator's memory M is simply for how many past timesteps the agent remembers other agents' actions. Operationally, the ABM has each appropriator record the actions of every other appropriator in its social network for time period M. The experiment manipulates the value of M to determine whether a history of cooperation improves the prospects for managing the CPR.

To allow appropriator agents to learn whether the population of resources is growing, appropriators use one of three information (I) rules. The first, the "ego" information rule, is that an appropriator measures the change in the population of resources within the appropriator's harvesting area but does not share its information with other harvesters. Because the resource agents are mobile, one would expect different appropriators using the I_{ego} rule to make different decisions to harvest or not: one appropriator might find many resources nearby and conclude the overall system is healthy, while another may find no resources in the vicinity and conclude the resource population is stressed. A second *I* rule, called the network rule, allows appropriators to share information about the ecosystem among all appropriators within its network neighborhood *N*. By sharing information with other appropriators, the community should have a better (albeit still incomplete) understanding of population trends in the ecosystem. The final *I* rule is a global rule: the model endows appropriator agents with complete information about trends in the resource population. This should be a best case scenario: full knowledge of the current state of the resource should allow appropriators to optimize the expected future yields of the resource. For payoffs, an appropriator agent receives a benefit of one unit of wealth for each resource unit it harvests, but pays a penalty if it chooses not to harvest. Because this penalty represents the opportunity costs of failing to amortize the appropriator's investment, the model measures the penalty as one-fifth the value of the technology parameter C. Thus, as technology grows more efficient, appropriators pay higher opportunity costs. To understand how appropriators learn, the model assumes appropriators are homogenous except for their strategies: all appropriators have the same values of C, M, and I for a given run of the simulation. Table 5.1 lists the ABM's parameters and range of values for experimental manipulations.

Because they have memories of past actions, appropriator agents can adapt to the actions of other appropriators. An appropriator's strategy S is a rule that determines whether or not the appropriator harvests resources. Each appropriator's strategy is encoded as a long bit string (a list of 1's and 0's) with a 1 indicating the appropriator will harvest. At each step in time, every appropriator observes all appropriators in its social network and determines which appropriators are harvesting. It then interprets the pattern of actions of its network neighbors to determine which position on its strategy bit string to check. For example, suppose an appropriator has a memory of length $m = 2$ and has $n = 4$ network neighbors. The appropriator's memory of its network's actions will be a list of length $m \times n$, such as [1 0 1 1 1 0 0 1].[54] The appropriator parses its memory list by converting it from binary to decimal format; in this example, 10111001 becomes 185 in decimal form. The appropriator would then refer to the 185th item in its strategy bit string to determine whether to harvest: if the 185th item is a 1, the appropriator would then harvest all resources within radius C.[55]

After an initial period of one hundred timesteps in which the simulated ecosystem achieves a steady-state population of resources, appropriators may decide whether or not to harvest resources. To simplify the analysis, I assume all appropriator agents are altruists—that is, there is no free-riding. Appropriator agents will not harvest resources unless two conditions are satisfied: their information rule provides a measurement indicated a net

Table 5.1: Model parameters and expectations

Concept	Operational Measure	Parameter name	Simulated parameter values	Expectation	N of Sims
Appropriator's time horizons	Number of previous plays the appropriator remembers to inform current decision	Memory (M)	$1 \leq M \leq 5$	Longer memories produce higher payoffs	240 240 240 240 240
				Longer memories improve survival of ecosystem	
Harvesting technology	Efficiency of harvesting the resource: the radius in which an appropriator harvests all resources in a timestep	Technology (C)	$1 \leq C \leq 5$	More efficient technology causes higher payoffs	240 240 240 240 240
				More efficient technology reduces survival of ecosystem	
Knowledge of Ecosystem	Measure of change in the number of resources that informs the decision to harvest	Information (I) "Ego" rule: the agent measures change in resources only in its radius C	$I \in \{$ Ego, Network, Global $\}$	Ego rule produces higher payoffs but reduces ecosystem survival	400 400 400

COWS GROW TREES, NETS GROW FISH

	"Network" rule: the agent measures change as the average change in radius C for all agents in social network		Global rule improves survival of ecosystem
	"Global" rule: all agents measure change as the change in resources for the entire ecosystem		
Appropriator's Strategy	A rule to harvest (1) or not (0) depending upon the actions of an appropriator's network neighbors	Strategy (S)	A set of $m \times n$ elements drawn from a discrete distribution $U(0,1)$	Genetic algorithm will cause appropriators to "learn" better strategies and improve payoffs	1,200

Total simulations = 75 combinations × 16 experiments = 1,200 growth in the number of resources, and their strategy indicates they should harvest. The model simulates two forms of appropriator learning: adapting their harvesting strategies, and learning to trust or mistrust other appropriators in the social network. How do appropriators learn their strategies? One challenge is the potentially large number of possible strategies for appropriation. Recall that a strategy set is a function of the appropriator's number of neighbors n and the appropriator's memory m. An appropriator with one neighbor and one time period needs only a short strategy string: [0 1]. But an appropriator with a large network of, perhaps, ten neighbors and a memory of five time periods must choose from $2^{10 \times 5}$ possible strategies, or 1.1 quadrillion choices. Obviously, appropriators cannot test every possible strategy. To simulate how actors learn effective strategies from such a large domain of choices, the ABM uses a genetic algorithm. First, from an initial population of randomly generated strategies S, actors will try each strategy once but will only select (or try again in the future) harvesting strategies that are effective, measured as the appropriator's average payoff (the mean number of resource agents harvested per timestep). Second, actors will "cross over" or combine strategies that they have selected as good performers. Finally, actors will mutate their strategies, or in other words will randomly try something different with some low probability. Because harvesters have only two choices for any position in the strategy set (1 = harvest or 0 = not), the mutation procedure chooses a random position in the strategy and flips a 1 to 0 or a 0 to 1. In essence, the genetic algorithm used in this model simulates actor learning and adaptation as a trial and error process over repeated runs of the model.[56] That is, each appropriator agent tests a population of strategies, runs the genetic algorithm, and repeats the cycle for "generations" (again, invoking the language of genetics). This simulates important features Ostrom has identified to explain how real world actors solve problems of managing CPRs: "Appropriators engage in a considerable amount of trial-and-error learning,"[57] and, "Humans may not be able to analyze all situations fully but . . . will be able to draw on inherited capabilities to learn norms of behavior, particularly reciprocity."[58] The genetic algorithm encodes these inherited capabilities, or "folk knowledge [that] must be preserved and passed along from one generation to the next,"[59] as strategy sets that appropriators have selected as fit performers, have recombined, and have mutated. Table 5.2 provides plain language pseudo code to explain the order of procedures the ABM executives for all appropriator, resource, and patch agents, as well as details about how the genetic algorithm instructs appropriator agents to select fit strategies.

Appropriator agents use the genetic algorithm not only to learn new effective strategies but also to change their social networks. Under the $I_{network}$ rule, appropriators learn about the health of the ecosystem from their network neighbors. For this reason, appropriators have an incentive to organize

Table 5.2. Pseudo code for the fisheries model

Initialization:
Create 20 *appropriator agents* and distribute them randomly in a 33 × 33 ecosystem
  endow them with *wealth* W = 20 units
  endow them with a *memory* of length M
  connect to N other actors with fixed p (manipulations: p = 0.1, 0.3, 0.6 or 0.9)
  endow them with a *strategy* of length $2^{M \times N}$
Create 150 *resource agents*:
  endow them with an *energy budget* E where $E \sim N(20,3)$
  endow them with an *age* A where $A \sim U(1,10)$
  distribute them randomly in the ecosystem
Endow *patches* with a random amount of *food* F where $F \sim N(10,3)$
  Repeat 5 times: diffuse half of *food* endowment equally to patches in Moore neighborhood

Execution:
Loop until the number of resources is 0 or *time* = 400, whichever comes first:
  Each resource agent:
    moves toward the patch with the most *food*
    decrements *energy* endowment by 1
    increments *age* by 1
    consumes 5 units of *food* or the amount of food on the patch, whichever is less
    reduces the patch *food* endowment by 5 or amount of food on patch, whichever is less
    repeats for each other resource agent within a radius of one patch:
      reproduce with p = .25 if the resource agent has an *energy* amount of > 10
        divide *energy* by two
        endow offspring with *energy* of parent; set offspring *age* to 1
    dies if *age* A greater than a random value drawn from N(70,5)
  Each patch:
    replenishes *food* at rate of 0.4 units per timestep
    repeats 5 times: diffuse half of *food* endowment equally to patches in Moore neighborhood
  Each appropriator agent (after *time* = 100):
    measures the *rate of change in number of resources* during period *memory* M using one of the following *information rules* I:
      if I = ego, measure change in radius *technology* C
      if I = network, measure average change in radius C for all network neighbors
      if I = global, measure change in entire system
    if *rate of change* is increasing, appropriates all resources in radius *technology* C
      increments *wealth* by 1 unit for each resource appropriated
      decrements *wealth* by −0.2 × C
End Loop

continued on next page

Table 5.2. *Continued.*

Genetic Algorithm:
Initialization:
　Endow each appropriator with a population of:
　　40 random social networks
　　40 random appropriation rules
　Run Initialization and Execution for each of 40 populations = 1 generation
　Loop for 40 generations:
　　At the end of each generation, each appropriator agent:
　　　Selects the fittest social network and appropriation rules using a fitness
　　　　proportionate selection criterion
　　　Runs a crossover procedure that:
　　　　Allows fit appropriators to exchange strategies
　　　　Crosses fit appropriation strategies for a given appropriator
　　　　Crosses fit social networks for a given appropriator
　　　　Allows appropriators to cross strategies and networks with each other
　　　Mutates strategies and social networks with $p = .005$
　　　Repopulates each appropriator's social networks, appropriation rules
　End Loop

their social relations in a way that improves their knowledge about the health of ecosystems. Each appropriator's network is simply a bit string of twenty positions, with 1 indicating the appropriator is attached to another appropriator at that position on the list (i.e., a 1 in the fourth position tells the appropriator to include appropriator 4 in its social network). It is important to note that the simulated social networks are directed rather than undirected networks. That is, ties among appropriators are not necessarily reciprocal: appropriator 1 might consider appropriator 4 a neighbor and will receive information from him, but appropriator 4 does not necessarily receive information from appropriator 1. When the simulation initializes, it endows appropriators with a set of forty random social networks.[60] Appropriators then measure which social network configurations give high payoffs from harvesting and which perform poorly. At the end of each generation of forty runs, appropriators use the selection, crossover, and mutation procedures of the genetic algorithm to produce new social networks. This learning process among the appropriators is analogous to building trust. That is, appropriator agents gradually learn which neighbors provide useful information about the health of the ecosystem, and which neighbors do not. One expects that appropriators using the $I_{network}$ rule will build social networks that differ significantly from the initial random networks.

In addition to adapting over time and building informative social networks, the simulation allows appropriators to learn from the examples of other appropriators. In half the experiments, the simulation enables appropriator agents to exchange strategies with other appropriators. In these experiments, whenever an appropriator agent runs the genetic algorithm it identifies neighbors in its social network whose average score exceeds the appropriator's score. With a probability of .25 (i.e., one out of every four higher-scoring neighbors on average), the appropriator will use a crossover procedure to swap strategy bit strings. This crossover of strategies between appropriators allows agents to mimic other high-scoring agents by adopting some of their strategies. Over the course of several generations, such mimicry should on average produce similar strategies throughout the population of appropriators, though of course such similarity in strategies does not necessarily imply every appropriator will score higher. For example, an appropriator might copy another who is quick to harvest, leading to a proliferation of strategies that overharvest the resource and reduce long-term expected payoffs. So the effect of mimicry is unclear a priori: it could either improve or reduce appropriator scores. For this reason, it is a useful method for creating a richer simulation of adaptive behavior of appropriators who learn in two ways: by adjusting their strategies in response to feedback from the ecosystem, and by mimicking the strategies of high-scoring appropriators.

Because the genetic algorithm uses forty strategy sets and social network sets for each of forty generations, a single run of the simulation constitutes 1,600 repeated trials by appropriator agents. For each run, the ABM measures both the performance of appropriators and the health of the ecosystem. This allows the analysis to assess tradeoffs between microlevel incentives and macrolevel performance. The ABM collects data on several dependent measures that fall into three categories. First, the simulation measures appropriator scores. An appropriator's score is the average number of resources per tick harvested during the final generation (or final forty trials) of the run. Because appropriator strategies may produce short-run gains but collapse the ecosystem, the standardized measure divides appropriator scores by three hundred, the maximum possible number of timesteps during which appropriators can harvest. Second, the simulation records the social network structure in the final trial of a simulation. I use social network analysis software to measure several features of the social network structure, including average path length (a measure of distance between actors in the network) and clustering coefficient (a measure of how actors group together).[61] Finally, the ABM records the survival time of the simulated ecosystem and whether or not the system collapsed. The simulation assumes that if the ecosystem survives until four hundred simulated timesteps, the appropriators have successfully devised strategies and social networks to manage the ecosystem indefinitely.[62]

The model holds constant a number of factors that researchers hypothesize may affect the preservation of CPRs. Most important is the number of appropriators. Although other studies note that the number of actors critically influences the likelihood of free-riding,[63] the ABM keeps the number of appropriators fixed at twenty. The model also keeps resource boundaries fixed: the simulated "ecosystem" contains a continuous space of 33 X 33 patches. Because the simulated system "wraps around" (that is, the shape of the space is technically a torus, such that agents who exit the left side of the world reappear on the right side), the model cannot test for the effects of fuzzy boundaries on the management of CPRs.[64] For this reason, the risks and unpredictability of flows of resources in the model arise strictly from the mobility of resource agents, not from boundary issues.

FINDINGS AND DISCUSSION

To understand how appropriators learn to manage the CPR, I repeated the simulation sixteen times for each of seventy-five combinations of parameter values, for a total of 1,200 observations.[65] The experiment incrementally changed each parameter in the ABM and compared the resulting distributions of the dependent measures to a set of baseline simulations. Each baseline run simulates appropriator strategies and learning with model parameters at their minimum values: appropriator agents have a memory of only one previous period of play; their technology is relatively inefficient (harvesting only in a radius of one unit of space); and they have incomplete information about the ecosystem using the ego information rule. The first row of Table 5.3 reports the parameter values for the baseline simulation. Under these conditions, appropriators achieve an average score of .003 resource units harvested per timestep, or an average of about one resource unit per appropriator per simulation. This suggests that the altruistic appropriators were very cautious: incomplete information from the ego rule induces appropriators to forego harvesting. For this reason, in all sixteen runs of the baseline simulation, the ecosystem survived the full simulated time of four hundred timesteps.

The subsequent rows of Table 5.3 report how incremental increases in the values of the simulation parameters affects appropriators' payoffs, the structure of their social network, and the probability of ecological collapse. The memory parameter clearly improves appropriators' payoffs: in all four increments, appropriators harvested between eighty-four and eighty-eight times more resources than the baseline simulation. Of note, however, is the finding that the effect of memory on appropriators' scores is nonlinear. Appropriator payoffs improve dramatically when the experiment increments memories from one to two previous timesteps, but subsequent increases in memory provide smaller increases in appropriators' scores that diminish to statistical insignificance. As expected, the length of an appropriator's

Table 5.3. Experimental results: t-test and chi-square comparisons of parameters and interactions to baseline simulation ($^*p < .05$, $^{**}p < .01$, $^{***}p < .001$). Note: table does not include all possible interaction effects.

Manipulation		Dependent Measure					
Parameter	Value (% max)	Player Scores (mean)	Clustering Coefficient	Average Path Length	Survival Time	Frequency of Collapse	N
Baseline (M=20%, C=20%, I = Ego)		.003	.47	1.59	400	0	16
Memory (M)	40%	.253***	.46	1.57	400	0	16
	60%	.263***	.46	1.61	400	0	16
	80%	.257***	.48	1.55	400	0	16
	100%	.251***	.47	1.57	400	0	16
Technology (C)	40%	.373***	.47	1.57	326***	5*	16
	60%	.069***	.49	1.54	129***	16***	16
	80%	.091***	.50*	1.55	138***	15***	16
	100%	.109***	.45	1.62	114***	16***	16
Information (I)	Network	.001	.47	1.56	400	0	16
	Global	.0003	.46	1.61	400	0	16

continued on next page

Table 5.3. Continued.

Manipulation		Dependent Measure					
Parameter	Value (% max)	Player Scores (mean)	Clustering Coefficient	Average Path Length	Survival Time	Frequency of Collapse	N
Parameter Interactions							
Network×Tech	40%	.384***	.46	1.60	372	2	16
Network×Tech	60%	.083***	.50*	1.53*	146***	15***	16
Network×Tech	100%	.109***	.47	1.56	113***	16***	16
Network×Memory	40%	-.027***	.53***	1.49**	400	0	16
Network×Memory	60%	-.040***	.55***	1.46***	400	0	16
Network×Memory	100%	-.039***	.53	1.42***	400	0	16
Global×Tech	40%	.380***	.47	1.57	294***	7**	16
Global×Tech	60%	.089***	.48	1.56	131***	16***	16
Global×Tech	100%	.109***	.48	1.55	114***	16***	16
Global×Memory	40%	-.011***	.46	1.58	400	0	16
Global×Memory	60%	-.017***	.47	1.58	400	0	16
Global×Memory	100%	-.052***	.48	1.56	400	0	16
I=Network × C=3 × M=5		.253***	.50	1.51**	276***	8*	16
I=Network × C=5 × M=5		.078***	.50	1.45**	123***	16***	16
I=Global × C=3 × M=5		.171***	.47	1.56	230***	13***	16
I=Global × C=5 × M=5		-.002	.48	1.56	150***	16***	16
Total		.150	.49	1.54	241	733	1200

memory does not significantly increase the risk of ecological collapse. In all four experimental manipulations of the memory parameter (sixty-four total simulations), the ecosystem survived.

Experimental variations of the technology parameter suggest that harvesting efficiency has an inverted u-shaped relationship with player scores. An increment in harvesting efficiency from 20 to 40 percent of the maximum value leads to a significant increase in appropriators' scores. Under this manipulation, appropriator agents harvested an average of 112 resources per run of the simulation, more than one hundred times the baseline value. This makes intuitive sense: an increase in efficiency should lead to more harvesting for the same effort. Yet the increased efficiency comes with greater risks of ecological collapse: Table 5.3 shows that even with harvesting technology that is only 40 percent efficient, the risk of collapse increased significantly (five of sixteen simulations ended in collapse, compared to none in the baseline simulations). The experiment shows, furthermore, that as technology becomes even more efficient, the risk of ecological collapse quickly outweighs the benefits of increased efficiency. As the experiment increments the technology efficiency parameter to 60 percent, 80 percent, and then 100 percent of the maximum value, appropriators' average scores remain significantly higher than the baseline simulation but are significantly lower than the best average scores at the 40 percent value. This is because efficient technology increases the risk of ecological collapse. As the data show, the average survival time of the ecosystem becomes significantly shorter with each experimental increment of the technology parameter, and the frequency of collapse grows. For the 60 percent, 80 percent, and 100 percent experiments, the appropriators exhausted the resource agents forty-seven out of forty-eight total simulations. Without resources to harvest, the appropriators naturally received lower scores. That is to say, their short-term gains in welfare arising from technological efficiency came at the expense of zero expected future gains.

Somewhat unexpectedly, increases in appropriator information about the ecosystem did not significantly improve player scores (though as expected, neither did they increase the risk of ecological collapse). Neither the "network" information rule nor the "global" information rule significantly improved appropriators' payoffs from harvesting. This unexpected finding may arise, however, from interactions among the model's parameters: the information rule may have significant effects under certain conditions of appropriator memories and technological efficiency, but not others. To test for such interaction effects, the experiment simultaneously increased the information rule (to "network" and then to "global") and the technology parameter. It then repeated the same simultaneous increments for combinations of the information and memory parameters.

The results of these experimental manipulations provide clear evidence of interactive effects between the network information rule and the technology parameter. With the network rule active and the technology parameter set to 40 percent of maximum value, appropriators score significantly higher than in the baseline simulations but with no significant increase in the risk of ecological collapse. However, the risk of collapse increases significantly when technology values of 60 percent and greater interact with the network rule. It appears, then, that the network information rule improves both appropriator payoffs and reduces the risk of ecological collapse at a very specific value of technological efficiency. The network rule also interacts with the memory parameter, but in ways opposite of the network-technology interaction. As players' memories of past actions grow under the network rule, appropriators tend to score significantly *lower* than the baseline simulation. They actually receive on average slightly negative scores ranging from −0.01 to −0.05, implying that the opportunity costs of not harvesting are penalizing appropriator agents. This is surprising. It appears that when the network and global information rules are active, appropriators with longer memories learn strategies that are extremely cautious. One interpretation of this caution is that appropriators have learned a nearly optimal strategy. They reduce the risks of ecological collapse to near zero while minimizing their opportunity costs almost to zero. In other words, they devise a Pareto solution that ideal-type altruists would choose.

Interactive effects also help explain how appropriators learn to restructure the social network. Because the network rule provides appropriators information through their network neighbors, the expectation is that appropriators will build a social network that is significantly different than under either the ego or the global information rule. The findings reported in Table 5.3 support this expectation. In three of the six experimental manipulations of interactions involving the network rule, appropriators reorganize their social networks to have a higher clustering coefficient. Likewise, in four of the six manipulations the resulting social networks have shorter average path lengths than the baseline simulations. In the resulting social networks, appropriators have significantly fewer neighbors on average but also have fewer steps between each other than in the random networks that characterize the baseline simulation. This suggests that appropriators have learned to build networks that are more like small-world social networks (with short path lengths but higher clustering) than purely random networks.[66] These findings appear to affirm the expectation that social networks manage information about the ecosystem more efficiently than other information rules.

The global information rule also interacts with technological efficiency to produce significantly higher but decreasing appropriator scores, a pattern similar to the interaction between the network rule and technology. Likewise, the global rule interacts with memory to produce significantly lower appropriator payoffs, a pattern also seen in the network-memory interaction. While interactions with the global rule significantly affect appropriator scores, however, they have no significant effect on the social network structure. In all six manipulations, interactions with the global rule produce measures of clustering and path lengths that are statistically indistinguishable from the baseline case. One would expect this: under the I_{global} rule, appropriators have complete information about the health of the population of resource agents. Because an appropriator's network neighbors provide no additional information, the appropriator agents have no incentive to reorganize their social ties. Finally, as with interactions involving the network rule, interactions between the global rule and technological efficiency significantly increase the risk of ecological collapse, while interactions with the memory parameter have no effect on the risk of collapse.

These findings illustrate that the technological efficiency parameter has the greatest effect on three dependent measures: player scores, survival time of the ecosystem, and the frequency of collapse. The effect of technology is similar for all three information rules. As expected, it is the only parameter that affects the likelihood of the system's collapse. The memory parameter improves player scores for the baseline ego information rule, but, paradoxically, lowers appropriator scores under the network and global information rules. Information rules impact player scores and the frequency of system collapse only by interacting with the technology and memory variables. A surface plot illustrates these interactions. Figure 5.1 displays the average appropriator score for each combination the memory and technology variables; to compare effects of the information rule, it provides one surface plot for each of the three information rules. Figure 5.2 similarly displays the average ecosystem survival time for each combination of memory and technology for the three information rules. Both figures illustrate the strong effect of technological efficiency on simulated outcomes. As noted above, in Figure 5.1 one can see the inverted u-shaped effect of technological efficiency; under all three information rule, players score highest with technological efficiency at the 40 percent of maximum level, with scores quickly tailing off at higher levels of efficiency. Likewise, in Figure 5.2, one can see that values of the technology parameter greater than 40 percent greatly reduce the average survival time of the ecosystem.

While the technology parameter is important, however, it is not determinative. Appropriators with better information about the system clearly learn to manage the risks of collapse. To understand the effect of information rules, one can compare the three surface plots in each figure. In Figure 5.1, appropriators who use the network and global information rules have average lower scores for the 40 percent value of technology, but appear to

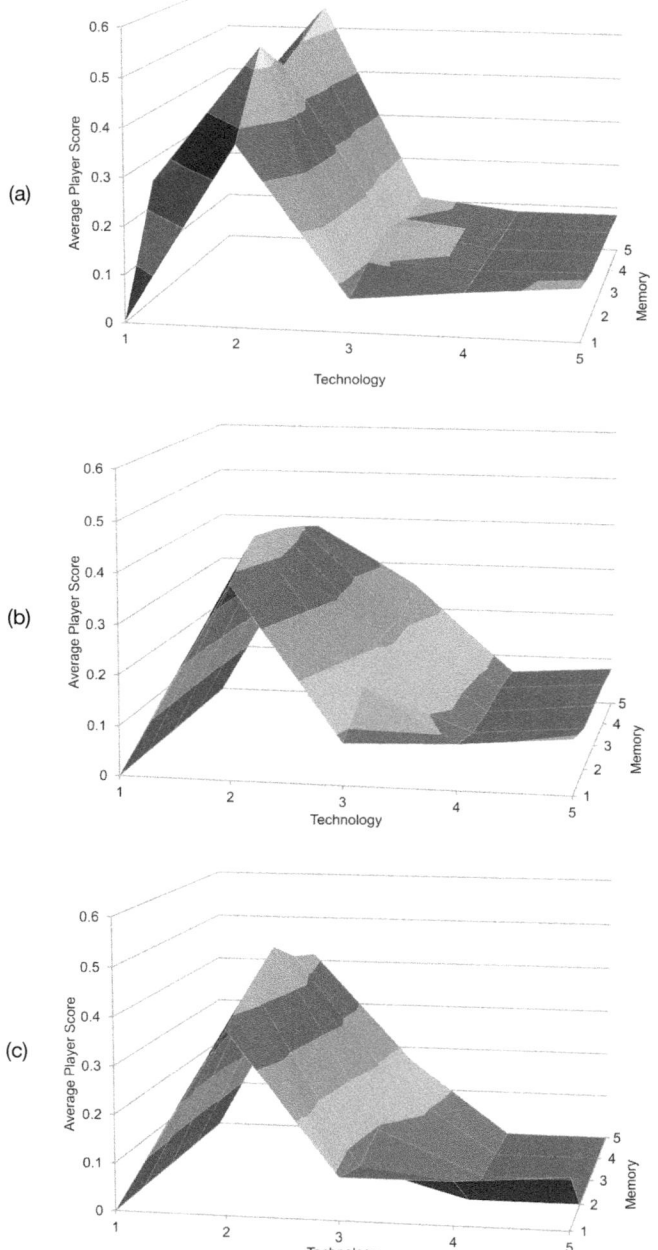

Figure 5.1. Mean appropriator scores for each information rule, by technology and memory: (a) ego rule; (b) network rule; (c) global rule.

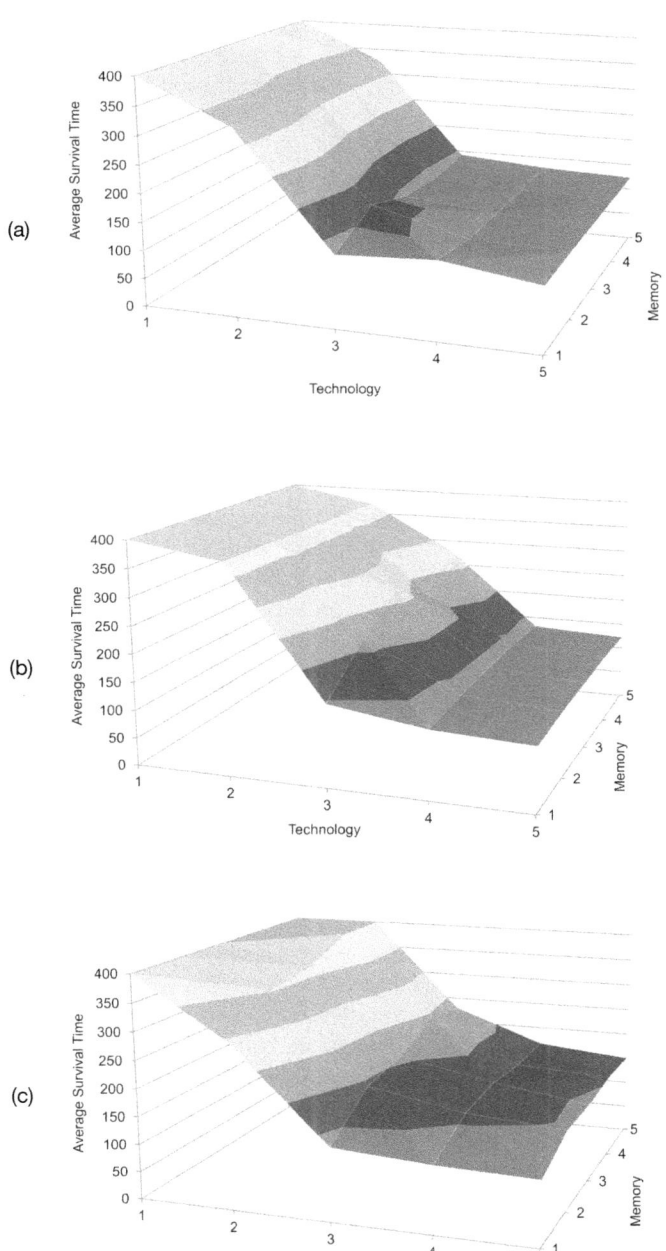

Figure 5.2. Average survival time for each information rule, by technology and memory: (a) ego rule; (b) network rule; (c) global rule.

score higher on average when technology is in the 60 percent range. One explanation for this finding is apparent in Figure 5.2. Under the ego information rule (Figure 5.2a) the average survival time falls drastically when the experiment increases technology from 40 percent to 60 percent maximum. Yet when appropriators receive better information under the network and global rules, they improve the average survival time for intermediate values of technology. This is apparent in the surfaces in Figures 5.2b and 5.2c, which decline less dramatically between the 40 percent and 80 percent values for the technology parameter. Together with Figure 5.1, this illustrates that appropriators have learned to trade off high payoffs for an increased likelihood of survival in the ecosystem.

Finally, both sets of figures illustrate the surprising impact of the memory parameter and its interaction complexity. The mean appropriator scores in Figures 5.1b and 5.1c illustrate that the memory parameter has an inverted u-shaped effect on player scores when technology = 2. Paradoxically, when technology = 3 the memory parameter improves appropriator scores under the global and network information rules, but *reduces* appropriator scores when technology = 5. The memory parameter shows similar effects on survival time, as illustrated in Figure 5.2. Under all three information rules, memory has no effect on survival time when technology = 5. At intermediate technology levels (2 and 3), memory significantly improves survival time under the network and global rule, but not under the ego rule. Together, these findings suggest appropriators' history of cooperation exhibits interactive complexity. Such a history improves both individual payoffs and social welfare, but only under when technology is neither too inefficient nor too efficient, and only when players share information about the system.

Figure 5.3 illustrates how the different information rules influence the tradeoff between individual payoffs and sustainment of the common pool resource. This figure reports the average appropriator scores (measured on the left vertical axis) and the average percentage of simulations that resulted in collapse (on the right vertical axis) for all simulated values of the memory and technology parameters. Appropriators achieve their highest payoffs under the ego information rule, but of course their successful harvesting increases the risk of ecosystem collapse. Nearly two out of every three simulations under the ego information rule result in the exhaustion of the resource. Thus, under the ego information rule appropriators develop high-payoff but high-risk strategies. Conversely, the global information rule produces low appropriator payoffs but intermediate risks, with more than 60 percent of the simulations resulting in resource exhaustion. With the network information rule, by contrast, appropriators learn strategies that yield intermediate payoffs but relatively low risks of collapse. Although more than half the simulations under this information rule still produce resource

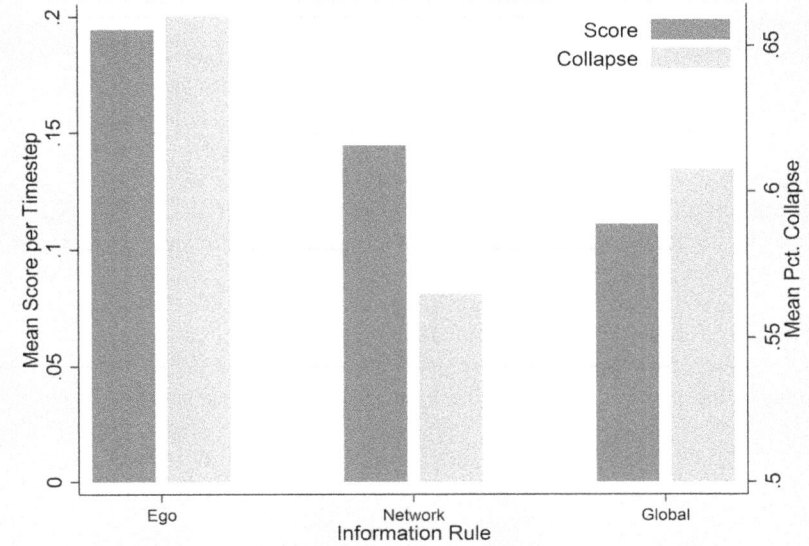

Figure 5.3. Mean appropriator score standardized per time step and percentage of simulations in which the ecosystem collapsed, by information rule

exhaustion, this is the lowest rate of failure of the three information rules. When appropriators use the network information rule, furthermore, they receive average payoffs that are significantly higher than when appropriators use the global information rule.[67] This is an interesting paradox: appropriators with less than complete information outperform appropriators with complete information about the status of the ecosystem. The chapter returns to this point later.

The experimental results in Table 5.3 are informative but not complete. They do not list all possible interactions between simulation parameters, and they compare outcomes only to the baseline simulation in which parameters assume their minimum value. Another approach is to conduct regression analysis, which reports the partial effect of each simulation parameter when holding the other parameters constant at their mean values. Regression also allows for testing for interaction affects across a range of parameter values and to control for the effects of modeling assumptions.[68] The subsequent analysis thus uses information from all 1,200 simulations. Of course, regression analysis requires the strong assumption that the effects of parameters are linear; as the discussion above shows, this is the case for neither the technology efficiency nor the memory parameter. For this reason, the subsequent analysis offers the regression analysis tentatively and advises the reader to use caution interpreting the results.[69] Tables 5.4 and 5.5 present estimated partial effects of the parameters, interaction effects, and controls for modeling assumptions. Each model presented in the tables uses ordinary least-squares regression (OLS) with robust standard errors. Table 5.4 presents the partial effects on three measures of appropriator scores. Table 5.5 presents the partial effects on measures of the social network appropriators construct during the simulation.

The results in table 5.4 affirm the importance of technological efficiency to managing the CPR. Somewhat surprisingly, the technology parameter significantly reduces the average of appropriators' scores, as well as the average scores of the best and worst performing appropriators. This probably indicates the regression models are capturing the downward sloping portion of the inverted u-shaped relationship between technological efficiency and appropriator scores. That is, increasingly efficient technology reduces

Table 5.4. Estimated partial effect of parameters, interactions terms, and controls on player payoffs, OLS regression with robust standard errors ($^{*}p < .05, ^{**}p < .01, ^{***}p < .001$)

Variable	Mean of Average Scores, Final Generation	Best Average Score, Final Generation	Worst Average Score, Final Generation
Memory	0.02**	0.03*	0.01***
Efficiency of Technology	−0.06***	−0.09***	−0.03***
Information: Network Rule Dummy	−0.17***	−0.24**	−0.13***
Information: Global Rule Dummy	−0.11**	−0.17*	−0.08***
Memory-Network Rule Interaction	−0.01	0.00	−0.02***
Memory-Global Rule Interaction	−0.02**	−0.02	−0.02***
Technology-Network Rule Interaction	0.05***	0.07***	0.04***
Technology-Global Rule Interaction	0.03***	0.06***	0.01**
Crossover of appropriators dummy	0.00	0.01	0.00
Connection Bias	0.00	0.01	0.00
constant	0.33***	0.68***	0.05**
N	1,200	1,200	1,200
r^2	0.17	0.06	0.24

appropriator scores indirectly, by collapsing the ecosystem and destroying the possibility for long-term gains. Both information rules have significant effects that are opposite of those of the technology parameter. The network and global information rules significantly reduce all three measures of appropriator scores while increasing the number of resources in the system. This suggests that appropriators learn to reduce their personal payoffs in order to sustain the system. Interestingly, interaction effects between information rules and the technology parameter significantly improve appropriators' scores beyond the partial effect of technology alone. This demonstrates that, as expected, improved information makes appropriators more effective. As appropriators improve their memory of past actions in their social network, they significantly increase their payoffs. This is consistent with previous studies that find a history of cooperation improves the chances for preserving CPRs. Interestingly, the technology parameter also interacts with the network and global information rules (the intercept term of the regression model captures the ego rule, which is the baseline information rule); these interaction terms significantly improve appropriators' scores. Finally, the results show that these partial effects obtain when controlling for differing densities for the initial random social networks. That is, the assumptions necessary for model construction do not significantly change the interpretation of the parameters of theoretic interest.

The estimated partial effects in Table 5.5 demonstrate that appropriator agents learn from each other by significantly altering the structure of their social ties. The crossover simulation parameter, which models the process of imitation among appropriators, is a significant predictor of eight of the nine measures of network structure. When appropriators learn to mimic other successful appropriators, they build a social network with a significantly smaller clustering coefficient, significantly longer path lengths, fewer links, and less density, ceteris paribus. That is to say, mimicry among appropriators produces social networks that are less efficient and *less* like small worlds, a somewhat surprising finding. One possibility for this, however, is that the different information rules may specify when appropriators build more efficient networks. It may be that appropriators build small world social networks only under the network information rule. Conversely, under the ego and global information rules, they build more centralized social networks. The interaction terms reported in Table 5.5 support this interpretation. The interaction between appropriators' memory and the network information rule illustrates that, when the network rule is active, appropriators who have histories of cooperation build a social network with significantly shorter path lengths. The network rule also significantly increases the clustering coefficients of social networks. Together, these results suggest that appropriators build networks that have fewer clusters and greater distances between appropriators.

Table 5.5. Estimated partial effects of model parameters, interaction terms, and controls on measures of social network structure, OLS regression with robust standard errors (*$p < .05$, **$p < .01$, ***$p < .001$)

Variable	Average Path Length	Clustering Coefficient	Efficiency	Betweenness	Closeness
Memory	0.00	0.00	0.00	0.00*	-0.01*
Efficiency of Technology	0.00	0.00	0.00	0.00	-0.01
Information: Network Rule Dummy	-0.03	0.03*	0.02	-0.01	-0.05
Information: Global Rule Dummy	0.01	-0.01	0.00	-0.01	-0.07**
Memory–Network Rule Interaction	-0.03***	0.00	-0.01	0.00	0.01
Memory–Global Rule Interaction	0.00	0.00	0.00	0.00	0.02**
Technology–Network Rule Interaction	0.01	-0.01	0.00	0.00	0.01
Technology–Global Rule Interaction	0.00	0.00	0.00	0.00	0.00
Crossover of appropriators dummy	0.08***	-0.06***	-0.05***	0.06***	0.00
Connection Bias	0.01	0.06***	0.06***	-0.01	0.03
Constant	1.53***	0.47***	0.85***	0.04***	0.30***
N	1200	1200	1200	1200	1200
r^2	0.19	0.21	0.14	0.34	0.01

Dependent Measure

Dependent Measure (continued)

Variable	In Degree Centralization	Out Degree Centralization	Density	Link Count
Memory	0.00	0.00	0.00	0.06
Efficiency of Technology	0.01*	-0.01*	0.00	0.05
Information: Network Rule Dummy	0.04*	-0.05**	0.03*	12.23*
Information: Global Rule Dummy	0.00	-0.02	0.00	-1.31
Memory–Network Rule Interaction	-0.01**	0.01	0.00	0.52
Memory–Global Rule Interaction	0.00	0.01*	0.00	0.02
Technology–Network Rule Interaction	0.00	0.01*	-0.01	-2.47
Technology–Global Rule Interaction	0.00	0.00	0.00	0.58
Crossover of appropriators dummy	0.16***	-0.04***	-0.08***	-30.18***
Connection Bias	0.02**	0.02*	0.06***	23.17***
Constant	0.18***	0.26***	0.47***	178.62***
N	1200	1200	1200	1200
r^2	0.49	0.08	0.31	0.31

But under the network information rule, the resulting networks are more like small world networks: appropriators on average are closer in path lengths to every other appropriator, and they tend to have tightly knit groups with a high density of connections, or "cliques" in the language of social network theory. All these findings obtain, furthermore, when controlling for the probability of connection in the random networks generated at the beginning of each simulation. That is to say, appropriators tend to develop small world–like networks under the network information rule irrespective of whether they start with a dense or a sparse initial social network.

These findings illustrate the partial effects of parameters on appropriator scores and on social network structure, but do not directly indicate the effects on the survival of the ecosystem. To examine this question, Table 5.6 presents the results from an event history model. Such models, sometimes called hazard models, assess the effects of hypothesized factors on both the likelihood of an event and its timing.[70] I use the lognormal distribution for the hazard function, or the shape of the probability distribution to characterize the likelihood of ecological collapse. Table 5.6 presents the estimated partial effects of model parameters, with statistically significant partial effects listed in bold type. As expected, the results show that technological efficiency greatly increases the likelihood of ecological collapse: the negatively signed estimated coefficient indicates that the efficiency of technology parameter significantly reduces survival time. Technological efficiency also interacts with the network information rule to significantly increase the risks of collapse: the interaction term has a negative sign, indicating that the interaction term shortens survival time. This suggests that, ceteris paribus, technology has a greater impact on survivability of the ecosystem under the network information rule than under either the ego or the global information rules. Paradoxically, however, the network information rule also reduces the risk of collapse. The positively signed estimated coefficient indicates the network rule significantly lengthens the survival time of the ecosystem. Finally, the length of appropriators' memories does significantly improve survival of the ecosystem, but only when appropriators have complete knowledge of the state of the resource population from the I_{global} rule.

Together, the statistical findings in Tables 5.3 through 5.6 suggest some important theoretical findings. Foremost is the importance of information: how actors share information about ecological complexity strongly affects their rewards and the prospects for successfully managing collective goods. When using information only from their social networks, the appropriators balanced the competing goals of personal and collective welfare. They improved their payoffs, achieving better average payoffs than when they had complete information. They also effectively managed the risks of ecological collapse, achieving lower frequencies of collapse than when they acted

Table 5.6. Estimated partial effects of model parameters, interaction terms, and controls on likelihood of collapse (lognormal survival time model with robust standard errors). Significant variables listed in bold type.

No. of subjects = 1200
No. of failures = 733
Time at risk = 289425
Log pseudolikelihood = −582.098

$N = 1200$
Wald $\chi^2(10) = 2294.15$
$(P > \chi^2) < .0001$

Variable	Estimated Coefficient	Robust Std. Err.	z	$P > z$	95% Conf. Interval	
Memory	0.001	0.015	0.090	0.931	−0.028	0.030
Efficiency of Technology	**−0.420**	**0.015**	**−28.310**	**0.000**	**−0.449**	**−0.391**
Information: Global Rule Dummy	−0.055	0.105	−0.530	0.597	−0.261	0.150
Information: Network Rule Dummy	**0.292**	**0.108**	**2.690**	**0.007**	**0.079**	**0.504**
Memory–Network Rule Interaction	0.042	0.022	1.910	0.056	−0.001	0.086
Memory–Global Rule Interaction	**0.096**	**0.021**	**4.610**	**0.000**	**0.055**	**0.137**
Technology–Network Rule Interaction	**−0.073**	**0.021**	**−3.530**	**0.000**	**−0.114**	**−0.033**
Technology–Global Rule Interaction	−0.005	0.020	−0.260	0.794	−0.044	0.033
Crossover of Appropriators Dummy	−0.027	0.024	−1.110	0.265	−0.075	0.021
Connection Bias	0.048	0.040	1.190	0.233	−0.031	0.127
constant	6.606	0.081	81.720	0.000	6.448	6.765
/ln_sig	−0.970	0.026	−37.980	0.000	−1.020	−0.920
sigma	0.379	0.010	0.360	0.398		

egoistically and when they had complete information. This is an important paradox: players do better both individually and collectively when they have less than complete information about the effects of their collective behavior. Why is this? Two answers are possible. One is that, when actors have complete information, they increase the risk of mutual interference. In the experiment, simulations that use the global information rule tend to produce patterns of harvesting in which all appropriators either harvest or rest at the same time.[71] Such everyone-or-no-one patterns of action may unintentionally induce larger stresses to the ecosystem, which in turn perturbs the predictability of their payoffs. As in the real world, the simulated players may find these stresses increasingly difficult to manage. Scientists have found, for example, that human harvesting of common pool resources tends to induce greater variability in the population of resources.[72] Such human-induced oscillations increase the uncertainty in payoffs that appropriators receive, and may lead to overharvesting. A second and related possible answer is that players with incomplete information, as under the social network rule, are less likely to induce ecological fluctuations that increase the risk of collapse. Because players organize into smaller cliques that harvest together, these groups induce smaller perturbations in the resource and hence have more predictable resource flows. Social networks may also provide "information processing" about the ecosystem—in effect, appropriators build a social network that more effectively calculates trends in the flow of the resource. Just as markets can calculate equilibrium prices and prediction markets can predict influenza outbreaks,[73] so too can the design of institutions calculate relatively stable and optimal solutions to collective action problems. In other words, networks as a whole develop knowledge that no individual appropriator possesses. This is an interesting example of emergent behavior and is consistent with real world examples of collective knowledge.

How can social networks process information about ecological complexity? In part, this may arise from their structure. The experiment showed that appropriators tend to self-organize into clusters like small world networks. Researchers have found that small world networks tend to be more robust to disruptions.[74] Although this previous research has discussed the survival of small world networks in terms of the removal of a given actor from the network, one might also consider the effect of variability of information on information processing. The structure of small world networks may allow them to dampen out rather than magnify large fluctuations in information. A node that perceives such a fluctuation is unlikely on average to pass this anomalous information to many other nodes. This is because, in small world networks, the fraction of peripheral actors is much greater than the fraction of "hub" actors who pass information to other cliques in the social network. In the simulated ecosystem, for example, a randomly chosen appropriator might observe a spike in the population of resources because he happens to be in an area where resource agents are clustering around abundant food. The appropriator might conclude that the ecosystem is booming and that harvesting is unlikely to damage it, but this may simply be an accident of chance. On average, this appropriator will have only a few neighbors with whom to share the good news. For this reason, fewer appropriators receive bad information and thus are less likely to overharvest. This explanation suggests that small world networks may be fault tolerant in another respect: they manage the flow of information among actors by limiting the passage of anomalous information. In systems characterized by both large variations and human-induced oscillations—for example, the financial services industry, pandemics, or protests—such information management can greatly aid collective action. Just as the Maasai noted that cows grow trees and elephants grow grass, (social) nets help grow fish.

The efficiency of harvesting technology has paradoxical effects both on the rewards appropriators receive and on the survivability of the ecosystem. On the one hand, increases in appropriation improve the information the community has about the health of the resource, but too many appropriators will overharvest and increase temptations to free-ride.[75] The experiment replicated this paradox, illustrating that appropriators maximize their welfare at low to intermediate levels of technological efficiency, but that the returns on efficiency quickly diminish and eventually harm overall welfare. A second interpretation concerns the opportunity costs appropriators pay when deciding not to harvest. The simulation assumed that opportunity costs increase constantly and proportionally to technological efficiency. This assumption may drive the observed effect in the simulation of the technological efficiency parameter. Because appropriator agents face higher penalties for not appropriating, the model may induce them to adopt riskier strategies that almost always lead to ecological collapse. In the real world, however, appropriators may realize economies of scale with efficient technologies that diminish opportunity costs such that the lost opportunities do not scale proportionately with increasing efficiency. While the simulation may suffer from a restrictive assumption about opportunity costs, however, there nevertheless may be an important theoretical insight. Because real world appropriators may have to amortize their capital investments in efficient but expensive harvesting technologies, they may face greater pressures to free-ride irrespective of their concerns about long-term sustainability of the common pool resource. To put it another way: competition among appropriators may induce capital investment strategies that considerably shorten their shadows of the future.

Although a history of cooperation may help appropriators conserve resources, such a history has strong requirements for information—not only must acts of cooperation be public knowledge, but actors must also have a relatively complete understanding of the ecosystem's dynamics. With a shortened time horizon, appropriators have less opportunity to build a history of cooperation. As discussed in chapter 3, extensive experimental research and formal game theory have found that players who have iterated interaction tend to produce better social outcomes. The simulations here tested the effects of iteration by endowing appropriators with memory of past actions and the ability to adapt strategies—for example, to punish greed and reward caution. The simulated appropriators exhibited three types of learning: they adapted their strategies, mimicked each other, and built ties with other appropriators analogous to trust. When the simulation endowed players with memory, they learned strategies that improved their individual average payoffs. But the effect of memory on the ecosystem—that is, on the changing structure of rewards players receive—is subtle. Improved memories of past actions did not always significantly improve the survivability of the ecosystem, and hence future expected rewards. Rather, a history of cooperation among appropriators may improve the sustainability of common pool resources, but only when appropriators have relatively complete knowledge the ecosystem. When players have less than complete information about the environment in which they are interacting, iteration and histories of cooperation are less important. This may explain why, for example, actors find it easier to manage resources with relatively predictable flows like irrigation systems but cannot effectively manage unpredictable flows, such as the Caspian Sea sturgeon. This observation has important implications for many types of collective action problems characterized by interaction complexity. For example, although banking regulators have a long history of cooperation under the Basel framework, their incomplete information about the organization and evolution of the financial services industry may render their collaborative history irrelevant to the design of future institutions. The next chapter explores this example.

CONCLUSIONS

The simulation presented in this chapter is highly idealized in several ways, and arguably is not a valid representation of real world social-ecological complexity. A more realistic simulation would introduce the possibility of free-riding behavior and heterogeneous actor capabilities. The study models a particular kind of CPR characterized by a mobile resource for which storage is not possible. Many types of CPRs, however, are stationary, allow for storage, or both—forests and grazing lands are fixed in space, while mobile resources such as irrigation waters may be stored in reservoirs. Nonstationary, non-storable CPRs present a particularly difficult collective action problem to appropriators because they induce greater unpredictability about resource flows. However, more complete information and reliable resource flows likely will produce different appropriation strategies, different forms of social networks, and varying risks of ecological collapse. That is to say, one simply cannot assume that "easier" collective action problems will produce higher player payoffs and more clustered social networks with shorter path lengths. Such logic assumes an absence of interactions between social and ecological factors. For this reason, a more complete model that accurately represents actors' behaviors and emergent outcomes needs a greater heterogeneity of actor capabilities and, arguably, requires more empirically driven modeling.

These concerns notwithstanding, the simulation of the common pool resource illustrates how different rules for sharing information affect cooperative strategies; how appropriators learn new strategies, adapt through mimicry, and build social ties that efficiently process information; and how appropriators change the environment and the payoffs they receive. Although common pool resources are only one type of collective action problem, they represent a broad range of phenomena in world politics characterized by boundedly rational actors learning about and adapting to problems with incomplete information in situations that lack centralized authority or planning—precisely conditions that characterize popular protests such as the Arab Spring, asset bubbles in financial markets, the harvesting of the forests of the Amazon, and many other contemporary challenges. Many forms of polycentric governance in world politics today have emerged to manage such collective action problems, from transnational networks of advocacy groups to terrorist organizations to the growing trade in illicit goods. Social-ecological complexity as a research program can help us understand how actors manage to cooperate and improve their welfare in such issue areas. Nowhere is such an understanding more pressing than in the management of global financial crises.

SIX

TOO BIG TO COMPROMISE

*Did Eleven Banks Block Reform
during the Great Recession?*

Just as species and harvesters coevolve in an ecosystem, firms, consumers, and products adapt, learn, and change in markets. Their coevolutionary dynamics can produce market efficiencies through network effects, complementary technologies, and economies of scale, but also lead to immense global firms, oligopolistic competition, and market distortions. Like natural ecosystems, markets may exhibit qualities of punctuated equilibrium, or "long periods of relative stability, or evolutionary change, interrupted by short periods of quick and extensive, or revolutionary, change."[1] The ecological perspective helps explain why firms' fortunes may rise and fall with breathtaking suddenness. For example, Finnish communications firm Nokia once was the largest manufacturer of mobile phones in the world but saw its profits fall 49 percent in the three years following Apple's introduction of the iPhone.[2] There are numerous examples of firms experiencing a reversal of fortune, but nowhere have the extensive, sudden, and catastrophic changes in markets—the "extinction events" of creative destruction—been more consequential than in global finance.

During the crucible of the 2008 financial crisis, Rahm Emanuel—newly designated chief of staff for President-elect Barack Obama—told the *Wall Street Journal*, "You never want a serious crisis to go to waste. . . . The crisis provides the opportunity for us to do things that you could not do before."[3] With the collapse of Lehman Brothers and its chilling effect on credit markets, one pressing area for reform was banking regulation. By early

2009, many world leaders anticipated a broad consensus on the need to prevent banks that are "too big to fail" from causing national credit crises to spread globally. Then-UK prime minister Gordon Brown told the Scottish Labour Conference in March 2009 that he saw "an emerging consensus on how we strengthen the global regulation of our financial markets to prevent any recurrence of the collapse that has caused so much damage to economies around the world."[4] The Basel Committee on Banking Supervision, the intergovernmental body in which governments negotiate rules for the global banking system, began discussions on strengthening the then-existing regime known as the Basel II Agreement. The twenty-seven members of the European Union agreed in July 2009 to create a European Systemic Risk Board to resolve disagreements among national banking regulators, an agreement so promising that French president Nicolas Sarkozy called it a "complete change in Anglo-Saxon strategy."[5] In September 2009, Josef Ackermann, the chief executive of Deutsche Bank, expressed his support for increased capital adequacy ratios to buffer banks from financial contagion.[6]

Yet just two weeks later, and just a year removed from the failure of Lehman, negotiations on a new, stronger international banking regime began to unravel. Contradicting Ackermann's support for a strengthened regime, several German bankers and regulators expressed concerns that the proposed Basel III Agreement would impose rules on capital adequacy that would harm many German banks.[7] By the time the Basel Committee announced the Basel III rules in September 2010, negotiators had considerably weakened the regime. Many observers concluded that the new regime did not provide sufficient protection against another global contagion of bank failures.[8] Rather than seizing the opportunity the 2008 crisis presented, then, governments agreed to an anodyne regime with a lengthy implementation schedule that failed to solve the problem of banks that are "too big to fail." One observer of the negotiations wryly lamented that "perhaps the best that can be said is that the attempt to clip the wings of the banking behemoths is so modest that the law of unintended consequences may be equally modest in its impact."[9]

Why did states create a weak banking regime after the 2008 financial crisis? The Basel III Agreement of 2010 illustrates an important feature of global politics: though actors learn and adapt to solve complex problems, this coevolution may produce perverse outcomes. Consider a number of puzzling features of the Basel III Agreement. While the agreement did require banks to increase their capital adequacy ratios, it preserved some of the most controversial and criticized rules that had weakened the previous Basel II regime. Most importantly, both agreements leave unspecified the risk-weighting formulas that banks use to assess the health of their asset portfolios, relying instead on banks themselves to identify risk formulas.[10] In this respect, like its predecessors the Basel III regime arguably commits a fallacy of composition: "By neglecting the macro-prudential aspects of regulation—the possibility that individual banks may appear sound while the system as a whole is unsafe—these agreements have, if anything, magnified systemic risk."[11] Even more puzzling, however, are the surprising positions different governments took during the Basel negotiations. While the United States, Britain, Canada, and Switzerland favored higher capital adequacy standards, Japan, France, Italy, and Germany all resisted increasing the requirements for capitalization. Germany's opposition to a stronger regime is particularly surprising. Not only do German banks enjoy about a 5 percent share of the international banking market, but they also occupy a relatively central position in global banking. Using data from the Bank of International Settlements, von Peter calculates that Germany hosts a large number of multinational banks that have large intrafirm cross-border activities—only British and French banks exhibit higher centrality in the global financial network.[12] The German financial industry consequently is particularly susceptible to transnational financial crises. Curiously, however, despite their initial support for a stronger regime, German negotiators ultimately succeeded in securing a multilateral agreement that includes a lengthy implementation schedule: signatories are obligated to meet the strengthened capital adequacy standards only by 2019.

The weak Basel III regime presents an interesting theoretical puzzle for scholars of world politics. For one, it belies the argument that states create regimes in response to crises: national economic interests alone do not explain why some states favored while others opposed a strong regime. While the 2008 financial crisis may have been a necessary condition for regime change, it was hardly sufficient. Likewise, the crisis response argument cannot explain why "even if the leading [banking] nations were to agree, they might end up converging on the wrong set of regulations."[13] Agreement does not necessarily mean better regulation, particularly if regimes do not create enforcement rules to prevent national regulators from turning a blind eye to onerous commitments.[14] To understand weak regimes, then, scholars must look beyond economic analysis.

This chapter argues that the Basel III Agreement illustrates how a few actors located centrally in business networks can change global outcomes. The terms of the final agreement reflect the politics of the banking sector in Germany. Negotiations about the global banking regime represent a variant of the classic Battle of the Sexes game, as discussed in chapter 4, in which players agree on a common aversion but have conflicting interests over the distribution of gains from cooperation. To understand the particular distribution of gains from Basel III, the chapter hypothesizes that eleven regional, publicly owned banks in Germany blocked a stronger global banking regime. These banks enjoyed particularly influential bargaining strength in the sectoral politics of German finance that derived from their centrality in the country's financial exchange networks. To test this hypothesis, this chapter uses an ABM of bilateral negotiations between the United States and Germany. The model uses network data about the structure of interbank lending in each country to simulate the network of financial institutions. The model illustrates that Germany's financial industry may be characterized by a few centrally positioned banks that may influence the processes of interest formation and articulation among German banks. In this respect, the chapter makes two contributions. First, rather than taking the interests of sectoral players as a given, it examines how market relationships may influence the learning of sectoral actors during international bargaining. In this respect, it problematizes interest formation in sectoral politics. Second, it uses the formal methods of social network analysis to map market relationships among sectoral actors. It illustrates how such market relationships shape the bargains that firms may strike among themselves and with national regulators. In this respect, the chapter elaborates on traditional arguments about sectoral politics and regulatory capture by illustrating how a specific social network can shape international negotiations independent of the preferences of sectoral actors. This has broad theoretical import: agreement or discord on international regimes may reflect the specific network structure of industrial sectors. If so, scholars who conduct social network analysis may increasingly help us understand patterns of cooperation and institutionalization in world politics.

The chapter starts with a brief overview of the history of the Basel III Agreement. It proceeds to explain why existing structural and state-level explanations for international banking regimes cannot sufficiently account for the puzzling weakness of the Basel III regime. To explain the surprising influence of German banks on the Basel outcome, the chapter hypothesizes that variations in the network structure of national financial systems allows some state regulators to enjoy independence from sectoral influence while the banking sector captures others. To test the plausibility of its network argument, it turns to an ABM of interest formation using empirical data on the structure of interbank financial transactions in the United States and in Germany. The chapter analyzes some preliminary data from the model and proposes elaborations on the model to capture the strategic bargaining of sectoral actors. It concludes with a brief theoretical discussion of the implications of domestic economic networks for our understanding of international bargaining, cooperation, and conflict.

A BRIEF HISTORY OF THE BASEL REGIME

The post-1973 global political economy witnessed a growth in international financial transactions that greatly exceeded the simultaneous growth in the trade in commodities, goods, and services. Indeed, one estimate of global financial flows found that every ten days financial markets trade an amount of wealth equal to an entire year's worth of trade in goods.[15] The growing financial services industry has led both to very large banks capable even of lending to sovereign countries, and to banks with global reach through partnerships, direct investment in foreign markets, or both. As a consequence, national banking systems have grown interdependent, giving rise to the risk of financial "contagion," or the reverberation of bank failures across sovereign boundaries. Such risks became manifest during Mexico's default crisis of 1982, which threatened the solvency of several large American banks that lent to the Mexican government. As Lall documents, despite the Mexican crisis, the U.S. banking industry resisted congressional pressures for greater regulation of their lending practices. They feared losing market share to European and Japanese banks which enjoyed the competitive advantages of less stringent capitalization requirements. Given the competitive consequences of disparate national regulations, American policymakers concluded that only a coordinated approach to regulation would preserve the competitive position of New York City's financial services sector.[16] To negotiate such a multilateral regime, the United States turned to the Basel Committee on Banking Supervision. The Basel Committee in turn derived from the Bank of International Settlements, and since 1974 allowed for banking regulators of the G10 countries to meet and discuss shared interests. Under the committee's procedures, the United States and other leading financial powers agreed to the first Basel accord in 1988.

It is worth noting that U.S. competitive concerns as much as worries about contagion drove the Basel I agreement.[17] These concerns find expression in the agreement's rules for assessing banks' exposure to risk, codified as two ratios of the bank's capital to its risk-weighted assets. The first ratio, or "tier I" capital, included "high quality" capital—principally, the bank's retained earnings and common stock. Tier II capital includes general provisions; loan-loss reserves; instruments with hybrids of debt and equity; undisclosed reserves; and subordinated debt.[18] In part, the distinction between types of bank capital reflects differences in national regulatory regimes, but also indicates how regulators found a way to compromise.[19] That is, the Basel framework established capital adequacy rules that provided national regulators enough flexibility to protect the competitiveness of their banks. Concerns about the orderly management of bank failures and the prevention of failures that cascade across sovereign borders assumed less importance in the final agreement.

The original Basel accord, and the Basel II Agreement that superseded it in 2004, both suffered from their rules governing the risk-weighting of a bank's loan portfolios. These rules allowed a bank holding a low-risk loan to reserve less than the standard required capital for the principal of the loan. Such risk-weighting allowed banks to exploit the difference between statutorily required capital reserves and the actual risk of the loan.[20] Compounding these rules were provisions that allowed the banks themselves to calculate their risk weights—the so-called advanced internal ratings-based approach. This self-regulation introduced unintended risks into financial systems. Lall finds, for example, that under Basel II larger banks actually reduced their capital obligations by a large amount (more than 25 percent) while smaller banks had slightly higher obligations.[21] Large banks achieved such reductions in their regulatory obligations by moving liabilities off their balance sheets through, among other mechanisms, packaging high-risk loans into securities. Among these were the mortgage-backed collateralized debt obligations that contributed fundamentally to the 2008 financial crisis. The Basel II rules in particular encouraged substantial overleveraging among banks: in 2009, for example, Citigroup's ratio of on- and off–balance sheet obligations to its tier I capital reached an estimated fifty-six to one.[22]

In the wake of the 2008 crisis, regulators and bankers alike concluded that the Basel II accord suffered both from inadequate capital adequacy ratios and from its provision for banks to calculate their own risk weights instead of relying on independent assessment of exposure to risk. Leaders of the twenty-seven states comprising the Basel Committee met throughout the summer of 2010 to reform the rules. Despite the apparent consensus on the inadequacy of the Basel II regime, however, negotiations on a successor regime quickly exposed fundamental disagreements about banking regulation. On one side, Canadian and Swiss negotiators joined American regulators in calling both for larger tier I capital adequacy ratios and for only the highest quality capital to be counted under tier I obligations. Germany, Japan, Italy, and France took a more moderate position, preferring lower capital adequacy standards and a longer schedule for implementing the accords. This position reflected the relatively undercapitalized position of German, Japan, Italian, and French banks, though each country's financial sector lacked sufficient capital for different reasons. French banks relied on an instrument called contingent convertible capital—that is, capital available only under emergency circumstances—to satisfy their regulatory obligations. Italian banks rely on shareholder registries for common equity, which limit their ability to raise capital from new investors. Japanese banks long have relied on lower quality debt-equity securities (in tier II) to meet their statutory requirement, but the proposed Basel III rules would limit this practice. Japanese and Italian banks also expressed concern that slow projected economic growth would limit their capacity to meet the proposed higher standards through retained profits. Finally, German negotiators and some German banks opposed the proposed higher standards. The German position reflected the problem of the *Landesbanken*, or regional banks that traditionally have focused on wholesale banking services in local communities. These banks typically have relied on state investment to meet their capital obligations. Not only would such state investment no longer count toward a bank's capital adequacy, but it also effectively forecloses outside investments as public offerings are unlikely to find takers.[23] For this reason, one leading German banker estimated that about one-half of the German banking system could not turn to capital markets to raise the equity necessary to meet the proposed Basel III standards.[24]

When the Basel Committee announced the new Basel III rules on September 12, 2010, many observers concluded the new regime failed to meet the goals that leaders had identified in the wake of the 2008 crisis. The rules raised the minimum ratios for common equity relative to risk-weighted assets: from 2 percent under Basel II to 4.5 percent. Banks must have 8 percent total capital (tier I plus tier II) relative to risk-weighted assets. Yet despite the apparent strengthening of capital requirements, the agreement fell short of expectations in three ways. First, some observers argue that even with the raised capital standards, the Basel III Agreement still places the ratio so low that it fails to discourage banks from overleveraging themselves. The low ratio also fails to assure sufficient liquidity among banks to manage crises without public intervention in credit markets.[25] Second, the agreement left the question of risk-weighting formulas untouched, reverting to the Basel II rules under which banks have an incentive to find low-weighted risk assets such as government debt. This is perhaps ironic: despite the sovereign debt crises plaguing the European Union during 2010, the Basel rules assign public debt issues a risk weight of zero. This allows banks to lend to governments with no change in their capitalization commitments. States obvious want continued access to capital markets at interest rates that do not fully reflect risks of sovereign default. Finally, the Basel III Agreement established a lengthy period for implementation. The first phase of increases in capital standards occurred on January 1, 2013; states must meet the final minimum capital requirements with buffers by January 1, 2019. The old tier II capital rules—which particularly aided Japanese, Italian, and German publicly owned banks in meeting the adequacy standards—will be phased out by 2021.[26]

This brief summary suggests the Basel III regime is a Pareto-improving but nonetheless imperfect set of rules and procedures. A Princeton economist summarized the agreement well: "More capital, better capital, a leverage ratio, and a liquidity requirement are all important steps forward. But the unwarranted reliance on rating agencies, the disgraceful internal risk models of banks, and the disastrous [structured investment vehicles] should have been easy marks for reformers."[27] Yet policymakers left these risky features of international finance untouched.

EXPLANATIONS FOR A WEAK FINANCIAL REGIME

At first, one might conclude that an economic explanation would suffice to explain the Basel III Agreement. Well-capitalized banks and their national regulators supported stronger capital standards, while undercapitalized banks opposed higher standards and, failing that, supported a lengthy implementation phase for the rules. Yet the economic argument cannot explain either the positions of national negotiators, nor important differences among banks within the leading economic powers. Germany's opposition to Basel III belies its position in the global banking services industry as a bridge between national financial markets. France opposed Basel III on the grounds that its banks relied upon contingent convertible capital. Like France, Canada supported including contingent convertible capital in the new capital adequacy obligations, but nonetheless supported the final agreement that did not include such an accommodation.[28] Like Germany, Swiss banks relied substantially on public funds to meet their capital obligations, yet the Swiss supported the new Basel rules that many German publicly funded banks opposed. Even banks in the United States exhibited some surprising resistance to the rules. The U.S. Bankers Association for Finance and Trade pressured the Basel Committee to ease the proposed rules on "forward provisioning," or the requirement that banks build up capital buffers during upswings in the economy.[29] The disagreements within and among countries on the Basel regime suggest that economic explanations alone are insufficient to explain the rules adopted in September 2010. Other explanations for the adoption of a weak banking regime are similarly unsatisfying.

Hegemonic stability theory explains international regimes as the creation of a single great power in the world system. Charles Kindleberger offers the seminal argument that links the distribution of state power to the general organization of the global economy. He argues that hegemons provide the public goods necessary for a liberal international economic order including the coordination of macroeconomic policies, particularly exchange rates; a sizeable domestic market that facilitates demand stimulus during times of global economic distress; the enforcement of trade rules; and sufficient liquidity to act as a lender of last resort.[30] Eichengreen tests this argument specifically for monetary regimes but finds that the presence of a hegemon is insufficient to explain variations in monetary regimes from the nineteenth and twentieth centuries.[31] Traditional criticisms of hegemonic theories emphasize their inability to explain the sources of a hegemon's preferences for an open trade or monetary system—hegemons may not necessarily act as responsible shepherds of the liberal trading regime. Wood makes this argument specifically about the Basel regime, suggesting that American influence on the Basel rules reflects not the interests of the global system but instead those of its banks.[32] These arguments suggest two possible structural explanations for the weak Basel III rules. Following Wood's argument, one might assert that American negotiators pressured other states to adopt rules that favored U.S. banks but did not protect against future crises. Alternatively, a structural argument might emphasize the relative decline of U.S. economic power, particularly following the 2008 crisis that originated in the American domestic financial services industry. Given its weakened economic condition, one might argue the United States is no longer a hegemon and is incapable of providing liberal regimes. Yet these structural arguments cannot explain several aspects of the Basel III rules. For one, hegemonic theorists themselves disagree on the attributes of a hegemon; the theory is "more of an intuitive idea based on a particular reading of history than a scientific theory."[33] For another, it is not clear that the Basel III regime reflects U.S. preferences. American negotiators in 2010 did indeed achieve the higher capital adequacy requirements they sought, but achieved neither the expedited implementation schedule they sought nor the reform of the rules for risk-weighting. In this respect, structural arguments that emphasize American hegemonic influence cannot explain the curious compromise banking regulators struck in September 2010.

A related argument emphasizes differing national preferences over the tradeoffs inherent in regulating finance. Rodrik suggests that states will differ in their preferred points along an "efficiency frontier" that trades financial stability for innovation in financial services.[34] Tarullo similarly argues that "the potential gains [from banking regulation] are of different types, and the more complete the realization of one goal may come at the expense of others. Moreover, the relative importance of these various gains will be evaluated differently by groups within each country."[35] This reasoning suggests that the Basel III rules reflect not economic theory or market efficiency but instead a compromise among regulators who differ in the preferences among these tradeoffs. If this argument is correct, however, why would states agree to global regulation in the first place? Presumably, states that disagree on the balance between financial stability and innovation could adopt national regimes that reflect their preferred tradeoff. A global regime would be unnecessary at best and counterproductive at worst. This line of reasoning suggests that any regime should reflect instead a set of "meta" rules regarding transparency of regulation rather than new regulatory obligations for governments and banks.[36] The tradeoff argument also tends to understate the transboundary consequences of weak national regulations that prompted the original Basel rules in the first place.

To move beyond inadequate explanations that emphasize structural factors, a number of researchers have examined the domestic politics of banking regulation. Kapstein explains the Basel regime as the result of struggle between publics demanding adequate protection against financial crises and banks seeking to minimize the costs of regulation to their international competitiveness.[37] By contrast, Kane uses a principal-agent model to illustrate how differences between small and large banks shaped the Basel regime. Because banking rules added similar financial burdens to all banks, smaller banks suffered greater costs to their international competitiveness. Kane suggests that the final regime reflected the pressures of smaller banks on regulators to protect their commercial interests.[38] In one of the more detailed discussions of the Basel II negotiations, Lall explains how large banks in the United States enjoyed advantages that allowed them to capture the policymaking process. Because regulators consulted the largest banks at the earliest stages of making policy, a small number of banks shaped the policymaking process in a way that precluded the interests of the broader population of American banks. Larger banks also enjoyed informational advantages: smaller banks had fewer resources to understand capital adequacy rules, while a disinterested and uninformed American public failed to hold regulators to account. This absence of accountability and the advantages of early participation allowed a small number of banks—five, with a combined 36 percent share of the market—to assure a relatively weak Basel II regime.[39] Because the procedures through which regulators consult with industry remain largely unchanged, Lall presciently forecast that the Basel III accords would suffer from a similar regulatory capture.

By emphasizing the domestic politics of international negotiations, these arguments offer several advantages over the more parsimonious structural explanations. The domestic analyses of the Basel regime identify important sectoral divides among banks in the United States, Germany, Italy, and elsewhere. They also offer an explanation for why negotiators' positions and leaders' preferences changed during the course of the Basel negotiations. Yet these explanations also are insufficient for several reasons. They do not explain why some countries suffer from regulatory capture while others do not: Why did American and German negotiators emphasize the interests of only some banks, while Swiss, British, and Canadian bankers arguably exhibited independence from the sectoral politics of their domestic constituents? This observation begs an antecedent yet important question that domestic analyses so far have not addressed: Why are some banks "large" or influential to begin with? This question suggests a partial circularity to arguments that emphasize domestic factors: we know banks are "large" not only because they have sizeable assets, but also because they have captured regulators and negotiators. In this respect, domestic arguments fail to identify adequate measures of policy influence that differentiate among market participants. To understand why some banks but not others shaped the Basel negotiations, researchers need first to separate measures of policy influence from post hoc assessments of outcomes.

This chapter proposes that the weak Basel regime reflects the preferences of the *Landesbanken*, the eleven regional banks controlled by state governments and one of the three officially recognized groups of banks (the others are private banks and cooperative banks). Though small in number, the network structure of financial relationships between banks in Germany may have afforded the *Landesbanken* considerable influence on German positions during the Basel negotiations. While scholars have yet to tell the complete history of bargaining among German banks, one might argue that it was unnecessary for the *Landesbanken* to capture regulators as Lall suggests, nor to exercise veto power.[40] Instead, as hubs in the German financial network, the *Landesbanken* enjoyed considerable power to shape the preferences of other banks, just as the network of appropriators in the simulated common pool resource in chapter 5 shaped others' preferences. The network explanation offers an advantage over existing explanations: by emphasizing bargaining among different banks, it can explain the evolution of the German negotiating position during the Basel process.

FINANCIAL SECTORAL POLITICS AS A NETWORK

All firms organize themselves into productive relationships with other firms that one might loosely characterize as a "network"—supplier relationships are one such example.[41] Whereas producer-supplier relationships may change fluidly as market conditions mandate, networks among banks tend to be more stable over the long term. These financial networks arise in response to two pressures: the process of industrialization and the management of risks inherent in lending.

Some states have built networks among banks to facilitate industrialization. Historical institutionalists suggest that the organization of banking reflects the unique challenges each state faced at the time of industrialization. In late industrializers, the relative scarcity of capital causes markets to underinvest in the modernization process. To redress this, states must play an active role in directing capital to modernization, both directly to industry and through public ownership and management of banks. In his seminal study on late industrializers, Gerschenkron explains the organization of banks in nineteenth-century Germany as a response to the need for long-run investment in the economy. To catch up with the Britain and the United States, Germany could not wait as banks built capital from retained profits. For this reason, in late industrializers the state actively organized both the financial sector and created industrial-banking conglomerates to minimize firms' costs and risks of borrowing.[42] In Germany, this state-directed organization of production and finance became known as *strukturpolitik*. Kurth suggests that during the twentieth century, as the capital intensity of modern industries increased, states encouraged new financial innovations including the creation of investment banks and deregulation of financial services.[43] These arguments help explain differences in the organization of the banking industries in the United States and Germany. American banking originally evolved as a response to market forces rather than state direction. While the state increasingly played a role in regulating American financial services, it rarely took ownership of banks. This market-based approach to finance explains several features of the American banking system: the separation of finance and industry (which antitrust regulators reinforce); the evolution of multipurpose banks rather than specialized ones; and, as discussed below, a relatively decentralized network of interbank relationships. By contrast, the modern German finance industry reflects both a tradition of state involvement and a history of industrial-banking conglomerates. German banks may rely on public finances for capital, and they often have close relationships with German firms. A tiered structure also characterizes the German banking network: while private commercial banks serve investment and commercial needs nationally and internationally, publicly owned banks tend to be organized regionally. Savings banks in Germany serve local commercial needs, are locally managed, and belong to regional conglomerates (*Sparkassen*) that in turn belong to one of the *Landesbanken*. The types of German banks also differ in their exposure to international markets and long-term lending. Savings banks tend to focus on long-term lending and domestic markets, while commercial banks have greater exposure to international markets and short-term lending. *Landesbanken* reside in between savings banks and commercial banks in both their international investments and their dependence on long-term loans.[44] An important consequence of this specialization and regional organization of banks is an interbank network characterized by a few influential banks— that is, banks with relatively high betweenness in the interbank network. While this network structure may allow for the efficient allocation of capital among financial institutions, risks of contagious bank defaults arise from this pattern of a few, highly central institutions.

    Banks also create networks to manage the risks of their asset portfolios. Transaction cost economics can help explain how banks use the interbank network to manage the inherent risks of lending.[45] To lessen the risk of default, banks have three strategies for spreading the risk of their loans: self-insurance through the amassment of a large capital reserve; reliance on public insurance from the state; and market-based insurance. Because the risk of default on any given loan is typically quite small, a large capital reserve tends to be inefficient with high opportunity costs. For this reason, banks historically have turned either to public insurance or to the market. Two contracting strategies characterize market-based solutions to risk management. Banks may engage in interbank lending to manage their capital reserves, or they can create securities to sell to investors. As electronic payment systems have become more secure and essentially costless, modern banks engage in large volumes of daily interbank lending. Securitization is a more recent market innovation, though one that has received increasing scrutiny from regulators due to its apparent influence on the 2008 financial crisis.[46] Of course, although analytically distinct the state-based and market-based approaches to managing risk are interdependent. States regulate the interbank market, and may shape other market-based approaches—Basel II's unintended encouragement of securitization is one such example. More important, perhaps, is the problem of moral hazard: investors in banks tend to underestimate risks because they expect governments will not let them fail. Thus, large banks that are too big to fail, for example, can borrow at lower rates than smaller banks.

Market-based approaches to managing lending risks create both direct and indirect networks among banks. In principle, banks could lend to any other bank in a given financial sector, suggesting that banking networks would be random in nature. Empirical studies have found, however, that the interbank lending network is neither random nor "complete" (that is, not all banks lend to every other bank). Allen and Babus note that although interbank lending tends to respond to credit market conditions and evolve over time, banks nevertheless tend to trade with only a subset of banks in the industry. They attribute this structure to the transaction costs associated with interbank lending: because these costs are not zero, banks find it costly to switch to new trading partners.[47] Perhaps more important are indirect linkages among banks. Because banks tend to hold similar asset portfolios, their capitalization levels tend to move together as market prices change. This creates risks that banks cannot necessary manage through interbank lending. When a distressed bank sells assets, for example, it weakens the capitalization of other banks through the depression of asset prices. This can create negative feedbacks in bank capitalization: banks may sell assets preemptively to bolster their capitalization, but these sales in turn distress the portfolios of other banks.[48] Thus, the transaction costs of managing the risks inherent in lending encourage banks to build both explicit networks of interbank lending, and implicit networks of asset portfolios.

Several empirical studies of banking networks have examined how network structures affect the likelihood of contagion during crises. Analyzing balance sheet information or data on overnight interbank loans, scholars have measured the properties of the interbank networks in Austria,[49] Germany,[50] Italy,[51] Japan,[52] the United States,[53] Switzerland,[54] and the United Kingdom.[55] These studies have found that incomplete networks are more susceptible to cascading failures among banks.[56] Likewise, concentrated networks may be more prone to failure.[57] For example, Upper and Worms estimate that a single bank failure in Germany could adversely affect 15 percent of the assets in the banking system. Capturing the centrality of *Landesbanken* to the German network, the study also finds that the failure of one of the *Landesbanken* could cause more than one thousand savings banks to fail and impact 60 percent of the total assets in the banking system.[58] If anything, these studies may understate the true risk of interbank networks because researchers assume banks tend to spread risk more evenly across the network than they actually do.[59] These studies illustrate that while interbank lending effectively manages the risks of small-scale defaults, some interbank network structures are prone to propagating larger shocks. This creates perverse incentives in banking: the safety provided by networks reduces the incentives to close inefficient banks,[60] while during crises banks and regulators may be willing to bail out insolvent banks to prevent the entire network from collapsing.[61] Of course, this latter perversity gained widespread public attention when, during the 2008 crisis, U.S. regulators and politicians lamented that the government was compelled to aid several large banks.

To my knowledge, few researchers have examined how the interbank network structure affects the sectoral politics of the industry. Howlett is one, though his analysis of the Canadian banking industry characterizes the policy network by its receptivity to new actors and new ideas rather than a formal representation of financial interdependencies among banks.[62] The paucity of studies on the relationship between market networks and policy advocacy perhaps reflects an unexamined assumption: Do networks derived from market exchange necessarily affect the pattern of policy advocacy? In my view, this is a question researchers have not adequately theorized or investigated. One might object that just because banks lend to each other, they do not necessarily share interests nor do they influence each other's policy positions. Nevertheless, political economy scholarship long has acknowledged that large firms have the resources and organization to influence policy. To the degree that networks confer to firms advantages in terms of resources and information, the study of global politics will benefit from understanding how market networks shape political outcomes.

SIMULATING THE BASEL III NEGOTIATIONS

To examine the influence of the interbank network on the Basel III Agreement, I extend the ABM of two-level bargaining games from chapter 3 to simulate negotiations between the United States and Germany.[63] This framework allows the researcher to specify the preferences of both states and domestic actors, and to explain policy outcomes as the result of bargaining at the domestic level (which Putnam refers to as level II), the interstate level (level I), and across levels.

To measure outcomes of the negotiations, the simulation awards payoffs based on the Battle of the Sexes games discussed in chapter 4. In this classic game, players share a common aversion—that is, they agree they are better off with cooperation than without it. But the players disagree over the distribution of gains from cooperation, and hence prefer different outcomes. Because this game combines mixed incentives for cooperation and competition, scholars argue it characterizes a range of cooperation problems in world politics.[64] The Basel negotiations exhibited a similar combination of incentives for cooperation and competition. After the 2008 crisis, governments clearly agreed that the status quo was undesirable—that is, states shared a common aversion. But the proposals to reform banking regulations clearly had distributive consequences. Under Basel II, banks in different countries adopted different mixes of tier I and tier II capital. To meet the proposed higher capital requirements of Basel III, countries in which the banks had thinner capital bases would bear a higher burden of strengthening the global financial system. For this reason, Japanese, Italian, and German banks anticipated they would pay higher costs for the proposed rules. Conversely, most large banks in the United States and Canada met the revised standards without having to raise any additional capital. This meant that American negotiators in Basel could advocate higher standards and a short implementation schedule with little opposition from U.S. banks.

Figure 6.1 presents both the classic Battle of the Sexes game and the extended game the simulation uses to award payoffs to players.[65] The extended game reflects the fact that regulators at Basel negotiated about two dimensions of the agreement: the new levels of capitalization banks would meet (labeled the "strength" of the regime) and the deadlines by which banks and regulators would have to meet the new standards (the "implementation" of the regime). Though simplified, this extended game captures the four possible outcomes of the Basel negotiations: (1) the status quo of no agreement or coordination, represented by (0, 0) payoffs in the Basel game matrix; (2) a modest revision to capital standards, or a "weak" regime (1, 3); (3) a "strong" regime with higher capital adequacy standards, but a slow implementation schedule to allow banks to adjust to the new rules (2, 2); and (4) a strong regime with an expedited implementation schedule (3, 1). The figure indicates cardinal payoffs for the United States and Germany, but these are merely suggestive. In fact, the history of bargaining during the 2010 negotiations suggests that different actors had differing orders of preference over these outcomes. At the state level, U.S. regulators supported a strong regime with an expedited implementation schedule, while their German counterparts preferred either a weak regime or, failing that, a lengthy phase-in of a stronger regime. Likewise, banks differed in their preferred outcomes. While American banks preferred better enforcement of the existing rules, if negotiators were to agree to a newer regime, American banks wanted stronger rules that preserved their market advantage in capitalization. German banks, on the other hand, appeared divided. Private commercial banks with considerable exposure to international lending supported the principle of higher capital standards, but expressed concern about the consequences on publicly owned savings banks and *Landesbanken*. For this reason, private commercial banks preferred a longer implementation of the strengthened rules. Finally, the *Landesbanken* preferred a regime with the relatively weak rules, like those of Basel II, which allowed for public investments to count

(a) Classic Game

		Player 2	
		Mountains	Ocean
Player 1	Mountains	2, 1	0, 0
	Ocean	0, 0	1, 2

Payoffs = (player 1, player 2)

(b) Basel Simulation Extension

		Germany		
		Weak Regime	Strong regime, slow implementation	Strong regime, fast implementation
United States	Weak Regime	1, 3	0, 0	0, 0
	Strong regime, slow implementation	0, 0	2, 2	0, 0
	Strong regime, fast implementation	0, 0	0, 0	3, 1

Payoffs = (United States, Germany)

Figure 6.1. Battle of the sexes game and extensions for the Basel simulation, with cardinal payoffs.

toward the banks' capital obligations. Failing that, the *Landesbanken* wanted a slower implementation schedule that would give them adequate time to build their capital. Table 6.1 lists these actors and the orders of their preferences.

To simulate the policy networks among banks, the ABM uses empirical data on the network structure of the overnight interbank market. For the United States, I use the data from Soramaki et al., who examined daily interbank transactions for nearly seven thousand U.S. banks during the fourth quarter of 2004. Column (i) of Table 6.2 reports the network properties Soramaki et al. found.[66] Because the data show relatively short average path lengths among banks but relatively high clustering, the researchers conclude the U.S. interbank network exhibits small world properties. Unfortunately, data on the interbank structure in Germany is less readily available. Upper and Worms use balance sheet information to measure the aggregate structure among different categories of banks in Germany. Examining data from more than three thousand banks, they demonstrate that the banking industry exhibits a two-tier structure, with local savings and cooperative banks largely trading with their regional *Landesbanken* or commercial banks but not with each other.[67] This analysis suggests that the interbank network in Germany exhibits the hub-and-spoke structure that characterizes scale-free networks.[68] Unfortunately, the study does not report bank-level data about the structure of the network. The Austrian interbank market has received considerable attention from researchers, however, and offers a reasonable proxy for the structure of the German interbank market. Like the German industry, the Austrian system includes savings and cooperative banks that tend to focus on local commercial banking; a tiered structure with a central bank for each federal state; a pattern of vertical relationships between local and regional banks; and a history of public investment.[69] Boss et al. conclude that "even

Table 6.1. Actors' orders of preferences.

Actor	Order
U.S. policy makers	D > C > B > A
U.S. banks	A > D > C > B
German policy makers	B > C > D > A
German private banks	C > D > B > A
German landesbanken	B > C > D > A

Outcomes:

A = status quo
B = weak regime
C = strong regime, slow implementation
D = strong regime, fast implementation

though the Austrian interbank market is small it is structurally very similar to the interbank systems in many European countries, including the large economies of Germany, France, and Italy."[70] For these reasons, the ABM uses data on the interbank network in Austria as a proxy for the network structure of German finance. Column (ii) of Table 6.2 reports the network properties of the Austrian industry. Most of the data come from Schmitz and Puhr's study of daily interbank transactions.[71] Because they do not report clustering, however, I rely on Boss et al.'s estimate of the clustering coefficient.[72] The data illustrate that the Austrian network has short path-length distances among banks comparable to the path lengths in the American industry, but has both fewer average links per bank (i.e., lower degree) and lower "clustering," or the probability that any two network-neighbor banks are both connected to a third bank. This low clustering captures the tiered structure of the Austrian network; most banks tend to trade with a few central hubs in the network. Although Boss et al. conclude the network exhibits properties of a small world network, the relatively low clustering is more characteristic of a scale-free network structure.[73]

To simulate the different sizes and structures of the American and German banking networks, the analysis used Network Workbench Tool v. 1.0, a free social network analysis software package.[74] The Workbench generated a small world network of two hundred nodes with average degree, clustering, and path lengths similar to the real world U.S. interbank network. To capture the tiered structure and low clustering of the German

Table 6.2. Measures of the actual and simulated interbank networks.

	(i)	(ii)	(iii)	(iv)
	Actual		Simulated	
	U.S.	Austria	U.S.	Germany
Nodes (n)	5,086	575	200	100
Links (m)	76,614	1,427	3,160	560
Connectivity	0.30%	0.43%	7.94%	5.65%
Average Degree	15.2	7.3	15.8	5.6
Power Law Exponent (γ)	2.11	0.62 to 2.01	2.18	1.91
Average Path Length	2.62	2.2	2.65	2.6
Average Eccentricity	4.67	3.0	3.99	3.83
Clustering Coefficient	0.53	0.12	0.53	0.14

Sources: Soramaki (fn. 52) for the United States; Boss et al. (fn. 45) and Schmitz and Puhr (fn. 70) for Austria.

network, I generated a scale-free network of one hundred nodes.[75] Columns (iii) and (iv) in Table 6.2 list the properties of the simulated networks. Because Soramaki et al. found about twice as many nodes in the American interbank network than Upper and Worms identified in the German industry, the simulated U.S. network is twice the size of the simulated German network.[76] The simulated networks are comparable to their real world counterparts in most measures except for connectivity, which measures the density of ties as a percentage of the total number of possible relationships. Because the ABM simulates smaller networks, to have the same average number of links to other banks the networks by definition must be denser. Despite this difference from the actual network, the simulated networks nevertheless are relatively sparsely connected. The ABM uses the simulated networks to initialize the relationships among banking agents in the model. To simplify the analysis, it assumes the network is symmetrical and that ties are unweighted. While this assumption ignores the volume and frequency of transactions in the interbank market, the ABM seeks to simulate political behavior of banks rather than their commercial transactions. For this reason, the simulated symmetrical, unweighted networks are a reasonable representation of political networks in the industry.

The ABM includes two classes of agents: banks and negotiators. Negotiators play the Basel game represented in Figure 6.1(b) with each other. At initialization, the model assigns each bank agent a random order of preferences representing the four outcomes of the Basel game: (a) the status quo; (b) a weak regime; (c) a strong regime with lengthy implementation; and (d) a strong regime with a quick implementation. Negotiator agents have preferences that reflected the real-world Basel negotiators: the simulated American negotiator prefers $d > c > b > a$, while the German negotiator prefers $b > c > d > a$. By construction, the Basel game's extension of the Battle of the Sexes dilemma has multiple possible equilibria. Because the simulation extends the game to a large-n cooperation problem, and because bank agents have differing preferences, the equilibrium solution of the game will reflect how bank agents bargain with other agents in their network neighborhood. Of course, the idea that bank agents "bargain" suggests that they must be willing to learn from other agents and change their preferences. To capture this process of bargaining and learning, the simulation implements a simple procedure. Agents identify the plurality choice of their network neighborhood; if the plurality choice is not the agent's preferred outcome, with some probability less than 1 the agent will reorder its preferences by promoting the local plurality choice.[77] Negotiator agents then play the Basel game with each other. If a negotiator's constituency has a majority choice, the negotiator plays that choice with some probability less than 1; otherwise, it plays its preferred choice. The two negotiator choices determine the position in the game matrix in Figure 6.1 and the payoffs agents receive. Because bank agents have varying preferences, they will receive different payoffs for the same outcome. For example, suppose negotiator agents play different choices; the outcome is no agreement. A bank agent that prefers an agreement would receive a payoff of zero, while a bank agent that prefers the status quo would receive a positive payoff. Each simulation repeats the game two hundred times. Table 6.3 presents the pseudo code for the agent-based model.

The analysis repeated the simulation 1,500 times and systematically varied the parameters that govern the sensitivity of banks to the preferences of their network neighbors and of negotiators to their constituent banks. Higher values indicate a greater likelihood that a bank (or negotiator) will reorder preferences to accommodate the interests of network neighbors (or constituents). To test for the influence of the *Landesbanken*, the model iden-

Table 6.3. Pseudo code for the Basel III model

Initialization
    Create 200 U.S. bank agents and 100 German bank agents
        Connect them to network neighbors using simulated network structures
        Endow them with random preference order from [a b c d]
            Endow high-centrality German banks with preference order [b c d a]
        Give banks a sensitivity p_B to preferences of network neighbors
    Create one U.S. negotiator and one German negotiator
        Connect them to their "constituency" (banking network)
        Endow them with preferences: U.S. = [d c b a]; Germany = [b c d a]
        Give them a sensitivity p_N to the preferences of their constituents

Execution
    Loop until time = 200
        Each bank agent:
            Checks plurality choice of network neighborhood
            If plurality choice is not preferred outcome, reorder preferences with
                probability p_B
            Play first preferred choice
        Each negotiator agent:
            Checks plurality choice of constituent network
            If constituency has a majority preference, play that choice with
                probability p_N
                  Otherwise, play first preferred choice
        Identify game outcome
        Update agent scores according to order of preferences

tifies the five nodes in the simulated German banking network with the highest betweenness centrality—that is, the bank agents that on average are on the shortest path between any other two banks.[78] In the simulated network, these nodes occupy positions similar to the central positions of the *Landesbanken* in the German interbank market. Half the simulations endowed these banks with the same starting preferences: $b > c > d > a$. That is, the "hub" banks in the German network will prefer a weak regime, followed by a strong regime with lengthy implementation; a strong regime with quick enactment; and no agreement. It is important to note that these high-centrality banks are not "intransigent" in the sense that they maintain fixed preferences. Like all other banks in the simulation, these bank agents update their preference orders dynamically in response to changes in the preferences of their network neighbors. They differ from the other simulated German bank agents only in their position in the network and in that the simulation does not randomize their initial preference orders. Otherwise, all other banks in both the U.S. and German networks receive random preference orders. If the hypothesis is correct, in the 750 simulations with fixed preferences of the high-betweenness German banks one would expect (1) the German collective choice is more likely to reflect the preferences of the high-betweenness banks; and (2) if the negotiators agree to a stable social choice, the outcome of the bargaining will reflect the preferences of the high-betweenness German banks.

SOME RESULTS

Table 6.4 presents the results of the experimental manipulations of the ABM parameters. For statistical comparison, the baseline simulation places the sensitivity parameters at a low value (10 percent of minimum) and assigns random preferences to the high-betweenness German banks. The columns labeled (i) through (iv) present the mean values of the dependent variables for a given parameter set: (i) the average payoffs the banks receive from the game; (ii) the probability that negotiators agree to a Pareto-improving equilibrium solution to the game, irrespective of which of the three equilibria it is; (iii) the probability that the German bargaining position is in favor of a weak regime, irrespective of whether the U.S. negotiator agrees to it; and (iv) the probability that the weak regime becomes the agreed outcome between negotiators. The table's rows present the values of the experimental manipulations and interactions.

A quick glance at column (iii) in the table illustrates that, as hypothesized, the high-centrality German banks significantly affect both the majority choice of all the German banks and the probability that negotiators will choose a regime that accommodates German preferences. In all thirty

Table 6.4. Experimental results with comparisons to baseline simulation ($^*p < .05$, $^{**}p < .01$, $^{***}p < .001$)

Manipulation		Dependent Measure				
Parameter	Value (% max)	(i) Average Bank Payoffs	(ii) Probability P of Any Agreement	(iii) P German choice = b	(iv) P equilibrium = b, b	N
Baseline (10%, 10%, no)		89.20	0.13	0.27	0.03	30
Bank sensitivity (Pb)	30%	134.83	0.23	0.50	0.07	30
	50%	143.28	0.23	0.40	0.13	30
	70%	205.57**	0.40*	0.23	0.07	30
	90%	130.89	0.23	0.33	0.07	30
Negotiator sensitivity (Pn)	30%	106.58	0.20	0.53*	0.10	30
	50%	112.91	0.33	0.50	0.17	30
	70%	66.06	0.07	0.87**	0.00	30
	90%	22.54**	0.10	0.97**	0.07	30
Fixed preferences of central German banks?	Yes	156.23	0.33	1.00***	0.33**	30

Paramter Interactions

Fixed preferences × Bank sensitivity	10%	77.65	0.11	0.97***	0.11	150
Fixed preferences × Bank sensitivity	50%	74.85	0.11	0.95***	0.09	150
Fixed preferences × Bank sensitivity	90%	91.06	0.11	0.97***	0.11	150
Fixed preferences × Negotiator sensitivity	10%	140.04	0.23	0.97***	0.23*	150
Fixed preferences × Negotiator sensitivity	50%	87.78	0.11	0.95***	0.10	150
Fixed preferences × Negotiator sensitivity	90%	13.78**	0.01**	0.99***	0.01	150
Bank sensitivity × Negotiator sensitivity	50% × 10%	150.47	0.25	0.67***	0.20*	60
Bank sensitivity × Negotiator sensitivity	90% × 10%	117.72	0.20	0.65***	0.10	60
Bank sensitivity × Negotiator sensitivity	10% × 50%	95.47	0.20	0.72***	0.12	60
Bank sensitivity × Negotiator sensitivity	10% × 90%	17.41**	0.05	0.97***	0.03	60
Total		*86.40*	*0.14*	*0.80*	*0.08*	*1500*

simulations in which the sensitivity parameters assumed their baseline values but high-centrality German banks received the fixed preferences of [$b > c > d > a$], the collective choice of the German banks was b, which in the Basel game represents the weakest possible regime other than the status quo. When the fixed preferences of high-centrality bank agents interacts with both the bank sensitivity and the negotiator sensitivity parameters, the probability of German agents choosing option b is significantly higher in all cases, ranging from .95 to .99. Of course, these figures represent only the effect of bank preferences on the German negotiating position. To get some sense of the effect on bargaining outcomes with the simulated American negotiator, column (iv) presents the likelihood of the negotiators agreeing to the weak regime represented by the game outcome of b, b (that is, both negotiators selecting option b). In the thirty simulations in which the five high-centrality banks had fixed preferences, the game's outcome was ten times more likely to be the weak regime than the baseline simulation—about one-third of these simulations resulted in an agreement to the b, b regime. The preferences of the high-centrality bank agents interact with negotiator sensitivities in surprising ways, furthermore. In the 150 simulations in which high-centrality banks had fixed preferences and negotiators were relatively insensitive to constituent preferences, nearly one in four simulations resulted in the weak regime agreement. This is puzzling: Why would insensitive negotiators be more likely to accommodate the preferences of the high-centrality banks? One possibility is that, paradoxically, the insensitivity of negotiators magnifies the bargaining advantages that high-centrality banks enjoy. With less receptivity to constituent preferences, those banks that prefer outcomes other than the weak regime are less likely to influence negotiators. But high-centrality banks are better positioned to take advantage of the rare occasions when negotiators listen to constituents. This is a counterintuitive but potentially important theoretical point: in multilateral talks, negotiators who are relatively free of societal pressures may in fact be more likely to represent particularistic rather than general interests.

Interestingly, the sensitivity of negotiators significantly increases the likelihood of the German agents choosing outcome b independent of the fixed preferences of the highly central banks. This is surprising: in these experiments, the simulation randomizes the preferences of all German banks. One would expect no significant differences from the distribution of German collective choices in the thirty baseline simulations. This may be an artifice, however, of the relatively small number of simulations the chi-square tests use.

Otherwise, only a few parameter values have significant effects on the dependent measures. For example, only two of the nineteen manipulations produce significant differences in the probability of negotiator agents achieving an agreement. This is to be expected: with banks receiving randomly assigned preferences, one would expect payoffs and the probability of negotiated agreements to vary uniformly across simulations. In terms of the payoffs the simulated banks receive from the Basel game, one surprise is that they receive significantly lower payoffs than the baseline simulation when negotiators are highly sensitive to the preferences of banks.[79] In three manipulations—when negotiators' sensitivity is set to 90 percent maximum value, and when high negotiator sensitivity interacts with the bank agents' sensitivity and with the fixed preferences of high centrality German bank agents—bank agents receive significantly lower payoffs than the baseline simulation. Conversely, there is some evidence that when banks are relatively accommodating of each other's preferences, they may receive significantly higher payoffs. There are two possible explanations for this paradoxical finding. One is that negotiators may be too accommodating: in multilateral discussions, a negotiator who changes positions frequently may actually shift negotiations away from stable equilibrium agreements. That is, overly solicitous negotiators may fail to capture the potential gains of cooperation. The other is that negotiators may quickly settle on positions that satisfy domestic constituents, but which will not win ratification from other states. These observations suggest that in multilateral talks, successful negotiators must strike a balance between accommodation of domestic constituents and the necessity of making binding commitments to international partners. Statesmen who are too accommodating may paradoxically contribute to discord more than they foster agreements. That being said, the data show that in the Basel game, the simulated negotiators who are highly sensitive to constituents are no more and no less likely to strike bargains with other negotiators.

One drawback of the experimental manipulations in Table 6.4 is that they use relatively few observations for each statistical test. Statistically speaking, a test based on only sixty of the 1,500 simulations may inflate the standard errors by discarding information from the other simulations. As discussed in chapter 5, regression analysis, by contrast, can use information from all 1,500 simulations to calculate standard errors. This offers an alternative method for testing the relationships between the simulation parameters and outcomes of interest. Table 6.5 presents the results of a multinomial logit model that estimates the effects of simulation parameters on the four possible outcomes of the Basel game. In 87 percent of the simulations, the negotiator agents failed to reach an agreement. Of the remaining simulations, in about 8 percent of the cases they agreed to the weak regime; in about 4 percent they agreed to the strong regime with fast implementation. They agreed to the strong regime with slow implementation in only sixteen of 1,500 simulations, just over 1 percent. The estimates in Table 6.5

Table 6.5. Multinomial logit estimates of effect of simulation parameters on Basel game outcomes. Outcome a, a (no agreement) is the comparison group.

					N = 1500	
					LR χ^2 (9) = 138.8	
					$P > \chi^2$ = 0.00	
Log likelihood = −657.67					Pseudo R^2 = 0.0955	
	Coef.	Std. Err.	z	$P>\vert z\vert$	95% Conf. Interval	
Choice = b, b						
Negotiator Sensitivity	−2.39	0.38	−6.25	0.00	−3.13	−1.64
Bank Sensitivity	−0.31	0.35	−0.89	0.37	−0.99	0.37
Fixed preferences	0.48	0.20	2.38	0.02	0.08	0.87
Constant	−1.50	0.27	−5.64	0.00	−2.02	−0.98
Choice = c, c						
Negotiator Sensitivity	−3.17	1.09	−2.91	0.00	−5.31	−1.04
Bank Sensitivity	1.66	0.96	1.73	0.08	−0.22	3.55
Fixed preferences	−2.78	1.04	−2.68	0.01	−4.81	−0.75
Constant	−3.41	0.73	−4.67	0.00	−4.84	−1.98
Choice = d, d						
Negotiator Sensitivity	−1.62	0.53	−3.06	0.00	−2.66	−0.58
Bank Sensitivity	0.07	0.51	0.13	0.89	−0.92	1.06
Fixed preferences	−2.87	0.60	−4.80	0.00	−4.04	−1.70
Constant	−1.84	0.36	−5.05	0.00	−2.55	−1.12

compare outcomes to the baseline case of no agreement. The multinomial logit analysis largely affirms the findings of the experimental manipulations. As hypothesized, fixed preferences among the high-centrality German bank agents significantly increase the likelihood of the negotiators agreeing to the weak regime equilibrium. These fixed preferences also significantly reduce the likelihood of the two strong regime outcomes (c, c and d, d) relative to the baseline case of no agreement. Interestingly, the multinomial logit analysis also suggests that ceteris paribus, negotiators' sensitivity significantly *reduces* the likelihood of any agreement. Negotiator agents who accommodate the simulated constituencies appear to create more problems than they solve. Conversely, banks that accommodate the preferences of their network neighbors appear to affect the likelihood only of outcome (c, c), the strong regime/slow implementation choice. Otherwise, banks that are sensitive to network neighbors have no effect on either the weak regime or strong regime/fast implementation outcomes, when controlling for other simulation parameters.

Both the logit analysis and the experimental manipulations support the chapter's hypothesis that a few banks centrally located in the financial network of Germany could affect the outcome of the Basel negotiations. That five bank agents in a scale-free network of one hundred bank agents could tip the collective choice to their preferred outcome is a testament to the power of networks. It also is consistent with Putnam's hypothesis that, when playing two-level games, negotiators faced with strong domestic preferences are more likely to strike a favorable bargain in multilateral talks, while negotiators with considerable flexibility find they make more concessions than they receive. The simulation of the Basel game reproduced these dynamics: the U.S. negotiator agent, whose constituents always had randomized preferences, secured an agreement for one of its top two preferred outcomes in only one of every twenty simulations.

INDUSTRY NETWORKS AND INTERNATIONAL REGIMES

One can plausibly argue that because the network structure of the banking industry in Germany exhibits greater centralization than the American industry, a small number of German banks enjoy a privileged influence on policy and regulatory debates. While taxpayers and policymakers may lament that some banks are too big to fail, perhaps they should consider the risks of banks that are too big to compromise. From their central positions in daily market transactions, some banks may shape public policy in ways that reflect neither the common interest nor the exigencies of international regulation. Independent of regulatory capture, a small number of banks may shape the policy debate by controlling the information that negotiators receive from the industry. The analysis above makes a plausible case that this explains the curiously feckless Basel III Agreement. In the wake of the greatest global financial crisis in eight decades, leading banking nations concluded an agreement that allowed banks to continue to calculate their own risk weights and to take up to a decade to meet the new capital adequacy standards. The agreement may protect the commercial interests of undercapitalized banks, but it reflects neither the lessons of 2008 nor the demands of citizens, regulators, or taxpayers. Computational social science can help us understand this perverse outcome.

Of course, the simulation presented here is a highly stylized representation of the negotiations that led to the Basel III Agreement. It makes a number of assumptions that may limit the validity of its findings. In the absence of data on the German interbank market, it uses network data from the similar Austrian interbank network. For this reason, it may introduce unknown sources of bias. The simulation also assumes that the relationships in the interbank market resemble policy networks. This is a reasonable assumption: as a method of scholarship, political economy regularly infers actors' preferences from market position, and economists often use the Herfindahl index of market size to infer a firm's influence on public policy and regulation. The use of formal network data is a natural extension of these traditions. Nevertheless, it is important to qualify the chapter's claims: the simulation shows that a bank's centrality may be *sufficient* to influence multilateral negotiations, but it is not *necessary*. That is, during the Basel negotiations, the *Landesbanken* and other firms may have influenced the final agreement through mechanisms unrelated to their network position. Scholars will need to complement simulation with case studies and other empirical methods if we are to understand the relationship between market-driven networks and policy networks.

The model also fails to capture a number of important nuances of the actual negotiations during the Basel process. For one, the simulation's assignment of random preferences to bank agents does not reflect the preferences of the actual banking sectors in the United States and Germany. One could easily revise the simulation to include information on the actual distribution of preferences among actors. More importantly, agents in the simulation do not behave strategically. They do not remember past plays of the game, nor do they "learn" to play strategies that provide better payoffs, as the players in the games in chapter 4 did. As illustrated there, players who iterate games and have a sizeable discount rate or "shadow of the future" are more likely to play cooperative strategies. A revision of the game could use insights from the genetic algorithms of chapter 4 to simulate the processes of learning and strategic decision making. Bank agents and negotiator agents alike could use their payoffs from the simulated game to evolve new strategies that optimize their payoffs. It may be that, with such learning, agents identify equilibrium outcomes that yield higher returns over the long run. If when using such simulation methods the game finds that agents still choose the weak regime outcome, it would affirm this chapter's finding of the importance of high-centrality banks. There is no a priori reason to expect such a finding, however. A model that simulates agent learning no doubt would suggest revisions to our understanding of the Basel negotiations and of multilateral negotiations in general.

Finally, the model ignores an important element of contemporary financial networks in the real world: transnational linkages. Others have shown how negotiators may bargain directly with members of the opposing negotiator's constituency, and how constituents may work together across sovereign boundaries to shape the outcomes of multilateral talks. Such transnational politics in the banking industry may have surprising effects. Von

Peter shows, for example, that the German industry as a whole is much more central to the global banking network than the American industry.[80] This global network data potentially allows for a more complete two-level games simulation. By incorporating network data about transnational linkages among banks, the model may simulate how transnational alliances emerge in support of particular regimes but not others.

Even the simple model presented here, however, shows how social networks can affect the prospects for cooperation in world politics. Market-driven networks may produce unexpected tradeoffs between efficiency and advocacy. Network scholars have demonstrated that scale-free networks, such as those that typify domestic interbank lending, are robust to random failures such as the insolvency of a random bank, but are vulnerable to cascading events when hubs fail much as Lehman Brothers' failure froze both the investment banking and commercial credit markets. In this respect, market networks have evolved to manage but not eliminate risk. Yet those same network structures may produce perverse patterns of policy advocacy. By affording prestige and centrality to specific market actors, they may deprive policymakers of knowledge about the preferences of actors throughout an industry. Similarly, leaders may find it harder to build coalitions in support of particular policies when a few privileged actors control access to market-derived networks. This suggests an important complement to the idea of network externalities: in addition to stimulating positive returns to producers of networked goods, they may produce policy advantages that preserve market position. Worries about firms being too big to fail occur during crises; but firms that are too big to compromise advocate policies every day.

Although intrabank lending tends to follow similar patterns and create a relatively stable social structure, this need not be so. In principle, regulators and bank leaders can change lending practices to assure no one bank enjoys a high degree of prestige or centrality in a financial network, or in policy decisions. Other global networks are, however, more difficult to rewire. Characterized by highly specific assets and high switching costs, global networks in transportation and telecommunication tend to be relatively fixed, at least in the short to medium run. Because these networks transcend national borders, furthermore, state-based regulation is particularly challenging. For these reasons, the dynamics of these infrastructure networks—particularly the cascading surprises that spill across sovereign boundaries—seem to be an inevitable feature of global politics, as the next chapter discusses.

SEVEN

NETS OF INSECURITY

Trade Networks, Cascading Failures, and Economic Vulnerability

In November 2012, the U.S. National Research Council released a study assessing the vulnerability of the U.S. electricity grid to deliberate disruption. Such are the magnitude of concerns about a possible "digital Pearl Harbor" that the council delayed publication of the report for five years while the U.S. Department of Homeland Security classified the entire report in 2008, even after its experts concluded the report contained no information that could inform would-be attackers.[1] The NRC report noted that "if they could gain access, hackers could manipulate SCADA [supervisory control and data acquisition] systems to disrupt the flow of electricity, transmit erroneous signals to operators, block the flow of vital information, or disable protective systems."[2] In conjunction with a physical disruption to the grid, an incapacitating cyberattack could "deny large regions of the country access to bulk system power for weeks or even months," possibly resulting in "hundreds or even thousands of deaths due to heat stress or extended exposure to extreme cold."[3]

Contemporary globalization consists of the worldwide movement of images, goods, money, information, and people. Nearly simultaneous reductions in transportation costs and increase in telecommunications capacity has facilitated this growth in worldwide exchange.[4] Yet these flows do not occur in a vacuum: global exchanges rely upon telecommunications, transportation, information technology, and energy networks that, such as the U.S. power grid, have specific physical and network properties.

Although such networks provide considerable efficiencies in trade and transportation, such efficiencies may come at the cost of our increasing reliance on networks. As the NRC report suggests, policymakers and scholars alike are increasingly concerned with how the properties of these networks may distribute costs as well as benefits across societies. As these complex networks have evolved to meet the demands of consumers, they have assumed structures that are efficient but not very robust—that is, when they experience disruptions, they may take some time to resume their efficient operation. They also transmit the costs of disruptions to geographically distant locations. For example, the Northeast Blackout of 2003, triggered by erroneous power readings in Indiana, caused power outages not only in the Midwest but also the Northeast as well as Ontario and Quebec in Canada, affecting fifty million people. In March 2008, the government of Haiti increased inspections of cargo through its ports in part to fight corruption, and in part to interdict the transshipment of narcotics to the United States. The inspections led not only to rotting and putrid food shipments on docks in Port-Au-Prince, but also to a backlog of containers in the Port of Miami as shippers had nowhere to store goods in Haiti.[5] In another recent telling example, in September 2011 a utility worker at a power substation in Yuma, Arizona, removed a faulty piece of monitoring equipment. The resulting cascade of power outages blacked out electricity throughout San Diego and much of Baja Mexico, leaving ATMs, traffic lights, 911 call centers, and the San Diego airport powerless.[6] The Japanese earthquake and tsunami in March 2011 closed ports in Yokohama and Tokyo, disrupting the supply of automotive parts to assembly plants in the United States.[7] By one estimate, the disruptions caused a 39 percent decline in automotive parts shipped from Japan in March 2011, and cost manufacturers around the world $17.2 billion over the three months after the earthquake.[8] These examples illustrate how, in a world of global networks, geographically distant disruptions may produce proximate costs in ways that confound our traditionally territory-based understanding of world politics.

To illustrate the dynamics of such cascading failures in global networks, this chapter uses an agent-based model of the United States air transportation network. Previous research has found that air transportation networks exhibit the properties of a small world scale-free network.[9] Because such networks tend to have a few large "hubs," or nodes with a large number of links, they tend to be robust to random failures but sensitive to targeted disruptions such as a terrorist attack. To understand the failure modes of the U.S. air transportation network, this chapter uses a genetic algorithm to act as a "smart terrorist"—the GA learns which attack strategies produce the largest disruption in air transportation for the least amount of effort. The chapter proceeds as follows. First, it shows how existing scholarship tends to view the physical infrastructure of international trade as irrelevant to the distribution of gains in world politics. It then reviews prior research on network failures, differentiating between studies that examine static metrics of network structure and those that measure dynamic flows across networks. The chapter then reviews the structure of the U.S. air transportation network, using data from the U.S. Department of Transportation's Bureau of Transportation Statistics (BTS). These data confirm prior research that characterizes air transportation network as a scale-free network. The analysis uses the BTS data to seed an ABM of the dynamic flow of passengers through the air transportation network. Given the large number of possible failure modes arising from the combinations of disrupted nodes, the analysis uses a genetic algorithm to llustrate how a few apparently minor airports (such as Santiago, Chile) can nevertheless produce surprising backlogs in the flow of passengers in the United States. These findings show how researchers can combine network analysis, evolutionary computation, and agent-based modeling to study the dynamics of global networks, whether of trade, communications, or energy.

THEORIZING ABOUT INFRASTRUCTURE NETWORKS

Globalization theory offers some insights into the origins of and potential consequences of worldwide networks. Many scholars posit that globalization represents an important, post–World War II change in world politics.[10] While there are several definitions of economic globalization, I borrow Scholte's definition. Globalization is the reconfiguration of social relations arising from the ability of people to pursue transplanetary, instantaneous, and simultaneous social relations.[11] This "deterritorialization" of social relations arises in part from global trade and communication networks. One way to examine the rise of a "networked society" is to study the properties of that society's networks.[12] Consider the U.S. air transportation network. This network is highly interconnected, providing more than two hundred cities around the world with air services to more than five hundred airports in the United States. Air transportation of both people and goods is increasingly important to high-value industries such as microelectronics and finance. A disruption to trade networks may have consequences far beyond the bottom line of manufacturers and passengers, furthermore: it may fundamentally affect the wealth and power of trading states. As key scholars of globalization note, "If, in the past, trade sometimes formed an enclave largely isolated from the rest of the national economy, it is now an integral part of the structure of national production in all modern states."[13] Despite this awareness of the conceptual importance of global networks, only recently have scholars examined whether and how the structure of global networks affects wealth and power among global actors, whether nation-states, firms, cities, or individuals.

One reason for this is that globalization theory tends to focus on state-based measures of global exchanges in goods, services, and capital. Several scholars have tested hypotheses about globalization pertaining to trade liberalization,[14] development and poverty,[15] and interstate warfare.[16] Networked interactions among nonstate actors, or between state and nonstate actors, have received less attention despite the growing awareness that terrorist organizations, for example, understand how modern economies depend upon network infrastructures. After 9/11, some experts found that Al Qaeda shifted its strategy to attack economic targets both in the Middle East and in the West, particularly the oil industry and shipping.[17] Al Qaeda's leadership has argued explicitly that such economic terrorism will harm American power.[18] Such economic terrorism is not new; the Provisional IRA explicitly identified transportation networks, energy infrastructures, and financial institutions as targets.[19] These examples suggest that nonstate actors may understand that exponential growth in network size and flows may provide states with both benefits and vulnerabilities. This chapter seeks to understand how network disruptions will directly affect states that depend upon these infrastructures. What will happen in the system when its airports are attacked in many different ways? This work promises to expand our theoretical understanding of the under-studied links between economic globalization and vulnerability.

Although the effect of trade on interstate relations has long been a central concern of international relations theory, theorists usually assume that the physical mechanisms of trade are inconsequential to state interests and behavior. IR theory requires a better explanation for the mechanisms of interdependence and their effect on world politics.[20] Hegemonic theorists and neo-mercantilists have long debated how that trade redistributes power between states. The former claim that free trade disproportionately favors the largest trading states, while the latter assert free trade typically favors rising powers.[21] Commercial liberals have argued that trade increases the expected costs of interstate conflict and thus mitigates the relative-gains pressures of anarchy. Some scholars find that growing trade interdependence, the spread of democracy, and international organizations combine to reduce interstate violence.[22] The interdependence literature draws the important distinction between sensitivity and vulnerability interdependence. "Sensitivity" interdependence refers to the speed with which policy changes affect interdependent states: "How quickly do changes in one country bring costly changes in another, and how great are the costly effects?"[23] By contrast, "vulnerability" interdependence refers to the costs to actors of foregoing an interdependent relationship. The term thus captures the availability and costliness of alternative relationships.[24] While interdependence and other theories are centrally concerned with trade, however, these theories typically disregard the actual infrastructure of trade that changes state interests or capacities. This observation suggests that mainstream IR theory offers little guidance on thinking about global networks.

Some globalization theorists have suggested that computational social science can help us understand how global processes may redistribute costs among nation-states. Several theorists have argued that complex system theory's interest in nonlinear dynamics may explain how small perturbations might "reverberate" or cause "cascading disruptions"—dynamics that researchers have noticed in other forms of globalization.[25] As Rosenau suggests, there is now a "widespread understanding that unexpected events are commonplace, that anomalies are normal occurrences, that minor incidents can mushroom into major outcomes."[26] Yet, while globalization scholars are interested in such effects, including "contagion," "the boomerang," and the metaphorical "butterfly effect," much of their discussion tends to be heuristic and metaphorical.[27] This chapter seeks to explore these dynamics methodically. Can one observe contagion and the butterfly effect on a simulated global network? The analysis here explores to what extent small perturbations, represented by various small disruptions in our simulations, produce major effects on national vulnerability.

The NRC report about the U.S. power grid is only the latest expression of policymakers' concerns with the vulnerability of networks.[28] However, to date studies of networks have ironically tended to ignore the properties of the networks themselves. Some have focused only on how attacks occurring on U.S. territory can affect American vulnerability.[29] Others have used methods of static analysis, essentially ignoring the possibility of interaction effects among components of a network.[30] This is odd precisely because networks take advantage of such interaction effects to generate economies of scale and exponential gains in efficiency. By contrast, a dynamic model of a transnational network can offer a more realistic view of potential nonlinear dynamics. It can also facilitate theory building about the impact of global networks on state vulnerability.[31]

At the broadest level, the analysis contributes to the debate among scholars who disagree about the impact of globalization on international politics. For instance, while some see it as generating positive effects such as decreased interstate war,[32] others see it as weakening states and making them vulnerable.[33] Cooley, for one, hypothesizes that "globalization increases the security threat posed by non-state actors by weakening the capacity" of states to cope with transnational actors, such as terrorist groups.[34] Similarly, Mueller argues that it constrains the autonomy of states, even of the American hegemon, and their freedom of action from outside forces.[35] By studying the U.S. air transportation network, the chapter's hypothesis testing can provide insights into whether, and to what extent, highly interconnected systems that constitute and enable economic globalization make nation-states more vulnerable.

METHODS OF ANALYZING NETWORK FAILURE

Prior research suggests that several properties of a network may affect its vulnerability to disruption. Early studies of network failure tended to use static analysis. By measuring a network's degree distribution, density, and the size and number of its components—that is, a subset of the graph in which any node can reach another through some existing path—researchers can compare the structure of a network before and after the removal of a given node. In effect, this method allows researchers to compare how different networks "break apart." One such study compared random accidental failures of a node (as might occur in a power grid, for example) and attacks that targeted hub nodes. It found that in random networks, random failures tend to break the network into more, smaller components. By contrast, scale-free networks tend to be more robust to random failures but less so to attacks.[36]

One problem with the static analysis of networks is that it tends to ignore several important features of networks, not the least of which is the volume of flows across edges. These flows may vary both across pairs of nodes as well as over time between any two given nodes. For example, trade flows between Mumbai and Mombasa probably are smaller than those between Shanghai and Los Angeles. Likewise, trade between Shanghai and Los Angeles follows seasonal variations, peaking in the fall to anticipate the rise in U.S. consumer spending each December. Hence, flows across nodes vary both within the network and over time. To capture these features, dynamic network analysis recently has examined how flows fluctuate through a network. Research has shown that the small world network structure allows for efficient, parallel transmission of information or resources, including the transmission of disruptions to other nodes. For example, one study found that small world social networks are particularly efficient at transmitting diseases.[37] Another method of analyzing dynamics is to create weighted network models, in which the edges between nodes are weighted by some measure of their traffic.[38] Many networks exhibit such heterogeneity across nodes and edges; transportation networks, information systems, and power grids all have edges with varying flows. Using Monte Carlo simulation, the study of weighted networks can estimate the probability of failures. Several recent studies have used weighted network models to assess network robustness in general,[39] in transportation networks,[40] and on the Internet and in power grids.[41]

It is useful to note that some complex global networks respond to geopolitical factors as well as technological and economic ones. For example, one study found that the global air transportation network exhibits a surprising feature: the most connected cities in the network are not necessarily those that are the most "central" to the network (in the sense that they are on the shortest path length between other airports).[42] One consequence of this structure is that the smaller nodes may act as a bridge between different communities within the network, much as Anchorage is a critical bridge to the Alaskan air transportation subnetwork. These smaller bridge nodes may play a disproportionately large role in dynamic processes, whether the transportation of passengers or computer parts, the spread of infectious diseases, or the contagion of cascading power outages.

Policymakers have expressed their concern about the robustness of global networks, not only because failures are costly but also because network vulnerabilities may lie elsewhere outside their jurisdiction. For example, Title X of the Implementing Recommendations of the 9/11 Commission Act of 2007 (which became P.L. 110-53 with President Bush's signature on August 3, 2007) calls for a national database on U.S. transportation assets whose loss "would have a negative or debilitating effect on the economic security, public health, or safety of the United States."[43] Similarly, the U.S. National Infrastructure Protection Plan raises the prospect that transportation disruptions could generate cascading failures in U.S. infrastructure.[44] Too often, however, policymakers have ignored the properties of networks that make these systems vulnerable. For example, a review of the Defense Critical Infrastructure Program Assessment Benchmarks for maritime transport focuses on physical security of specific ports, but does not address the networked characteristics that actually make the maritime shipping system vulnerable.[45]

One drawback of the analysis of weighted networks is that such models typically assume that the weights assigned to vertices or edges are constant. While this is a useful simplifying assumption, it is unrealistic: the demand for electricity is greater on hot days than moderate ones; the highways on Thanksgiving tend to be more crowded than on a Tuesday in October. For this reason, weighted network models may suffer from a lack of external validity. Another challenge for dynamic analysis is interaction effects among nodes: Which combinations of failed nodes produce a greater likelihood of network fragmentation? Agent-based modeling (ABM) offers a useful alternative method for analyzing these networks because weighted networks exhibit the properties of a complex adaptive system. Global networks typically have a large number of actors who interact repeatedly over time, and have cause-effect relationships that exhibit nonlinear relationships due to feedback, exponential growth, and interaction among parameters. Because failures in such global networks are, thankfully, rare, simulation methods allow for experimentation in the absence of good empirical data on failure events.[46]

To illustrate how complex networks may transmit costs among countries, this study uses data from the U.S. Department of Transportation's Bureau of Transportation Statistics to simulate the movement of people on international flights to and from the United States. The ABM also employs a genetic algorithm to identify "small" disruptions that produce cascading network failures. The algorithm identifies conditions under which disruptions elsewhere in the international network produce large economic losses to the United States.

DATA ABOUT THE U.S. AIR TRANSPORTATION NETWORK

The Bureau of Transportation Statistics (BTS) in the U.S. Department of Transportation collects monthly data on air transportation within the United States and between the U.S. and cities with direct service to American airports.[47] The data include not only the names of the origin and destination airports of each route but also the airlines servicing the route; the available seats; the number of passengers flown; the amount of freight and mail flown; the distance and air time; and the load factor (the ratio of passenger miles to available seat miles). It is important to note that the BTS data record charter as well as regularly scheduled flights, so there likely is some small variation in the network structure from month to month. Nevertheless, the data are a reasonably valid representation of the contemporary U.S. air transport network. The analysis uses the data for February 2011 to construct a weighted network using the origin and destination airports as nodes and the passengers flown as weights for the edges. Table 7.1 summarizes the

Table 7.1. Summary statistics of the U.S. air route network.

Measure	Value
Nodes	797
Edges	12,745
Density	0.0201
Average Total Degree	36.88
Median Total Degree	12
Power Law Exponent	1.434
Average Path Length	3.093
Clustering Coefficient	0.652

properties of the network. These data suggest the U.S. air transport network approximates the structure of a scale-free network. A number of airports in the dataset were "isolates," or had no scheduled or charter flights in February 2011. Several other city-pairs were "pendants"—that is, they were components unconnected to the rest of the network. After removing these, the network consists of 797 airports (nodes) and 12,745 "city pairs" or routes (edges). The average number of in- and out-routes (i.e. total degree) is 36.88; the median total degree of 12 suggests a skewed distribution that typifies a scale-free network. Figure 7.1 shows the log-log plot of the out degree distribution and is visually similar to the distribution of scale-free networks.

Researchers disagree about how best to determine whether empirical data scale according to a power law. I used the estimation technique proposed by Clauset, Shalizi, and Newman and found the U.S. air transport network's scaling exponent γ is approximately 1.43.[48] This estimate approximates the scaling exponent that other studies have found for the global air transportation network ($\gamma \approx 1$);[49] China's network ($\gamma \approx 1.7$);[50] and that of India ($\gamma \approx 2.2$).[51] Each of the studies concludes these networks

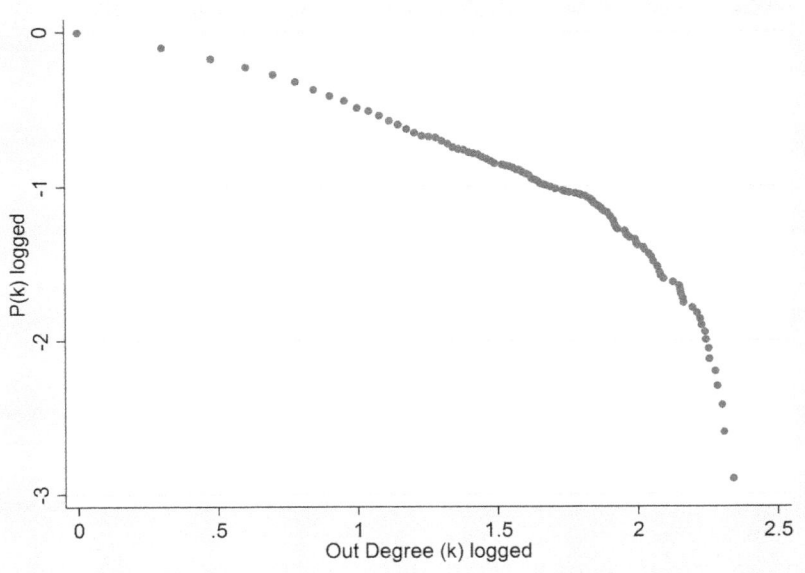

Figure 7.1. Log-log plot of the distribution of out degrees.

all exhibit scale-free properties. Similarly the BTS data suggests the U.S. air transportation network, along with its international city-pairs, also is a scale-free network.

THE MODEL AND GENETIC ALGORITHM

Using the BTS data, I created an agent-based model in which agents represent airports in the network. Each airport agent has a set of out-links to the destination airport agents recorded in the BTS dataset. Each link has a weight w equal to the daily number of passengers who transited that route. Because the BTS data is aggregated by month, the weight equals one twenty-eighth of the reported passengers on a given route in February 2011. The simulation gives each airport an initial endowment of passengers equal to the sum of the weights of its in-links. At each step in simulated time (the time step is equivalent to one day in the real world network) airports "send" a number of passengers to their network neighbors equal to the weight of each out-link. Airport agents keep track of the stock of passengers at each step in simulated time: the stock S is equal to the difference of the summed in-link weights and out-link weights: $S = \Sigma w_i - \Sigma w_o$. It is important to note that, in the simulation results presented here, the weights remain constant throughout the simulation. But there is no necessary reason for the ABM to have such a restriction. Indeed, one of the advantages of this method of network analysis is that one can easily reprogram the simulation so that weights vary stochastically according to a schedule (such as fluctuations in passenger volume weekly or seasonally) or by drawing from a known statistical distribution.

Each airport agent has a throughput capacity equal to 1.25 times the sum of its in-link weights. This is equivalent to assuming that each airport is operating at 80 percent of full capacity. This capacity parameter gives airport agents some ability to send excess passengers to its network neighbors in the event of a backlog—that is, each out-link from an airport has extra "seats" with which to move passengers if $\Delta S > 0$. The capacity parameter is comparable to the average load factor of routes in February 2011 (which was approximately 0.7). By assuming that airports are operating at less than capacity, the network should exhibit some ability to recover from a disruption, as airport agents not directly affected by a disruption can use excess capacity to move a backlog of passengers. Conversely, as the capacity constraint grows toward 100 percent, one expects backlogs will build. Although it would be interesting to simulate the effect of variations in capacity on network backlogs, to focus on disruptions the simulation keeps the capacity constraint constant across airport agents and across experiments. Table 7.2 presents the pseudo code for the ABM.

Table 7.2. Pseudo code for the air transportation network model

Initialization
    Create airport agents
        Endow with a neighborhood of other airports, based on BTS statistics
        Endow with a stock of passengers = sum of out-link weights
        Endow with a maximum capacity = 1.25 times sum of in-link weights
    Create link agents between airport neighbors
        Endow with a weight = sum of passengers on the route from BTS data

Execution
    Loop
        Disable airport(s) and incident links as indicated by genetic algorithm strategy
        Ask airport agents
            "Send passengers": set stock = stock − Σ out-link weights that are not disabled
            "Receive passengers":
                If stock < capacity
                      Set stock = stock + Σ in-link-weights that are not disabled
                Otherwise, set stock = capacity
        Measure system
            Overall and change in average stock of passengers per airport
            Overall backlog of passengers
            Overall and change in average stock of passengers per U.S. airport
            Overall backlog of passengers at U.S. airports
    End Loop

Genetic Algorithm
    Initialization
        Choose number n of airports to disrupt, with $1 \leq n \leq 5$
        Create a set of 50 strategies
            Randomly select set of n airports outside U.S.
            Randomly select an attack time t such that $t \sim U(60 \leq t < 90)$
    Run Execution once for each of 50 strategies = one generation
    Loop for 50 generations
        At the end of each generation, create 40 new strategies:
            Select the best strategies measured by
                (a) average passenger backlog for U.S. airports;
                (b) total U.S. passenger backlog / number of disabled links
            Cross selected strategies with $p = .75$
            With $p = .005$, replace an airport in the strategy with a randomly
                selected one
        Create a set of 10 new strategies, per initialization procedure
    End Loop

To examine how disruptions affect flows on the simulated network, the model uses a genetic algorithm (GA). For simulations characterized by both large numbers of parameter combinations and interaction effects, factorial designs can be quite time-consuming. In the analysis of large complex networks, factorial designs can be prohibitively slow, particularly when one wishes to account for interaction effects among nodes. For example, when Chicago O'Hare Airport is snowed in, there likely will be a considerable backlog in the network; but when both Chicago and Atlanta Hartsfield Airport are closed, the backlogs may be exponentially larger. To generalize the example, a factorial design that wished to identify an optimal combination of two airport nodes to remove would have to test 797 × 796 = 634,412 combinations. To study a three-node combination, the number of experiments grows to 5×10^8.

GAs can efficiently explore the modes of disruption. The algorithm acts as an "optimal terrorist" of sorts, exploring the system to discover which disruption strategies produce the largest backlog in the system. In each experiment, the GA optimizes against one of two fitness criteria: the average number of passengers backlogged at U.S. airports, and the total number of backlogged passengers in U.S. airports divided by the number of out-links disabled by the GA's disruption. It measures these criteria for ninety steps (simulated days) after a disruption. The former fitness criterion measures macrolevel effects across the entire network. The latter criterion, by contrast, encourages the GA to be efficient by finding the greatest backlog for the smallest attack—essentially a minimax strategy. In a sense, by penalizing the GA for picking the largest airports, this latter criterion is equivalent to looking to trigger a network avalanche, much as the shutdown of a power generation plant in suburban Cleveland triggered cascading failures in the Northeast power grid in 2003.

The GA starts with an initial set of fifty random strategies—a "strategy" is simply a list of airports to remove from the network (e.g., Tegucigalpa, Tokyo, Toronto). Because I am interested in how disruptions in geographically distant locations may affect the United States, the GA's strategies consist only of airports outside of the United States (there are 207 such airports in the BTS data). The model runs the simulation once for each strategy, disabling the airports as well as their in- and out-links. It then measures that strategy's performance using one of the two the fitness criteria. After testing all fifty initial strategies (a "generation") the GA uses a selection procedure to populate forty strategies for the next generation. In half of the experiments, the GA uses a simple tournament selection that compares the fitness of two randomly chosen strategies. In the other half, the GA uses a fitness proportionate selection rule, in which the probability of a strategy surviving to the next round is higher for better performing strategies. As the simulation evolves, the GA creates novel strategies in three ways. First, after every tournament selection the winning strategies cross over with a probability of .75. Second, at the end of every generation, after the algorithm selects its fittest strategies the GA mutates each allele on a fit strategy with a probability of .005. Finally, the selection tournament provides only forty fit strategies for subsequent generations. The remaining ten strategies are randomly generated ones, assuring that in each generation fit strategies compete against 20 percent new strategies. Figure 7.2 is a box plot of fitness by generation for one of the experiments; the hollow circles represent the median fitness for each generation. By the twenty-second generation, the GA has found an optimal strategy that survives and becomes the median strategy by the end of the experiment. The figure also clearly shows how the median value increases and the interquartile range grows with each passing generation. This is the value of a GA: it simultaneously improves strategies while exploring a range of alternative strategies.

An experiment consists of the GA testing fifty generations of fifty strategies each, for a total of 2,500 simulations per experiment. To test for interaction effects, the GA ran experiments in which it selected a single node; two nodes; and three nodes for removal. I conducted twelve total

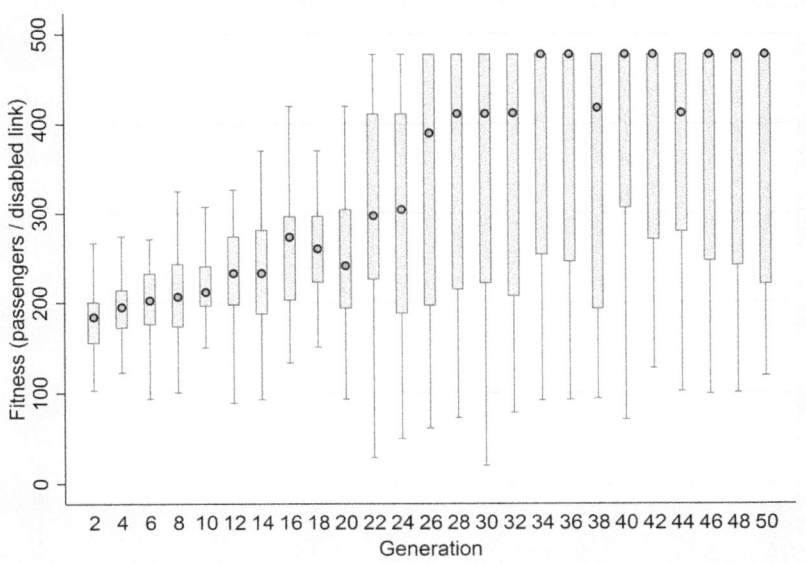

Figure 7.2. Box plot of strategy fitness by GA generation.

experiments: three types of strategy (one, two, or three airports attacked) × two fitness criteria (total backlog versus backlog / disabled node) × two selection rules (tournament versus fitness proportionate). For each experiment I recorded both the measures of network performance and the final generation of fifty strategies.

FINDINGS

Table 7.3 reports the frequency with which airport nodes appeared in the strategies of the final generation of the GA. Recall that each generation included fifty strategies, and that the twelve experiments varied disruption strategies from one airport to a combination of three airports. For this reason, the GA identifies an average of one hundred optimal airport nodes in each experiment's final generation, for a total of 1,200 selected nodes. For k successes in n trials with a probability of success of p, the binomial mass function is $p^k \times (1-p)^{(n-k)}$. Because the GA selects from only the 207 non-U.S. airports, $p = 1 \div 207 = .0048$. Thus, the probability the GA of randomly selects an airport thirteen times in 1,200 trials is about .006. Table 7.3(a) reports the airports the GA selected with a frequency that is significantly greater than random selection at $p < .01$; only eleven airports appear with a frequency greater than thirteen. Table 7.3(b) reports the selected airports for the total backlog criterion, while 7.3(c) lists the airports when the GA sought to optimize the total backlog per disabled link.

The results illustrate how the GA found airports that can disrupt flows in the air transport network even though they are not central to the network. The airport with the highest betweenness centrality (that is, the probability that the airport lies on the shortest path between all other vertices) is Toronto at .0045. This is an expected result: the BTS data reports only traffic to and from U.S. airports but not, for example, between Toronto and Vancouver. By construction, then, all non-U.S. airports in the simulation have low betweenness centrality. Nonetheless, the results also show how the GA selects relatively "small" airports in the network. Toronto has the greatest number of connections to the U.S. network with seventy-two out-links; Cancun has forty-three and Montego Bay twenty-six. Santiago, Mumbai, Brisbane, Birmingham, Abu Dhabi, and Santa Marta all have three or fewer out-links to the United States. In terms of flows, Toronto sent an average of about 12,000 passengers to the United States per day in February 2011, Tokyo sent about 10,000, and Cancun about 8,500. These are obviously rather small portions of the daily network flow of about 1.9 million passengers.

A comparison of tables 7.3(b) and 7.3(c) illustrates how the GA found different strategies when optimizing different criteria. To create the

Table 7.3. Results of the GA experiments.

Node		N	Percent
(a) All Experiments			
Tokyo (Narita)		193	16.08
Santiago, Chile		108	9.00
Toronto (Pearson)		74	6.17
Brisbane		48	4.00
Seoul (Inchon)		43	3.58
Birmingham, UK		38	3.17
Montego Bay		36	3.00
Abu Dhabi		34	2.83
Cancun		28	2.33
Mumbai		19	1.58
Santa Marta, Colombia		16	1.30
	Total	1200	100.00
(b) Criterion = Total Passenger Backlog			
Tokyo (Narita)		143	23.83
Toronto (Pearson)		74	12.33
Seoul (Inchon)		39	6.50
Montego Bay		36	6.00
Cancun		26	4.33
	Subtotal	600	100.00
(c) Criterion = Backlog per Disabled Link			
Santiago, Chile		108	18.00
Tokyo (Narita)		50	8.33
Brisbane		48	8.00
Birmingham, UK		37	6.17
Abu Dhabi		34	5.67
	Subtotal	600	100.00

greatest total backlog of passengers, the GA identified large foreign airports with both lots of connections to the United States and relatively large passenger flows. Tokyo's Narita Airport and Inchon Airport in Seoul are important gateways from Asia to North America. Likewise, Toronto serves as a bridge between the Canadian and American air transportation networks. Surprisingly, the GA selected no European airports to disrupt. Equally surprising is its selection of Montego Bay and Cancun. Because the model uses

BTS data from February 2011, the GA might be capturing winter travel to these vacation destinations. Yet their inclusion may also reveal some of the structural properties of the U.S. network. As Caribbean destinations, Cancun and Montego Bay form a cluster in the network because numerous large hubs in the United States are connected to both, including Atlanta, Dallas-Fort Worth, Newark, both New York airports, Chicago O'Hare, and Miami. Indeed, the two airports share twenty-three U.S. destinations. This suggests that, although individually the Cancun and Montego Bay airports are relatively small, the interaction effect of a simultaneous disruption creates congestion in major hub airports in the United States.

Table 7.3(c) shows the GA results when it optimized a minimax criterion: the most disruption for the least number of disabled links. The results illustrate that, although large airports can create sizeable disruptions to passenger flows, such disruptions are relatively "costly" in the sense that they require disabling many links. When measured on a per-link basis, smaller airports may have a greater impact. Santiago, Chile, is connected to only three U.S. airports; Brisbane and Abu Dhabi each are connected to only two. Yet because of the scale-free nature of the air transportation network, the hub structure allows relatively small nodes such as Santiago to introduce perturbations that the hub then transmits through the network.

Although table 7.3 presents the frequency with which the GA selects specific airports to disrupt, it does not summarize the frequency with which the GA selects specific strategies. In eight of the twelve experiments, the GA combined the disruption of two or three airports outside the United States. An examination of these strategies should indicate whether the GA identified interaction effects among airports. Table 7.4 reports the most frequently selected strategies, and reveals a few surprises. Although Tokyo and Montego Bay may be geographically distant, their passenger flows intersect at a number of hub airports, including Atlanta, Chicago O'Hare, Dallas-Fort Worth, and Los Angeles. These hubs also connect Seoul, Tokyo, and Toronto. More surprising is the strategy to disrupt both Aguascalientes, Mexico, and San Salvador. Though quite small, both Latin American airports feed traffic through Atlanta and Dallas-Fort Worth. Similarly, Toronto and Santa Marta, Colombia, are connected through Miami and JFK Airport in New York. All of these examples suggest that combinations of disruptions can produce nonlinear effects by pushing the passenger backlog of a U.S. hub airport above the capacity threshold.

Finally, it is interesting to note that although the combination of Brisbane and Santiago is the second most frequently selected strategy, they share no link neighbors. To fly from Brisbane to Santiago via the United States, a passenger would have to transit either LAX or JFK first, and then Miami, Atlanta, or Dallas-Fort Worth. The frequency with which the GA

Table 7.4. Most frequently selected strategy sets.

Strategy	N	Percent
Montego Bay, Tokyo	36	9.00
Brisbane, Santiago	34	8.50
Seoul, Tokyo, Toronto	32	8.00
Abu Dhabi, Birmingham, Santiago	29	7.25
Aguascalientes, San Salvador	10	2.50
Santa Marta, Toronto	10	2.50
Total	400	100.00

selected this strategy suggests the possibility of second-order interaction effects. By simultaneously disrupting Santiago and Brisbane, the GA may induce backlogs that build first in one U.S. hub airport and then in another. In this respect, hub airports can act as multipliers for disruptions, magnifying the cascades of backlogged passengers. Anyone who has faced a "weather" delayed flight on a sunny day is familiar with these second-order effects.

Although these findings are interesting, the simplifying assumptions of the simulation limit their generality. Foremost is the assumption that the U.S. air transportation system is a discrete network. Of course, it is merely a subnetwork of the global air transportation system. As the 2010 eruption of the Eyjafjallokull volcano in Iceland demonstrated, delays in the European subnetwork can reverberate in the United States. With data on both the structure of and traffic across the global air transportation network, the GA might identify other, more effective modes of disruption. Similarly, the simulation would benefit from finer-grained measures of the network's dynamics. The simulation presented here used daily passenger flows to affix constant weights to links in the network. Likewise, it assumes a constant capacity constraint across airports and across time. Although the BTS aggregates data by month, it may be possible to measure the variation in passenger flows among airports in the system. Such data would allow the model to simulate daily and seasonal variations in passenger traffic, and by extension the variation in capacity constraints at airports. With such a refinement, the GA could search not only for optimal disruptions but also for an optimal time at and sequence with which to disrupt the airports. It is likely that the sequence and timing of disruptions is just as important as the nodes the GA disrupts.

What are the financial costs to nation-states of the disruptions identified by the GA? The results above do not quantify the backlog as a percentage of total throughput in the system, nor do they estimate the financial costs of such delays. It may be, for example, that although the GA has identified simultaneous disruptions of Brisbane and Santiago as an optimal disruption strategy, this may create backlogs of only a few hundred passengers per day. A more realistic simulation would measure the financial costs of disruptions. After all, airlines and regulators ultimately are more concerned about financial losses than the number of individuals who are inconvenienced. These costs may be considerable. The Air Transport Association estimates that in 2011, a one-minute delay of a flight produces about $75 in direct costs to airlines plus another $0.65 in opportunity costs to passengers.[52] To quantify this in terms of the simulation results presented above, one experiment in which the GA disabled Seoul, Tokyo, and Toronto produced about 39,400 passenger delay days (i.e., one passenger delayed one day) or a daily average of about 438 passengers. The costs to passengers alone would be about $410,000 per day. Using data like these, the GA could select among the most costly strategies rather than merely those that affect flows the most.

Finally, in the real world networks are adaptive. Although asset specificity and capital costs may limit the short-term adaptation of networks such as energy grids, other networks may be much more adaptive, including transportation networks. In this respect, the simulation would benefit from "smart" airport agents. In the current implementation of the simulation, an airport agent simply moves its passenger backlog to all its network neighbors—in effect, it assumes passengers are homogeneous when, in the real world, they differ in their destinations. Obviously, this implementation is unrealistic: Chicago O'Hare cannot reroute a Des Moines passenger through Columbus because that passenger probably will end up back in Chicago. One useful extension of the model would be to endow airports with evolutionary learning as well, so that they can dynamically evolve strategies for dispensing with passenger backlogs. In effect, airport agents would coevolve strategies with the disruption strategies created by the optimal terrorist GA.

CONCLUSIONS

Complex global networks behave in surprising ways. When such networks span the borders of nation-states—and many utility, information, and transportation networks do—they may produce unintended costs that governments cannot control. While the static analysis of the structural properties of such networks can reveal subgraphs, bridging nodes, and other critical features, it tends to overlook dynamic flows through the network. To understand cascading failures, researchers can turn to computational social science. Because many global complex weighted networks have evolved in response to market demands, furthermore, they have developed scale-free properties that are highly efficient for moving information, people, and goods, but that may not be very robust in the face of disruptions. For this reason, researchers and policymakers alike need methods to analyze how complex weighted networks respond to disruptions. Using the U.S. air transportation system as an example, this chapter illustrates how researchers can simulate differing failure modes for global networks. By focusing on disruptions at non-U.S. airports, the analysis demonstrates how disruptions may interrupt flows at points in the network that are geographically distant. This is not only costly to individual, firms, and governments, but it also demonstrates that individual governments cannot manage network effects on their own. The United States air transportation network relies upon efficient networks in Europe and Asia, just as those regions depend upon safe and efficient transportation in the United States. In the absence of international coordination in the management and security of complex networks, nasty surprises will inevitably occur. The concluding chapter turns to the question of whether and how theorists and policymakers alike can understand the myriad surprises of world politics today.

EIGHT

CONCLUSIONS

Self-Organization in World Politics

Although complexity and self-organization are ubiquitous in world politics today, scholars have largely ignored this reality. Of course, the observation that the world is "complex," surprising, and unpredictable is hardly novel.[1] This awareness of the complexity of world politics has failed, however, to produce a meaningful research agenda for two reasons. One is that we have failed to recognize homologous processes—positive and negative feedback, massively parallel interactions, reinforcement and evolutionary learning, path dependence, and others—that occur in many domains of world politics, from financial crises and resource depletion to civil conflict and revolutionary cascades. This failure arises in part from the reductive methods in social sciences, and in part from the organization of scientific inquiry into disciplines and subfields. The research program on global complexity is deficient for another reason: we tend to assume that the outcomes of collective action are independent of the spatial and temporal patterns of interaction. In fact, the networked structure of social relations—among banks, firms, transportation hubs, negotiators, elites, activists, and myriad others—can give rise to unexpected forms of self-organization that may become locked in and resistant to change. The goal of this book is to elucidate how similar mechanisms produce self-organization at all scales of world politics, from neighborhoods and fishing villages to intergovernmental organizations and global trade. Such "scale invariance"—the fractal-like similarity of organization across scales of politics—is itself a product of complex social systems.

To investigate self-organization in world politics, computational methods are invaluable tools. Ideas from complex systems theory, evolutionary computation, and network theory can help us think about three important questions about world politics: How do actors in world politics learn and adapt? How do they construct social structures that both create opportunities for some and restrict possibilities for others? What do these processes tell us about the changes wrought by globalization, their durability, and their permanence? Informing these questions is an implied criticism of theories of world politics. The field's reliance on hierarchical levels of analysis emphasizing individuals, state institutions, and the anarchic structure of world politics—with an implied focus on stability—is insufficient. Such an ontological ordering of our theories tends to obscure important interactions across the levels of analysis. Our reliance on these levels challenges us to make inferences about individuals using aggregate data, or conversely to infer structural properties from the attributes and behaviors of individual actors. Although this criticism of the levels Waltz famously labeled man, the state, and war is hardly new, today social scientists have a range of new tools that allow us to analyze the interactions across levels.[2] The methods of computational social science introduce a formalization and rigor that heretofore we have not had. Computational social science thus offers a new way of conceptualizing, testing, and understanding hypotheses about structuration, learning, and change in world politics.

To appreciate the importance of interaction effects across levels of analysis, the student of world politics need look no farther than the dinner plate that greets her at the end of the day. Twice since 2007, global food prices have spiked, particularly for grains that are an important staple of most people's diet. The drivers of the "food crisis" are myriad, including changes in diet and demand from the growing middle class in India and China, and the recurrent droughts in grain-producing regions including the Midwest of the United States. Yet the rise in food prices is a story of unintended effects—of the micro decisions that produce worldwide changes no one necessarily intended. In 2011, the National Academy of Sciences reviewed a range of scholarship on the relationship between grain prices and biofuels technologies that the U.S. government has subsidized. The NAS concluded that 20 to 40 percent of the rise in global food prices was due to grains being diverted for use in biofuels.[3] Because the world's poor spend a higher proportion of their income on food, they bear a disproportionate burden of these U.S. energy subsidies, with more of the world's poor now "food insecure" than prior to the rise in prices in the mid-2000s.[4] Yet the consequences of biofuels extend beyond their impact on individuals. Developing states that import grains face growing trade deficits they can finance only by cutting spending on the social services on which the poor rely. Growing food insecurity has in turn fueled social unrest, most notably in Egypt:

> When prices skyrocketed even higher late last year [in 2010], Mubarak and rulers like him responded the way they always had, by announcing a panicked round of handouts. This time it didn't work: Rioters rejected the arrangement and demanded regime change, nor just a quick meal. The dictators had failed to understand . . . that food is not only something to eat, but a symbol of something larger—freedom, justice, security, call it what you will. In the end, it's about much more than bread.[5]

Egypt's protesters had learned the lessons of Tunisia's uprising in January 2011, and in turn inspired protests in Libya, Yemen, Syria, and Bahrain. This unrest in the Middle East subsequently contributed to instability in global oil prices as speculators hedged against possible interruptions in supply through the Persian Gulf. Thus, in a half-decade, a global feedback loop closed itself: U.S. concerns about affordable energy triggered the revolutions across North Africa and the Middle East that raised energy prices. The unintended consequences of biofuels demonstrate, furthermore, why students of world politics need to understand interactions across issues and across levels. A small change in U.S. energy policy triggered learning and adaptation among citizens across the Arab world. The contagion of the revolutions contributed to pervasive crises of authority that have fundamentally restructured the Middle East. Biofuel subsidies tell the story of learning, adaptation, agents and structures, and change in world politics.

LEARNING AND ADAPTATION

Whether individuals, policymakers, firms, nongovernmental organizations, or sovereign states, actors in world politics learn and adapt in ways that make the world dynamic and unpredictable. In situations "in which people's behavior or people's choices depend on the behavior or the choices of other people, [and] that usually don't permit any simply summation or extrapolation to the aggregates," actors face a problem of information: What do others prefer? As Jervis notes, such strategic thinking entails "consciously react[ing] to others and anticipat[ing] what they think others will do."[6] As chapter 3 illustrated, one consequence of this strategic learning is preference cycles in which individual preferences remain relatively constant but aggregate into intransitive social choices that are inherently unstable and unpredictable.

While learning and adaptation may give rise to social conflict, however, it may also give rise to important forms of cooperation. Actors often deliberately "use reason and persuasion in their efforts to devise better rules" to govern collective action problems.[7] They may also identify opportunities for Pareto-improving joint actions. Chapter 4's analysis of distributive games illustrates how repeated interaction allows actors to learn about each other's preferences. Beyond the importance of iteration, furthermore, the analysis in chapters 4 and 5 demonstrated the importance of mimesis—of actors adopting the strategies of others. The simulations of distributive games and of common pool resources showed how agents may adopt the best strategies and discard ineffective ones. One consequence of mimetic learning is that actors in world politics identify evolutionary "niches" in which to thrive. For example, Chinese fans of rock music have found creative ways to criticize the Communist Party: "Even if the authorities still insist on approving lineups in advance, rejections are infrequent, organizers say, partly because more musicians perform in English, which can challenge all but the most learned censors."[8] As in natural ecosystems, in world politics actors may collaborate to shared advantage even as their beliefs and apparent interests diverge. For example, in Germany Jewish, Christian, and Muslim groups joined together to protest a court's ruling that circumcision violates the rights of the child. Together, religious communities viewed the decision as "an attack by secular society on religious ritual, on faith itself."[9]

One consequence of such learning and adaptation is that actors increasingly provide collective goods without resort to the compulsory authority of the nation-state. Chapter 5 illustrated how simulated harvesters devised strategies and rules that allowed them to preserve fisheries, even without the capacity to enforce bargains or punish each other with tit-for-tat-style strategies of retaliation. This decentralized form of governance, so different from the bureaucratized and hierarchical state, characterizes the recent global emergence of parallel structures of governance and production.[10] For example, one estimate suggests that the global "self-reliance" or informal economy of gray-market products—those products that are legal products, but the consumption of which governments do not tax or otherwise regulate—may be worth around $10 trillion per year.[11] By 2020, nearly two out of every three jobs in the world will be in this unregulated, untaxed, and ungoverned economy.[12] To understand global governance as whole, then, we must understand how actors learn to solve collective action problems in the absence of enforceable agreements. As the chapters in this book have shown, both social networks and actors' learning, adaption, and mimesis affect whether groups succeed in providing the collective goods that governments today seem incapable of providing.

AGENTS AND STRUCTURES

The informal economy is but one example of an emergent global system beyond the control of sovereign states. As actors learn and adapt, they induce positive feedback mechanisms that intensify the process of creating such structures. The result is a form of globalization that no one intends and that seems ungovernable, what Giddens called a juggernaut: "a runaway engine of enormous power which, collectively as human beings, we can drive to some extent but which also threatens to rush out of our control and which could rend itself asunder."[13] Some of these self-reinforcing structures are productive and socially beneficial, including the agglomeration of industries in specific geographic locations such as Bollywood in Mumbai, Silicon Valley in California, or an emerging "iHub" in Nairobi.[14] For every virtuous circle of endogenous economic growth, however, one can find a vicious cycle. Across the U.S.-Mexico border, recursive flows of northbound narcotics and southbound guns produce an intensifying structure of violence that resists coordinated policing efforts across the border. Drug cartels offer another example of structuration in world politics. They have used the same global business strategies as licit industries, including diversifying into human trafficking, partnering with other producers of illicit goods, and using global financial services to launder and repatriate their revenues.[15] The result is a set of business relationships that states cannot easily disentangle from their legitimate businesses. The global illicit economy as a whole shows how the actions of individuals produce structures that grow, intensify, and become locked in. Because crime retards development, societies plagued by illicit activities suffer from both a lack of investment and from lost tax revenues. Yet the lack of development creates the persistent poverty that drives individuals into the illicit economy, closing the vicious cycle. The incentives are perfectly perverse, and defy interventions by governments. As Giddens suggested, as human beings we can only hope to shape these processes, which threaten to spin out of control.

Chapters 4 and 6 showed how social systems may create structures that resist change. The analysis of the intrabank lending networks demonstrated how market relationships in Germany afford some banks bargaining power that is disproportionate to their size. Although social scientists have long understood how minority interests may predominate in collective choices, the analysis of U.S. and German banking networks illustrated how market relationships themselves may shape the processes of aggregating social preferences, irrespective of the advantages of group size. The ABM in chapter 4 illustrated, furthermore, how "noise" can play an important role in creating social structures. When playing the rules of the road game, for example, players with shorter memories scored higher than players who possessed a memory of past play and constantly evolved strategies. Paradoxically, social actors with more information may actually overcompensate to the point that actors continually tip the group away from Pareto-improving solutions. The study of common pool resources in chapter 6 found a similar effect of noise on group performance. One important role of social networks, then, is to mediate the information that actors receive about others' preferences. Some network structures—particularly scale-free forms characterized by actors who are information hubs—allow actors to escape the trap of mutual interference. Together, these findings illustrate how collective action problems in world politics exhibit tipping dynamics. Because social choices tend to evolve toward stable equilibria, many forms of social interaction in world politics become institutionalized through repeated interactions. That is, they become structures resistant to change, whether that is the concentration of production in industrial hubs or an intensifying drug war on Mexico's northern border.

One illustrative example of such robust structuration is Italy's continued problems with tax evasion. When Chinese immigrants gradually entered the lower end of Italy's fashion industry, they started repatriating their profits to China, nearly $1.5 million per day by one estimate. "What seems to gall some Italians most," *The New York Times* observed, "is that the Chinese are beating them at their own game—tax evasion and brilliant ways of navigating Italy's notoriously complex bureaucracy."[16] By refining the practices of local merchants and taking advantage of global financial flows, Chinese immigrants have reproduced and intensified Italy's institutionalized tax evasion. Such widespread disregard of state authority finds expression in the most surprising places. Although the Iranian government prohibits satellite television dishes, for example, as many as half the households in Tehran own them.[17] In general, actors in world politics produce structures that challenge the authority of the nation-state. These structures may be socially beneficial like the International Committee to Ban Land Mines; socially harmful, like the global drug trade; or somewhere in between, like the informal economy. In all cases, however, social actors organized into massively parallel networks of exchange and communication that contrast with and may challenge the centralized, bureaucratized authority of the nation-state.

CHANGE IN WORLD POLITICS

Gilpin offers a useful typology of change in world politics.[18] Regular exchanges, processes, and flows among actors in world politics is simply "interaction" change. Examples include changing balances of trade, shifts in military alliances, and the distribution of foreign aid through international organizations. "Systemic" change is a "change in the form of control or governance of an international system."[19] "Systems" change is the most fundamental form, involving a change in the nature of the actors constituting world politics and in the rules, orders, or principles that govern their interactions. Many globalization theorists argue that the technological, financial, ideational, media, and demographic flows that reorganize social relations on a transplanetary scale indeed are causing a systems change, engendering a parallel world of heterogeneous actors who sometimes complement, and sometimes challenge, the authority of sovereign nation-states.[20] To Gilpin's types of change, one could add a dialectic conception of change in world politics. In a Hegelian sense, change represents the synthesis of opposing social forces in which the nation-state is only one element. Because these forces emerge, build, and interact over time, change is not a linear or incremental process, but rather one characterized by the sudden, dramatic reordering of institutions.[21] The dialectic conception of change in world politics emphasizes moments of crisis and discontinuity, much as the concept from evolutionary biology of punctuated equilibrium emphasizes moments of sudden change in the forms and anatomical structures of species. Computational social science offers students of world politics a set of tools to understand each of these types of change, but the focus here is on the emergence of the new actors, rules, and principles that are reorganizing world politics.

One need only review changes in the global organization of production and finance to have some sense of the emergence of new actors and rules. Even as global flows of money vastly exceed the value of trade of goods and services, the global financial crisis has spurred changes worldwide in how communities think about money. In the developing world, people have created informal financial institutions to supplement ineffective national and international banks. For many of the world's poor, the ubiquitous mobile phone is more than a means of communication. It also is a savings account. Telecommunications firms in Kenya now hold deposits that subscribers can access from their phones. In earthquake-devastated Haiti in 2010, the Mercy Corps, a U.S.-financed relief and development organization, distributed cash once a month to Haitians' mobile phones for recipients to use at local merchants.[22] Even in the world's wealthiest economies, innovative communities are reconfiguring the relationship between states and markets. The citizens of Oberhausen, Germany, for example, have addressed the problem of insufficient liquidity by creating their own currency, the "coal." Locals can earn coals through voluntary work and use them to redeem goods and services from local merchants. The local group that organized the coal economy received inspiration from Conjunto Palmeiras in Brazil, which has used its own local currency for more than a decade. Residents of Berkshire County, Massachusetts, likewise have devised a local currency.[23] In each case, communities have found ways to create liquidity when national governments have chosen not to. Arguably, these parallel institutions of economic governance are more than simply a convenience. Increasingly, governments and citizens alike come to rely on the public goods they provide. These shared expectations institutionalize these practices and rules. In other words, the practices become an accepted, taken-for-granted part of peoples' lives. This durable social fact contributes to the bifurcation of structures of governance in world politics.

Computational social science also alerts students of world politics to the potential for the sudden, dramatic changes in world politics that dialectics emphasize. Though we cannot predict precisely when and where such events will occur, as with earthquakes we can observe the building forces and anticipate, however imprecisely, imminent moments of disjuncture. For example, one can foresee several potential tipping points in the Eurozone crisis that would dramatically restructure the European Union, if indeed it would survive such a regime shift. While Greece's exit from the currency union might limit the EU's financial obligations as well as expedite Greece's resolution of its balance of trade deficit, such an exit would dramatically increase the borrowing costs for Spain and Italy because investors would consider their sovereign default more likely. Increased borrowing costs in turn would require Spain and Italy to reduce government spending yet again, a painful choice in economies that already suffer from high unemployment. The positive feedback cycle is cruelly counterproductive: austerity reduces macroeconomic output, depressing tax revenues, and increasing the likelihood of default. Yet the threat of sovereign default drives up bond yields and requires more austerity, starting the cycle anew. Perhaps it is unsurprising, then, that some leaders of Catalonia have called for "fiscal sovereignty" from the Spanish central government.[24] Beyond the obvious economic consequences of such an outcome, Catalonia's push for autonomy could feed separatist sentiment in the Basque region as well as in other national communities elsewhere in the European Union. These self-reinforcing mechanisms intensify the crisis in the EU to the point that, in Giddens's words, events may rush out of the control of leaders. Such cascades could rend irreparably the institutions of both the EU and its constituent nation-states. Whether this is systemic change (in the form of control or governance of Europe) or systems change (a shift in the nature and types of actors in world politics) depends in large part on the actors' learning and the processes of structuration.

By definition, such sudden changes in institutions, practices, rules, and actors are rare. One of the advantages of computational social science is that its simulation methods can supplement empirical methods when rare events produce scarce useable data. Chapter 7 illustrated how one can study the infrequent but nonetheless important breakdown of international networks. Chapter 5's examination of common pool resources allowed the harvesting agents to suffer the collapse of their simulated ecosystem many times in order to learn the practices and identify the relationships that sustain the ecosystem. In general, when empirical observations may question conventional assumptions (such as whether people are rational utility-maximizers), simulation methods can help researchers evaluate competing explanations for these surprising empirical findings.[25]

THEORIZING WITHOUT THEORY

Computational social science does not offer a theory of world politics (or for that matter, a theory of microeconomics or for any other social science discipline). It does not specify important research questions or derive hypotheses. It is silent on the question of who the relevant actors are. Yet, like rational choice theory before it, computational social science offers the student of world politics a set of concepts and methods of inquiry with which to examine global dynamics, a way of theorizing without becoming beholden to existing theories. By calling attention to the social phenomenon of emergence, complex systems theory can help us understand the behaviors that actors use to build social structures. Network theory can help us formally examine the interdependencies of actor preferences and interests, reminding us that people do not exist in an abstract space. Rather, they think and behave based on cues they receive from family, neighbors, colleagues, and even strangers they may meet at a public protest. At a minimum, by formalizing our assumptions about social network structure, we can examine how sensitive our findings are to differing assumptions. Evolutionary computation reminds us to think of actor learning as a continuous process. Actors in world politics do not necessarily learn in a discrete fashion, switching from "ignorant" to "knowledgeable" in an instant. Rather, actors constantly adapt and coevolve with each other, such that each continuously exists along a continuum between ignorant and knowledgeable. To understand a range of questions in world politics, from the Arab Spring to the collapse of fisheries, we need to conceive of actor learning as an iterative, ongoing process. Like rational choice theory, computational social science complements rather than substitutes for existing theories of world politics. Computational social science diverges from rational choice, however, on the question of how to think about the relationship between behavior and interests. While rational choice theorists make assumptions about interests to infer actors' behaviors, the computational social scientist makes assumptions about actors' behavior in order to study the process of learning and the emergence of interests.

That computational social science is not a theory of world politics is, I think, one reason to commend it. For one, because the field evolved from developments in a range of fields including economics, physics, biology, and computer science, it is intrinsically capable of assessing interaction affects that cross the boundaries of academic disciplines, such as climate change and food scarcity. For another, our traditional emphasis on the nation-state arguably makes us insensitive to the heterogeneity of actor types that typify world politics. The very language of the "nonstate" actors by contradistinction affords conceptual primacy to the nation-state, even if such pride of place may not be appropriate for some questions in world politics. This habit of theorists is, in Kuhn's sense, "normal" social science because theorists take new actors and incorporate them within the existing paradigm of state-centric theories.[26] By contrast, from its origins computational social science has embraced actor heterogeneity. It seeks to understand how different actor types may interact to produce social structures. Finally, the very nature of computational social science offers "a disciplined openness both to reaffirming established concepts where appropriate and to replacing them with new formulations where necessary."[27] In this time of adaptation and change in world politics, the observer can reaffirm and replace concepts only if our scholarship is equally adaptive. The complex system we call social science is up to the task.

NOTES

CHAPTER ONE. THE GYRE

1. Lindsey Hoshaw, "Afloat in the Ocean, Expanding Islands of Trash," *The New York Times*, Nov. 10, 2009, D2.
2. Thomas M. Kostingen, "The World's Largest Dump: The Great Pacific Garbage Patch," *Discover*, July 2008.
3. Ibid.
4. Ibid.
5. Garrett Hardin, "The Tragedy of the Commons," *Science*, Dec. 13, 1968, 1243–48.
6. Melanie Mitchell, *Complexity: A Guided Tour* (New York: Oxford University Press, 2010), 94–111.
7. Amy R. Poteete, Marco A. Janssen, and Elinor Ostrom, *Working Together: Collective Action, the Commons, and Multiple Methods in Practice* (Princeton: Princeton University Press, 2010), 58.
8. Robert Axelrod, *The Complexity of Cooperation: Agent-Based Models of Computation and Collaboration* (Princeton: Princeton University Press, 1997); Lars-Erik Cederman, *Emergent Actors in World Politics* (Princeton: Princeton University Press, 1997); and Robert Jervis, *System Effects: Complexity in Political and Social Life* (Princeton: Princeton University Press, 1997). See also James N. Rosenau, *Distant Proximities: Dynamics beyond Globalization* (Princeton: Princeton University Press, 2003), ch. 9.
9. Ian S. Lustick, Dan Miodwonik, and Roy J. Eidelson, "Secessionism in Multicultural States: Does Sharing Power Prevent or Encourage It?" *American Political Science Review* 98, no. 2 (May 2004): 211.
10. James Pethica, ed., *Yeats's Poetry, Drama, and Prose: Authoritative Texts, Contexts, Criticisms* (New York: W. W. Norton, 2000), 76.
11. Jack Snyder, "Civil-Military Relations and the Cult of the Offensive, 1914 and 1984," *International Security* 9, no. 1 (Summer 1984): 108–46; Stephen Van Evera, "The Cult of the Offensive and the Origins of the First World War," *International Security* 9, no. 1 (Summer 1984): 58–107.
12. Barbara Tuchman, *The Guns of August* (New York: Ballantine, 1994); and Jack S. Levy, "Organizational Routines and the Causes of War," *International Studies Quarterly* 30, no. 2 (June 1986): 193–222. For criticisms of these arguments,

see Scott D. Sagan, "1914. Revisited: Allies, Offense, and Instability," *International Security* 11, no. 2 (Fall 1986): 151–75; and Marc Trachtenberg, "The Meaning of Mobilization in 1914," *International Security* 15, no. 3 (Winter 1990/91): 120–50.

13. Jack S. Levy, "Preferences, Constraints, and Choices in July 1914," *International Security* 15, no. 3 (Winter 1990/91): 151–86.

14. James N. Rosenau, *Turbulence in World Politics: A Theory of Change and Continuity* (Princeton: Princeton University Press, 1990), 27.

15. Ibid.

16. For example, social psychologist Howard Levanthal studied Yale University students' attitudes toward tetanus inoculations. He found that students who received a booklet with a map to the campus health clinic and a schedule of times when free shots were available were significantly more likely to get vaccinations than students who did not have a map to the clinic. For a brief discussion, see Malcolm Gladwell, *The Tipping Point: How Little Things Can Make a Big Difference* (New York: Little, Brown, 2002), 96–98.

17. "A Doctor in Your Pocket," *The Economist*, April 16, 2009.

18. Anand Giridharadas, "Africa's Gift to Silicon Valley: How to Track a Crisis," *The New York Times*, March 14, 2010, WK3.

19. Ibid.

20. "After the Fall," *The Economist*, November 13, 2008. See also Felix Salmon and David A. Johnson, "A Formula for Disaster," *Wired* 17, no. 3 (March 2009): 74.

21. "Marching off to Cyberwar," *The Economist*, Dec. 4, 2008.

22. Demetri Sevastopoulo, "Chinese Hack into White House Network," *Financial Times*, Nov. 6, 2008.

23. Nazila Fathi, "Iran's Opposition Seeks More Help in Cyberwar with Government," *The New York Times*, March 18, 2010.

24. Tom A. Peter, "Cyber Spy Network with Global Reach Raises Alarms," *Christian Science Monitor*, March 29, 2009; John Markoff, "Vast Spy System Loots Computers in 103 Countries," *New York Times*, March 29, 2009.

25. "Battle Is Joined," *The Economist*, April 23, 2009.

26. Mark Mazzetti, "Senators Warned of Terrorist Attack on U.S. by July," *The New York Times*, Feb. 3, 2010; Christopher Beam, "Cyberspace Invaders: Is a Cyber-Attack an Act of War?" Slate.com, Nov. 7, 2008, accessed Aug. 11, 2010, http://www.slate.com/id/2204123/; "Battle Is Joined"; "Marching off to Cyberwar."

27. Jon Cohen, "Employers Advised on Swine Flu; Local Colleges Making Plans," *Washington Post*, Aug. 19, 2009, A06.

28. Joshua M. Epstein, "Modelling to Contain Pandemics," *Nature*, Aug. 6, 2009, 687.

29. Ibid.

30. For a good discussion of this point, see Jan Aart Scholte, *Globalization: A Critical Introduction*, 2nd ed. (New York: Palgrave MacMillan, 2005), 59–64.

31. Ibid, ch. 6.

32. Kenneth Waltz, *Man, The State, and War* (New York: Columbia University Press, 1954). See also Patrick Thaddeus Jackson and Daniel Nexon, "Globalization, the Comparative Method, and Comparing Constructions," in *Constructivism*

and Comparative Politics, ed. Daniel M. Green (Armonk, NY: M. E. Sharpe, 2002), 88–120.

33. Mitchell, *Complexity*, 13.
34. Jervis, *System Effects: Complexity in Political and Social Life*, 6.
35. Ibid.
36. For a good introduction to these ideas, see Steven Johnson, *Emergence: The Connected Lives of Ants, Brains, Cities, and Software* (New York: Scribner, 2001).
37. John H. Miller and Scott Page, *Complex Adaptive Systems: An Introduction to Computational Models of Social Life* (Princeton: Princeton University Press, 2007), 10.
38. David Knoke and Song Yang, *Social Network Analysis: Second Edition* (Los Angeles: Sage, 2008).
39. A. S. Klovdahl et al., "Social Networks and Infectious Disease: The Colorado Springs Study," *Social Science & Medicine* 38, no. 1 (Jan. 1994): 79–88. Malcolm Gladwell offers an accessible discussion of this study as well as how social networks communicated syphilis in Baltimore; see *The Tipping Point*, ch. 1.
40. Gerald F. Davis et al., "The Small World of the American Corporate Elite, 1982–2001," *Strategic Organization* 1, no. 3 (Aug. 2003): 301–26.
41. Michael Jensen, "The Role of Network Resources in Market Entry: Commercial Banks' Entry into Investment Banking, 1991–1997," *Administrative Science Quarterly* 48, no. 3 (Sept. 2003): 466–97.
42. Uwe Cantner and Holger Graf, "The Network of Innovators in Jena: An Application of Social Network Analysis," *Research Policy* 35, no. 4 (May 2006): 463–80.
43. Spencer Moore et al., "International NGOs and the Role of Network Centrality in Humanitarian Aid Operations: A Case Study of Coordination during the 2000 Mozambique Floods," *Disasters* 27, no. 4 (Dec. 2003): 305–18.
44. Michelle A. Benson, "Dyadic Hostility and the Ties That Bind: State-to-State versus State-to-System Security and Economic Relationships," *Journal of Peace Research* 41, no. 6 (Nov. 2004): 659–76.
45. Knoke and Yang 2008, 6.
46. Ibid.
47. Mancur Olson, *The Logic of Collective Action: Public Goods and the Theory of Groups* (Cambridge: Harvard University Press, 1971).
48. Rosenau, *Distant Proximities*; and Margaret E. Keck and Kathryn Sikkink, *Activists beyond Borders: Advocacy Networks in International Politics* (Ithaca: Cornell University Press, 1998), 1.
49. Ronnie Lipschutz, "Reconstructing World Politics: The Emergence of Global Civil Society," *Millennium: Journal of International Studies* 21, no. 3 (1992): 390.
50. Keck and Sikkink, *Activists beyond Borders*.
51. Toshiyuki Nakagaki et al., "Maze-Solving by an Amoeboid Organism," *Nature*, Sept. 28, 2000, 470.
52. Cecile Rohwedder, "Deep in the Forest, Bambi Remains The Cold War's Last Prisoner," *The Wall Street Journal*, Nov. 4, 2009.

53. Rosenau, for one, argues "What is needed is a model organized around the central premise in which the form and direction of micro action is conceived to spring from a combination of habits that perpetuate continuity and orientations that allow for thoughtful estimates and are open to change." *Turbulence in World Politics*, 228.

54. John R. Alford, Carolyn L. Funk and John R. Hibbing, "Are Political Orientations Genetically Transmitted?" *American Political Science Review* 99, no. 2 (June 2005): 153–67; Nicos Nicolau et al., "Is the Tendency to Engage in Entrepreneurship Genetic?" *Management Science* 54, no. 1 (Jan. 2008): 167–79.

55. Thomas R. Frieden et al., "The Emergence of Drug-Resistant Tuberculosis in New York City," *The New England Journal of Medicine* 328, no. 8 (Feb. 25, 1993): 521–26.

56. Jensen, "The Role of Network Resources."

57. Gladwell (2002) provides one example: "In the mid-1990s . . . in the pool halls and roller skating-rinks of East St. Louis, Missouri, there was a man named Darrell 'Boss Man' McGee. He was big—over six feet—and charming, a talented skater, who wowed young girls with his exploits on the rink. . . . Between 1995 and 1997, when he was shot dead by an unknown assailant, he slept with at least 100 women and—it turned out later—infected at least 30 of them with HIV." Gladwell, *The Tipping Point*, 20.

58. Paul R. Milgrom, Douglas C. North, and Barry R. Weingast, "The Role of Institutions in the Revival of Trade: The Law Merchant, Private Judges, and the Champagne Fairs," *Economics and Politics* 2, no. 1 (March 1990): 1–23.

59. Ian Urbina, "Views of 'JihadJane' Were Unknown to Neighbors," *The New York Times*, March 10, 2010.

60. John Seigenthaler, "A False Wikipedia 'Biography,'" *USA Today*, Nov. 29, 2005.

61. Jim Giles, "Internet Encyclopaedias Go Head to Head," *Nature*, Dec. 15, 2005, 900–901.

62. Ibid.

63. See "John Seigenthaler," Wikipedia, accessed June 20, 2014, http://en.wikipedia.org/wiki/John_Seigenthaler; and "Wikipedia Seigenthaler biography incident," Wikipedia, accessed June 20, 2014, http://en.wikipedia.org/wiki/Wikipedia_biography_controversy.

64. Farhad Manjoo, "The Netflix Prize Was Brilliant: Google and Microsoft Should Steal the Idea," Slate.com, Sept. 22, 2009, accessed Aug. 13, 2010, http://www.slate.com/id/2229225/.

65. "A Doctor in Your Pocket."

66. Jeremy Ginsberg et al., "Detecting Influenza Epidemics Using Search Engine Query Data," *Nature*, Feb. 19, 2009, 1012–14.

67. Shishir Nagaraja and Ross Anderson, "The Snooping Dragon: Social Malware Surveillance of the Tibetan Movement," University of Cambridge Computer Laboratory Technical Report No. 746, UCAM-CL-TR-746 (Cambridge, UK: March 2009), 8.

68. P. M. Polgreen et al., "Use of Prediction Markets to Forecast Infectious Disease Activity," *Clinical Infectious Diseases* 44 (Jan. 2007): 272–79.

69. "Political Landscape 2008," washingtonpost.com, accessed June 20, 2014. Realclearpolitics.com has an electoral college map using the same data at "Real Clear Politics Electoral College," realclearpolitics.com, accessed Aug. 20, 2010, http://www.realclearpolitics.com/epolls/maps/obama_vs_mccain/?map=10.

70. Evie Stone, "Rudin's Call: Obama 291, McCain 247," NPR.org, November 3, 2008, accessed Aug. 13, 2010, http://www.npr.org/blogs/politics/2008/11/rudins_call_obama_291_mccain_2.html.

71. For examples that are still available, see "The Electoral Map: Key States," *The New York Times* online, November 4, 2008, accessed Aug. 20, 2010, http://elections.nytimes.com/2008/president/whos-ahead/key-states/map.html?scp=1&sq=2008%20electoral%20college&st=cse; "Electoral College Calculator," *The Wall Street Journal* online, Nov. 2, 2008, accessed Aug. 20, 2010, Online resource available at http://online.wsj.com/public/resources/documents/info-flash08.html?project=POLCALCULATOR; and "State-by-State Glance at the Electoral College Map," Foxnews.com, October 29, 2008, accessed Aug. 20, 2010, http://www.foxnews.com/wires/2008Oct29/0,4670,Roadto270States,00.html.

72. Intrade's markets actually predicted 364 for Obama and 174 for McCain because its market for Nebraska only allowed for contracts on which candidate would win the entire state. However, Nebraska allows candidates to split its electoral votes; Obama won the second congressional district and thus picked up one of the states' four electoral votes. Although Intrade's markets incorrectly forecasted Obama would win Missouri and McCain would win Indiana, because both states have eleven electoral votes, Intrade's overall predicted electoral college split remained accurate.

73. Leighton Vaughan Williams, "How to Forecast an Election (And How to Win One!)" accessed May 7, 2009, http://www.pollingreport.com/lvw_bet.htm; "Did Intrade Correctly Predict the 2008 Presidential Election?" accessed, Aug. 13, 2010, http://electoralmap.net/analysis.php.

74. David M. Lazer, R. Kennedy, Gary King, and A. Vespignani, "The Parable of Google Flu: Traps in Big Data Analysis," *Science*, March 14, 2014, 1203–1205.

75. James Surowiecki, *The Wisdom of Crowds: Why the Many Are Smarter than the Few and How Collective Wisdom Shapes Business, Economies, Societies, and Nations* (New York: Doubleday, 2004).

76. Rosenau, *Turbulence in World Politics*; James N. Rosenau and W. Michael Fagen, "A New Dynamism in World Politics: Increasingly Skillful Individuals," *International Studies Quarterly* 41, no. 4 (Dec. 1997), 655–86; and Rosenau, *Distant Proximities*.

77. Rosenau, *Distant Proximities*, ch. 1.

78. Fathi, "Iran's Opposition Seeks More Help."

79. Daniel W. Drezner, "Weighing the Scales: The Internet's Effect on State-Society Relations," *Brown Journal of World Affairs* 16, no. 2 (Spring-Summer 2010): 34.

80. Giridharadas, "Africa's Gift to Silicon Valley."

81. "Marching off to Cyberwar," 2008.

82. Symantec, *Symantec Global Internet Security Threat Report: Trends for 2009*, vol. XV, April 2010; *Browser Security Comparison: A Quantitative Approach*, Dec.

14, 2011, accessed Nov. 17, 2012, http://www.accuvant.com/sites/default/files/images/webbrowserresearch_v1_0.pdf.

83. David C. Earnest, "Growing a Virtual Insurgency: Using Massively Parallel Gaming to Simulate Insurgent Behavior," *The Journal of Defense Modeling and Simulation: Applications, Methodology, Technology* 6, no. 2 (2009): 55–67.

84. Jim Giles, "Challenges of being a Wikipedian," *Nature*, Dec. 15, 2005, 901.

85. W. Brian Arthur, *Increasing Returns and Path Dependence in the Economy* (Ann Arbor: University of Michigan Press, 1994); W. Brian Arthur, "Positive Feedbacks in the Economy," *McKinsey Quarterly* 1 (1994): 81–95.

86. Stephen M. Walt, "Fads, Fevers and Firestorms," *Foreign Policy* 121 (Nov.-Dec. 2000): 34–42.

87. "After the Fall," Nov. 2008.

88. "Stage prop," Jan. 28, 2010.

89. Ibid.

90. M. Mitchell Waldrop, "The Trillion Dollar Vision of Dee Hock: The Corporate Radical Who Organized Visa Wants to Dis-Organize Your Company," *Fast Company* 5 (Oct. 31, 1996).

91. James N. Rosenau, *Along the Domestic-Foreign Frontier: Exploring Governance in a Turbulent World* (New York: Cambridge University Press, 1997), 38.

92. "Obama '08: The Official iPhone Application." Accessed Aug. 24, 2009, available at http://my.barackobama.com/page/content/iphone.

93. Gladwell, *The Tipping Point*, 30–88.

94. Joseph A. Schumpeter, *Capitalism, Socialism, and Democracy* (New York: Harper and Row, 1976).

95. Ernest K. Gann, *Fate is the Hunter* (New York: Touchstone, 1961), 129–30.

96. Charles Perrow, *Normal Accidents: Living with High-Risk Technologies* (New York: Basic Books, 1984).

97. William Langewieshe, "The Devil at 37,000. Feet," *Vanity Fair*, Jan. 2009, 86–141.

98. Ibid.

99. Jervis, *System Effects*, 19.

100. Reinhard Selten et al., "Experimental Investigation of Day-to-Day Route-Choice Behaviour and Network Simulations of Autobahn Traffic in North Rhine-Westphalia," in *Human Behavior and Traffic Networks*, ed. Michael Schreckenberg and Reinhard Selden (Berlin: Springer-Verlag, 2004), 1–21.

101. Peter Bonsall, "The Influence of Route Guidance Advice on Route Choice in Urban Networks," *Transportation* 19, no. 1 (Feb. 1992): 1–23.

102. Miller and Page note, "The idea that imperfection is a productive way to navigate multiple equilibria has been shown in many contexts. . . . This research indicates that allowing mistakes (especially if they are not too costly or occur early in the search process) helps systems escape less productive outcomes and converge on more productive ones. Less perfection is often more in these types of systems." Miller and Page, *Complex Adaptive Systems*, 108.

103. " 'Phantom' Traffic Jams that Cause Misery for Motorists Can Be Caused by Just ONE Driver," *Daily Mail* (London), April 3, 2010. See also M. R. Flynn et

al., "Self-Sustained Nonlinear Waves in Traffic Flow," *Physical Review E* 79, no. 5 (May 2009).

104. Timothy Ferris, *The Whole Shebang* (New York: Touchstone, 1997), 177.

105. Ibid, 167.

106. Robert Gilpin, *The Global Political Economy: Understanding the International Economic Order* (Princeton: Princeton University Press, 2001), 108–22.

107. Uri Wilensky and Mitchel Resnick, "Thinking in Levels: A Dynamic Systems Approach to Making Sense of the World," *Journal of Science Education and Technology* 8, no. 1 (1999): 10.

108. Giles, "Challenges of Being a Wikipedian," 901.

109. Kimberley A. Strassel, "The Climate Change Climate Change: The Number of Skeptics Is Swelling Everywhere," *The Wall Street Journal*, June 26, 2009, A13.

110. Biologist Stephen Jay Gould typically receives credit for coining the phrase "punctuated equilibrium," although Niles Eldredge co-authored with Gould two of the foundational papers. In biology, punctuated equilibrium refers to the process of change in the morphology of species. Rather than gradual evolutionary change, Gould and Eldredge found in the fossil record that the shapes and forms of species maintain long historical periods of stability ("stasis") followed by very sudden and dramatic changes. In general, the phrase "punctuated equilibrium" characterizes processes with sudden, discontinuous, or "breakpoint" changes rather than gradualism. See Niles Eldredge and Stephen J. Gould, "Punctuated Equilibria: An Alternative to Phyletic Gradualism," *Models in Paleobiology* 82 (1972): 82–115; and Stephen J. Gould and Niles Eldredge, "Punctuated Equilibria: The Tempo and Mode of Evolution Reconsidered," *Paleobiology* 3, no. 2 (Spring 1977): 115–51.

111. Robert K. Forscher, "Chaos in the Brickyard," *Science*, Oct. 18, 1963, 339.

112. See Rosenau, *Distant Proximities*, ch. 3 for an excellent discussion of this point.

113. For example, the financial crisis had a greater impact in Europe than in Asia, despite comparable levels of trade in goods between the United States and both continents. See M. Lander, "The Financial Crisis is Spreading to Europe," *The New York Times*, Oct. 1, 2008.

114. Scholte (*Globalization*, 51) finds that the earliest academic treatments of globalization emerged in the early 1980s. Although social scientists used some simulation methods such as system dynamics modeling in the 1960s, Gilbert and Troitzsch find that "in the early 1990s the situation changed radically, mainly as a result of the development of multi-agent models which offered the promise of simulating autonomous individuals and the interactions between them." Gilbert and Troitzsch, *Simulation for the Social Scientist*, 8.

115. Wilensky and Resnick, "Thinking in Levels," 18.

CHAPTER TWO. AGENTS AND NETWORKS

1. Waltz, *Man, the State, and War*.

2. R. B. J. Walker, *Inside/outside: International Relations as Political Theory* (New York: Cambridge University Press, 1993).

3. Stephen Gill, ed., *Gramsci, Historical Materialism and International Relations* (New York: Cambridge University Press, 1993).
4. Rosenau, *Along the Domestic-Foreign Frontier*, 304–305; Scholte, *Globalization*, 64–67.
5. Keck and Sikkink, *Activists beyond Borders*, 1.
6. Ronnie Lipschutz, "Reconstructing World Politics: The Emergence of Global Civil Society," *Millennium: Journal of International Studies* 21, no. 3 (1992): 390.
7. David Lazer et al., "Computational Social Science." *Science*, Feb. 6, 2009, 721–23. See also Joshua M. Epstein and Robert Axtell, *Growing Artificial Societies: Social Science from the Bottom Up* (Washington, DC: Brookings Institution Press, 1996).
8. Walker, *Inside/outside*, 100.
9. Walker, *Inside/outside*; Jeffrey T. Checkel, "The Constructivist Turn in International Relations Theory," *World Politics* 50, no. 2 (1998): 324–48.
10. Vendulka Kubalkova et al., *International Relations in a Constructed World* (Armonk, NY: M. E. Sharpe, 1996); Colin Wight, *Agents, Structures, and International Relations: Politics as Ontology* (New York: Cambridge University Press, 2006), 14–61.
11. Waltz, *Man, the State, and War*.
12. Anthony Giddens, *The Constitution of Society: Outline of the Theory of Structuration* (Berkeley: University of California Press, 1986); Alexander E. Wendt, "The Agent-Structure Problem in International Relations Theory," *International Organization* 41, no. 3 (1987); Gill, *Gramsci, Historical Materialism, and International Relations*.
13. Alexander Wendt, "Levels of Analysis vs. Agents and Structures: Part III," *Review of International Studies* 18 (1992): 181–85.
14. Rosenau, *Turbulence in World Politics*; R. Keith Sawyer, *Social Emergence: Societies as Complex Systems* (New York: Cambridge University Press, 2005), 196–97.
15. Waltz, *Man, the State, and War*; Kenneth N. Waltz, *Theory of International Politics* (New York: McGraw-Hill, 1979); Wendt, "Levels of Analysis vs. Agents and Structures"; Gill, *Gramsci, Historical Materialism, and International Relations*, 24; Wight, *Agents, Structures, and International Relations*.
16. Wendt, "Levels of Analysis vs. Agents and Structures."
17. Walker, *Inside/outside*, 81–99.
18. Wendt, "Levels of Analysis vs. Agents and Structures."
19. Sawyer, *Social Emergence*, 77.
20. Wendt, "Levels of Analysis vs. Agents and Structures," 182.
21. Stanley Wasserman and Katherine Faust, *Social Network Analysis: Methods and Applications* (New York: Cambridge University Press, 1994), 30–33; David Knoke and Song Yang, *Social Network Analysis*, 2d ed. (Los Angeles: Sage, 2008), 15–20.
22. "After the Fall," *The Economist*, Nov. 13, 2008.
23. Ibid.
24. Felix Salmon, "Recipe for Disaster: The Formula That Killed Wall Street," *Wired*, Feb. 23, 2009, 74; emphases added.
25. Robert Lucas, "In Defence of the Dismal Science," *The Economist*, Aug. 6, 2009. Such a hypothetical forecasting tool would be an interesting example of

the "double hermeneutic," whereby social scientific knowledge enters popular consciousness and alters the very behavior about which it theorizes. Giddens presciently links the double hermeneutic to processes of globalization. Anthony Giddens, *The Consequences of Modernity* (Stanford: Stanford University Press, 1991), 15–16.

26. Anthony Giddens, *Social Theory and Modern Sociology* (Stanford: Stanford University Press, 1987).

27. The field of behavioral economics, of which Lucas is a pioneer, seeks to understand and model economic behavior that deviates from classic assumptions of rational choice utility theory.

28. John H. Miller and Scott E. Page, *Complex Adaptive Systems: An Introduction to Computational Models of Social Life* (Princeton: Princeton University Press, 2007), 108.

29. "The Worm Turns," *The Economist*, Dec. 4, 2008.

30. Gilpin, *The Global Political Economy*, 112–17.

31. "After the Fall."

32. David C. Earnest, Steve Yetiv, and Stephen M. Carmel, "Contagion in the Transpacific Shipping Network: International Networks and Vulnerability Interdependence," *International Interactions* 38, no. 5 (2012): 571–96.

33. Rosenau, *Distant Proximities*, 60.

34. Scholte, *Globalization*, 64–67.

35. Markoff, "Vast Spy System Loots Computers in 103 Countries." Regarding cyberattacks, "attribution is difficult because there is no agreed upon international legal framework for being able to pursue investigations down to their logical conclusion, which is highly local."

36. "Marching off to Cyberwar."

37. Alan Cowell, "Deadly Bird Flu Confirmed in British Turkeys," *New York Times*, Feb. 4, 2007, 16.

38. Waltz, *Man, the State, and War*.

39. Rosenau, *Turbulence in World Politics*.

40. Jackson and Nexon, "Globalization, the Comparative Method, and Comparing Constructions," 90.

41. Giddens, *The Constitution of Society*; Sawyer, *Social Emergence*, 127–30 and 132–35.

42. Jackson and Nexon, "Globalization, the Comparative Method, and Comparing Constructions," 104.

43. Ibid.

44. Karl W. Deutsch, *The Nerves of Government: Models of Political Communication and Control* (London: Free Press of Glencoe, 1963).

45. Thomas C. Schelling, *Micromotives and Macrobehavior* (New York: Norton, 1978).

46. Herbert A. Simon, "A Behavioral Model of Rational Choice," *Quarterly Journal of Economics* 69, no. 1 (Feb. 1955): 99–118.

47. Barry Hughes, *World Futures: A Critical Analysis of Alternatives* (Baltimore: Johns Hopkins University Press, 1985); and Barry Hughes, *International Futures: Choices in the Creation of a New World Order* (Boulder: Westview, 1993).

48. Walker, *Inside/outside*.

49. Ibid.; Gill, *Gramsci, Historical Materialism, and International Relations*; and Wendt, "The Agent-Structure Problem in International Relations Theory."

50. Indeed, two prominent theorists have argued that complex systems theory can help us understand dynamics of international politics. See Jervis, *System Effects*; and Rosenau, *Distant Proximities*, 205–31.

51. Sawyer, *Social Emergence*, 198.

52. Ibid., 198–207.

53. Wasserman and Faust, *Social Network Analysis*, 4.

54. Knoke and Yang, *Social Network Analysis*, 4.

55. Ibid., 7.

56. Ibid.

57. Ibid., 5–6.

58. Ibid., 6.

59. Ibid.

60. Knoke and Yang, *Social Network Analysis*, offers a good introduction. See also Wasserman and Faust, *Social Network Analysis: Methods and Applications*.

61. Duncan J. Watts and Steven H. Strogatz, "Collective Dynamics of 'Small World' Networks," *Nature*, June 4, 1998, 440–42.

62. Albert-Laszlo Barabasi and Reka Albert, "Emergence of Scaling in Random Networks," *Science*, Oct. 15, 1999, 509–12.

63. Ibid.; Albert-Laszlo Barabasi and Eric Bonabeau, "Scale-Free Networks," *Scientific American*, May 2003, 60–69.

64. Watts and Strogatz, "Collective Dynamics"; Duncan J. Watts, "Networks, Dynamics, and the Small World Phenomenon," *American Journal of Sociology* 105, no. 2 (Sept. 1999): 493–527; Duncan J. Watts, *Small Worlds: The Dynamics of Networks Between Order and Randomness* (Princeton: Princeton University Press, 1999); A. Barrat, M. Barthelemy, R. Pastor-Satorras, and A. Vespignani, "The Architecture of Complex Weighted Networks," *Proceedings of the National Academy of Sciences* 101, no. 11 (Jan. 8, 2004): 3747–52.

65. William I. Robinson and Jerry Harris, "Towards a Global Ruling Class? Globalization and the Transnational Capitalist Class," *Science & Society* 64, no. 1 (Spring 2000); Leslie Sklair, *The Transnational Capitalist Class* (Oxford: Blackwell, 2001); William K. Carroll and Colin Carson, "The Network of Global Corporations and Elite Policy Groups: A Structure for Transnational Capitalist Class Formation?" *Global Networks* 3, no. 1 (Feb. 2003): 29–57; and Jeffrey Kentor, "The Growth of Transnational Corporate Networks: 1962–1998," *Journal of World Systems Research* 11, no. 2 (Dec. 2005): 263–86.

66. Samuel P. Huntington, "Dead Souls: The Denationalization of the American Elites," *The National Interest* 75 (Spring 2004): 5–18.

67. John Micklethwait and Adrian Wooldridge, *A Future Perfect: The Challenge and Promise of Globalization* (New York: Random House, 2000), 242.

68. Keck and Sikkink, *Activists beyond Borders*.

69. Miller and Page, *Complex Adaptive Systems*, 95.

70. M. E. J. Newman, "The Structure and Function of Complex Networks," *SIAM Review* 45, no. 2 (May 2003): 167–256.

71. Mitchel Resnick, *Termites, Turtles, and Traffic Jams: Explorations in Massively Parallel Microworlds* (Cambridge: MIT Press, 1999); Steven Johnson, *Emergence: The Connected Lives of Ants, Brains, Cities, and Software* (New York: Scribner, 2001).

72. Michael Wines, "China's Growth Leads to Problems Down the Road," *The New York Times*, Aug. 27, 2010, A4; M. R. Flynn et al., "Self-Sustained Nonlinear Waves in Traffic Flow," *Physical Review E* 79, no. 5 (May 2009).

73. Epstein, "Modelling to Contain Pandemics."

74. J. Doyne Farmer and Duncan Foley, "The Economy Needs Agent-Based Modelling," *Nature*, Aug. 6, 2009, 685–86.

75. See M. Mitchell Waldrop, *Complexity: The Emerging Science at the Edge of Order and Chaos* (New York, Touchstone, 1992); and Miller and Page, *Complex Adaptive Systems*, for good introductions to complex systems theory.

76. Epstein and Axtell, *Growing Artificial Societies*, 35.

77. Ibid., 52.

78. Steven Strogatz, *Sync: The Emerging Science of Spontaneous Order* (New York: Hyperion, 2003).

79. Toshiyuki Nakagaki et al., "Intelligence: Maze-Solving by an Amoeboid Organism," *Nature*, Sept. 28, 2000, 470.

80. W. Brian Arthur, *Increasing Returns and Path Dependence in the Economy* (Ann Arbor: University of Michigan Press, 1994); W. Brian Arthur, "Positive Feedbacks in the Economy," *McKinsey Quarterly* 1 (1994): 81–95.

81. Massimo Daniele Sapienza, "An Experimental Approach to the Study of Banking Intermediation: The Banknet Simulator," in *Economic Simulations in Swarm: Agent-based Modelling and Object Oriented Programming*, ed. Benedikt Stefansson and Francesco Luna (Dordrecht: Kluwer, 2000).

82. Miller and Page, *Complex Adaptive Systems*, 42.

83. Scholars disagree about whether there is a "theory" or "science" of complexity. Mitchell (*Complexity*, 14) asserts there is not yet a science of complexity, though definitional and conceptual debates among scholars may be a harbinger of an emerging science. Sawyer nevertheless argues that "complex systems may have laws and properties at the global level that cannot be reduced to lower-level, more basic sciences" and suggests complexity is a paradigm. R. Keith Sawyer, *Social Emergence: Societies as Complex Systems* (New York: Cambridge, 2005), 4.

84. Rosenau and Fagen, "A New Dynamism in World Politics."

85. Beth A. Simmons and Zachary Elkins, "The Globalization of Liberalization: Policy Diffusion in the International Political Economy," *American Political Science Review* 98, no. 1 (Feb. 2004): 171–89.

86. Michael C. Horowitz, "Nonstate Actors and the Diffusion of Innovations: The Case of Suicide Terrorism," *International Organization* 64, no. 1 (Winter 2010): 33–64.

87. Emanuel Adler, "The Emergence of Cooperation: National Epistemic Communities and the International Evolution of the Idea of Nuclear Arms Control," *International Organization* 46 (Dec. 1992): 101–45.

88. Peter Haas, "Introduction: Epistemic Communities and International Policy Coordination," *International Organization* 46, no. 1 (Dec. 1992): 1–35; Jef-

frey W. Knopf, "The Importance of International Learning," *Review of International Studies* 29 (2003): 185–207.

89. Michael W. Macy and Andreas Flache, "Beyond Rationality in Models of Choice," *Annual Review of Sociology* 21 (1995): 83.

90. Brian J. McGill and Joel S. Brown, "Evolutionary Game Theory and Adaptive Dynamics of Continuous Traits," *Annual Review of Ecology, Evolution, and Systematics* 38 (2007): 403–35.

91. David M. Kreps, *Game Theory and Economic Modelling* (Oxford: Clarendon, 1990), 97; emphasis in original.

92. Ibid., 101.

93. George J. Mailath and Larry Samuelson, *Repeated Games and Reputations: Long-Run Relationships* (Oxford: Oxford University Press, 2006), 69–71.

94. Robert Boyd and Jeffrey P. Lorberbaum, "No Pure Strategy is Evolutionarily Stable in the Repeated Prisoner's Dilemma Game," *Nature*, May 7, 1987, 58–59. Game theory borrows this phrase from ecology. An "evolutionarily stable" strategy is one that, once it becomes dominant in a population, will defeat any other possible strategy by natural selection alone. The concept is a refinement of the Nash equilibrium for use in evolutionary biology because species do not exercise rational foresight. Hence, rational choice theory cannot explain an equilibrium solution in evolutionary biology.

95. Robert Axelrod, *The Evolution of Cooperation* (New York: Basic Books, 1984).

96. Vladimir Akimov and Mikhail Soutchanski, "Automata Simulation of N-Person Social Dilemma Games," *Journal of Conflict Resolution* 38, no. 1 (March 1994): 138–48; Martin A. Nowak and Karl Sigmund, "Tit for Tat in Heterogeneous Populations," *Nature*, Jan. 16, 1992, 250–53; Martin A. Nowak and Robert M. May, "Evolutionary Games and Spatial Chaos," *Nature*, Oct. 29, 1992, 826–29; Miklos N. Szilagyi and Zoltan C. Szilagyi, "Non-Trivial Solutions to the N-Person Prisoner's Dilemma," *Systems Research and Behavioral Science* 19, no. 3 (May/June 2002): 281–90; Shao-Meng Qin et al., "Effect of Memory on the Prisoner's Dilemma Game in a Square Lattice," *Physical Review E* 78, no. 4 (2008); and Conrad Power, "A Spatial Agent-Based Model of N-Person Prisoner's Dilemma Cooperation in a Socio-Geographic Community," *Journal of Artificial Societies and Social Simulation* 12, no. 1 (January 2009).

97. Macy and Flache, "Beyond Rationality in Models of Choice," 86.

98. Ibid., 87.

99. Samuel Bowles, "Did Warfare Among Ancestral Hunter-Gatherers Affect the Evolution of Human Social Behaviors?" *Science*, June 5, 2009, 1293–98; John T. Scholz and Cheng-Lung Wang, "Learning to Cooperate: Learning Networks and the Problem of Altruism," *American Journal of Political Science* 53, no. 3 (July 2009): 572–87.

100. Ian S. Lustick, "Agent-Based Modelling of Collective Identity: Testing Constructivist Theory," *Journal of Artificial Societies and Social Simulation* 3, no. 1 (Jan. 2000).

101. Ernst B. Haas, *Beyond the Nation-State: Functionalism and International Organization* (Stanford: Stanford University Press, 1964); Ernst B. Haas, *When Knowledge Is Power: Three Models of Change in International Organizations* (Berkeley:

University of California Press, 1990); John Meyer et al., "World Society and the Nation-State," *The American Journal of Sociology* 103, no. 1 (July 1997): 144–81.

102. John Gerard Ruggie, "Continuity and Transformation in the World Polity: Toward a Neorealist Synthesis," in *Neorealism and Its Critics*, ed. Robert O. Keohane (New York: Columbia University Press, 1986), 131–57.

103. Miller and Page, *Complex Adaptive Systems*, 42.

104. Wight, *Agents, Structures, and International Relations*, 107.

105. Schelling, *Micromotives and Macrobehavior*, 147–66; Epstein and Axtell, *Growing Artificial Societies*, 165–70; Miller and Page, *Complex Adaptive Systems*, 143–46.

106. Wendt, "Levels of Analysis vs. Agents and Structures: Part III."

107. Miller and Page, *Complex Adaptive Systems*, 225.

108. Wendt, "Levels of Analysis vs. Agents and Structures: Part III;" Wight, *Agents, Structures, and International Relations*, 103–106.

109. Miller and Page, *Complex Adaptive Systems*, 299.

110. Jackson and Nexon, "Globalization, the Comparative Method, and Comparing Constructions," 104.

111. Sawyer, *Social Emergence*, 198.

112. Benjamin Radcliffe, "The Structure of Voter Preferences," *The Journal of Politics* 55, no. 3 (Aug. 1993): 714–19; Kurt Taylor Gaubatz, "Intervention and Intransitivity: Public Opinion, Social Choice, and the Use of Military Force Abroad," *World Politics* 47, no. 4 (July 1995): 534–54.

113. For a good start, see Robert Gilpin, *War and Change in World Politics* (New York: Cambridge University Press, 1983); and Rosenau, *Turbulence in World Politics*.

114. Wendt, "The Agent-Structure Problem in International Relations Theory"; Wendt "Levels of Analysis vs. Agents and Structures: Part III;" and Wendt, "Anarchy Is What States Make of It: The Social Construction of Power Politics," *International Organization* 46, no. 2 (Spring 1992).

115. Gilpin, *War and Change in World Politics*, 9–49.

116. Wendt "Levels of Analysis vs. Agents and Structures: Part III," 184.

117. Indeed, Farmer and Foley argue agent-based modeling is an essential tool of behavioral economics. Farmer and Foley, "The Economy Needs Agent-Based Modelling."

118. Miller and Page, *Complex Adaptive Systems*, 197.

119. Matthew J. Hoffmann, *Ozone Depletion and Climate Change: Constructing a Global Response* (Albany: State University of New York Press, 2005).

120. Lustick, "Agent-Based Modeling."

121. Dan Miodownik, "Cultural Differences and Economic Incentives: an Agent-Based Study of Their Impact on the Emergence of Regional Autonomy Movements," *Journal of Artificial Societies and Social Simulation* 9, no. 4 (October 2006).

122. Jackson and Nexon, "Globalization, the Comparative Method, and Comparing Constructions," 109.

123. Miller and Page, *Complex Adaptive Systems*, 220.

124. See Robert Axtell et al., "Aligning Simulation Models: A Case Study and Results," *Computational and Mathematical Organization Theory* 1, no. 2 (Feb. 2006): 123–41; Robert Ernest Marks, "Validating Simulation Models: A General

Framework and Four Applied Examples," *Computational Economics* 30, no. 3 (Oct. 2007): 265–90; Scott Moss and Bruce Edmonds, "Sociology and Simulation: Statistical and Quantitative Cross-Validation," *American Journal of Sociology* 110, no. 4 (Jan. 2005); and Klaus G. Troitzsch, "Validating Simulation Models," Proceedings of the 18th Simulation Multiconference (Erlangen, Germany: Society for Modeling & Simulation International, 2004), among others.

125. Rosenau, *Distant Proximities*, 214–17.

126. Gunnar Myrdal, *Rich Lands and Poor: The Road to World Prosperity* (New York: Harper, 1957), vii; Miller and Page, *Complex Adaptive Systems*, 216; W. Brian Arthur, "Competing Technologies, Increasing Returns, and Lock-In by Historical Events," *Economic Journal* 99, no. 334 (March 1989): 116–31.

127. For this reason, agent-based modeling is one type of object-oriented program (OOP) in the jargon of computer science. Agent-based modeling software uses object-oriented languages such as C++ or Java. RePast, Swarm, MASON, and NetLogo are four of the most extensively used ABM software.

128. Miller and Page, *Complex Adaptive Systems*, 80.

129. Epstein and Axtell, *Growing Artificial Societies*; Miller and Page, *Complex Adaptive Systems*, 66–68.

130. Epstein, "Modelling to Contain Pandemics."

131. Robert Axelrod, *The Complexity of Cooperation: Agent-Based Models of Computation and Collaboration* (Princeton: Princeton University Press, 1997), 3–4.

132. Epstein and Axtell, *Growing Artificial Societies*, 177.

133. John H. Holland, "Genetic Algorithms," *Scientific American*, July 1998, 66–72; Melanie Mitchell, *An Introduction to Genetic Algorithms* (Cambridge: MIT Press, 1998).

134. Robert Axelrod, "An Evolutionary Approach to Norms," *American Political Science Review* 80, no. 4 (Dec. 1986): 1095–1111.

135. See, for example, Robert Axelrod, "The Evolution of Strategies in Iterated Prisoner's Dilemma," in *Genetic Algorithms and Simulated Annealing*, ed. L. Davis (Los Altos, CA: Kaufman, 1987), 32–41; Axelrod, *The Complexity of Cooperation*; and Gilbert and Troitzsch, *Simulation for the Social Scientist*, 195–236.

136. Edward Lorenz, "Deterministic Nonperiodic Flow," *Journal of Atmospheric Sciences* 20 (1963): 130–41.

137. Thomas B. Pepinsky, "From Agents to Outcomes: Simulation in International Relations," *European Journal of International Relations* 11, no. 3 (Sept. 2005): 367–94.

138. Lustick et al., "Secessionism in Multicultural States."

139. Ibid.

140. James D. Fearon, "Counterfactuals and Hypothesis Testing in Political Science," *World Politics* 43, no. 2 (Jan. 1991): 169–95; Pepinsky, "From Agents to Outcomes"; Gary King and Langche Zeng, "The Dangers of Extreme Counterfactuals," *Political Analysis* 14, no. 2 (Summer 2006): 131–59.

141. Marc V. Simon and Harvey Starr, "Extraction, Allocation, and the Rise and Decline of States: A Simulation of Two-Level Security Management," *The Journal of Conflict Resolution* 40, no. 2 (June 1996): 272–97.

142. John H. Miller, "Active Nonlinear Tests (ANTs) of Complex Simulation Models," *Management Science* 44, no. 6 (June 1998): 820–30. The model Miller tests is from Dennis L. Meadows et al., *Dynamics of Growth in a Finite World* (Cambridge: Wright-Allen Press, 1974).

143. Pepinsky, "From Agents to Outcomes."

144. "The significance of this shift is that students no longer need to search only for unique answers, which may be true or false in themselves. They can spend their time trying to compare theories against other theories." Uri Wilensky and Kenneth Reisman, "Thinking Like a Wolf, a Sheep, or a Firefly," *Cognition and Instruction* 24, no. 2 (June 2006): 192. One could say the same thing about social scientists.

145. L. Booth Sweeney and John D. Stearman, "Thinking about Systems: Student and Teacher Conceptions of Natural and Social Systems," *System Dynamics Review* 23, no. 2/3 (Summer/Fall 2007): 285–312.

146. Wilensky and Reisman, "Thinking Like a Wolf," 4.

147. Ibid, 10.

148. Powner notes that undergraduates have "an intuitive understanding of the nature of knowledge and reality" that makes learning the scientific method relatively easy. Leanne C. Powner, "Teaching the Scientific Method in the Active Learning Classroom," *PS: Political Science & Politics* 39, no. 3 (July 2006): 521.

149. To illustrate the potential for younger students to learn about complex systems, researchers have had some success in teaching high school and middle school students the ideas and methods of complex systems theory. See Wilenksy and Reisman, "Thinking Like a Wolf"; Wilensky and Resnick, "Thinking in Levels." For a review of prior research on the relationship between age and systems thinking, see also Michael J. Jacobson and Uri Wilensky, "Complex Systems in Education: Scientific and Educational Importance and Implications for the Learning Sciences," *The Journal of the Learning Sciences* 15, no. 1 (Jan. 2006): 11–34.

150. Robert L. Goldstone, "The Complex Systems See-Change in Education," *The Journal of the Learning Sciences* 15, no. 1 (Jan. 2006): 41.

151. For a discussion of these traditions, see Scott Moss, "Alternative Approaches to the Empirical Validation of Agent-Based Models," *Journal of Artificial Society and Social Simulation* 11, no. 1 (Jan. 2008).

152. Ibid.

153. For example, see Joshua M. Epstein, *Generative Social Science: Studies in Agent-Based Computational Modeling* (Princeton: Princeton University Press, 2006).

154. Scott Moss and Bruce Edmonds, "Sociology and Simulation: Statistical and Quantitative Cross-Validation," *American Journal of Sociology* 110, no. 4 (Jan. 2005).

155. Daniel Diermeier, "Arguing for Computational Power," *Science*, Nov, 9, 2007, 918.

156. Lazer et al., "Computational Social Science."

157. Pepinsky, "From Agents to Outcomes"; David C. Earnest and James N. Rosenau, "Signifying Nothing? What Complex Systems Can and Cannot Tell Us about Global Politics," in *Complexity in World Politics: Concepts and Methods of a New Paradigm*, ed. Neil E. Harrison (Albany: State University of New York Press, 2006).

158. Pepinsky, "From Agents to Outcomes," 375–76.
159. Cederman, *Emergent Actors in World Politics*, 62–63.
160. See Axtell et al., "Aligning Simulation Models"; Marks, "Validating Simulation Models"; Moss and Edmonds, "Sociology and Simulation"; and Troitzsch, "Validating Simulation Models."
161. Paul Windrum, Giorgio Fabiolo and Alessio Moneta, "Empirical Validation of Agent-Based Models: Alternatives and Prospects," *Journal of Artificial Societies and Social Simulation* 10, no. 2 (March 2007).
162. Axtell et al., "Aligning Simulation Models"; Troitzsch, "Validating Simulation Models."
163. Roberto Leombruni and Matteo Richiardi, "Why Are Economists Skeptical about Agent-Based Simulations?" *Physica A: Statistical Mechanics and Applications* 355, no. 1 (Sept. 2005): 103–109.
164. Marks, "Validating Simulation Models."
165. Moss and Edmonds, "Sociology and Simulation."
166. Cederman, *Emergent Actors in World Politics*, 62–63.
167. Ibid, 63.
168. "A Model Approach: More Development Work Is Needed to Help Computer Simulations Inform Economic Policy," *Nature*, Aug. 6, 2009, 667.
169. Nigel Gilbert, *Agent-Based Models* (Thousand Oaks, CA: Sage, 2008), 54.
170. George E. P. Box and Norman R. Draper, *Empirical Model-Building and Response Surfaces* (New York: John Wiley and Sons, 1987), 74.
171. D. Scott Bennett, "Governments, Civilians, and the Evolution of Insurgency: Modeling the Early Dynamics of Insurgencies," *Journal of Artificial Societies and Social Simulation* 11, no. 4 (Oct. 2008).
172. Lustick, Miodownik, and Eidelson. "Secessionism in Multicultural States."
173. Armando Geller and Scott Moss, "Growing QAWM: An Evidence-Driven Declarative Model of Afghan Power Structures," *Advances in Complex Systems* 11, no. 2 (April 2008): 321–35.
174. Axelrod, *The Complexity of Cooperation*, 124–44.
175. Lars-Erik Cederman, "Modeling the Size of Wars: From Billiard Balls to Sandpiles," *American Political Science Review* 97, no. 1 (Feb. 2003): 135–50.
176. Epstein, "Modelling to Contain Pandemics."
177. Miller and Page, *Complex Adaptive Systems*, 217; Matthew O. Jackson, "Networks and Economic Behavior," *Annual Review of Economics* 1 (2009): 489–513.

CHAPTER THREE. THE ADVANTAGE OF SIZE

1. Kenneth J. Arrow, *Social Choice and Individual Values* (New York: Wiley, 1963); Duncan Black, "On the Rationale of Group Decision-making," *Journal of Political Economy* 56, no. 1 (Feb. 1948): 23–34; Maurice Duverger, *Party Politics and Pressure Groups: A Comparative Introduction*, trans. David Wagoner (New York: Thomas Y. Crowell, 1972); and William H. Riker, "The Number of Political Parties: A Reexamination of Duverger's Law," *Comparative Politics* 9, no. 1 (Oct. 1976): 93–106.

2. Michihiro Kandori, George J. Mailath, and Rafael Rob, "Learning, Mutation, and Long Run Equilibria in Games," *Econometrica* 61, no. 1 (1993): 29–56; H. Peyton Young, "The Evolution of Conventions," *Econometrica* 61, no. 1 (1993): 57–84; and H. Peyton Young, *Individual Strategy and Social Structure: An Evolutionary Theory of Institutions* (Princeton: Princeton University Press, 1998).

3. Robert D. Putnam, "Diplomacy and Domestic Politics: The Logic of Two-Level Games," *International Organization* 42, no. 3 (Summer 1988): 427–60; Peter B. Evans, Harold K. Jacobson, and Robert D. Putnam, eds., *Double-Edged Diplomacy: International Bargaining and Domestic Politics* (Berkeley: University of California Press, 1993); Helen V. Milner, *Interests, Information, and Institutions: Domestic Politics and International Relations* (Princeton: Princeton University Press, 1997).

4. Robert Axelrod and Robert O. Keohane, "Achieving Cooperation under Anarchy: Strategies and Institutions," *World Politics* 38, no. 1 (Oct. 1985): 226–54; Stephen D. Krasner, "Global Communications and National Power: Life on the Pareto Frontier," *World Politics* 42, no. 3 (April 1991): 336–66; Lisa L. Martin, "Interests, Power, and Multilateralism," *International Organization* 46, no. 4 (Aug. 1992): 765–92; and Arthur Stein, "Coordination and Collaboration: Regimes in an Anarchic World," *International Organization* 36, no. 2 (Spring 1982): 299–324.

5. Andrew Moravcsik, "Taking Preferences Seriously: A Liberal Theory of International Politics," *International Organization* 51, no. 4 (Autumn 1997): 513–53; Joe D. Hagan and Margaret D. Hermann, eds., "Leaders, Groups, and Coalitions: Understanding the People and Processes in Foreign Policymaking," *International Studies Review (Special Edition)* (Malden, MA: Blackwell, 2001).

6. Robert O. Keohane, *After Hegemony: Cooperation and Discord in the World Political Economy* (Princeton: Princeton University Press, 1984); John Gerard Ruggie, "Multilateralism: Anatomy of an Institution," *International Organization* 46 (Summer 1992): 561–98.

7. Rosenau, *Distant Proximities*, 357–65.

8. Audie Klotz, "Norms Reconstituting Interests: Global Racial Equality and U.S. Sanctions against South Africa," *International Organization* 49, no. 3 (Summer 1995): 451–78; Keck and Sikkink, *Activists Beyond Borders*.

9. Mancur Olson, *The Logic of Collective Action: Public Goods and the Theory of Groups* (Cambridge: Harvard University Press, 1971); Miles Kahler, "Multilateralism with Small and Large Numbers," *International Organization* 46, no. 3 (Summer 1992): 681–708.

10. Keck and Sikkink 1998, fn. 8.

11. Putnam, "Diplomacy and Domestic Politics"; John S. Odell, "International Threats and Internal Politics: Brazil, the European Community, and the United States, 1985–1987," in Evans, Jacobson, and Putnam, *Double-Edged Diplomacy*.

12. In fact, one can treat this theoretical disagreement as a variable property of a complex adaptive system. As several scholars have noted, states' sensitivity to relative gains (and hence the prospects for cooperation) vary across issue areas. This variation in sensitivity itself is an important emergent property of a complex adaptive system of nation-states. David A. Baldwin, ed., *Neorealism and Neoliberalism: The Contemporary Debate* (New York: Columbia University Press, 1993).

13. Mitchell Waldrop, *Complexity: The Emerging Science at the Edge of Order and Chaos* (New York, Touchstone, 1992).
14. John H. Holland, "Complex Adaptive Systems," *DAEDALUS* 121, no. 1 (Winter 1992): 17–30.
15. Alexander Wendt, "Anarchy Is What States Make of It: The Social Construction of Power Politics," *International Organization* 46, no. 2 (Spring 1992): 391–425.
16. Cederman, *Emergent Actors in World Politics*.
17. Uri Wilensky, "NetLogo Voting Model," Center for Connected Learning and Computer-Based Modeling, Northwestern University, Evanston, IL; Johannes Kottnau and Claudia Pahl-Wostl, "Simulating Political Attitudes and Voting Behavior," *Journal of Artificial Societies and Social Simulation* 7, no. 4 (Oct. 2004); Mary Lynn Reed, "Political Modeling and Election Simulations," *Dr. Dobb's Journal* (Oct. 2004):16–27.
18. Putnam, "Diplomacy and Domestic Politics." I developed the model using NetLogo version 3.1.4, a free agent–based modeling environment developed at Northwestern University; Uri Wilensky, NetLogo v. 3.0. Center for Connected Learning and Computer-Based Modeling, Northwestern University, Evanston, IL.
19. Putnam "Diplomacy and Domestic Politics," 452–54.
20. Duncan Snidal, "Cooperation versus Prisoners' Dilemma: Implications for International Cooperation and Regimes," *American Political Science Review* 79, no. 4 (Dec. 1985): 923–42; Martin, "Interests, Power and Multilateralism"; Rick K. Wilson and Carl M. Rhodes, "Leadership and Credibility in N-Person Coordination Games," *Journal of Conflict Resolution* 41, no. 6 (Dec. 1997): 767–91; Kenneth W. Abbott and Duncan Snidal, "Why States Act through Formal International Organizations," *Journal of Conflict Resolution* 42, no. 1 (Feb. 1998): 3–32; Walter Mattli and Tim Buthe, "Setting International Standards: Technological Rationality or Primacy of Power?" *World Politics* 56, no. 1 (Oct. 2003): 1–42.
21. The basic coordination game has two equilibria and hence no unique solution (though it does have a mixed-strategy equilibrium). The three-choice game is a trivial extension of the two-choice game. Formally, the two-person three-choice coordination game is:

		Actor B		
		Left	*center*	*right*
Actor A	*up*	3, 3	0, 0	0, 0
	middle	0, 0	2, 2	0, 0
	down	0, 0	0, 0	1, 1

Payoffs: (A, B)

22. Benjamin Radcliffe, "The Structure of Voter Preferences," *The Journal of Politics* 55, no. 3 (Aug. 1993): 714–19; Kurt Taylor Gaubatz, "Intervention and Intransitivity: Public Opinion, Social Choice, and the Use of Military Force Abroad," *World Politics* 47, no. 4 (July 1995): 534–54.
23. Martin, "Interests, Power, and Multilateralism."

24. Krasner, "Global Communications and National Power."
25. Putnam, "Diplomacy and Domestic Politics," 434.
26. The choice of upper limit to the number of negotiators is an arbitrary one. I chose 40 merely for ease of computation and interpretation. One can quickly rewrite the model, however, to examine a counterfactual with a large number of negotiators and constituencies, such as negotiations among the 150 World Trade Organization members during the Doha development round.
27. Olson, *The Logic of Collective Action*; Kahler, "Multilaterlaism with Small and Large Numbers."
28. Odell, "International Threats and Internal Politics."
29. Putnam, "Diplomacy and Domestic Politics."
30. Watts, *Small Worlds*.
31. Evans, Jacobson, and Putnam, *Double-Edged Diplomacy*; Milner, *Interests, Information, and Institutions*.
32. See Odell, "International Threats and Internal Politics" for an interesting study of these dynamics.
33. John H. Miller, "Active Nonlinear Tests (ANTs) of Complex Simulation Models," *Management Science* 44, no. 6 (June 1998): 820–30.
34. Holland, "Complex Adaptive Systems."
35. The simulation allows the researcher to choose one of two types of tournaments. One is a simple pairwise tournament; the other is a fitness proportionate tournament. For an introduction to these methods, see Mitchell, *An Introduction to Genetic Algorithms*.
36. Miller ("Active Nonlinear Tests") has shown that the active nonlinear test efficiently explores the parameter space of nonlinear models provided the fitness landscape has a single or a few fitness peaks. If not, the test may converge on suboptimal peaks in the fitness landscape, though the genetic crossover routine minimizes this risk.
37. Olson, *The Logic of Collective Action*.
38. Kahler, "Multilateralism with Small and Large Numbers."
39. Duncan Snidal, "Relative Gains and the Patterns of International Cooperation," *American Political Science Review* 85, no. 3 (Sept. 1991): 701–26; Duncan Snidal, "International Cooperation among Relative Gains Maximizers," *International Studies Quarterly* 35, no. 4 (Dec. 1991): 387–402.
40. Keck and Sikkink, *Activisits beyond Borders*.
41. Watts, *Small Worlds*, particularly ch. 8.
42. John M. Owen, "How Liberalism Produces Democratic Peace," *International Security* 19, no. 2 (Fall 1994): 87–125; Kurt Taylor Gaubatz, "Democratic States and Commitment in International Relations," *International Organization* 50, no. 1 (Winter 1996): 109–39.
43. Mark Granovetter, "The Strength of Weak Ties," *American Journal of Sociology* 78, no. 6 (May 1973): 1360–80; Mark Granovetter, "The Strength of Weak Ties: A Network Theory Revisited," *Sociological Theory* 1 (1983): 201–33.
44. Timur Kuran, "Now Out of Never: The Element of Surprise in the East European Revolutions of 1989," *World Politics* 44, no. 1 (Oct. 1991): 7–48; Susanne Lohmann, "The Dynamics of Information Cascades: The Monday Demonstrations in Leipzig, East Germany, 1989–1991," *World Politics* 47, no. 1 (Oct. 1994): 42–101.

45. Mark Granovetter, "Threshold Models of Collective Behavior," *American Journal of Sociology* 83, no. 6 (May 1978): 1420–43.
46. Putnam, "Diplomacy and Domestic Politics," 450.
47. Kenneth A. Schultz, "Domestic Opposition and Signalling in International Crises," *American Political Science Review* 92, no. 4 (Dec. 1998): 829–44.
48. Putnam "Diplomacy and Domestic Politics," 454–55.
49. Young, *Individual Strategy and Social Structure*, 144.
50. See, for example, Robert Axelrod, "The Evolution of Strategies in Iterated Prisoner's Dilemma," in *Genetic Algorithms and Simulated Annealing*, ed. L. Davis (Los Altos, CA: Kaufman, 1987), 32–41; Robert Axelrod, *The Complexity of Cooperation: Agent-Based Models of Competition and Collaboration* (Princeton: Princeton University Press, 1997); and Nigel Gilbert and Klaus G. Troitzsch, *Simulation for the Social Scientist* (Philadelphia: Open University Press, 1999), 195–236.
51. Putnam, "Diplomacy and Domestic Politics."
52. Beth A. Simmons, "International Law and State Behavior: Commitment and Compliance in International Monetary Affairs," *American Political Science Review* 94, no. 4 (Dec. 2000): 819–35.
53. Pepinsky, "From Agents to Outcomes," 380.
54. Ibid., 379–85.

CHAPTER FOUR. DIVIDING THE PIE

1. Robert Pahre, "Multilateral Cooperation in an Iterated Prisoner's Dilemma," *Journal of Conflict Resolution* 38, no. 2 (June 1994): 326–52; David C. Earnest, "Coordination in Large Numbers: An Agent-Based Model of International Negotiations," *International Studies Quarterly* 52, no. 2 (June 2008): 363–82.
2. Thomas C. Schelling, *Micromotives and Macrobehavior* (New York: W. W. Norton, 1960), 172–73.
3. Ibid., 172.
4. Brian Skyrms and Robin Pemantle, "A Dynamic Model of Social Network Formation," *Proceedings of the National Academy of Sciences* 97, no. 16 (August 2000): 9340.
5. Conrad Power, "A Spatial Agent-Based Model of N-Person Prisoner's Dilemma Cooperation in a Socio-Geographic Community," *Journal of Artificial Societies and Social Simulation* 12, no. 1 (Jan. 2009).
6. Robert Axelrod, *The Complexity of Cooperation: Agent-Based Models of Competition and Collaboration* (Princeton: Princeton University Press, 1997).
7. Frank Schweitzer, Laxmidhar Behera, and Heinz Muhlenbein, "Evolution of Cooperation in a Spatial Prisoner's Dilemma," *Advances in Complex Systems* 5, no. 2–3 (June-Sept. 2002): 269–99; Shao-Meng Qin, Yong Chen, Xiao-Ying Zhao, and Jian Shi, "Effect of Memory on the Prisoner's Dilemma Game in a Square Lattice," *Physical Review E* 78, no. 4 (Oct. 2008).
8. Martin A. Nowak and Karl Sigmund, "Tit for Tat in Heterogeneous Populations," *Nature*, Jan. 16, 1992, 250–53.
9. Vladimir Akimov and Mikhail Soutchanski, "Automata Simulation of N-Person Social Dilemma Games," *Journal of Conflict Resolution* 38, no. 1 (March 1994): 138–48.

10. J. Alonso, A. Fernandez, and H. Fort, "Prisoner's Dilemma Cellular Automata Revisited: Evolution of Cooperation under Environmental Pressure," *Journal of Statistical Mechanics* 06 (2006): 06013.

11. Power, "A Spatial Agent-Based Model."

12. Masanao Matsushima and Takashi Ikegami, "Evolution of Strategies in the Three-Person Iterated Prisoner's Dilemma Game," *Journal of Theoretical Biology* 1, no. 7 (Nov. 1998): 65.

13. Skyrms and Pemantle, "A Dynamic Model of Social Network Formation."

14. For a good introduction to network and graph theory, see Watts, *Small Worlds*.

15. Duncan J. Watts and Stephen H. Strogatz, "Collective Dynamics of 'Small World' Networks," *Nature*, June 4, 1998, 409–10.

16. Mark Granovetter, "The Strength of Weak Ties," *American Journal of Sociology* 78, no. 6 (May 1973): 1360–80.

17. Hisashi Ohtsuki et al., "A Simple Rule for the Evolution of Cooperation on Graphs and Social Networks," *Nature*, May 25, 2006, 502–505.

18. F. C. Santos and J. M. Pacheco, "Scale-Free Networks Provide a Unifying Framework for the Emergence of Cooperation," *Physical Review Letters* 95, no. 9 (Aug. 26, 2005). Barabasi and Albert pioneered the study of scale-free networks. Barabasi and Albert, "Emergence of Scaling in Random Networks."

19. Olson, *The Logic of Collective Action*.

20. Miles Kahler, "Multilateralism with Small and Large Numbers," *International Organization* 46, no. 3 (Spring 1992): 681–708.

21. Pahre, "Multilateral Cooperation."

22. Duncan Snidal, "Relative Gains and the Pattern of International Cooperation," *American Political Science Review* 85, no. 3 (Sept. 1991): 923–42; Duncan Snidal, "International Cooperation among Relative Gains Maximizers," *International Studies Quarterly* 35, no. 4 (Dec. 1991): 387–402.

23. William B. G. Liebrand, "The Effect of Social Motives, Communication, and Group Size on Behaviour in an N-Person Multi-State Mixed-Motive Game," *European Journal of Social Psychology* 14, no. 3 (July/Sept. 1984): 239–64.

24. Kreps, *Game Theory and Economic Modelling*, 101.

25. Robert Boyd and Jeffrey P. Lorberbaum, "No Pure Strategy Is Evolutionarily Stable in the Repeated Prisoner's Dilemma Game," *Nature*, May 7, 1987, 58–59.

26. David C. Earnest and Kurt Taylor Gaubatz, "Modeling, Simulation, and the Social Sciences: An Agenda for Integration" (paper presented to the 2007 Simulation Integration Workshop Conference, Simulation Interoperability Standards Organization, Norfolk, VA, March 25–30, 2007).

27. Axelrod, *The Evolution of Cooperation*.

28. See also Nowak and Sigmund, "Tit for Tat in Heterogeneous Populations"; Martin A. Nowak and Robert M. May, "Evolutionary Games and Spatial Chaos," *Nature*, Oct. 29, 1992, 826–29; Akimov and Soutchanski, "Automata Simulation of N-Person Social Dilemma Games"; Miklos N. Szilagyi and Zoltan C. Szilagyi, "Non-Trivial Solutions to the N-Person Prisoners' Dilemma," *Systems Research and Behavioral Science* 19, no. 3 (May/June 2002): 281–90; Qin et al., "Effect of Memory on the Prisoner's Dilemma Game"; and Power, "A Spatial Agent-Based Model of N-Person Prisoner's Dilemma Cooperation."

29. Snidal, "Relative Gains and the Pattern of International Cooperation."
30. Stephen D. Krasner, "Global Communications and National Power: Life on the Pareto Frontier," *World Politics* 43, no. 3 (April 1991): 336–66.
31. Lisa L. Martin, "Interests, Power, and Multilateralism," *International Organization* 46, no. 4 (Autumn 1992): 765–92.
32. Arthur A. Stein, "Coordination and Collaboration: Regimes in an Anarchic World," *International Organization* 36, no. 2 (March 1982): 299–324.
33. Charles Lipson, "International Cooperation in Security and Economic Affairs," *World Politics* 37, no. 1 (Oct. 1984): 1–23; Axelrod and Keohane, "Achieving Cooperation under Anarchy"; Snidal, "Relative Gains and the Pattern of International Cooperation"; and Snidal, "International Cooperation among Relative Gains Maximizers."
34. Watts and Strogatz, "Collective Dynamics of 'Small World' Networks."
35. Steven Strogatz, *Sync: The Emerging Science of Spontaneous Order* (New York: Hyperion, 2003), 249.
36. Barabasi and Albert, "Emergence of Scaling in Random Networks."
37. Technically, a scale-free network is one in which the distribution of the number of connections of the nodes follows a power law.
38. Santos and Pacheco, "Scale-Free Networks Provide a Unifying Framework."
39. Richard Matthew and George Shambaugh, "The Limits of Terrorism: A Network Perspective," *International Studies Review* 7, no. 4 (Dec. 2005): 617–27.
40. Matsushima and Ikegami, "Evolution of Strategies"; Skyrms and Pemantle, "A Dynamic Model of Social Network Formation."
41. Szilagyi and Szilagyi, "Non-Trivial Solutions"; Power, "A Spatial Agent-Based Model of N-Person Prisoner's Dilemma Cooperation."
42. Axelrod, *The Evolution of Cooperation*.
43. Mitchell, *Complexity*, 17–21; Axelrod, "The Evolution of Strategies in the Iterated Prisoner's Dilemma."
44. Axelrod, *The Evolution of Cooperation*.
45. Mitchell has a good discussion of this point (*Complexity*, 18–19). In brief, each negotiator must have a strategy for any possible sequence of play. With a memory of length m and a two-choice two-person game, the shortest possible strategy length is 2^{2m}. Thus, with a memory length of 1, there are four possible outcomes of a prisoner's dilemma: both cooperate, both defect, defect-cooperate, and cooperate-defect. With a memory of 2, there are sixteen possible strategies, and so on. The problem is that above a memory of 5 (implying 1,024 possible scenarios) the computation required to generate, select, crossover, and mutate strategy sets becomes considerable.
46. Axelrod, *The Evolution of Cooperation*; Qin et al., "Effect of Memory on the Prisoner's Dilemma Game."
47. Boyd and Lorderbaum, "No Pure Strategy is Evolutionarily Stable."
48. There are a couple of possible explanations for this. One is that players may play different cooperative strategies and hence have large Hamming distances (for example, if one plays all cooperation and the other plays tit-for-tat for twenty iterations, they will have a Hamming distance of 10). Yet they are still cooperating. A second possibility concerns how the genetic algorithm generates new strategies.

Because each strategy is a map for all possible outcomes of the previous play, it may be a very long bit string: a memory of length three implies a bit-string of sixty-four positions. Yet as players evolve and cooperate, they may call only two or three of those sixty-four strategies. So the Hamming distance may reflect bits that differ in positions that neither player ever calls. If so, then the measure of Hamming distance tends to understate the level of agreement.

49. It is important to note that this is a small sample of the parameter space. The simulation allows the researcher to simulate problems with as few as two or as many as fifty negotiators. Negotiators' memories may vary between one and five previous plays of the game. With four possible network structures and four games, this implies 3,072 parameter sets. I simulated only 192 parameter sets. Thus, I infer the results presented here from a sample of about 6 percent of the parameter space, albeit a sample that deliberately varies parameters of interest between low and high values.

50. Olson, *The Logic of Collective Action*.

51. Matsushima and Ikegami, "Evolution of Strategies"; Skyrms and Pemantle, "A Dynamic Model of Social Network Formation."

52. Santos and Pacheco, "Scale-Free Networks Provide a Unifying Framework."

53. Joseph M. Grieco, "Anarchy and the Limits of Cooperation: A Realist Critique of the Newest Liberal Institutionalism," *International Organization* 42, no. 3 (Summer 1988): 485–507.

54. Axelrod's version of the prisoner's dilemma was:

		Player 2	
		Cooperate	Defect
Player 1	Cooperate	3, 3	0, 5
	Defect	5, 0	1, 1

Payoffs: Player 1, Player 2

Axelrod, "The Evolution of Strategies."

55. Szilagyi and Szilagyi, "Non-Trivial Solutions to the N-Person Prisoners' Dilemma"; Power, "A Spatial Agent-Based Model of N-Person Prisoner's Dilemma Cooperation."

56. Matsushima and Ikegami, "Evolution of Strategies"; Skyrms and Pemantle, "A Dynamic Model of Social Network Formation."

CHAPTER FIVE. COWS GROW TREES, NETS GROW FISH

1. Richard A. Carey, *The Philosopher Fish: Sturgeon, Caviar, and the Geography of Desire* (New York: Counterpoint, 2005); C. J. Chivers, "Corruption Endangers a Treasure of the Caspian," *The New York Times*, Nov. 28, 2005, 1.

2. Chivers, "Corruption Endangers Treasure of the Caspian"; Jennifer A. Devine, Krista D. Baker and Richard L. Haedrick, "Deep-Sea Fishes Qualify as Endangered: A Shift from Shelf Fisheries to the Deep Sea Is Exhausting Late-Maturing Species that Recover only Slowly," *Nature*, Jan. 2006, 29.

3. Chivers, "Corruption Endangers Treasure of the Caspian."

4. Ellen K. Pikitch et al., "Status, Trends, and Management of Sturgeon and Paddlefish Fisheries," *Fish and Fisheries* 6, no. 3 (Sept. 2005): 233–65.
5. David G. Green and Suzanne Sadedin, "Interactions Matter—Complexity in Landscapes and Ecosystems," *Ecological Complexity* 2 (2005): 118.
6. Peter J. Mumby et al., "Fishing, Trophic Cascades, and the Process of Grazing on Coral Reefs," *Science*, Jan. 2006, 98–101.
7. Jervis, *System Effects*, 49. Jervis in turn cites David Western, "The Balance of Nature," *Wildlife Conservation* 96, no. 2 (March/April 1993): 54.
8. For a good introduction to endogenous growth theory, see Gilpin, *The Global Political Economy*, 108–48.
9. John W. Meyer et al., "World Society and the Nation-State," *The American Journal of Sociology* 103, no. 1 (July 1997): 144–81.
10. David Kreps argues, "Some (important) sorts of games have many equilibria, and the theory is no help in sorting out whether any one is the 'solution' and, if one is, which one is." Kreps, *Game Theory and Economic Modelling*, 97. See also Brian J. McGill and Joel S. Brown, "Evolutionary Game Theory and Adaptive Dynamics of Continuous Traits," *Annual Review of Ecology, Evolution, and Systematics* 38 (2007): 403–35.
11. Hardin, "The Tragedy of the Commons."
12. Elinor Ostrom, "Coping with Tragedies of the Commons," *Annual Review of Political Science* 2, no. 1 (1999): 493–535.
13. Rosenau notes the growth of "multicentric governance" alongside state-based governance, asserting that "informal and noninstitutional forms of authority (spheres) [that] may emerge at least to supplement, if not to replace, the long-established formal and institutionalized structures of authority." Rosenau, *Distant Proximities*, 294. Likewise, Scholte argues that globalization has given rise to "polycentric" governance that "disperses regulation across multiple substate, state, suprastate and private sites, as well as dense networks that interlink these many points of governance." Scholte, *Globalization*, 141.
14. Arun Agrawal, "Sustainable Governance of Common-Pool Resources: Context, Methods, and Politics," *Annual Review of Anthropology* 32 (2003): 244.
15. Olson, *The Logic of Collective Action*.
16. Ibid.
17. For a good introduction, see Elinor Ostrom, *Governing the Commons: The Evolution of Institutions for Collective Action* (Cambridge: Harvard University Press, 1990).
18. Hardin, "The Tragedy of the Commons."
19. Ostrom, *Governing the Commons*.
20. Agrawal, "Sustainable Governance."
21. Olson, *The Logic of Collective Action*; Robert Wade, *Village Republics: Economic Conditions for Collective Action in South India* (New York: Cambridge University Press, 1994).
22. Arun Agrawal and Sanjeev Goyal, "Group Size and Collective Action: Third-party Monitoring of Common-pool Resources," *Comparative Political Studies* 34, no. 1 (Feb. 2001): 63–93.

23. Jean-Marie Baland and Jean-Philippe Platteau, *Halting Degradation of Natural Resources: Is There a Role for Rural Communities?* (Oxford: Oxford University Press, 1996), ch. 12; Ostrom, *Governing the Commons*, ch. 2.

24. Ostrom, *Governing the Commons*, 21–34.

25. Ibid., 45.

26. Ostrom, "Coping with Tragedies," 518–19.

27. Ibid., 520.

28. David Southgate, Rodrigo Sierra, and Lawrence A. Brown, "The Causes of Tropical Deforestation in Ecuador: A Statistical Analysis," *World Development* 19, no. 9 (September 1991): 1145–51; cited in Baland and Platteau, *Halting Degradation*, 28.

29. Daniel Pauly et al., "Toward Sustainability in World Fisheries," *Nature*, Aug. 8, 2002, 689–95.

30. Agrawal, "Sustainable Governance."

31. Tom Teitenberg, "The Tradable Permits Approach to Protecting the Commons: What Have We Learned?" in *The Drama of the Commons*, ed. Elinor Ostrom et al. (Washington, DC: National Academy Press, 2002): 197–232.

32. Ostrom, *Governing the Commons*, 12–13.

33. Ibid., 13–14.

34. Ibid., 497.

35. Wade, *Village Republics*.

36. Agrawal, "Sustainable Governance," 254.

37. In game theoretical terms, players have incomplete information because they are uncertain about each other's payoffs. Dynamic games of incomplete information typically have Nash equilibria or mixing strategies.

38. James Wilson, "Scientific Uncertainty, Complex Systems, and the Design of Common-Pool Institutions," in *The Drama of the Commons*, ed. Elinor Ostrom et al. (Washington, DC: National Academy Press, 2002), 327–59.

39. Ibid., 340.

40. Ostrom, "Coping with Tragedies," 507–508.

41. Wilson, "Scientific Uncertainty," 341.

42. Axelrod, *The Evolution of Cooperation*.

43. Baland and Platteau, *Halting Degradation*.

44. Pauly et al., "Toward Sustainability in World Fisheries."

45. Ostrom, "Coping with Tragedies," 507.

46. Agrawal, "Sustainable Governance."

47. Ostrom, "Coping with Tragedies," 508.

48. Lustick, Miodownik, and Eidelson, "Secessionism in Multicultural States," 211–12.

49. Ostrom, "Coping with Tragedies," 509.

50. Agrawal, "Sustainable Governance," 255.

51. Ostrom, "Coping with Tragedies," 519.

52. Wilson, "Scientific Uncertainty," 334.

53. Ostrom, "Coping with Tragedies"; Wilson, "Scientific Uncertainty"; Poteete, Janssen, and Ostrom, *Working Together*.

54. In general, the length of an appropriator's strategy will be $2^{m \times n}$.

55. This method of encoding appropriator strategies requires each appropriator to have a strategy bit string long enough to accommodate every possible configuration of actions by its social network neighbors. The length of the strategy bit string is $2^{M \times N}$. For small networks and short memories, this is a manageable length. However, because $M_{max} = 5$ and $N_{max} = 19$ (theoretically, an agent could have all other appropriators as social network neighbors), for some simulations appropriators may require S of length 295. As a practical matter, the NetLogo software with which I encoded the model cannot parse integers larger than 253 digits. For most simulations, however, this presents no problem. My verification of the model estimates that in half the simulations, appropriators have an initial network of more than 10 neighbors. But in only 20 percent of these simulations will appropriators have a memory endowment of 5. Thus, I estimate that the bit string implementation of S is a problem in only about 10 percent of the simulations. To guard against run-time errors, the model code includes a procedure that uses the logarithm of the decimal formatted memory value to refer to the position on the strategy bit string. This allows appropriators to have S of lengths less than 253 digits.

56. That is, each appropriator agent tests a "population" of forty strategies, runs the genetic algorithm, and repeats the cycle for forty "generations" (again, invoking the language of biology and offspring). Forty strategies times forty generations gives 1,600 total runs of the model.

57. Ostrom, *Governing the Commons*, 34.

58. Ibid., 507–508.

59. Ibid., 33.

60. Because the density of the network (i.e., the proportion of actual ties to total possible ties) is sensitive to the assumptions about the random process of network initialization, the experiment tests random social networks generated with initial probabilities of attachment of 0.1, 0.3, 0.6, and 0.9.

61. I recorded these data using ORA, a free social network analysis tool. Kathleen M. Carley, "ORA Organization Risk Analyzer v. 2.0," (Pittsburgh: Center for Computational Analysis of Social and Organizational Systems, Carnegie Mellon University, 2010).

62. The subsequent data support this assumption. Of the 733 simulations in which the appropriator agents collapsed the ecosystem, the longest-lived such simulation was 250 timesteps, precisely halfway between the beginning of harvesting at $t = 100$ and the arbitrary truncation of the simulation at $t = 400$.

63. Olson, *The Logic of Collective Action*; Ostrom, "Coping with Tragedies"; Agrawal and Goyal, "Group Size and Collective Action."

64. Agrawal, "Sustainable Governance," 254.

65. The information rule has three possible values and the memory parameter has five discrete values. For simplicity, I assumed five discrete values for the technological efficiency parameter. This implies $5 \times 5 \times 3 = 75$ total parameter combinations.

66. Duncan J. Watts and Steven H. Strogatz, "Collective Dynamics in 'Small-World' Networks," *Nature*, June 4, 1998, 440–42.

67. The mean payoff for the $I_{network}$ rule is .1445 resources per appropriator per timestep. The mean value for the I_{global} rule is .1110. The t-statistic is 2.886 with a p-value of .002.

68. In this study, the two assumptions for which the analysis controls are the density of the initial random networks (labeled as "connection bias" to imply the effect of the probability of connection at the time of model initialization); and whether appropriators share strategies using a crossover procedure in the genetic algorithm, labeled "crossover of appropriators dummy."

69. One other concern is the presence of multicollinearity among regressors, which increases the probability of finding no significant effects where some may in fact occur. Correlation analysis found high correlations between the two information rule dummy variables and their interaction terms. For this reason, the regression results reported in Tables 5.4 through 5.6 probably understate the true effects of information on appropriator scores, social network structure, and ecosystem survival. This suggests that the regression approach adopted here is conservative, and is unlikely to find effects when in fact none exist.

70. Janet M. Box-Steffensmeier and Bradford S. Jones, "Time Is of the Essence: Event History Models in Political Science," *American Journal of Political Science* 41, no. 4 (Oct. 1997): 1414–61.

71. I compared ten simulations in which appropriators used the global information rule to ten in which they used the network rule. I conducted an ANOVA test of the 3,870 timesteps during which appropriators could harvest. The global rule produced significantly greater variation in the number of appropriators at any given timestep: $F = 75.48$, $p < .0001$. This is consistent with the speculation that the global rule induces greater variation in the number of harvesters at any given timestep.

72. Pauly et al., "Toward sustainability," 690–91.

73. P. M. Polgreen et al., "Use of Prediction Markets to Forecast Infectious Disease Activity," *Clinical Infectious Diseases* 44 (Jan. 2007): 272–79.

74. Barabasi and Bonabeau, "Scale-Free Networks."

75. Ostrom, "Coping with Tragedies," 509.

CHAPTER SIX. TOO BIG TO COMPROMISE

1. Rajiv Sabherwal, Rudy Hirschheim, and Tim Goles, "The Dynamics of Alignment: Insights from a Punctuated Equilibrium Model," *Organization Science* 12, no. 2 (March-April 2001): 179. See also Mark J. Roe, "Chaos and Evolution in Law and Economics," *Harvard Law Review* 109, no. 3 (Jan. 1996): 641–68.

2. Matthew Lynn, "The Fallen King of Finland," *Bloomberg BusinessWeek*, Sept. 20–26, 2010, 7–8.

3. Gerald F. Seib, "In Crisis, Opportunity for Obama," *Wall Street Journal*, Nov. 21, 2008, A2.

4. "Scottish Conference: Brown Presents his Blueprint for International Banking Reform," *The Scotsman*, March 6, 2009.

5. "An EU Fudge on Bank Reform," *The Economist*, July 19, 2009.

6. James Wilson, "Deutsche Bank Adds to Calls for Tough Capital Regulations," *Financial Times*, Sept. 9, 2009, 22.

7. James Wilson, "German Bankers Fear Impact of New Rules," *Financial Times*, Sept. 21, 2009, 4.

8. See for example Stephen Foley, "Tricky Lessons Yet to Be Learnt by International Regulators; The View from Wall Street," *The Independent* (London),

Sept 14, 2010, 36; Katherine Griffiths, "New Bank Rules Are Too Weak to Work, Says Myners," *The Times* (London), Sept. 15, 2010, 37; George Melloan, "Basel's Illusions; The New Basel III Banking Agreement Is Unlikely to Instill Safety into Complex Human Transactions," *The National Post* (Canada), Sept. 15, 2010, FP17; and Leigh Skene, "Basel III Won't Save Us from Another Banking Crisis," FT.com, Sept 16, 2010.

    9. John Plender, "Banks Let off the Hook as Flawed Model Is Preserved," *Financial Times*, July 15, 2009, 22.

    10. "Third Time's the Charm?" *The Economist*, Sept. 13, 2010.

    11. Dani Rodrik, "A Plan B for Global Finance," *The Economist*, March 12, 2009.

    12. Specifically, German banks exhibit the third highest "betweenness centrality," a network measure of the frequency with which German banks lie on the shortest path between two otherwise unconnected locations. Goetz von Peter, "International Banking Centres: A Network Perspective," *BIS Quarterly Review* (Dec. 2007): 33–34.

    13. Rodrik, "A Plan B for Global Finance."

    14. Marc Levinson, "Faulty Basel: Why Diplomacy Won't Keep the Financial System Safe," *Foreign Affairs* 89, no. 3 (May 2010).

    15. Scholte, *Globalization*, 166.

    16. Ranjit Lall, "Reforming Global Banking Rules: Back to the Future?" Paper presented at the Danish Institute for International Studies, DIIS Working Paper 2010 (16): 9.

    17. Ibid.

    18. For a good introduction to the tier I and tier II rules, see Daniel K. Tarullo, *Banking on Basel: The Future of International Financial Regulation* (Washington, DC: Peterson Institute for International Economics, 2008), 55–57.

    19. Ibid., 57.

    20. Lall, "Reforming Global Banking Rules," 10.

    21. Ibid., 11–12.

    22. Niall Ferguson, "Diminished Returns," *The New York Times Magazine*, May 17, 2009.

    23. Patrick Jenkins, "German Banks Try to Fend off Basel III," *Financial Times*, Sept. 6, 2010.

    24. Brooke Masters, "Fears for German Banks under New Rules," *Financial Times*, Sept. 9, 2010.

    25. Robert H. Wade, "The Great Slump: What Comes Next?" *Economic and Political Weekly*, Nov. 20, 2010, 57–58.

    26. Basel Committee on Banking Supervision, "Group of Governors and Heads of Supervision Announces Higher Global Minimum Capital Standards," Bank for International Settlements (Basel, Switzerland): Sept. 12, 2010. Press release. See also Huw Jones, "Snap Analysis: Implementation Key to Basel III Success," Reuters, Sept. 12, 2010.

    27. Alan S. Binder, "Two Cheers for the New Bank Capital Standards; Why Do We Still Rely on Rating Agencies, and Why Are We Still Allowing Lehman Brothers Levels of Leverage?" *The Wall Street Journal*, Sept. 29, 2010.

28. Alan Beattie and Tom Braithwaite, "Leading Nations Agree to Disagree on Bank Tax," *Financial Times*, April 24, 2010.
29. Lall, "Reforming Global Banking Rules," 33; Brooke Masters, "Impact of Basel III: Trade Finance May Become a Casualty," *Financial Times*, Oct. 19, 2010.
30. Charles Kindleberger, *The World in Depression, 1929–1939* (Berkeley: University of California Press, 1973).
31. Barry Eichengreen, "Hegemonic Stability Theories of the International Monetary System," in *Can Nations Agree? Essays on International Economic Cooperation*, ed. Ralph Bryant (Washington, DC: The Brookings Institution, 1989), 255–98.
32. Duncan Wood, *Governing Global Banking: The Basel Committee and the Politics of Financial Globalization* (Aldershot: Ashgate 2005).
33. Gilpin, *Global Political Economy*, 94.
34. Rodrik, "A Plan B for Global Finance."
35. Tarullo, *Banking on Basel*, 6.
36. Indeed, Rodrik suggests that competing national regulatory systems make more sense economically and politically than a global regime. Rodrik, "A Plan B for Global Finance."
37. Ethan B. Kapstein, "Architects of Stability? International Cooperation among Financial Supervisors," *BIS Working Papers* no. 199 (2006).
38. Edward J. Kane, "Connecting National Safety Nets: The Dialects of the Basel II Contracting Process," *Atlantic Economic Journal* 35, no. 4 (Nov. 2007): 399–409.
39. Lall, "Reforming Global Banking Rules."
40. Ibid.
41. For a good introduction, see Ian Wilkinson, *Business Relating Business: Managing Organisational Relations and Networks* (Northampton, MA: Edward Elgar, 2008).
42. Alexander Gerschenkron, *Economic Backwardness in Historical Perspective* (Cambridge: Harvard University Press, 1962).
43. James Kurth, "The Political Consequences of the Product Cycle: Industrial History and Political Outcomes," *International Organization* 33, no. 1 (Dec. 1979): 1–34.
44. Christian Upper and Andreas Worms, "Estimating Bilateral Exposures in the German Interbank Market: Is There a Danger of Contagion?" *European Economic Review* 48 (2004): 827–49.
45. Oliver Williamson, *The Economic Institutions of Capitalism: Firms, Markets, Relational Contracting* (New York: Free Press, 1985).
46. "Basel III: Third Time's the Charm?"; Paul Krugman, *The Return of Depression Economics and the Crisis of 2008* (New York: W. W. Norton, 2009).
47. Franklin Allen and Ana Babus, "Networks in Finance," in *The Network Challenge: Strategy, Profit, and Risk in an Interlinked World*, ed. Paul R. Kleindorfer and Yoram (Jerry) Wind (Upper Saddle River, NJ: Pearson, 2009).
48. Helmut Elsinger, Alfred Lehar, and Martin Summer, "Risk Assessment for Banking Systems," paper presented to the 2003. European Finance Association annual convention, Glasgow, Scotland, Aug. 20–23, 2003.

49. Michael Boss et al., "Network Topology of the Interbank Market," *Quantitative Finance* 4 (Dec. 2004): 677–85.
50. Upper and Worms, "Estimating Bilateral Exposures."
51. Giulia De Masi et al., "Fitness Model for the Italian Interbank Market," *Physical Review E* 74 (2006); Giulia Iori et al., "A Network Analysis of the Italian Overnight Money Market," *Journal of Economic Dynamics and Control* 32 (2008): 259–78.
52. Hajime Inaoka et al., "Self-Similarity of Banking Network," *Physica A* 339 (2004): 621–34.
53. Kimmo Soramaki et al., "The Topology of Interbank Payment Flows," *Physica A* 379 (2007): 317–33.
54. George Sheldon and Martin Mauer, "Interbank Lending and Systemic Risk: An Empirical Analysis for Switzerland," *Swiss Journal of Economics and Statistics* 134, no. 4 (1998): 685–704.
55. Simon Wells, "U.K. Interbank Exposures: Systemic Risk Implications," *Financial Stability Review* (Dec. 2002): 175–82.
56. Allen and Babus, "Networks in Finance."
57. Erlend Nier et al., "Network Models and Financial Stability," *Journal of Economic Dynamics and Control* 31 (2007): 2033–60.
58. Upper and Worms, "Estimating Bilateral Exposures," 844.
59. Allen and Babus, "Networks in Finance," 373.
60. Franklin Allen and Douglas Gale, "Financial Contagion," *Journal of Political Economy* 108, no. 1 (Feb. 2000): 1–33.
61. Yaron Leitner, "Financial Networks: Contagion, Commitment, and Private Sector Bailouts," *Journal of Finance* 60, no. 6 (Dec. 2005): 2925–53.
62. Michael Howlett, "Do Networks Matter? Linking Policy Network Structure to Policy Outcomes: Evidence from Four Canadian Policy Sectors 1990–2000," *Canadian Journal of Political Science* 35, no. 2 (June 2002): 235–67.
63. Robert D. Putnam, "Diplomacy and Domestic Politics: The Logic of Two-Level Games," *International Organization* 42, no. 3 (Summer 1988): 427–60.
64. Stephen D. Krasner, "Global Communications and National Power: Life on the Pareto Frontier," *World Politics* 43, no. 3 (April 1991), 336–66.
65. The formulation for the classic game comes from ibid.
66. Soramaki et al., "The Topology of Interbank Payment Flows," 324.
67. Upper and Worms, "Estimating Bilateral Exposures," 836–37.
68. Barabasi and Bonabeau, "Scale-Free Networks."
69. Boss et al., "Network Topology of the Interbank Market," 679.
70. Ibid., 682.
71. Stefan W. Schmitz and Claus Puhr, "Risk Concentration, Network Structure, and Contagion in the Austrian Real Time Interbank Settlement System," in *Simulation Studies of Liquidity Needs, Risks and Efficiency in Payment Networks*, ed. Harry Leinonen (Helsinki: Bank of Finland, 2007).
72. Boss et al., "Network Topology of the Interbank Market," 682.
73. Ibid.
74. NWB Team, *Network Workbench Tool*, Indiana University, Northeastern University, and University of Michigan (2006).

75. The Network Workbench Tool implements a Watts-Strogatz algorithm for small world networks and the Barabasi-Albert algorithm for scale-free networks.

76. Soramaki et al., "The Topology of Interbank Payment Flows"; Upper and Worms, "Estimating Bilateral Exposures."

77. This is similar to the learning algorithm negotiator agents used in the coordination game model in chapter 3.

78. The centrality betweenness (CB) values of the five nodes are 0.26, 0.16, 0.11, 0.09, and 0.07. No other node in the network has a CB score greater than or equal to .07.

79. This may also reflect the relatively small number of simulations with which to test for significant differences—in all t-tests and chi-square tests, the number of observations ranges from 60 to 180. Given the variability in the data, this may be an insufficient number of observations to tease out meaningful differences.

80. Von Peter, "International Banking Centres," 37.

CHAPTER SEVEN. NETS OF INSECURITY

1. Douglas Birch, "Lights Out: A Newly Declassified Report Shows How Vulnerable America's Electrical Grid Is," *Foreign Policy*, Nov. 14, 2012.

2. National Research Council, *Terrorism and the Electric Power Delivery System* (Washington, DC: National Academies Press, 2012), 2.

3. Ibid., 1.

4. David Held et al., *Global Transformations: Politics, Economics, and Culture* (Stanford: Stanford University Press, 1999), 170.

5. Jonathan M. Katz and Jennifer Kay, "Red Tape Cutting off Food," *The Virginian-Pilot*, March 7, 2008.

6. Ian Lovett, "1.4. Million Lose Electricity in Area around San Diego," *The New York Times*, Sept. 9, 2011, A20.

7. Keith Bradsher, "Shipping Lines Pull Back from Japan," *The New York Times*, March 25, 2011, B1.

8. Cameron A. MacKenzie, Joost R. Santos, and Kash Barker, "Measuring Changes in International Production from a Disruption: Case Study of the Japanese Earthquake and Tsunami," *International Journal of Production Economics* 138, no. 2 (Aug. 2012): 293–302.

9. L. A. N. Amaral, A. Scala, M. Barthelemy, and H. E. Stanley, "Classes of Small-World Networks," *Proceedings of the National Academy of Sciences* 97, no. 31 (Oct. 10, 2000): 11149–52; R. Guimera and L. A. N. Amaral, "Modeling the World-Wide Airport Network," *The European Physical Journal B* 38, no. 2 (March 2004): 381–85.

10. Rosenau, *Turbulence in World Politics*; Rosenau, *Distant Proximities*; Neil E. Harrison, *Complexity in World Politics: Concepts and Methods of a New Paradigm* (Albany: State University of New York Press, 2006).

11. Scholte, *Globalization: A Critical Introduction*, 16–17.

12. Manuel Castells, *The Rise of the Network Society* (Malden, MA: Blackwell, 1996).

13. Held et al., *Global Transformations*, 149.

14. Beth A. Simmons and Zachary Elkins, "The Globalization of Liberalization: Policy Diffusion in the International Political Economy," *American Political Science Review* 98, no. 1 (Feb. 2004): 171–89.

15. Nancy Brune and Geoffrey Garrett, "The Globalization Rorschach Test: International Economic Integration, Inequality, and the Role of Government," *Annual Review of Political Science* 8 (2005): 399–423.

16. Scholte, *Globalization: A Critical Introduction*, ch. 9.

17. Bruce Hoffman, "The Changing Face of Al Qaeda and the Global War on Terrorism," *Studies in Conflict & Terrorism* 27, no. 6 (Nov. 2004): 553–54; Gal Luft and Anne Korin, "Terrorism Goes to Sea," *Foreign Affairs* 83, no. 6 (Nov./Dec. 2004): 64–65.

18. Steven A. Yetiv, *The Petroleum Triangle: Oil, Globalization and Terror* (Ithaca: Cornell University Press, 2011): 193–97.

19. Brian A. Jackson, Lloyd Dixon, and Victoria A. Greenfield, *Economically Targeted Terrorism: A Review of the Literature and a Framework for Considering Defensive Approaches* (Santa Monica: RAND Corporation, 2007), 13–21.

20. Edward D. Mansfield and Brian M. Pollins, "The Study of Interdependence and Conflict: Recent Advances, Open Questions, and Directions for Future Research," *Journal of Conflict Resolution* 45, no. 6 (Dec. 2001): 834–59.

21. Raymond Vernon, *Sovereignty at Bay: The Multinational Spread of U.S. Enterprises* (New York: Basic Books, 1971); Robert Gilpin, *War and Change in World Politics* (New York: Cambridge University Press, 1983).

22. Bruce M. Russett and John R. Oneal, *Triangulating Peace: Democracy, Interdependence, and International Organizations* (New York: Norton, 2001).

23. Robert O. Keohane and Joseph S. Nye, *Power and Interdependence: World Politics in Transition* (Boston: Little, Brown, 1977), 12.

24. Ibid., 13.

25. Rosenau, *Turbulence in World Politics*; Rosenau, *Distant Proximities*; Jervis, *System Effects*; Zeev Maoz, "Network Polarization, Network Interdependence, and International Conflict, 1816–2002," *Journal of Peace Research* 43, no. 4 (July 2006): 391–411.

26. Rosenau, *Distant Proximities*, 209.

27. Lorenz, "Deterministic Nonperiodic Flow"; Stephen M. Walt, "Fads, Fevers, and Firestorms," *Foreign Policy* 121 (Dec. 2000): 34–42.

28. U.S. Public Law 110-53, 110th Cong., 1st sess., *Implementing Recommendations of the 9/11. Commission Act of 2007* (Aug. 3, 2007); U.S. Department of Homeland Security, *National Infrastructure Protection Plan* (Washington, DC: U.S. GPO, 2006); U.S. Department of Defense. Office of the Assistant Secretary of Defense for Homeland Defense, *Defense Critical Infrastructure Program Assessment Benchmarks* (Washington, DC: U.S. GPO, 2007).

29. Mark Gerencser, Jim Weinberg, and Don Vincent, *Port Security War Game: Implications for U.S. Supply Chains* (Vienna, VA: Booz-Allen Hamilton, 2003).

30. Organization for Economic Cooperation and Development, Directorate for Science Technology and Industry, *Security in Maritime Transport: Risk Factors and Economic Impact* (Paris: OECD Publication Services, 2006); Michael D. Greenberg

et al., *Maritime Terrorism: Risk and Liability* (Washington, DC: RAND Corporation, 2006); U.S. Congressional Budget Office, *The Economic Costs of Disruptions in Container Shipments* (Washington, DC: U.S. GPO, March 29, 2006).

31. Axelrod, *The Complexity of Cooperation*.
32. Russett and Oneal, *Triangulating Peace*.
33. David Held and Anthony McGrew, *Globalization/Anti-Globalization* (Malden, MA: Blackwell, 2002), 24.
34. Alexander Cooley, "Globalization and National Security after Empire: The Former Soviet Space," in *Globalization and National Security*, ed. Jonathan Kirshner (New York: Routledge, 2006), 208.
35. Karl P. Mueller, "The Paradox of Liberal Hegemony: Globalization and U.S. National Security," in *Globalization and National Security*, ed. Jonathan Kirshner (New York: Routledge, 2006), 144.
36. Barabasi and Bonabeau, "Scale-Free Networks."
37. Watts, *Small Worlds*.
38. A. Barrat et al., "The Architecture of Complex Weighted Networks"; Wen-Xu Wang and Guanrong Chen, "Universal Robustness Characteristics of Weighted Networks against Cascading Failure," *Physical Review E* 77, no. 2 (Feb. 2008); Yaru Dang and Wenjing Li, "Comparative Analysis on Weighted Network Structure of Air Passenger Flow of China and US," *Journal of Transportation Systems Engineering and Information Technology* 11, no. 3 (June 2011): 156–62.
39. E. Estrada, "Network Robustness to Targeted Attacks: The Interplay of Expansibility and Degree Distribution," *The European Physical Journal B* 52, no. 4 (Aug. 2006): 563–74; Wang and Chen, "Universal Robustness Characteristics."
40. Luca Dall'Asta, Alain Barrat, Marc Barthelemy, and Alessandro Vespignani, "Vulnerability of Weighted Networks," *Journal of Statistical Mechanics: Theory and Experiment* 2006, no. 4 (April 2006): 1–12; Keping Li, Ziyou Gao, and Baohua Mao, "A Weighted Network Model for Railway Traffic," *International Journal of Modern Physics* 17, no. 9 (Sept. 2006); Anna Nagurney and Qiang Qiang, "A Transportation Network Efficiency Measure that Captures Flows, Behavior, and Costs with Applications to Network Component Importance Identification and Vulnerability," *Proceedings of the POMS 18th Annual Conference* (Miami: Production and Operations Management Society, 2007).
41. R. Yang et al., "Optimal Weighting Scheme for Suppressing Cascades and Traffic Congestion in Complex Networks," *Physical Review E* 79, no. 2 (Feb. 2009).
42. R. Guimera et al., "The Worldwide Air Transportation Network: Anomalous Centrality, Community Structure, and Cities' Global Roles," *Proceedings of the National Academy of Sciences* 102, no. 22 (April 2005): 7794–99.
43. U.S. Public Law 110-53.
44. U.S. Department of Homeland Security, *National Infrastructure Protection Plan*.
45. U.S. Department of Defense, Office of the Assistant Secretary of Defense for Homeland Defense, *Defense Critical Infrastructure Program*, Directive 3020.40 (Washington, DC: U.S. GPO, 2005).

46. Lustick, Miodownik, and J. Eidelson, "Secessionism in Multicultural States."

47. "Air Carriers: T-100. International Market," U.S. Department of Transportation, Bureau of Transport Statistics, accessed September 9, 2011, http://www.transtats.bts.gov.

48. Aaron Clauset, Cosma Rohilla Shalizi, and M. E. J. Newman, "Power-Law Distributions in Empirical Data," *SIAM Review* 51, no. 4 (2009): 661–703.

49. Guimera and Amaral, "Modeling the Worldwide Airport Network."

50. W. Li and X. Cai, "Statistical Analysis of Airport Network of China," *Physical Review E* 69, no. 4 (April 2004).

51. Ganesh Bagler, "Analysis of the Airport Network of India as a Complex Weighted Network," *Physica A: Statistical Mechanics and Its Applications* 387, no. 12 (May 2008): 2972–80.

52. "Annual and Per-Minute Cost of Delays to U.S. Airlines," Air Transportation Association, accessed November 23, 2012, http://www.airlines.org/Pages/Annual-and-Per-Minute-Cost-of-Delays-to-U.S.-Airlines.aspx.

CHAPTER EIGHT. CONCLUSIONS

1. For example, Hans Morgenthau wrote that "the student of international politics must learn and never forget . . . that the complexities of international affairs make simple solutions and trustworthy prophecies impossible." Hans J. Morgenthau, *Politics among Nations: The Struggle for Power and Peace* (New York: Knopf 1973 [1948]): 4–6.

2. Kenneth N. Waltz, *Man, the State, and War* (New York: Columbia University Press, 1954).

3. Committee on Economic and Environmental Impacts of Increasing Biofuels Production. *Renewable Fuel Standard: Potential Economic and Environmental Effects of U.S. Biofuels Policy* (Washington, DC: National Academies Press, 2011), 131–32.

4. Timothy A. Wise, "US Corn Ethanol Fuels Food Crisis in Developing Countries," *Al-Jazeera*, Oct. 10, 2012.

5. Annia Ciezadlo, "Eat, Drink, Protest: Stories of the Middle East's Hungry Rumblings," *Foreign Policy* 186 (May/June 2011): 79.

6. Jervis, *System Effects*, 44.

7. Ostrom, "Coping with Tragedies," 524.

8. Andrew Jacobs, "In China Music Festivals, Hip Rock, and the State's Blessing," *The New York Times*, Oct. 24, 2010, 6.

9. Jack Ewing, "Some Religious Leaders See a Threat as Europe Grows More Secular," *The New York Times*, Sept. 19, 2012.

10. Rosenau, *Distant Proximities*, 62–63; Scholte, *Globalization*, 217–18.

11. Robert Neuwirth, *Stealth of Nations: The Global Rise of the Informal Economy* (New York: Anchor, 2012), 27.

12. Ibid., 19.

13. Giddens, *The Consequences of Modernity*, 139.

14. John Arlidge, "Tech's Big Beasts Eye Silicon Savanna," *The Sunday Times* (London), Aug. 12, 2012, 1.

15. Moises Naim, *Illicit: How Smugglers, Traffickers, and Copycats are Hijacking the Global Economy* (New York: Anchor, 2005), 65–85.

16. Rachel Donadio, "Stitched in Italy, by Chinese: Newcomers Redefine a Label," *The New York Times*, Sept. 12, 2010, 1.

17. Dexter Filkins, "TV Channel Draws Viewers, and Threats, in Iran," *The New York Times*, Nov. 20, 2010, 1.

18. Gilpin, *War and Change in World Politics*, 39–49.

19. Ibid., 40.

20. Rosenau, *Distant Proximities*; Scholte, *Globalization: A Critical Introduction*.

21. Randall D. Germain and Michael Kenny, "Engaging Gramsci: International Relations Theory and the New Gramscians," *Review of International Studies* 24, no. 1 (Jan. 1998): 3–21.

22. Nicholas D. Kristof, "I've Seen the Future (in Haiti)," *The New York Times*, Dec. 5, 2010, 10.

23. Simon Broll, "Making Money—New Currency Brings Hope to Debt-Stricken City," *Spiegel Online International*, March 16, 2012, accessed November 25, 2012, http://www.spiegel.de/international/zeitgeist/0,1518,821769,00.html.

24. Raphael Minder, "Catalan Vote Could Be a First Step toward Self-Rule," *The New York Times*, Nov. 23, 2012.

25. Poteete, Janssen, and Ostrom, *Working Together*, 194–212.

26. Thomas S. Kuhn, *The Structure of Scientific Revolutions* (Chicago: University of Chicago Press, 1965).

27. Rosenau, *Turbulence in World Politics*, 44.

REFERENCES

"A Doctor in Your Pocket." *The Economist*, April 16, 2009.
"A Model Approach: More Development Work Is Needed to Help Computer Simulations Inform Economic Policy." *Nature* 460 (August 2009): 667.
"After the Fall." *The Economist*, November 13, 2008.
"An EU Fudge on Bank Reform." *The Economist*, July 19, 2009.
"Basel III: Third Time's the Charm?" *The Economist*, September 13, 2010.
"Battle Is Joined." *The Economist*, April 23, 2009.
"Did Intrade Correctly Predict the 2008 Presidential Election?" Accessed August 13, 2010. http://electoralmap.net/analysis.php.
"Marching off to Cyberwar." *The Economist*, December 4, 2008.
"Obama '08: The Official iPhone Application." Accessed August 24, 2009. http://my.barackobama.com/page/content/iphone.
"Scottish Conference: Brown Presents his blueprint for international banking reform." *The Scotsman*, March 6, 2009.
"Stage Prop." *The Economist*, January 28, 2010.
"The Worm Turns." *The Economist*, December 4, 2008.
Abbott, Kenneth W., and Duncan Snidal. "Why States Act through Formal International Organizations." *Journal of Conflict Resolution* 42, no. 1 (February 1998): 3–32.
Accuvant Labs. *Browser Security Comparison: A Quantitative Approach*. Accessed June 20, 2014. http://www.accuvant.com/sites/default/files/images/webbrowserresearch_v1_0.pdf.
Adler, Emanuel. "The Emergence of Cooperation: National Epistemic Communities and the International Evolution of the Idea of Nuclear Arms Control." *International Organization* 46 (December 1992): 101–45.
Agrawal, Arun. "Sustainable Governance of Common-Pool Resources: Context, Methods, and Politics." *Annual Review of Anthropology* 32 (2003): 243–62.
———, and Sanjeev Goyal. "Group Size and Collective Action: Third-Party Monitoring of Common-Pool Resources." *Comparative Political Studies* 34, no. 1 (February 2001): 63–93.
Air Transportation Association. "Annual and Per-Minute Cost of Delays to U.S. Airlines." Accessed November 23, 2012. http://www.airlines.org/Pages/Annual-and-Per-Minute-Cost-of-Delays-to-U.S.-Airlines.aspx.
Akimov, Vladimir, and Mikhail Soutchanski. "Automata Simulation of N-Person Social Dilemma Games." *Journal of Conflict Resolution* 38, no. 1 (March 1994): 138–48.

Alford, John R., Carolyn L. Funk, and John R. Hibbing. "Are Political Orientations Genetically Transmitted?" *American Political Science Review* 99, no. 2 (June 2005): 153–67.

Allen, Franklin, and Ana Babus. "Networks in Finance." In *The Network Challenge: Strategy, Profit, and Risk in an Interlinked World*, edited by Paul R. Kleindorfer and Yoram (Jerry) Wind. Upper Saddle River, NJ: Pearson, 2009.

Allen, Franklin, and Douglas Gale. "Financial Contagion." *Journal of Political Economy* 108, no. 1 (February 2000): 1–33.

Alonso, J., A. Fernandez, and H. Fort. "Prisoner's Dilemma Cellular Automata Revisited: Evolution of Cooperation under Environmental Pressure." *Journal of Statistical Mechanics* 06 (2006): 06013.

Amaral, L. A. N., A. Scala, M. Barthelemy, and H. E. Stanley. "Classes of Small-World Networks." *Proceedings of the National-Academy of Sciences* 97, no. 31 (October 10, 2000): 11149–52.

Arlidge, John. "Tech's Big Beasts Eye Silicon Savanna." *The Sunday Times* (London), August 12, 2012.

Arrow, Kenneth J. *Social Choice and Individual Values*. New York: Wiley, 1963.

Arthur, W. Brian. "Competing Technologies, Increasing Returns, and Lock-In by Historical Events." *Economic Journal* 99, no. 334 (March 1989): 116–31.

———. *Increasing Returns and Path Dependence in the Economy*. Ann Arbor: University of Michigan Press, 1994.

———. "Positive Feedbacks in the Economy." *McKinsey Quarterly* 1 (1994): 81–95.

Axelrod, Robert. *The Complexity of Cooperation: Agent-Based Models of Competition and Collaboration*. Princeton: Princeton University Press, 1997.

———. *The Evolution of Cooperation*. New York: Basic Books, 1984.

———. "The Evolution of Strategies in the Iterated Prisoner's Dilemma." In *Genetic Algorithms and Simulated Annealing*, edited by Lawrence Davis, 32–41. London: Pitman, and Los Altos, CA: Morgan Kaufman, 1987.

———. "An Evolutionary Approach to Norms." *American Political Science Review* 80, no. 4 (December 1986): 1095–1111.

———, and Robert O. Keohane. "Achieving Cooperation under Anarchy: Strategies and Institutions." *World Politics* 38, no. 1 (October 1985): 226–54.

Axtell, Robert, Robert Axelrod, Joshua M. Epstein, and Michael D. Cohen. "Aligning Simulation Models: A Case Study and Results." *Computational and Mathematical Organization Theory* 1, no. 2 (February 2006): 123–41.

Bagler, Ganesh. "Analysis of the Airport Network of India as a Complex Weighted Network." *Physica A: Statistical Mechanics and Its Applications* 387, no. 12 (May 2008): 2972–80.

Baland, Jean-Marie, and Jean-Philippe Platteau. *Halting Degradation of Natural Resources: Is There a Role for Rural Communities?* Oxford: Oxford University Press, 1996.

Baldwin, David A., ed. *Neorealism and Neoliberalism: The Contemporary Debate*. New York: Columbia University Press, 1993.

Barabasi, Albert-Laszlo, and Reka Albert. "Emergence of Scaling in Random Networks." *Science* 286, no. 5439 (October 15, 1999): 509–12.

Barabasi, Albert-Laszlo, and Eric Bonabeau. "Scale-Free Networks." *Scientific American* 288 (May 2003): 60–69.
Barrat, A., M. Barthelemy, R. Pastor-Satorras, and A. Vespignani. "The Architecture of Complex Weighted Networks." *Proceedings of the National Academy of Sciences* 101, no. 11 (January 8, 2004): 3747–52.
Basel Committee on Banking Supervision. "Group of Governors and Heads of Supervision Announces Higher Global Minimum Capital Standards." Basel: Bank for International Settlements. September 12, 2010. Press release.
Beam, Christopher. "Cyberspace Invaders: Is a Cyber-Attack an Act of War?" Slate.com, November 7, 2008. Accessed August 11, 2010. http://www.slate.com/id/2204123/.
Beattie, Alan, and Tom Braithwaite. "Leading Nations Agree to Disagree on Bank Tax." *Financial Times*, April 24, 2010.
Bennett, D. Scott. "Governments, Civilians, and the Evolution of Insurgency: Modeling the Early Dynamics of Insurgencies." *Journal of Artificial Societies and Social Simulation* 11, no. 4 (October 2008).
Benson, Michelle A. "Dyadic Hostility and the Ties That Bind: State-to-State versus State-to-System Security and Economic Relationships." *Journal of Peace Research* 41, no. 6 (November 2004): 659–76.
Binder, Alan S. "Two Cheers for the New Bank Capital Standards; Why Do We Still Rely on Rating Agencies, and Why Are We Still Allowing Lehman Brothers Levels of Leverage?" *The Wall Street Journal*, September 29, 2010.
Birch, Douglas. "Lights Out: A Newly Declassified Report Shows How Vulnerable America's Electrical Grid Is." *Foreign Policy*, November 14, 2012.
Black, Duncan. "On the Rationale of Group Decision-Making." *Journal of Political Economy* 56, no. 1 (February 1948): 23–34.
Bonsall, Peter. "The Influence of Route Guidance Advice on Route Choice in Urban Networks." *Transportation* 19, no. 1 (February 1992): 1–23.
Boss, Michael, Helmut Elsinger, Martin Summer, and Stefan Thurner. "Network Topology of the Interbank Market." *Quantitative Finance* 4 (December 2004): 677–85.
Bowles, Samuel. "Did Warfare Among Ancestral Hunter-Gatherers Affect the Evolution of Human Social Behaviors?" *Science* 324 (June 2009): 1293–98.
Box, George E. P., and Norman R. Draper. *Empirical Model-Building and Response Surfaces*. New York: John Wiley and Sons, 1987.
Box-Steffensmeier, Janet M., and Bradford S. Jones. "Time Is of the Essence: Event History Models in Political Science." *American Journal of Political Science* 41, no. 4 (October 1997): 1414–61.
Boyd, Robert, and Jeffrey P. Lorberbaum. "No Pure Strategy Is Evolutionarily Stable in the Repeated Prisoner's Dilemma Game." *Nature* 327, no. 7 (May 7, 1987): 58–59.
Bradsher, Keith. "Shipping Lines Pull Back from Japan." *The New York Times*, March 25, 2011.
Broll, Simon. "Making Money—New Currency Brings Hope to Debt-Stricken City," *Spiegel Online International*, March 16, 2012.

Brune, Nancy, and Geoffrey Garrett. "The Globalization Rorschach Test: International Economic Integration, Inequality, and the Role of Government." *Annual Review of Political Science* 8 (2005): 399–423.
Cantner, Uwe, and Holger Graf. "The Network of Innovators in Jena: An Application of Social Network Analysis." *Research Policy* 35, no. 4 (May 2006): 463–80.
Carey, Richard A. *The Philosopher Fish: Sturgeon, Caviar, and the Geography of Desire.* New York: Counterpoint, 2005.
Carley, Kathleen M. "ORA Organization Risk Analyzer v. 2.0." Pittsburgh: Center for Computational Analysis of Social and Organizational Systems, Carnegie Mellon University, 2010.
Carroll, William K., and Colin Carson. "The Network of Global Corporations and Elite Policy Groups: A Structure for Transnational Capitalist Class Formation?" *Global Networks* 3, no. 1 (February 2003): 29–57.
Castells, Manuel. *The Rise of the Network Society.* Malden, MA: Blackwell, 1996.
Cederman, Lars-Erik. *Emergent Actors in World Politics.* Princeton: Princeton University Press, 1997.
———. "Modeling the Size of Wars: From Billiard Balls to Sandpiles." *American Political Science Review* 97, no. 1 (February 2003): 135–50.
Checkel, Jeffrey T. "The Constructivist Turn in International Relations Theory." *World Politics* 50, no. 2 (1998): 324–48.
Chivers, C. J. "Corruption Endangers a Treasure of the Caspian." *The New York Times,* November 28, 2005.
Ciezadlo, Annia. "Eat, Drink, Protest: Stories of the Middle East's Hungry Rumblings." *Foreign Policy* 186 (May/June 2011): 79.
Clauset, Aaron, Cosma Rohilla Shalizi, and M. E. J. Newman. "Power-Law Distributions in Empirical Data." *SIAM Review* 51, no. 4 (2009): 661–703.
Cohen, Jon. "Employers Advised on Swine Flu; Local Colleges Making Plans." *The Washington Post,* August 20, 2009.
Committee on Economic and Environmental Impacts of Increasing Biofuels Production. *Renewable Fuel Standard: Potential Economic and Environmental Effects of U.S. Biofuels Policy.* Washington, DC: National Academies Press, 2011.
Cooley, Alexander. "Globalization and National Security after Empire: The Former Soviet Space." In *Globalization and National Security,* edited by Jonathan Kirshner, 201–30. New York: Routledge, 2006.
Cowell, Alan. "Deadly Bird Flu Confirmed in British Turkeys." *New York Times,* February 4, 2007, 16.
Dall'Asta, Luca, Alain Barrat, Marc Barthelemy, and Alessandro Vespignani. "Vulnerability of Weighted Networks." *Journal of Statistical Mechanics: Theory and Experiment* 2006, no. 4 (April 2006): 1–12.
Dang, Yaru, and Wenjing Li. "Comparative Analysis on Weighted Network Structure of Air Passenger Flow of China and US." *Journal of Transportation Systems Engineering and Information Technology* 11, no. 3 (June 2011): 156–62.
Davis, Gerald F., Mina Yoo, and Wayne E. Baker. "The Small World of the American Corporate Elite, 1982–2001." *Strategic Organization* 1, no. 3 (August 2003): 301–26.

De Masi, Giulia, Giulia Iori, and Guido Caldarelli. "Fitness Model for the Italian Interbank Market." *Physical Review E* 74, no. 6 (2006).

Deutsch, Karl W. *The Nerves of Government: Models of Political Communication and Control.* London: Free Press of Glencoe, 1963.

Devine, Jennifer A., Krista D. Baker, and Richard L. Haedrick. "Deep-Sea Fishes Qualify as Endangered: A Shift from Shelf Fisheries to the Deep Sea is Exhausting Late-Maturing Species that Recover Only Slowly." *Nature* 439, no. 5 (January 2006): 29.

Diermeier, Daniel. "Arguing for Computational Power." *Science* 318 (November 2007): 918.

Donadio, Rachel. "Stitched in Italy, by Chinese: Newcomers Redefine a Label." *The New York Times*, September 12, 2010.

Drezner, Daniel W. "Weighing the Scales: The Internet's Effect on State-Society Relations." *Brown Journal of World Affairs* 16, no. 2 (Spring-Summer 2010).

Duverger, Maurice. *Party Politics and Pressure Groups: A Comparative Introduction.* Translated by David Wagoner. New York: Thomas Y. Crowell, 1972.

Earnest, David C. "Coordination in Large Numbers: An Agent-Based Model of International Negotiations." *International Studies Quarterly* 52, no. 2 (June 2008): 363–82.

———. "Growing a Virtual Insurgency: Using Massively Parallel Gaming to Simulate Insurgent Behavior." *The Journal of Defense Modeling and Simulation: Applications, Methodology, Technology* 6, no. 2 (2009): 55–67.

Earnest, David C., and Kurt Taylor Gaubatz. "Modeling, Simulation, and the Social Sciences: An Agenda for Integration." Paper presented at the 2007 Simulation Integration Workshop Conference, Norfolk, VA, March 25–30, 2007.

Earnest, David C., and James N. Rosenau. "Signifying Nothing? What Complex Systems Can and Cannot Tell Us about Global Politics." In *Complexity in World Politics: Concepts and Methods of a New Paradigm*, edited by Neil E. Harrison, 143–63. Albany: State University of New York Press, 2006.

Earnest, David C., Steve Yetiv, and Stephen M. Carmel. "Contagion in the Transpacific Shipping Network: International Networks and Vulnerability Interdependence." *International Interactions* 38, no. 5 (2012): 571–96.

Eichengreen, Barry. "Hegemonic Stability Theories of the International Monetary System." In *Can Nations Agree? Essays on International Economic Cooperation*, edited by Ralph Bryant, 255–98. Washington, DC: The Brookings Institution, 1989.

Eldredge, Niles, and Stephen J. Gould. "Punctuated Equilibria: An Alternative to Phyletic Gradualism." *Models in Paleobiology* 82 (1972): 82–115.

Elsinger, Helmut, Alfred Lehar, and Martin Summer. "Risk Assessment for Banking Systems." Paper presented to the 2003 European Finance Association annual convention, Glasgow, Scotland: August 20–23, 2003.

Epstein, Joshua M. *Generative Social Science: Studies in Agent-Based Computational Modeling.* Princeton: Princeton University Press, 2006.

———. "Modelling to Contain Pandemics." *Nature* 460 (August 2009): 687.

———, and Robert Axtell. *Growing Artificial Societies: Social Science from the Bottom Up*. Washington, DC: Brookings Institution Press, 1996.

Estrada, E. "Network Robustness to Targeted Attacks: The Interplay of Expansibility and Degree Distribution." *The European Physical Journal B* 52, no. 4 (August 2006): 563–74.

Evans, Peter B., Harold K. Jacobson, and Robert D. Putnam, eds. *Double-Edged Diplomacy: International Bargaining and Domestic Politics*. Berkeley: University of California Press, 1993.

Ewing, Jack. "Some Religious Leaders See a Threat as Europe Grows More Secular." *The New York Times*, September 19, 2012.

Farmer, J. Doyne, and Duncan Foley. "The Economy Needs Agent-Based Modelling." *Nature* 460 (August 2009): 685–86.

Fath., Nazila. "Iran's Opposition Seeks More Help in Cyberwar With Government." *The New York Times*, March 18, 2010.

Fearon, James D. "Counterfactuals and Hypothesis Testing in Political Science." *World Politics* 43, no. 2 (January 1991): 169–95.

Ferguson, Niall. "Diminished Returns." *The New York Times Magazine*, May 17, 2009.

Ferris, Timothy. *The Whole Shebang: A State-of-the-Universe(s) Report*. New York: Touchstone, 1997.

Filkins, Dexter. "TV Channel Draws Viewers, and Threats, in Iran." *The New York Times*, November 20, 2010.

Flynn, Morris R., Aslan R. Kasimov, J-C. Nave, Rodolfo R. Rosales, and Benjamin Seibold. "Self-Sustained Nonlinear Waves in Traffic Flow." *Physical Review E* 79, no. 5 (May 2009).

Foley, Stephen. "Tricky Lessons Yet to Be Learnt by International Regulators; The View from Wall Street." *The Independent* (London), September 14, 2010.

Forscher, Robert K. "Chaos in the Brickyard." *Science*, October 1963, 339.

Fox News. "State-by-state Glance at the Electoral College Map." Accessed August 20, 2010. http://www.foxnews.com/wires/2008Oct29/0,4670,Roadto270States,00.html.

Frieden, Thomas R., Timothy Sterling, Ariel Pablos-Mendez, James O. Kilburn, George M. Cauthen, and Samuel W. Dooley. "The Emergence of Drug-Resistant Tuberculosis in New York City." *The New England Journal of Medicine* 328, no. 8 (February 25, 1993): 521–26.

Gann, Ernest K. *Fate is the Hunter*. New York: Touchstone, 1961.

Gaubatz, Kurt Taylor. "Democratic States and Commitment in International Relations." *International Organization* 50, no. 1 (Winter 1996): 109–39.

———. "Intervention and Intransitivity: Public Opinion, Social Choice, and the Use of Military Force Abroad." *World Politics* 47, no. 4 (July 1995): 534–54.

Geller, Armando, and Scott Moss. "Growing QAWM: An Evidence-Driven Declarative Model of Afghan Power Structures." *Advances in Complex Systems* 11, no. 2 (April 2008): 321–35.

Gerencser, Mark, Jim Weinberg, and Don Vincent. *Port Security War Game: Implications for U.S. Supply Chains*. Vienna, VA: Booz-Allen Hamilton, 2003.

Germain, Randall D., and Michael Kenny. "Engaging Gramsci: International Relations Theory and the New Gramscians." *Review of International Studies* 24, no. 1 (January 1998): 3–21.

Gerschenkron, Alexander. *Economic Backwardness in Historical Perspective*. Cambridge: Harvard University Press, 1962.
Giddens, Anthony. *The Consequences of Modernity*. Stanford: Stanford University Press, 1990.
———. *The Constitution of Society: Outline of the Theory of Structuration*. Berkeley: University of California Press, 1986.
———. *Social Theory and Modern Sociology*. Stanford: Stanford University Press, 1987.
Gilbert, Nigel. *Agent-Based Models*. Thousand Oaks, CA: Sage, 2008.
———, and Klaus G. Troitzsch. *Simulation for the Social Scientist*. Philadelphia: Open University Press, 1999.
Giles, Jim. "Challenges of Being a Wikipedian." *Nature* 438, no. 7070 (December 15, 2005): 901.
———. "Internet Encyclopaedias Go Head to Head." *Nature* 438, no. 7070 (December 15, 2005): 900–901.
Gill, Stephen, ed. *Gramsci, Historical Materialism, and International Relations*. New York: Cambridge University Press, 1993.
Gilpin, Robert. *Global Political Economy: Understanding the International Economic Order*. Princeton: Princeton University Press, 2001.
———. *War and Change in World Politics*. New York: Cambridge University Press, 1983.
Ginsberg, Jeremy, Matthew H. Mohebbi, Rajan S. Patel, Lynnette Brammer, Mark S. Smolinski, and Larry Brilliant. "Detecting Influenza Epidemics Using Search Engine Query Data." *Nature* 457, no. 7232 (February 19, 2009): 1012–14.
Giridharadas, Anand. "Africa's Gift to Silicon Valley: How to Track a Crisis." *The New York Times*, March 14, 2010.
Gladwell, Malcolm. *The Tipping Point: How Little Things Can Make a Big Difference*. New York: Little, Brown, 2002.
Goldstone, Robert L. "The Complex Systems See-Change in Education." *The Journal of the Learning Sciences* 15, no. 1 (January 2006): 41.
Gould, Stephen J., and Niles Eldredge. "Punctuated Equilibria: The Tempo and Mode of Evolution Reconsidered." *Paleobiology* 3, no. 2 (Spring 1977): 115–51.
Granovetter, Mark. "The Strength of Weak Ties." *American Journal of Sociology* 78, no. 6 (May 1973): 1360–80.
———. "The Strength of Weak Ties: A Network Theory Revisited." *Sociological Theory* 1 (1983): 201–33.
———. "Threshold Models of Collective Behavior." *American Journal of Sociology* 83, no. 6 (May 1978): 1420–43.
Green, David G., and Suzanne Sadedin. "Interactions Matter—Complexity in Landscapes and Ecosystems." *Ecological Complexity* 2 (2005): 117–30.
Greenberg, Michael D., Peter Chalk, Henry H. Willis, Ivan Khilko, and David S. Ortiz. *Maritime Terrorism: Risk and Liability*. Washington, DC: RAND Corporation, 2006.
Grieco, Joseph M. "Anarchy and the Limits of Cooperation: A Realist Critique of the Newest Liberal Institutionalism." *International Organization* 42, no. 3 (Summer 1988): 485–507.
Griffiths, Katherine. "New Bank Rules Are Too Weak to Work, Says Myners." *The Times* (London), September 15, 2010.

Guimera, R., and L. A. N. Amaral. "Modeling the World-Wide Airport Network." *The European Physical Journal B* 38, no. 2 (March 2004): 381–85.

Guimera, R., S. Mossa, A. Turtschi, and L. A. N. Amaral. "The Worldwide Air Transportation Network: Anomalous Centrality, Community Structure, and Cities' Global Roles." *Proceedings of the National Academy of Sciences* 102, no. 22 (April 2005): 7794–99.

Haas, Ernst B. *Beyond the Nation-State: Functionalism and International Organization.* Stanford: Stanford University Press, 1964.

———. *When Knowledge Is Power: Three Models of Change in International Organizations.* Berkeley: University of California Press, 1990.

Haas, Peter. "Introduction: Epistemic Communities and International Policy Coordination." *International Organization* 46, no. 1 (December 1992): 1–35.

Hagan, Joe D., and Margaret D. Hermann, eds. "Leaders, Groups and Coalitions: Understanding the People and Processes in Foreign Policymaking." *International Studies Review* (Special Edition). Malden, MA: Blackwell, 2001.

Hardin, Garrett. "The Tragedy of the Commons." *Science* 162, no. 3859 (December 13, 1968): 1243–48.

Harrison, Neil E. *Complexity in World Politics: Concepts and Methods of a New Paradigm.* Albany: State University of New York Press, 2006.

Held, David, and Anthony McGrew. *Globalization/Anti-Globalization.* Malden, MA: Blackwell, 2002.

Held, David, Anthony McGrew, David Goldblatt, and Jonathan Perraton. *Global Transformations: Politics, Economics, and Culture.* Stanford: Stanford University Press, 1999.

Hoffman, Bruce. "The Changing Face of Al Qaeda and the Global War on Terrorism." *Studies in Conflict & Terrorism* 27, no. 6 (November 2004): 553–54.

Hoffmann, Matthew J. *Ozone Depletion and Climate Change: Constructing a Global Response.* Albany: State University of New York Press, 2005.

Holland, John H. "Complex Adaptive Systems." *DAEDALUS* 121, no. 1 (Winter 1992): 17–30.

———. "Genetic Algorithms." *Scientific American* 267 (July 1998): 66–72.

Horowitz, Michael C. "Nonstate Actors and the Diffusion of Innovations: The Case of Suicide Terrorism." *International Organization* 64, no. 1 (Winter 2010): 33–64.

Hoshaw, Lindsey. "Afloat in the Ocean, Expanding Islands of Trash." *The New York Times*, November 10, 2009.

Howlett, Michael. "Do Networks Matter? Linking Policy Network Structure to Policy Outcomes: Evidence from Four Canadian Policy Sectors 1990–2000." *Canadian Journal of Political Science* 35, no. 2 (June 2002): 235–67.

Hughes, Barry. *International Futures: Choices in the Creation of a New World Order.* Boulder: Westview, 1993.

———. *World Futures: A Critical Analysis of Alternatives.* Baltimore: Johns Hopkins University Press, 1985.

Huntington, Samuel P. "Dead Souls: The Denationalization of the American Elites." *The National Interest* 75 (Spring 2004): 5–18.

Inaoka, Hajime, Hideki Takayasu, Tokiko Shimzu, Takuto Ninomiya, and Ken Taniguchi. "Self-Similarity of Banking Network." *Physica A* 339 (2004): 621–34.

Iori, Giulia, Giulia De Masi, Ovidiu Vasile Precup, Giampaolo Gabbi, and Guido Caldarelli. "A Network Analysis of the Italian Overnight Money Market." *Journal of Economic Dynamics and Control* 32, no. 1 (2008): 259–78.

Jackson, Brian A., Lloyd S. Dixon, and Victoria A. Greenfield. *Economically Targeted Terrorism: A Review of the Literature and a Framework for Considering Defensive Approaches.* Santa Monica: RAND Corporation, 2007.

Jackson, Matthew O. "Networks and Economic Behavior." *Annual Review of Economics* 1 (2009): 489–513.

Jackson, Patrick Thaddeus, and Daniel Nexon. "Globalization, the Comparative Method, and Comparing Constructions." In *Constructivism and Comparative Politics*, edited by Daniel M. Green, 88–120. Armonk, NY: M. E. Sharpe, 2002.

Jacobs, Andrew. "In China Music Festivals, Hip Rock and the State's Blessing." *The New York Times*, October 24, 2010.

Jacobson, Michael J., and Uri Wilensky. "Complex Systems in Education: Scientific and Educational Importance and Implications for the Learning Sciences." *The Journal of the Learning Sciences* 15, no. 1 (January 2006): 11–34.

Jenkins, Patrick. "German Banks Try to Fend Off Basel III." *Financial Times*, September 6, 2010.

Jensen, Michael. "The Role of Network Resources in Market Entry: Commercial Banks' Entry into Investment Banking, 1991–1997." *Administrative Science Quarterly* 48, no. 3 (September 2003): 466–97.

Jervis, Robert. *System Effects: Complexity in Political and Social Life*. Princeton: Princeton University Press, 1997.

Johnson, Steven. *Emergence: The Connected Lives of Ants, Brains, Cities, and Software*. New York: Scribner, 2001.

Jones, Huw. "Snap Analysis: Implementation Key to Basel III Success." Reuters, September 12, 2010.

Kahler, Miles. "Multilateralism with Small and Large Numbers." *International Organization* 46, no. 3 (Spring 1992): 681–708.

Kandori, Michihiro, George J. Mailath, and Rafael Rob. "Learning, Mutation, and Long Run Equilibria in Games." *Econometrica* 61, no. 1 (January 1993): 29–56.

Kane, Edward J. 2007. "Connecting National Safety Nets: The Dialectics of the Basel II Contracting Process." *Atlantic Economic Journal* 35, no. 4 (November 2007): 399–409.

Kapstein, Ethan B. "Architects of Stability? International Cooperation among Financial Supervisors." *BIS Working Papers* 199, 2006.

Katz, Jonathan M., and Jennifer Kay. "Red Tape Cutting Off Food." *The Virginian-Pilot*, March 7, 2008.

Keck. Margaret E., and Kathryn Sikkink. *Activists beyond Borders: Advocacy Networks in International Politics*. Ithaca: Cornell University Press, 1998.

Kentor, Jeffrey. "The Growth of Transnational Corporate Networks: 1962–1998." *Journal of World Systems Research* 11, no. 2 (December 2005): 263–86.

Keohane, Robert O. *After Hegemony: Cooperation and Discord in the World Political Economy*. Princeton: Princeton University Press, 1984.

———, and Joseph S. Nye. *Power and Interdependence: World Politics in Transition*. Boston: Little, Brown, 1977.

Kindleberger, Charles. *The World in Depression, 1929–1939*. Berkeley: University of California Press, 1973.

King, Gary, and Langche Zeng. "The Dangers of Extreme Counterfactuals." *Political Analysis* 14, no. 2 (Summer 2006): 131–59.

Klotz, Audie. "Norms Reconstituting Interests: Global Racial Equality and U.S. Sanctions against South Africa." *International Organization* 49, no. 3 (Summer 1995): 451–78.

Klovdahl, Alden S., John J. Potterat, Donald E. Woodhouse, John B. Muth, Stephen Q. Muth, and William W. Darrow. "Social Networks and Infectious Disease: The Colorado Springs Study." *Social Science & Medicine* 38, no. 1 (January 1994): 79–88.

Knoke, David, and Song Yang. *Social Network Analysis: Second Edition*. Los Angeles: Sage, 2008.

Knopf, Jeffrey W. "The Importance of International Learning." *Review of International Studies* 29 (2003): 185–207.

Kostingen, Thomas M. "The World's Largest Dump: The Great Pacific Garbage Patch." *Discover*, July 2008.

Kottanau, Johannes, and Claudia Pahl-Wostl. "Simulating Political Attitudes and Voting Behavior." *Journal of Artificial Societies and Social Simulation* 7, no. 4 (October 2004).

Krasner, Stephen D. "Global Communications and National Power: Life on the Pareto Frontier." *World Politics* 42, no. 3 (April 1991): 336–66.

Kreps, David M. *Game Theory and Economic Modelling*. Oxford: Clarendon Press, 1990.

Kristof, Nicholas D. "I've Seen the Future (in Haiti)." *The New York Times*, December 5, 2010.

Krugman, Paul. *The Return of Depression Economics and the Crisis of 2008*. New York: W. W. Norton, 2009.

Kubalkova, Vendulka, Nicholas G. Onuf, and Paul Kowert. *International Relations in a Constructed World*. Armonk, NY: M. E. Sharpe, 1996.

Kuhn, Thomas S. *The Structure of Scientific Revolutions*. Chicago: University of Chicago Press, 1965.

Kuran, Timur. "Now Out of Never: The Element of Surprise in the East European Revolutions of 1989." *World Politics* 44, no. 1 (October 1991): 7–48.

Kurth, James. "The Political Consequences of the Product Cycle: Industrial History and Political Outcomes." *International Organization* 33, no. 1 (December 1979): 1–34.

Lall, Ranjit. "Reforming Global Banking Rules: Back to the Future?" Paper presented at the Danish Institute for International Studies, DIIS Working Paper 16 (2010).

Lander, M. "The Financial Crisis Is Spreading to Europe." *The New York Times*, October 1, 2008.

Langewieshe, William. "The Devil at 37,000 Feet." *Vanity Fair* 51, no. 1 (January 2009): 86–141.

Lazer, David, Alex Pentland, Lada Adamic, Sinan Aral, Albert-Laszlo Barabasi, Devon Brewer, Nicholas Christakis, Noshir Contractor, James Fowler, Myron Gutmann, Toby Jebara, Gary King, Michael Macy, Deb Roy, and Marshall Van Alstyne. "Computational Social Science." *Science* 323 (February 2009): 721–23.

Lazer, David, R. Kennedy, Gary King, and A. Vespgnani. "The Parable of Google Flu: Traps in Big Data Analysis." *Science* 343 (March 14, 2014): 1203–1205.

Leitner, Yaron. "Financial Networks: Contagion, Commitment, and Private Sector Bailouts." *Journal of Finance* 60, no. 6 (December 2005): 2925–53.

Leombruni, Roberto, and Matteo Richiardi. "Why Are Economists Skeptical about Agent-Based Simulations?" *Physica A: Statistical Mechanics and Applications* 355, no. 1 (September 2005): 103–109.

Levinson, Marc. "Faulty Basel: Why Diplomacy Won't Keep the Financial System Safe." *Foreign Affairs* 89, no. 3 (May 2010): 76–88.

Levy, Jack S. "Organizational Routines and the Causes of War." *International Studies Quarterly* 30, no. 2 (June 1986): 193–222.

———. "Preferences, Constraints, and Choices in July 1914." *International Security* 15, no. 3 (Winter 1990/91): 151–86.

Li, Keping, Ziyou Gao, and Baohua Mao. "A Weighted Network Model for Railway Traffic." *International Journal of Modern Physics* 17, no. 9 (September 2006).

Li, W., and X. Cai. "Statistical Analysis of Airport Network of China." *Physical Review E* 69, no. 4 (April 2004).

Liebrand, William B. G. "The Effect of Social Motives, Communication, and Group Size on Behaviour in an N-Person Multi-State Mixed-Motive Game." *European Journal of Social Psychology* 14, no. 3 (July/September 1984): 239–64.

Lipschutz, Ronnie. "Reconstructing World Politics: The Emergence of Global Civil Society." *Millennium: Journal of International Studies* 21, no. 3 (1992): 389–420.

Lipson, Charles. "International Cooperation in Security and Economic Affairs." *World Politics* 37, no. 1 (October 1984): 1–23.

Lohmann, Susanne. "The Dynamics of Information Cascades: The Monday Demonstrations in Leipzig, East Germany, 1989–1991." *World Politics* 47, no. 1 (October 1994): 42–101.

Lorenz, Edward. "Deterministic Nonperiodic Flow." *Journal of Atmospheric Sciences* 20 (1963): 130–41.

Lovett, Ian. "1.4 Million Lose Electricity in Area Around San Diego." *The New York Times*, September 9, 2011.

Lucas, Robert. "In Defence of the Dismal Science." *The Economist*, August 6, 2009.

Luft, Gal, and Anne Korin. "Terrorism Goes to Sea." *Foreign Affairs* 83, no. 6 (November/December 2004): 64–65.

Lustick, Ian S. "Agent-Based Modelling of Collective Identity: Testing Constructivist Theory." *Journal of Artificial Societies and Social Simulation* 3, no. 1 (January 2000).

———, Dan Miodownik, and Roy J. Eidelson. "Secessionism in Multicultural States: Does Power Sharing Prevent or Encourage It?" *American Political Science Review* 98, no. 2 (May 2004): 209–29.

Lynn, Matthew. "The Fallen King of Finland." *Bloomberg BusinessWeek* 4196 (September 20–26, 2010): 7–8.

MacKenzie, Cameron A., Joost R. Santos, and Kash Barker. "Measuring Changes in International Production from a Disruption: Case Study of the Japanese Earthquake and Tsunami." *International Journal of Production Economics*, 138, no. 2 (August 2012): 293–302.

Macy, Michael W., and Andreas Flache. "Beyond Rationality in Models of Choice." *Annual Review of Sociology* 21 (1995): 73–91.
Mailath, George J., and Larry Samuelson. *Repeated Games and Reputations: Long-Run Relationships*. Oxford: Oxford University Press, 2006.
Manjoo, Farhad. "The Netflix Prize Was Brilliant: Google and Microsoft should steal the idea." Slate.com. Accessed August 13, 2010. http://www.slate.com/id/2229225/.
Mansfield, Edward D., and Brian M. Pollins. "The Study of Interdependence and Conflict: Recent Advances, Open Questions, and Directions for Future Research." *Journal of Conflict Resolution* 45, no. 6 (December 2001): 834–59.
Maoz, Zeev. "Network Polarization, Network Interdependence, and International Conflict, 1816–2002." *Journal of Peace Research* 43, no. 4 (July 2006): 391–411.
Markoff, John. "Vast Spy System Loots Computers in 103 Countries." *New York Times*, March 29, 2009.
Marks, Robert Ernest. "Validating Simulation Models: A General Framework and Four Applied Examples." *Computational Economics* 30, no. 3 (October 2007): 265–90.
Martin, Lisa L. "Interests, Power, and Multilateralism." *International Organization* 46, no. 4 (August 1992): 765–92.
Masters, Brooke. "Fears for German Banks under New Rules." *Financial Times*, September 9, 2010.
———. "Impact of Basel III: Trade Finance May Become a Casualty." *Financial Times*, October 19, 2010.
Matsushima, Masanao, and Takashi Ikegami. "Evolution of Strategies in the Three-Person Iterated Prisoner's Dilemma Game." *Journal of Theoretical Biology* 1, no. 7 (November 1998): 53–67.
Matthew, Richard, and George Shambaugh. "The Limits of Terrorism: A Network Perspective." *International Studies Review* 7, no. 4 (December 2005): 617–27.
Mattli, Walter, and Tim Buthe. "Setting International Standards: Technological Rationality or Primacy of Power?" *World Politics* 56, no. 1 (October 2003): 1–42.
Mazzetti, Mark. "Senators Warned of Terrorist Attack on U.S. by July." *The New York Times*, February 3, 2010.
McGill, Brian J., and Joel S. Brown. "Evolutionary Game Theory and Adaptive Dynamics of Continuous Traits." *Annual Review of Ecology, Evolution, and Systematics* 38 (2007): 403–35.
Meadows, Dennis L., William W. Behrens, Donella H. Meadows, Roger F. Naill, Jorgen Randers, and Erich Zahn. *Dynamics of Growth in a Finite World*. Cambridge: Wright-Allen Press, 1974.
Melloan, George. "Basel's Illusions; The New Basel III Banking Agreement Is Unlikely to Instill Safety into Complex Human Transactions." *The National Post* (Canada), September 15, 2010.
Meyer, John W., John Boli, George M. Thomas, and Francisco O. Ramirez. "World Society and the Nation-State." *The American Journal of Sociology* 103, no. 1 (July 1997): 144–81.
Micklethwait, John, and Adrian Wooldridge. *A Future Perfect: The Challenge and Promise of Globalization*. New York: Random House, 2000.

Milgrom, Paul R., Douglas C. North, and Barry R. Weingast. "The Role of Institutions in the Revival of Trade: The Law Merchant, Private Judges, and the Champagne Fairs." *Economics and Politics* 2, no. 1 (March 1990): 1–23.

Miller, John H. "Active Nonlinear Tests (ANTs) of Complex Simulation Models." *Management Science* 44, no. 6 (June 1998): 820–30.

———, and Scott E. Page. *Complex Adaptive Systems: An Introduction to Computational Models of Social Life*. Princeton: Princeton University Press, 2007.

Milner, Helen V. *Interests, Information, and Institutions: Domestic Politics and International Relations*. Princeton: Princeton University Press, 1997.

Minder, Raphael. "Catalan Vote Could Be a First Step toward Self-Rule." *The New York Times*, November 23, 2012.

Miodownik, Dan. "Cultural Differences and Economic Incentives: An Agent-Based Study of Their Impact on the Emergence of Regional Autonomy Movements." *Journal of Artificial Societies and Social Simulation* 9, no. 4 (October 2006).

Mitchell, Melanie. *Complexity: A Guided Tour*. New York: Oxford University Press, 2009.

———. *An Introduction to Genetic Algorithms*. Cambridge: MIT Press, 1998.

Moore, Spencer, Eugenia Eng, and Mark Daniel. "International NGOs and the Role of Network Centrality in Humanitarian Aid Operations: A Case Study of Coordination During the Mozambique Floods." *Disasters* 27, 4 (December 2003): 305–318.

Moravcsik, Andrew. "Taking Preferences Seriously: A Liberal Theory of International Politics." *International Organization* 51, no. 4 (Autumn 1997): 513–53.

Morgenthau, Hans J. *Politics among Nations: The Struggle for Power and Peace*. New York: Knopf 1973 [1948].

Moss, Scott. "Alternative Approaches to the Empirical Validation of Agent-Based Models." *Journal of Artificial Society and Social Simulation* 11, no, 1 (January 2008).

———, and Bruce Edmonds. "Sociology and Simulation: Statistical and Qualitative Cross-Validation." *American Journal of Sociology* 110, no. 4 (January 2005): 1095–1131.

Mueller, Karl P. "The Paradox of Liberal Hegemony: Globalization and U.S. National Security." In *Globalization and National Security*, edited by Jonathan Kirshner, 143–170. New York: Routledge, 2006.

Mumby, Peter J., Craig P. Dahlgren, Alastair R. Harborne, Carrie V. Kappel, Fiorenzia Micheli, Daniel R. Burnbaugh, Katherine E. Holmes, Judith M. Mendes, Kenneth Broad, James N. Sanchirico, Kevin Buch, Steve Box, Richard W. Stoffle, and Andrew B. Gill. "Fishing, Trophic Cascades, and the Process of Grazing on Coral Reefs." *Science* 311 (January 2006): 98–101.

Myrdal, Gunnar. *Rich Lands and Poor: The Road to World Prosperity*. New York: Harper, 1957.

Nagaraja, Shishir, and Ross Anderson. "The Snooping Dragon: Social Malware Surveillance of the Tibetan Movement." University of Cambridge Computer Laboratory Technical Report No. 746, UCAM-CL-TR-746, Cambridge, UK: March 2009.

Nagurney, Anna, and Qiang Qiang. "A Transportation Network Efficiency Measure that Captures Flows, Behavior, and Costs with Applications to Network Component Importance Identification and Vulnerability." *Proceedings of the POMS 18th Annual Conference*. Miami, FL: Production and Operations Management Society, 2007.

Naim, Moises. *Illicit: How Smugglers, Traffickers, and Copycats are Hijacking the Global Economy*. New York: Anchor, 2005.

Nakagaki, Toshiyuki, Hiroyasu Yamada, and Agota Toth. "Maze-Solving by an Amoeboid Organism." *Nature* 407, no. 6803 (September 28, 2000): 470.

National Research Council. *Terrorism and the Electric Power Delivery System*. Washington, DC: National Academies Press, 2012.

Network Workbench Tool. Bloomington: Indiana University, Northeastern University, and University of Michigan, 2006.

Neuwirth, Robert. *Stealth of Nations: The Global Rise of the Informal Economy*. New York: Anchor, 2012.

The New York Times. "The Electoral Map: Key States." Accessed August 20, 2010. http://elections.nytimes.com/2008/president/whos-ahead/key-states/map.html?scp=1&sq=2008%20electoral%20college&st=cse.

Newling, Dan. "'Phantom' Traffic Jams that Cause Misery for Motorists Can Be Caused by Just ONE Driver." *Daily Mail* (London), April 3, 2010.

Newman, M. E. J. "The Structure and Function of Complex Networks." *SIAM Review* 45, no. 2 (May 2003): 167–256.

Nicolau, Nicos, Scott Shane, Lynn Chekas, Janice Hunkin, and Tim D. Spector. "Is the Tendency to Engage in Entrepreneurship Genetic?" *Management Science* 54, no. 1 (January 2008): 167–79.

Nier, Erlend, Jing Yang, Tanju Yorulmazer, and Amadeo Alentorn. "Network Models and Financial Stability." *Journal of Economic Dynamics and Control* 31 (2007): 2033–60.

Nowak, Martin A., and Karl Sigmund. "Tit for Tat in Heterogeneous Populations." *Nature* 355 (January 16, 1992): 250–53.

Nowak, Martin A., and Robert M. May. "Evolutionary Games and Spatial Chaos." *Nature* 359 (October 29, 1992): 826–29.

Odell, John S. "International Threats and Internal Politics: Brazil, the European Community, and the United States, 1985–1987." In *Double-Edged Diplomacy: International Bargaining and Domestic Politics*, edited by Peter B. Evans, Harold K, Jacobson, and Robert D. Putnam, 233–64. Berkeley: University of California Press, 1993.

Ohtsuki, Hisashi, Christoph Hauert, Erez Leiberman, and Martin A. Nowak. "A Simple Rule for the Evolution of Cooperation on Graphs and Social Networks." *Nature* 441 (May 25, 2006): 502–505.

Olson, Mancur. *The Logic of Collective Action and the Theory of Groups*. Cambridge: Harvard University Press, 1965.

Organization for Economic Cooperation and Development, Directorate for Science Technology and Industry. *Security in Maritime Transport: Risk Factors and Economic Impact*. Paris: OECD Publication Services, 2006.

Ostrom, Elinor. "Coping with Tragedies of the Commons," *Annual Review of Political Science* 2, no. 1 (1999): 493–535.

———. *Governing the Commons: The Evolution of Institutions for Collective Action.* Cambridge: Harvard University Press, 1990.

Owen, John M. "How Liberalism Produces Democratic Peace." *International Security* 19, no. 2 (Fall 1994): 87–125.

Pahre, Robert. "Multilateral Cooperation in an Iterated Prisoner's Dilemma." *Journal of Conflict Resolution* 38, no. 2 (June 1994): 326–52.

Pauly, Daniel, Villy Christensen, Sylvie Guenette, Tony J. Pitcher, U. Rashid Sumaila, Carl J. Walters, Reg Watson, and Dirk Zeller. "Toward Sustainability in World Fisheries." *Nature* 418 (August 2002): 689–95.

Pepinsky, Thomas B. "From Agents to Outcomes: Simulation in International Relations." *European Journal of International Relations* 11, no. 3 (September 2005): 367–94.

Perrow, Charles. *Normal Accidents: Living with High-Risk Technologies.* New York: Basic Books, 1984.

Peter, Tom A. "Cyber Spy Network with Global Reach Raises Alarms." *Christian Science Monitor*, March 29, 2009.

Pethica, James, ed. *Yeats's Poetry, Drama, and Prose: Authoritative Texts, Contexts, Criticisms.* New York: W. W. Norton, 2000.

Pikitch, Ellen K., Phaedra Doukakis, Liz Lauck, Prosanta Chakrabarty, and Daniel L. Erickson, "Status, Trends, and Management of Sturgeon and Paddlefish Fisheries." *Fish and Fisheries* 6, no. 3 (September 2005): 233–65.

Plender, John. "Banks Let off the Hook as Flawed Model Is Preserved." *Financial Times*, July 15, 2009.

Polgreen, Phillip M., Forrest D. Nelson, George R. Neumann, and Robert A. Weinstein. "Use of Prediction Markets to Forecast Infectious Disease Activity." *Clinical Infectious Diseases* 44 (January 2007): 272–79.

Poteete, Amy R., Marco A. Janssen, and Elinor Ostrom. *Working Together: Collective Action, the Commons, and Multiple Methods in Practice.* Princeton: Princeton University Press, 2010.

Power, Conrad. "A Spatial Agent-Based Model of N-Person Prisoner's Dilemma Cooperation in a Socio-Geographic Community." *Journal of Artificial Societies and Social Simulation* 12, no. 1 (January 2009).

Powner, Leanne C. "Teaching the Scientific Method in the Active Learning Classroom." *PS: Political Science & Politics* 39, no. 3 (July 2006): 521–24.

Putnam, Robert D. "Diplomacy and Domestic Politics: The Logic of Two-Level Games." *International Organization* 42, no. 3 (Summer 1988): 427–60.

Qin, Shao-Meng, Yong Chen, Xiao-Ying Zhao, and Jian Shi. "Effect of Memory on the Prisoner's Dilemma Game in a Square Lattice." *Physical Review E* 78, no. 4 (October 2008).

Radcliffe, Benjamin. "The Structure of Voter Preferences." *The Journal of Politics* 55, no. 3 (August 1993): 714–19.

Real Clear Politics. "Real Clear Politics Electoral College." Accessed June 19, 2014. http://www.realclearpolitics.com/epolls/maps/obama_vs_mccain/?map=10.

Reed, Mary Lynn. "Political Modeling and Election Simulations." *Dr. Dobb's Journal* (October 2004): 16–27.
Resnick, Mitchel. *Termites, Turtles, and Traffic Jams: Explorations in Massively Parallel Microworlds*. Cambridge: MIT Press, 1999.
Riker, William H. "The Number of Political Parties: A Reexamination of Duverger's Law." *Comparative Politics* 9, no. 1 (October 1976): 93–106.
Robinson, William I., and Jerry Harris. "Towards A Global Ruling Class? Globalization and the Transnational Capitalist Class." *Science & Society* 64, no. 1 (Spring 2000): 11–54.
Rodrik, Dani. "A Plan B for global finance." *The Economist*, March 12, 2009.
Roe, Mark J. "Chaos and Evolution in Law and Economics." *Harvard Law Review* 109, no. 3 (January 1996): 641–68.
Rohwedder, Cecile. "Deep in the Forest, Bambi Remains the Cold War's Last Prisoner." *The Wall Street Journal*, November 4, 2009.
Rosenau, James N. *Along the Domestic-Foreign Frontier: Exploring Governance in a Turbulent World*. New York: Cambridge University Press, 1997.
———. *Distant Proximities: Dynamics beyond Globalization*. Princeton: Princeton University Press, 2003.
———. *Turbulence in World Politics: A Theory of Change and Continuity*, Princeton: Princeton University Press, 1990.
———, and W. Michael Fagen. "A New Dynamism in World Politics: Increasingly Skillful Individuals." *International Studies Quarterly* 41, no. 4 (December 1997): 655–86.
Ruggie, John Gerard. "Continuity and Transformation in the World Polity: Toward a Neorealist Synthesis." In *Neorealism and Its Critics*, edited by Robert O. Keohane, 131–57. New York: Columbia University Press, 1996.
———. "Multilateralism: Anatomy of an Institution." *International Organization* 46 (Summer 1992): 561–98.
Russett, Bruce M., and John R. Oneal. *Triangulating Peace: Democracy, Interdependence, and International Organizations*. New York: Norton, 2001.
Sabherwal, Rajiv, Rudy Hirschheim, and Tim Goles. "The Dynamics of Alignment: Insights from a Punctuated Equilibrium Model." *Organization Science* 12, no. 2 (March-April 2001): 179–97.
Sagan, Scott D. "1914 Revisited: Allies, Offense, and Instability." *International Security* 11, no. 2 (Fall 1986): 151–75.
Salmon, Felix. "Recipe for Disaster: The Formula That Killed Wall Street." *Wired* 17, no. 3 (February 23, 2009): 74.
Santos, F. C., and J. M. Pacheco. "Scale-Free Networks Provide a Unifying Framework for the Emergence of Cooperation." *Physical Review Letters* 95, no. 9 (August 26, 2005).
Sapienza, Massimo Daniele. "An Experimental Approach to the Study of Banking Intermediation: The Banknet Simulator." In *Economic Simulations in Swarm: Agent-Based Modelling and Object Oriented Programming*, edited by Benedikt Stefansson and Francesco Luna. Dordrect: Kluwer, 2000.
Sawyer, R. Keith. *Social Emergence: Societies as Complex Systems*. New York: Cambridge University Press, 2005.

Schelling, Thomas C. *Micromotives and Macrobehavior.* New York: Norton, 1978.
Schmitz, Stefan W., and Claus Puhr. "Risk Concentration, Network Structure, and Contagion in the Austrian Real Time Interbank Settlement System." In *Simulation Studies of Liquidity Needs, Risks and Efficiency in Payment Networks,* edited by Harry Leinonen. Helsinki: Bank of Finland, 2007.
Scholte, Jan Aart. *Globalization: A Critical Introduction.* 2nd Edition. New York: Palgrave Macmillan, 2005.
Scholz, John T., and Cheng-Lung Wang. "Learning to Cooperate: Learning Networks and the Problem of Altruism." *American Journal of Political Science* 53, no. 3 (July 2009): 572–87.
Schultz, Kenneth A. "Domestic Opposition and Signaling in International Crises." *American Political Science Review* 92, no. 4 (December 1998): 829–44.
Schumpeter, Joseph A. *Capitalism, Socialism, and Democracy.* New York: Harper and Row 1976.
Schweitzer, Frank, Laxmidhar Behera, and Heinz Muhlenbein. "Evolution of Cooperation in a Spatial Prisoner's Dilemma." *Advances in Complex Systems* 5, no. 2-3 (June-September 2002): 269–99.
Seib, Gerald F. "In Crisis, Opportunity for Obama." *Wall Street Journal,* November 21, 2008.
Seigenthaler, John. "A False Wikipedia 'Biography.'" *USA Today,* November 29, 2005.
Selten, Reinhard, Michael Schreckenberg, Thorsten Chmura, Thomas Pitz, Sebastian Kube, Sigurour F. Hafstein, Roland Chrobok, Andreas Pottmeier, and Joachim Wahle. "Experimental Investigation of Day-to-Day Route-Choice Behaviour and Network Simulations of Autobahn Traffic in North Rhine-Westphalia." In *Human Behavior and Traffic Networks,* edited by Michael Schreckenberg and Reinhard Selden, 1–21. Berlin: Springer-Verlag, 2004.
Sevastopoulo, Demetri. "Chinese Hack into White House Network." *Financial Times,* November 6, 2008.
Sheldon, George, and Martin Mauer. "Interbank Lending and Systemic Risk: An Empirical Analysis for Switzerland." *Swiss Journal of Economics and Statistics* 134, no. 4 (1998): 685–704.
Simmons, Beth A. "International Law and State Behavior: Commitment and Compliance in International Monetary Affairs." *American Political Science Review* 94, no. 4 (December 2000): 819–35.
———, and Zachary Elkins. "The Globalization of Liberalization: Policy Diffusion in the International Political Economy." *American Political Science Review* 98, no. 1 (February 2004): 171–89.
Simon, Herbert A. "A Behavioral Model of Rational Choice." *Quarterly Journal of Economics* 69, no. 1 (February 1955): 99–118.
Simon, Marc V., and Harvey Starr. "Extraction, Allocation, and the Rise and Decline of States: A Simulation of Two-Level Security Management." *The Journal of Conflict Resolution* 40, no. 2 (June 1996): 272–97.
Skene, Leigh. "Basel III Won't Save Us from Another Banking Crisis." *FT.com,* September 16, 2010.
Sklair, Leslie. *The Transnational Capitalist Class.* Oxford: Blackwell, 2001.

Skyrms, Brian, and Robin Pemantle. "A Dynamic Model of Social Network Formation." *Proceedings of the National Academy of Sciences* 97, no. 16 (August 2000): 9340.
Snidal, Duncan. "Cooperation versus Prisoners' Dilemma: Implications for International Cooperation and Regimes." *American Political Science Review* 79, no. 4 (December 1985): 923–42.
———. "International Cooperation among Relative Gains Maximizers." *International Studies Quarterly* 35, no. 4 (December 1991): 387–402.
———. "Relative Gains and the Pattern of International Cooperation." *American Political Science Review* 85, no. 3 (September 1991): 701–26.
Snyder, Jack. "Civil-Military Relations and the Cult of the Offensive, 1914 and 1984." *International Security* 9, no. 1 (Summer 1984): 108–46.
Soramaki, Kimmo, Morten L. Bech, Jeffrey Arnold, Robert J. Glass and Walter E. Beyeler. "The Topology of Interbank Payment Flows." *Physica A* 379 (2007): 317–33.
Southgate, David, Rodrigo Sierra, and Lawrence A. Brown. "The Causes of Tropical Deforestation in Ecuador: A Statistical Analysis." *World Development* 19, no. 9 (September 1991): 1145–51.
Stein, Arthur A. "Coordination and Collaboration: Regimes in an Anarchic World." *International Organization* 36, no. 2 (March 1982): 299–324.
Stone, Edie. "Rudin's Call: Obama 291, McCain 247." NPR.org. Accessed August 13, 2010. http://www.npr.org/blogs/politics/2008/11/rudins_call_obama_291_mccain_2.html.
Strassel, Kimberley A. "The Climate Change Climate Change: The Number of Skeptics Is Swelling Everywhere." *The Wall Street Journal*, June 26, 2009.
Strogatz, Steven. *Sync: The Emerging Science of Spontaneous Order.* New York: Hyperion, 2003.
Surowiecki, James. *The Wisdom of Crowds: Why the Many Are Smarter than the Few and How Collective Wisdom Shapes Business, Economies, Societies, and Nations.* New York: Doubleday, 2004.
Sweeney, L. Booth, and John D. Stearman. "Thinking about Systems: Student and Teacher Conceptions of Natural and Social Systems." *System Dynamics Review* 23, no. 2/3 (Summer/Fall 2007): 285–312.
Symantec. *Symantec Global Internet Security Threat Report: Trends for 2009*, vol. XV. Accessed August 17, 2010. http://eval.symantec.com/mktginfo/enterprise/white_papers/b-whitepaper_internet_security_threat_report_xv_04-2010.en-us.pdf.
Szilagyi, Miklos N., and Zoltan C. Szilagyi. "Non-Trivial Solutions to the N-Person Prisoners' Dilemma." *Systems Research and Behavioral Science* 19, no. 3 (May/June 2002): 281–90.
Tarullo, Daniel K. *Banking on Basel: The Future of International Financial Regulation.* Washington, DC: Peterson Institute for International Economics, 2008.
Teitenberg, Tom. "The Tradable Permits Approach to Protecting the Commons: What Have We Learned?" In *The Drama of the Commons*, edited by Elinor Ostrom, Thomas Dietz, Nives Dolsak, Paul C. Stern, Susan Stonich, and Elke U. Weber, 197–232. Washington, DC: National Academy Press, 2002.

Trachtenberg, Marc. "The Meaning of Mobilization in 1914." *International Security* 15, no. 3 (Winter 1990/91): 120–150.
Troitzsch, Klaus G. "Validating Simulation Models." *Proceedings of the 18th Simulation Multiconference*. Erlangen, Germany: Society for Modeling & Simulation International, 2004.
Tuchman, Barbara. *The Guns of August*. New York: Ballantine Book, 1994.
U.S. Congressional Budget Office. *The Economic Costs of Disruptions in Container Shipments*. Washington, DC: GPO, March 29, 2006.
U.S. Department of Defense, Office of the Assistant Secretary of Defense for Homeland Defense. *Defense Critical Infrastructure Program*. Washington, DC: U.S. GPO, 2005.
———. *Defense Critical Infrastructure Program Assessment Benchmarks*. Washington, DC. U.S. GPO, 2007.
U.S. Department of Homeland Security. *National Infrastructure Protection Plan*. Washington, DC: U.S. GPO, 2006.
U.S. Department of Transportation. Bureau of Transport Statistics. "Air Carriers: T-International Market." Accessed September 11, 2011. http://www.transtats.bts.gov.
U.S. Public Law 110-53. 110th Cong., 1st sess. *Implementing Recommendations of the 9/11 Commission Act of 2007* (August 3, 2007).
Upper, Christian, and Andreas Worms. "Estimating Bilateral Exposures in the German Interbank Market: Is There a Danger of Contagion?" *European Economic Review* 48 (2004): 827–49.
Urbina, Ian. "Views of 'JihadJane' Were Unknown to Neighbors." *The New York Times*, March 10, 2010.
Van Evera, Stephen. "The Cult of the Offensive and the Origins of the First World War." *International Security* 9, no. 1 (Summer 1984): 58–107.
Vernon, Raymond. *Sovereignty at Bay: The Multinational Spread of U.S. Enterprises*. New York: Basic Books, 1971.
Von Peter, Goetz. "International Banking Centres: A Network Perspective." *BIS Quarterly Review* (December 2007): 33–34.
Wade, Robert H. "The Great Slump: What Comes Next?" *Economic and Political Weekly* XLV, no. 47 (November 20, 2010): 57–58.
Wade, Robert. *Village Republics: Economic Conditions for Collective Action in South India*. New York: Cambridge University Press, 1994.
Waldrop, M. Mitchell. *Complexity: The Emerging Science at the Edge of Order and Chaos*. New York: Touchstone, 1992.
———. "The Trillion Dollar Vision of Dee Hock: The Corporate Radical Who Organized Visa Wants to Dis-Organize Your Company." *Fast Company*, October 31, 1996.
Walker, R. B. J. *Inside/outside: International Relations as Political Theory*. New York: Cambridge University Press, 1993.
The Wall Street Journal. "Electoral College Calculator." Accessed August 20, 2010. http://online.wsj.com/public/resources/documents/info-flash08.html?project=POLCALCULATOR.

Walt, Stephen M. "Fads, Fevers, and Firestorms." *Foreign Policy* 121 (November-December 2000): 34–42.
Waltz, Kenneth N. *Man, the State, and War: A Theoretical Analysis*. New York: Columbia University Press, 1954.
———. *Theory of International Politics*. New York: McGraw-Hill, 1979.
Wang, Wen-Xu, and Guanrong Chen. "Universal Robustness Characteristics of Weighted Networks against Cascading Failure." *Physical Review E* 77, 2 (February 2008): 026101.
The Washington Post. "Political Landscape 2008," Accessed June 19, 2014. http://www.washingtonpost.com/wp-srv/politics/interactives/campaign08/index_bak.html.
Wasserman, Stanley, and Katherine Faust. *Social Network Analysis: Methods and Applications*. New York: Cambridge University Press, 1994.
Watts, Duncan J. "Networks, Dynamics, and the Small World Phenomenon." *American Journal of Sociology* 105, no. 2 (September 1999): 493–527.
———. *Small Worlds: The Dynamics of Networks between Order and Randomness*. Princeton: Princeton University Press, 1999.
———, and Stephen H. Strogatz. "Collective Dynamics of 'Small World' Networks." *Nature* 393, no. 6684 (June 4, 1998): 440–42.
Wells, Simon. "U.K. Interbank Exposures: Systemic Risk Implications." *Financial Stability Review* (December 2002): 175–82.
Wendt, Alexander E. "The Agent-Structure Problem in International Relations Theory." *International Organization* 41, no. 3 (1987): 335–70.
———. "Anarchy Is What States Make of It: The Social Construction of Power Politics." *International Organization* 46, no. 2 (Spring 1992): 391–425.
———. "Levels of Analysis vs. Agents and Structures: Part III." *Review of International Studies* 18 (1992): 181–85.
Western, David. "The Balance of Nature." *Wildlife Conservation* 96, no. 2 (March/April 1993): 52–55.
Wight, Colin. *Agents, Structures, and International Relations: Politics as Ontology*. New York: Cambridge University Press, 2006.
Wikipedia. "John Seigenthaler." Accessed June 19, 2014. http://en.wikipedia.org/wiki/John_Seigenthaler.
———. "Wikipedia Seigenthaler Biography Incident." Accessed June 19, 2014. http://en.wikipedia.org/wiki/Wikipedia_Seigenthaler_biography_incident.
Wilensky, Uri. "NetLogo Voting Model." Center for Connected Learning and Computer-Based Modeling, Northwestern University, Evanston, IL. Accessed June 20, 2014. http://ccl.northwestern.edu/netlogo/models/Voting.
———. NetLogo v. 3 through v. 5. Center for Connected Learning and Computer-Based Modeling, Northwestern University, Evanston, IL.
Wilenksy, Uri, and Kenneth Reisman. "Thinking like a Wolf, a Sheep, or a Firefly." *Cognition and Instruction* 24, no. 2 (June 2006): 171–209.
Wilensky, Uri, and Mitchel Resnick. "Thinking in Levels: A Dynamic Systems Approach to Making Sense of the World." *Journal of Science Education and Technology* 8, no. 1 (March 1999): 3–19.
Wilkinson, Ian. *Business Relating Business: Managing Organisational Relations and Networks*. Northampton: Edward Elgar, 2008.

Williams, Leighton Vaughan. "How to Forecast an Election (And How to Win One!)" Accessed May 7, 2009. http://www.pollingreport.com/lvw_bet.htm.
Williamson, Oliver. *The Economic Institutions of Capitalism: Firms, Markets, Relational Contracting*. New York: Free Press, 1985.
Wilson, James. "Deutsche Bank Adds to Calls for Tough Capital Regulations." *Financial Times*, September 9, 2009.
———. "German Bankers Fear Impact of New Rules." *Financial Times*, September 21, 2009.
Wilson, James. "Scientific Uncertainty, Complex Systems, and the Design of Common-Pool Institutions." In *The Drama of the Commons*, edited by Elinor Ostrom, Thomas Dietz, Nives Dolsak, Paul C. Stern, Susan Stonich, and Elke U. Weber, 327–59. Washington, DC: National Academy Press, 2002.
Wilson, Rick K., and Carl M. Rhodes. "Leadership and Credibility in N-Person Coordination Games." *Journal of Conflict Resolution* 41, no. 6 (December 1997): 767–91.
Windrum, Paul, Giorgio Fabiolo, and Alessio Moneta. "Empirical Validation of Agent-Based Models: Alternatives and Prospects." *Journal of Artificial Societies and Social Simulation* 10, no. 2 (March 2007).
Wines, Michael. "China's Growth Leads to Problems down the Road." *The New York Times*, August 27, 2010.
Wise, Timothy A. "US Corn Ethanol Fuels Food Crisis in Developing Countries." *Al-Jazeera*, October 10, 2012. Accessed November 24, 2012. http://www.aljazeera.com/indepth/opinion/2012/10/201210993632838545.html.
Wood, Duncan. *Governing Global Banking: The Basel Committee and the Politics of Financial Globalization*. Aldershot: Ashgate 2005.
Yang, Rui, Wen-Xu Wang, Ying-Cheng Lai, and Guanrong Chen. "Optimal Weighting Scheme for Suppressing Cascades and Traffic Congestion in Complex Networks." *Physical Review E* 79, no. 2 (February 2009).
Yetiv, Steven A. *The Petroleum Triangle: Oil, Globalization and Terror*. Ithaca: Cornell University Press, 2011.
Young, H. Peyton. "The Evolution of Conventions." *Econometrica* 61, no. 1 (1993): 57–84.
———. *Individual Strategy and Social Structure: An Evolutionary Theory of Institutions*. Princeton: Princeton University Press, 1998.

INDEX

Page numbers in italics refer to figures and tables.

9/11, 174, 177

ABC News, 6
ABM. *See* agent-based models
Abu Dhabi, 184, *185*, 186, *187*
accidents, 21
Ackermann, Josef, 142
active nonlinear test, 67–71, *69*, *71*, 73, 219n36
activists, 13, 58–59, 99, 191
actors: bounded rationality of, 104, 139; in complex systems, 4, 7–8, 11–13; and ecological complexity, 103–104, 110, 138; emergence and self-organization among, 4, 40–41, 45, 55, 82, 102, 104, 197; heterogeneity of, 55, 98, 139, 197–198; information sharing among, 134–137; learning of, 17, 41–42, 44, 58, 60, 99, 102–104, 111, 142, 192–194, 198–199; mutual constitution with structure, 45, 48, 60, 103, 192, 195–196, 199; nonstate, 174–175, 200; origins of preferences, 2–4, 45, 47, 55, 168, 199; represented as agents in models, 50, 53, 61–65, 70, 72, 74–75, 82, 116, 117, 119–120, 155–157, 168; sensitivity to relative gains, 97; and social choice dilemmas, 56–58, 77–78, 80, 82, 92, 97; in social networks, 6, 8–11, 20, 23–24, 26, 30, 33–38, 40, 59, 94–95, 143–144, 169, 173–174, 177, 196; and social preferences, 58–60; transnational, 175; as unit of analysis, 45, 55, 197–199. *See also* agents
adaptation: and co-evolution, 104, 193; in complex systems, 7–8, 13–16; and cooperation, 194; and evolutionary game theory, 40–41; and levels of analysis, 193; in networks, 10, 188; in politics, 36–37, 52, 200; simulated with genetic algorithms, 50, 88, 116
Adler, Emanuel, 41
Afghanistan, 55, 95
Africa, 193
agent-based models: advantages of, 50–52, 111; artificial societies versus evidence-driven, 52–53, 103; assumptions of, 61; and complex systems theory, 40, 111; as a computational method, 3, 49–51; and economics, 54, 213n117; and emergence, 49–51; and evolutionary game theory, 78, 173; and game theory, 49; and genetic algorithms, 50, 116, 178, 180; and geographic information science, 79; and imperfect information, 195–196; limitations of, 53–54; of networks, 155, 157–159, 172–173, 177, 180; of norm formation, 47; programming languages, 214n127; and pseudo code, 54–55, 116, 160; replication, 54–55; of social choice dilemmas,

agent-based models (*continued*)
58, 61, 82; of social-ecological complexity, 102–104, 111–113, 119–120; sufficiency versus necessity of, 53–54, 168; and two-level games, 144, 155; use in experimentation, 49–52, 59, 61, 161; validation of, 54–55, 215n151

agents: and agent-based models, 52–55, 61, 111; and complex adaptive systems, 60; and emergence, 40–41; and genetic algorithms, 74, 86, 90, 119, 231n77; heterogeneity versus homogeneity, 85, 98; learning of, 67, 74, 76, 111, 194; logical fallacies about, 46–47; and networks, 39–40; as simulated airports, 180, 181, 188; as simulated appropriators, 112–113, 115, 116–120, 117, 123–125, 131, 137, 199, 226n62; as simulated banks, 159–161, 160, 164–168; as simulated constituencies, 62–63, 66; as simulated natural resources, 111–112, 115, 116, 117, 120, 123, 125, 137; as simulated negotiators, 62–63, 66, 86, 159–160, 160, 164–166, 168; rationality assumption, 40, 47, 74, 111; relation to structures, 30–31, 38, 45, 48–49, 55, 195. *See also* actors

agent-structure debate, 25, 30–31, 35, 45–46, 48

Agrawal, Arun, 104, 106–107, 110

Aguascalientes, Mexico. *See* airports: Aguascalientes, Mexico

Air Transport Association, U.S., 188

air transportation network: Alaskan, 177; China, 179; global, 177; India, 179; United States 172–173, 176, 178–180

airports: Abu Dhabi, 184–186, 185, 187; Aguascalientes, Mexico, 186, 187; Atlanta Hartsfield, 182, 186; Birmingham (U.K.), 184, 185, 187; Brisbane, 184–188, 185, 187; Cancun, 184–186, 185; Chicago O'Hare 182, 186, 188; Dallas-Fort Worth, 186; Los Angeles, 186; Miami 186; Montego Bay, 184–186, 185, 187; Mumbai, 184, 185; New York JFK, 186; Newark, 186; San Salvador, 186, 187; Santa Marta, Colombia, 184–186, 185, 187; Santiago, 173, 184–188, 185, 187; Seoul-Inchon, 185, 185; Tokyo, 182, 184–188, 185, 187; Toronto Pearson, 182, 184, 185, 186, 187, 188

Akimov, Vladimir, 79
Al Qaeda, 174
alert fatigue, 21–22
Aleutian Islands, 1
algorithms: Watts-Strogatz, 231n75; Barabasi-Albert, 231n75. *See also* genetic algorithms
altruism, 44, 80, 113, 120, 124
Amazon River, 20–21, 106, 139
Anchorage, Alaska, 177
ANT. *See* active nonlinear test
Anti-Ballistic Missile Treaty, 41
antibiotics, 12
Apple, 18, 20, 141
appropriators. *See* agents: as simulated appropriators
Arab Spring, 57, 95, 139, 199
Arthur, W. Brian, 22
artificial society. *See* agent-based model: artificial societies versus evidence-driven
Atlanta. *See* airports: Atlanta Hartsfield
attribution problem, 6, 209n35
Austria: interbank network, 154, 157–158, 158, 167; Netflix prize, 14
automata, 79
Axelrod, Robert, 44, 50, 82, 87–89, 97, 223n54
Axtell, Robert, 41, 50

Babus, Ana, 153
bacteria. *See* slime mold
Bahrain, 193
Baland, Jean-Marie, 110
Baltimore, 203n39

INDEX

Bank of International Settlements (BIS), 143, 145
Bankers Association for Finance and Trade, U.S., 148
banks: capital adequacy ratio requirements, 24, 142–143, 145–150, 155, 167; commercial, 12, 152, 156–157; contingent convertible capital of, 146, 148; correlation of asset portfolios, 152–153; interbank lending, 19, 75, 144, 152–154, 157–159, 161, 167–169; *Landesbanken*, 147, 151–152, 154, 156–157, 157, 160–161, 168; interbank networks, 152, 154–155, 157–159, *158*, 167; risk-weighting formulas of, 146–147, 167; savings, 152, 154, 156–157
Barabasi, Albert-Laszlo, 221n18
Basel Accords: I (one), 138, 145–146, 150; II (two), 142, 146–147, 150, 153, 155; III (three), 104–105, 142–144, 147–150, 155, 167–168; ABM of negotiations, 155–159, *160*, 164–165, *166*; deficiencies, 146; As a regime, 150–151; risk-weighting formulas, 146–147; tier I versus tier II capital, 145
Basel Committee on Banking Supervision, 142, 145–148
Battle of the Sexes. *See* dilemmas: Battle of the Sexes
Bering Sea, 2
Berlin Wall, 12
betweenness. *See* network structure: betweenness
biology: complex systems theory and, 48; computational social science and, 200; evolutionary, 42, 50, 197, 207n110; evolutionary game theory and, 48, 212n94; and genetic algorithms, 50, 226n56
bird flu, 35
Birmingham, UK. *See* airports: Birmingham, UK
Bollywood, 195
Boss, Michael, 157–158, *158*

Box, George E. P., 55
Brazil: Conjunto Palmeiras, 197; Corumba, 20; population growth in, 106
Brisbane. *See* airports: Brisbane
Britain. *See* United Kingdom
Brown, Gordon, 142
BTS. *See* Bureau of Transportation Statistics
Bureau of Transportation Statistics, U.S., 173, 178, 180–182, *181*, 184, 186–187
butterfly effect, 50, 175

Cairo, 77
California, 195
campaigns, 5, 20
Canada: 2003 blackout, 172; Basel negotiations, 143, 148, 155; Catalina, Newfoundland and Labrador, 79; Netflix prize, 14; Ontario, 172; Quebec, 172
Cancun. *See* airports: Cancun
carbon trading, 97
Carnegie Mellon University, 11
carrying capacity, 112
CAS. *See* complex adaptive systems
cascades, 32, 72, 146, 172, 187, 191, 198
Caspian Sea, 101–102, 108, 138
Catalina. *See* Canada: Catalina, Newfoundland and Labrador
Caviar, 101, 108
Cederman, Lars-Erik, 54
Centers for Disease Control and Prevention, U.S., 15
centrality. *See* network structure: centrality
CERT. *See* Computer Emergency Response Team
Champagne fairs, 13
change: of Basel regime, 143, 150; in common pool resources, 103–104, 106–109, 111, 139; in complex adaptive systems, 8, 23, 40, 42–47, 50, 55, 60; and evolutionary game

change *(continued)*
  theory, 81, 92, 99; and genetic algorithms, 50; and interdependency, 8, 60, 174; international relations theories of, 25, 30–31, 35–36, 47, 49, 55, 72–73, 174–175, 196–198, 200; in markets, 141, 151, 153; in networks, 10, 17, 38, 173, 191, 195; and punctuated equilibria, 24, 207n110
chaord, 19
chaos, 19, 22, 104
Chicago. *See* airports: Chicago O'Hare
China: air transportation network, 179; and food crisis, 192; hackers from, 5, 15; immigrants from, 196; rock music fans, 194
Chivers, C. J., 101–102
Clauset, Aaron, 179
Cleveland, 182
climate change, 23, 51, 78, 200
cliques. *See* network structure: cliques
clustering coefficient. *See* network structure: clustering coefficient
code: for agent-based models 44, 53–54, 112–113; genetic algorithms, 116, 226n55; for replication, 54; pseudo 54, 66, 86, *117*, *160*, *181*
coevolution: among actors, 42, 47, 82, 88, 92, 99, 188, 199; actors with structure, 48, 79; in markets, 141–142; simulated with genetic algorithms, 67, 90
Columbus, Ohio, 188
common pool resources: agent-based models of, 111, 199; as collective action problem, 25, 105–106; conservation of, 102–103, 128, 137; effects of harvesting, 136; effects of information on actors, 108–109, 13, 138–139, 196; effects of social network structure, 151; effects of technology, 130; examples of, 105; fisheries, 25, 51, 105, 107–108, 110, *117*, 194, 199; forests, 104–108, 138–139; free-riding, 103–107, 113, 120, 137–138; grazing lands, 105, 107–108, 138; greenhouse gases, 104; hypotheses, 106–111, 119–120; irrigation systems, 104–105, 107–108, 138; and learning, 116, 120, 194; as nearly decomposable system, 109; properties of, 105, 138–139; self-organization among actors, 104
Commons, Tragedy of the. *See* Tragedy of the Commons
Communist Party (China), 194
competition: among banks, 141; and common pool resources, 137; and game theory, 155; in genetic algorithms, 67; and learning, 13–15; as selection mechanism, 12; and self-organization, 23
complex adaptive systems: agent-based models of, 49–51; common pool resources, 106; formation of actors' interests, 47–48; global social systems as, 7–8; networks as, 10, 177; properties of, 7–8, 40, 48, 60; sensitivity to relative gains, 217n12; social preferences, 60; social systems as, 7–8, 11–16, 18–19, 23, 26–27, 38, 46, 52, 191; in world politics, 4, 10–11, 30–32, 34–35
complex systems theory: applied to world politics, 7, 30–31, 35, 48–49, 55, 192, 210n50; and "change," 47; common pool resources, 109; computational social science, 45; defined, 40–41, 211n75; 211n83; learning about, 215n149; levels of analysis, 46; social construction as, 47–48, 199; and social network analysis, 36, 40
complexity theory. *See* complex systems theory
complexity: defined, 2; ecological, 23, 102–104, 107, 110–111, 134, 136, 138–139; and emergence, 45; interaction, 21, 111, 128, 138; and world politics, 2–3, 10, 37, 101–102, 191

computation, evolutionary, 173, 192, 199
computational methods, 3, 49, 192. *See also* agent-based models
computational social science: and agent-based models, 54; and cascades, 188; and collective action problems, 82, 167; as a field, 3, 35–36; elements of, 7, 31, 55; and world politics, 25–27, 31, 35, 37, 45–49, 175, 192, 197–200
Computer Emergency Response Team, 11
Condorcet, Marquis de, 58, 61
Condorcet decision problem, 61–62
conservation: of common pool resources, 24, 49, 101–102, 107, 137; in complex global social systems, 16–23; and evolutionary game theory, 43, 81; and genetic algorithms, 50; of information, 11–12, 17; mechanisms of, 15, 43, 81
constitution, mutual, 45–46, 79
construction, social, 30, 38, 110
contagion: financial, 142, 145, 154; globalization and, 175, 177; political, 19, 193
context preservation, problem of in game theory, 79–80, 93
Convention on International Trade in Endangered Species (CITES), 102
Cooley, Alexander, 175
cooperation: agent-based model of, 67, 69, 83, 85–90, 86, 89, 159, 222n45, 222n48; and Basel Accords, 151–155; common pool resources, 110, 112, 128, 131, 137–139; communication and, 58; emergence of, 63, 73, 82; gains from, 59, 61, 72, 97–98, 217n12; games, 25, 75, 77–80, 83, 84, 97–98, 143, 155, 223n54; information and, 85, 89, 139; international, 47, 83, 97; iteration, 79, 168; learning and, 58, 85, 92, 194; measurement of, 87–90;

networks and, 38, 83, 85, 90–94, 99, 144, 169; reciprocity and, 43–44
corruption, 101, 104, 108, 172
CPR. *See* common pool resources
creative destruction, 20, 22, 92, 141
CreditSights, 33
credit default swaps, 5, 32–33
crisis maps, 5, 17, 19
crisis: of 1914, 3; and change, 197; financial of 2008, 3, 19, 24, 26, 27, 32–33, 141–155, 167, 197, 207n113; Eurozone, 198; food, 192; Mexico default, 145
crossover. *See* genetic algorithms
cyberwar, 17
Czech Republic, 12

Dalai Lama, 6, 32
Darwin, Charles, 12
Defense Critical Infrastructure Program (U.S.), 177
degree: and air transportation networks, 178–179, *178*; in agent-based models, *158*; and banking, 158; distribution, 38–39, 176, *179*; and network density, 38, 176; defined, 38; in- versus out-, *133*; and path length, 84; total, 178–179
Diermeier, Daniel, 53
Des Moines, 188
Deutsch, Karl W., 36
Deutsche Bank, 142
Diffusion, 41
Digital Pearl Harbor, 6, 26, 171
dilemmas: Battle of the Sexes, 75, 77, 82–83, 84, 92, 94, 143, 155, 156, 159; of collective action, 22, 42–43, 77–87, 92, 97–99, 102–103; Condorcet, 58; Prisoner's, 43–44, 50, 77–80, 82–85, 84, 87, 89, 90, 91, 92–95, 96, 97–98, 212n94, 222n45, 223n54; Rules of the Road, 61, 77, 82–83, 84, 92–94, 93, 94, 195; second order, 106; security, 78; Stag Hunt, 77, 82–83, 84, 91, 92–95, 96

disease, 4, 6, 9, 11, 13, 35, 55, 176–177
distance: geographic, 17, 29, 34, 172, 178, 182, 186, 189; in networks, 17, 38, 119, 131, 158; social, 77
distant proximities, 34
distribution: of gains, 25–26, 34, 57–59, 61, 64, 67, 72–75, 78, 80, 82–83, 86, 94, 95–98, 143–144, 155, 172–173, 175, 194; lognormal, 134; of network nodes (degree), 38–39, 176, 179; normal, 112; probability, 43, 81–82, 134, 180; Poisson, 39; power law, 39, 222n37; of preferences, 63, 69, 164, 168; skewed, 179; spatial, 79, 109; of strategies, 42–43, 88, 89, 95, 99, 104; uniform, 66
Draper, Norman R., 55
dynamics: agent-structure, 35; bargaining, 167; coevolutionary, 141; of complex systems, 41, 52, 60; fragmenting, 19; of information, 72, 74; integrating, 19; interaction, 79; and levels of analysis, 51; in models, 53; of natural systems, 107, 138; in networks, 23, 36, 38, 65, 104, 169, 172–173, 176, 187; nonlinear, 19, 50, 102–104, 175; of preferences, 58, 76; in social systems, 55, 87, 97; system, 51; temporal, 82; in world politics, 3–4, 24, 26–27, 29–31, 37, 44, 55–56, 196, 199, 210n50, 219n32

East St. Louis, Missouri, 204n57
economics: behavioral, 40, 47, 209n27, 213n117; and complex systems, 40, 48; and computational social science, 26, 200; forecasting, 33; micro, 12, 199; and networks, 168; transaction costs, 152
economy: American, 6, 34; Brazilian, 197; German, 151–152; global, 26, 103, 145, 148; illicit, 195; informal, 194–196
ecosystems: as complex systems, 11, 23, 109; interaction with social systems, 101, 103; management of, 109; markets as, 141; model of, 111–138, *114–115*, *117*, *129*, 199, 226n62, 227n69; natural selection, 12; networks and, 136; player strategies as, 42; regime shifts, 109; technology, 110, 137; and world politics, 194
edges. *See* links
Edmonds, Bruce, 54
effects: feedback, 3; interaction, 3, 51, 111, 175, 177, 182, 192; nonlinear, 20, 35, 111, 186; network, 18, 20, 95, 141, 189; unintended, 192. *See also* butterfly effect
efficiency: in complex systems, 21; frontier, 149; of markets, 149, 169; of networks, 169, 175; of technology, 102, 112, 114, 123–125, 130, *132–133*, 134, *135*, 137, 226n65
Eichengreen, Barry, 148
Eldredge, Niles, 207n110
electricity, 10, 171–172, 177
Emanuel, Rahm, 141
emergence: and agent-based models, 76, 82; and complex systems 40–41, 49, 199; of cooperation, 63, 67, 73, 80, 85, 88, 98; defined, 8, 40; examples, 41; global, 194; of identities, 47, 55, 197; of interests, 199; and logical fallacies, 8; of norms, 47, 197; social, 11, 45, 99, 199
Encyclopedia Britannica, 13
endogenous growth theory, 22, 34
Epstein, Joshua M., 6, 41, 50
error: cognitive, 40; creative, 20–23; deliberate, 21
Estonia, 32
Europe, 3, 33, 189, 198, 207n113
European Union, 142, 147, 198
European Systemic Risk Board, 142
event history models. *See* regression: event history (hazard) models
evolution: of actors, 47, 188, 191, 194; biology, 50, 197, 207n110, 212n94; coevolution, 42, 67, 79, 90, 99, 141–142; in complex systems, 7, 19,

52; of networks, 99; of strategies, 81–82, 98, 151. *See also* game theory: evolutionary
evolutionarily stable strategy, 42, 44, 81–82, 99, 212n94
evolutionary computation, 173, 192, 199
experiments: absence of empirical data, 178; actor learning and, 104; with agent-based models, 50–52, 59, 183–184; in simulations, 43, 81; human subjects, 81; multiplayer games, 82; true vs. quasi-true, 51–52
exploration: in agent-based models, 51, 53; versus exploitation, 23; of parameter spaces, 43, 51, 67, 81, 92; and social theory, 24–25
externalities, 34, 102, 104, 107, 169
Eyjafjallokull (volcano), 187

fallacies: of composition, 8, 19, 32, 41, 46, 143; ecological, 8, 41, 46; and levels of analysis, 48
feedback: in complex systems, 3, 109; and learning, 42, 119, 195; negative, 41, 52, 153, 191; in networks, 177; positive, 2, 5, 14, 41, 52, 95, 191; in socio-ecological systems, 101–102; in world politics, 191, 193, 198
finance: asset bubbles, 139; assumption of composability, 19; as complex network, 25; in Germany, 152, 155–161, *157*, *158*; global crisis, 3, 141; industry, 173, 192, 197; interactions in, 2; network properties, 158; regime, 25, 142–151, 229n36; in the United States, 152, 155–161, *157*, *158*. *See also* banks
Firefox, 18
fish, 1, 101–103, 110, 137
fisheries. *See* common pool resources: fisheries
fitness proportionate selection. *See* genetic algorithm
fitness: criteria, 67, 71, 182; evolutionary game theory, 44; in genetic algorithms, 86, 90, 118, 182–184, *183*; landscape, 92, 219n36
Flache, Andreas, 44
flu. *See* influenza
Folk Theorem, 43
food crisis, 192–193
forests. *See* common pool resources: forests
Forscher, Bernard K., 24–26
Fox News, 16
France, 143, 146, 148, 158
free-riding, 103–107, 113, 120, 138

G10, 145
GA. *See* genetic algorithms
gains: relative 80, 97; sensitivity to, 97–98, 217n12
game theory: and agent-based modeling, 49–52; beach problem, 22; and biology, 42, 48, 212n94; chicken, 82; classical versus evolutionary, 42–44, 58, 77–78, 81; collaboration, 83, 93, 95; and complex systems, 40, 45, 46–48, 55; and computational social science, 26, 35–36; coordination, 25, 58, 61, 74–75, 80, 83, 92, 94, 95, 98, 218n21, 231n77; El Farol Bar problem, 22; evolutionary, 7, 30, 41–45; and genetic algorithms, 74; grim trigger strategy, 88; heterogeneous strategies, 81–82, 88; multiple equilibria, 81, 224n10; and networks, 48, 55, 79–80, 95; players' information, 85, 98; players' learning, 90, 138; shadow of the future, 103, 168; tit-for-tat strategy, 44, 88; two-player versus multiplayer, 25–26, 77–83, 85–87, 94–95; ultimatum game, 42. *See also* dilemmas
Gann, Ernest K., 20–21
generation. *See* genetic algorithms
genetic algorithms: active nonlinear test, 67–69; and actor learning, 50, 74, 87–88, 116–119, 168, 172–173, 178, 222n48; computational social

genetic algorithms *(continued)*
science, 3; crossover procedure, 50, 67. 118–119, 131, 219n36, 222n45, 227n68; and experimentation, 51, 90; generation, 67, 69, 86, 90, 92, 115, 118–119, 182–184, 226n56; models, 66, 86, 115, 118, 181, 182; mutation in, 50, 67, 116, 183, 222n45; pairwise versus fitness proportionate selection, 90–92, 219n35; population, 50, 81–82, 90, 116, 226n56; selection criteria, 90
geographic information science (GIS), 79
Georgia, 5, 32
Germany: banking network, 24, 142–144, 146–148, 150–152, 154–161, 167–169, 195, 228n12; Berlin Wall, 12; controversy about circumcision, 194; Jena, 9; *Landesbanken*, 147, 151–152, 154, 156–157, 160–161, 168; Oberhausen, 197; similarity to Austrian banking network, 157–158; *Sparkassen*, 152
Gerschenkron, Alexander, 151–152
GhostNet, 6, 15, 32
Giddens, Anthony, 33, 45, 49, 195, 198, 208n25
Gilbert, Nigel, 207n114
Gilkes, Kai, 33
Gill, Stephen, 37
Gilpin, Robert, 47, 196–197
Gladwell, Malcolm, 202n16, 203n39, 204n57
global positioning system, 21
Global Viral Forecasting Initiative, 14
globalization: and computational social science, 26–27, 31, 37; defined, 7, 35, 171, 173; and governance, 59, 159, 224n13; as a juggernaut, 195; ontology, 34, 45; and self-organization, 192; theory, 7, 10, 26–27, 29–31, 72, 173–176, 197, 207n114, 208n25
goods: collective, 4, 7, 10, 16, 26, 33, 78, 99, 102–103, 134, 194; public, 59, 99, 103, 105–106, 148, 198; public versus private, 105
Google, 14–15
Gould, Stephen J., 207n110
governance: coordination problems, 75; decentralized, 194; global, 47, 59, 194, 197–198; polycentric, 104, 107, 139, 224n13; and self-organization, 102–104
government: and common pool resources, 105; and complex global social systems, 4–6, 99, 103, 188–189; and computational social science, 37, 55; financial regime, 142–143, 147, 149–153; global financial crisis, 155; and informal economy, 194; levels of analysis, 76; and monetary policy, 197–198; and self-organization, 26; and social networks, 13, 17
Goyal, Sanjeev, 106
Granovetter, Mark, 80
graph theory. *See* network theory
grazing lands. *See* common pool resources: grazing lands
Great Pacific Garbage Patch, 1–2, 11, 102
Greece, 198
greenhouse gases. *See* common pool resources: greenhouse gases
Grieco, Joseph M., 97
gyre: as metaphor for world politics, 3–4, 23, 27, 99; "widening," 3. *See also* North Pacific Gyre

hackers. *See* patriotic hackers
Haiti, 5, 172, 197
Hamming distance, 86, 88, 90, 222n48
Hardin, Garrett, 2, 105
harvesters, 101, 108, 112, 141, 227n71
Hawaii, 1–2
hazard models. *See* regression: event history (hazard) models
hegemonic stability theory, 148–149, 174
Herfindahl index, 168

heterogeneity: of actors, 85, 98, 106, 108, 138–139, 197, 200; and fitness, 92; of networks, 176; of strategies, 82, 88, 92
hierarchy: of authority, 5; levels of analysis, 7, 192; versus parallelism, 17–18; of social organizations, 10, 34
HIV. *See* human immunodeficiency virus
Hock, Dee, 19
Hoffmann, Matthew J., 47
Holland, John, 60
Homeland Security, U.S. Department of, 171
homeostasis, 112
Howlett, Michael, 154
hub. *See* network structure: scale free
Hughes, Barry, 36
human immunodeficiency virus, 4, 204n57
Huntington, Samuel P., 39

Iceland, 187
Ikegami, Takashi, 79
incidence. *See* network theory
India, 2, 6, 179, 192
Indiana, 172, 205n72
influenza, 14–15, 136; bird, 35; swine, 6
information: cascades, 72; and common pool resources, 106–110; complete, 33, 134, 136, 139; conservation, 11–12, 50; in complex systems, 7, 40, 136; errors in, 21–22, 196; imperfect, 40, 60, 85, 92, 98; incomplete, 40, 73, 103, 136, 138–139, 225n37; and learning, 193; and networks, 10, 14, 17, 25, 33, 38, 72, 77, 80, 104, 136–137, 154, 167, 171, 188–189, 196; parallelism, 17, 19–20, 176; perfect, 85, 98; sharing, 102, 134, 139; systems, 4–6, 9, 13, 16, 32, 171, 176, 188
infrastructure, 5, 26, 169, 173–175, 177
innovation: in complex systems, 13–16; and creative errors, 20–23;
in economies, 197–198; and evolutionary game theory, 41–42, 81; and genetic algorithms, 50, 67; and massive parallelism, 17–18; mechanisms, 43, 81
institutionalism, 36–37, 47, 49, 59, 97–98
institutions: change of, 24, 197–198; and collective action problems, 62, 104, 136; and common pool resources, 106, 108–109, 111; European Union, 198; financial, 9, 19, 136, 144, 152, 174, 197; governance, 224n13; international, 59, 83, 108, 144; mutual constitution, 45–46, 55; and transparency, 72; as units of analysis, 35, 192; voting, 61, 75
interdependence: in complex social systems, 30, 40–41; decisions, 2; in finance, 19, 32, 145, 153–154; international, 60, 72, 174–175; networks as representations of, 8–11, 37; of payoffs, 59–60, 199; and segregation, 45; in social systems, 8; in systems, 8, 11, 21
International Committee to Ban Land Mines, 196
international relations theory, 23, 29, 34, 59, 82, 97, 174
internet, 9, 11, 13–14, 29, 34, 176
Internet Explorer, 18
internet protocol, 83
Intrade, 15–16, 205n72
iPhone. *See* Apple
Iran, 5, 17, 57, 196
Iraq, 95
irrigation systems. *See* common pool resources: irrigation systems
Israeli-Palestinian Peace Process, 97
Italy: Basel III regime, 143, 146, 150; financial network, 154, 158; risk of default, 198; tax evasion in, 196

Jackson, Patrick Thaddeus, 35–36, 46, 49

Jacobson, Michael J., 215n149
Japan, 1, 5, 143, 145–147, 154–155, 172
Jervis, Robert, 8, 21, 103, 193
JihadJane. *See* LaRose, Colleen R.

Kahler, Miles, 71, 80
Kane, Edward J., 150
Kapstein, Ethan B., 150
Keck, Margaret E., 72
Kennedy, John F., 13
Kennedy, Robert F., 13
Kenya, 5, 197
k-factor. *See* gains: sensitivity to
Kindleberger, Charles, 148
Krasner, Stephen D., 83
Kreps, David M., 42–43, 81, 224n10
Kuhn, Thomas S., 200
Kurth, James, 152
Kyoto Protocol, 97

Lall, Ranjit, 145–146, 150–151
Landesbanken. *See* Germany: *Landesbanken*
LaRose, Colleen R., 13
learning: in agent-based models, 52, 138; algorithms, 74, 85, 159–160, 231n77; and bounded rationality, 139; and collective action problems, 58, 92, 98, 104, 193–194; in complex systems, 7, 13, 40–41, 47, 104; computational social science, 31, 192; concern of political science, 36; evolutionary game theory, 41–42, 44, 188, 191, 199; genetic algorithms, 50, 87–88, 116, 118, 168; mimetic, 194; in multiplayer games, 82; and networks, 78, 144; simulation of, 48–49; trial-and-error, 104; and uncertainty, 109; in world politics, 47, 193, 198–199
Lehman Brothers, 141–142, 169
levels of analysis: and agent-based models, 51, 58, 76, 82; and agent-structure debate, 46; and complex systems, 35–37, 46; and computational social science, 31, 46, 48, 192; and logical fallacies, 46, 48; and network theory, 38; orthodox, 7, 10, 23, 27, 192; problem, 29, 31
Levanthal, Howard, 202fn16
Li, David X., 33
Libya, 57, 193
Liebrand, William B. G., 80
links: in agent-based models, 180, 181; defined, 9; and disruptions, 182, 184, 186; in financial networks, 158; in- versus out-, 180; and learning, 131; in scale-free networks, 172; versus nodes, 8–9; weights, 63, 65, 66, 70, 74, 159, 176–178, 180, 181, 187–189. *See also* network theory
Lipschutz, Ronnie, 30
liquidity, 147–148, 197–198
lobster, 107
lock-in, 35, 49
Los Angeles, 176. *See also* airports: Los Angeles
Los Angeles Times, 16
Lucas, Robert, 33, 209n27
Lustick, Ian S., 47

Maasai, 103, 137
Macy, Michael W., 44
Maine, 107
Man, The State, and War, 7, 35
markets: and agent-based models, 159; black, 101; carbon trading, 97; and common pool resources, 107; and community enforcement, 13; as complex adaptive systems, 141, 188; and corruption, 108; and diffusion, 41; efficiency of, 105, 136, 141, 149; emerging, 33; equilibrium in, 141; financial, 5, 9, 12–13, 19, 32–33, 139, 141–145, 147–148, 150, 152–153, 156; global, 11, 32; and governments, 103–104, 197; informal economy, 194; as networks, 9, 12–13, 144, 151, 154, 157–159, 167–169, 195; prediction, 15–16, 136, 205n72; and public goods, 105; and risk, 153

Marks, Robert E., 54
Martin, Lisa L., 62, 83
Marxism, 29
Massachusetts Institute of Technology, 52
Massachusetts, 197
massive multiplayer online role-playing games, 18
Matsushima, Masanao, 79
Matthew, Richard, 85
McCain, John, 5, 16, 205n72
McGee, Darrell "Boss Man," 204n57
memory: in agent-based models, 74, 76, 85, 86, 112–113, 117, 120–123, 131; collective, 11–12; computer, 6, 34; and cooperation, 89–90, 92, 93; and genetic algorithms, 87, 116, 222n45, 222n48, 226n55; interaction effects, 123–128, *126–127*, 131; and learning, 138, 196
Mercy Corps, 197
methodology: of computational social science, 30–31, 37, 48, 54–55, 78; individualism, 31; innovation, 7, 31; Monte Carlo, 176; tools, 23, 38–39, 47–48. *See also* agent-based models; simulation
Mexico: border with U.S., 195–196; financial crisis of 1982, 145; power outage, 172; public health, 5
Miami, 172. *See also* airports: Miami
Micromotives and Macrobehavior, 36
Miller, John H., 8, 41, 45–46, 48, 51, 67, 206n102, 219n36. *See also* active nonlinear test
Miodownik, Dan, 47
MIT. *See* Massachusetts Institute for Technology
Mitchell, Melanie, 87, 211n83, 219n35, 222n45
MMORPGs. *See* massive multiplayer online role-playing games
models: assumptions of, 49, 76, 129–130; artificial society, 52–53; behavioral, 6; evidence-driven, 52–53, 139; evolutionary, 99; formal, 48; system dynamics, 36, 207n114; validation, 87. *See also* agent-based models
Mombasa, 176
Money, 9, 14–16, 26, 42, 171, 197
Montego Bay. *See* airports: Montego Bay
Morgenstern, Oskar, 44
Morgenthau, Hans, 234n1
Moss, Scott, 52, 54
Mozambique, 9
Mubarak, Hosni, 193
Mueller, Karl P., 175
multilateralism, 57, 72, 80, 83, 97, 143, 145, 164–165, 167–168
multiplayer games. *See* game theory: two-player versus multiplayer
Mumbai, 175, 195. *See also* airports: Mumbai
mutation. *See* genetic algorithms: mutation
My Pet Jawa, 13

Nairobi, 195
Nassau grouper, 103
National Academy of Sciences, U.S., 192
National Infrastructure Protection Plan, U.S., 177
National Public Radio, 16
National Research Council, U.S., 171
NATO, 6
Nebraska, 205n72
negotiations: Basel agreements, 142–143, 146–151, 155–156, 159–161, 164–168; and game theory, 25, 61–62, 82, 85–88, 86, 97–98, 155; international, 60; and memory, 74; and networks, 144, 191; multilateral, 63, 72, 80, 97, 165, 168, 219n26; two-level games, 58–59, 61–65, 64, 67, 68, 69–76, 71
neighborhood: agents, 66, 79; Moore, 79, *117*; network, 112–113, 159, *160*, 181
Nerves of Government, The, 36

Netflix, 14, 18, 23
NetLogo, 218n18, 226n55
network analysis. *See* network theory
network structure: all-to-all, 90; average path length, 38–39, 119, 124, 157, 158, 178; betweenness centrality, 132, 152, 161, 184, 228n12, 231n78; centrality, 38, 143–144, 154, 160, 164–166, 168–169; cliques, 38, 134, 136; clustering coefficient, 38–39, 119, 124, 131, 158, 178; density, 38, 46, 65, 94, 99, 131, 133, 134, 159, 176, 178, 226n60, 227n68; eccentricity, 158; fully connected 40, 65, 83, 85, 86, 87, 91; nearest neighbor, 84, 86, 90–95, 91, 94, 96; random, 39, 118, 124, 131, 134, 153, 176, 226n60, 227n68; scale free, 39, 80, 84–85, 86, 87, 90–95, 91, 94, 96, 98, 157–159, 167, 169, 172–173, 176, 179–180, 186, 188, 196, 221n18, 222n37, 231n75; small world, 39, 65, 84, 86, 90–95, 91, 94, 96, 103–104, 131, 134, 136–137, 157–158, 172, 176, 231n75
network theory: and agent-based modeling, 40; and computational social science, 30–31, 35–37, 45, 55, 192, 199; and game theory, 48, 79–80; and graph theory, 8–9, 38, 79–80; and interdependencies, 9, 37; and logical fallacies, 46; and network structure, 65, 134; and structuration, 38
networks: as a heuristic, 29–30; financial, 143, 151–155, 157–159, 160, 161, 167–169, 195; global, 26, 169, 172–173, 175, 177–178, 188–189; social, 6, 9–10, 17, 20, 32–34, 38–40, 43–46, 48, 58, 65, 72, 77, 79–80, 83–85, 87, 93–95, 98, 103–104, 112–113, 114–115, 116, 118, 118–120, 124–125, 130–131, 132, 134, 136, 139, 144, 158, 169, 176, 194, 196, 199, 226n55, 226n60, 227n69; transportation, 26, 172–174, 176–180, 181, 185–189; weighted, 176–178, 188–189
New York City, 12, 145. *See also* airports: New York JFK
New York Times, The, 5, 16, 196, 205n71
Newman, M. E. J., 179
Nexon, Daniel, 35–36, 46, 49
nodes: in agent-based models, 158–159, 161, 178–179, 183–184; defined, 8–9, 38; and levels of analysis, 56; and information dynamics, 136; interaction effects, 182, 187; and network failure, 173, 176–177, 188; in physical networks, 10; in social networks, 17, 23, 36–37; and transportation hubs, 172
noise, 22, 61, 85, 92, 98, 195–196
Nokia, 141
nonlinearity: and agent-based models, 50–52, 111; butterfly effect, 50, 175; cascades, 175; in common pool resources, 106, 109, 111; and complex adaptive systems, 2, 8, 16, 175; contagion, 175; and empirical analysis, 58; in networks, 175, 177, 186; reverberation, 175; in world politics, 18–19, 23, 35, 102–103
non–state actors, 10, 60, 174, 200
norms: altruism, 44; and common pool resources, 109–110, 116; constitutive, 37, 47; massive parallelism and, 17–18; networks and, 10, 38; reciprocity, 62; regulative, 37, 47; sanctions, 80; in world politics, 72
North Pacific Gyre, 1–2, 27
Northeast Blackout of 2003, 172
Nowak, Martin A., 79

Obama, Barack, 5, 16, 19–20, 205n72
Occupy Movement, 4, 94
Odell, John S., 64
Olson, Mancur, 105–106
Ontario, Canada, 172
ontology: and agent-based models, 54; complex adaptive systems, 31, 41,

46; computational social science, 49; globalization, 34, 192; process, 35–36, 46; state-centric, 23, 29, 76
optimization: agent strategies, 92, 94, 113, 168; and genetic algorithms, 50, 90, 182, 184, 186
organization: and complex adaptive systems, 4, 10, 60; decentralized, 72; dynamics, 4; of finance, 138, 151–152; and globalization, 1–2, 7, 26, 197; hierarchical, 10, 34; and networks, 37, 40, 85; and nonstate actors, 10; self, 2–3, 5, 7, 16–18, 191–192; spatial, 79; state-directed, 152. *See also* emergence
organizations: "chaordic," 19; and complex adaptive systems, 8, 23, 60; and globalization, 7; humanitarian, 5; international, 16, 30, 60, 78, 174, 191; and learning, 14; networks, 10–11, 34; nongovernmental, 9–10, 193; terrorist, 139, 174
Oslo Peace Process. *See* Israeli-Palestinian Peace Process
Ostrom, Elinor, 104, 106–111, 116

Pacheco, J. M., 80, 85, 93
Pacific Ocean, 1–2, 11, 20
Page, Scott E., 8, 41, 45–46, 48, 206n102
Pahre, Robert, 80
pandemics, 6, 55, 137
parallelism: and agent-based models, 49; and common pool resources, 102, 107; in complex adaptive systems, 4, 40, 48, 60; massive, 16–18, 23; and networks, 77, 176; and nonstate actors, 10, 30; in world politics, 191, 194, 196
Pareto optimality, 46, 75, 124, 147, 161, 194, 196
parrotfish, 103
parsimony, 42, 78, 81
path dependence, 35, 49, 82, 191
path length. *See* network structure: average path length

patriotic hackers, 4–6, 13, 17, 32, 34
Pauly, Daniel, 107, 110
payoffs: Battle of the Sexes, 155–156, *156*, 160; cardinal versus interval, 87–88; common pool resources, 113, 114, 116, 118–120, 128, 130, 131, 136, 139; and complex adaptive systems, 60; coordination games, 59, 74–75; and distribution games, 85–87, *86*; and information, 98, 225n37; and learning, 79, 95, 128, 138, 168; and networks, 123–124, 129, 134, 226n67; Prisoner's Dilemma, 50; sensitivity to relative gains, 97–98; Stag Hunt, 83; ultimatum game, 42
Pemantle, Robin, 79
Pentagon, 5, 37
Pepinsky, Thomas B., 50, 54, 76
Perrow, Charles, 21
perturbations, 8, 50, 84, 136, 175, 186
Peter, Goetz von, 143, 169
pheromone tagging, 12
Platteau, Jean-Philippe, 110
players. *See* game theory
political economy, 48, 145, 154, 168
population: of agents, 50, 81, 112; banks, 150; common pool resources, 107, 110, 136–137; ecological inference problem, 46; learning in, 92; and networks, 84; selection from, 12, 90, 103; size, 106; strategies within, 42–44, 81–82, 88, 104, 212n94, 226n56
Port-Au-Prince, 172
power law, 39, *158*, *178*, 179, 222n37. *See also* network structure: scale free
Power, Conrad, 79
Pragmatic Chaos, 14
prediction markets, 15–16, 136
preferences: in agent-based models, 53, 60–67, *66*, 69–74, 155–168, *157*, *160*, *162*, *166*; in Basel negotiations, 149–151; in complex adaptive systems, 60; and computational social science, 55; cycles, 58–61, *62*, 75–76;

preferences *(continued)*
  formation, 44–45, 47–48; hegemonic, 149; and learning, 193–194; and levels of analysis, 3–4, 48; logical fallacies, 8, 46–47; and markets, 168, 195; and networks, 37–38, 77–78, 144, 196, 199; of states, 47, 57, 59, 72, 149
preservation: common pool resources, 101–103, 106–108, 110, 119, 131, 194; context, 79–80, 93; of information, 12, 116; institutions, 106
Prisoner's Dilemma. *See* dilemmas: Prisoner's
Project Masiluleke, 4
ProMED, 11
property rights, 107–108
protestors, 17, 57
Provisional IRA, 174
pseudocode: *See* code: pseudo
Puhr, Claus, 158
punctuated equilibria, 24, 48, 141, 197, 207n110
Putnam, Robert D., 58, 61–62, 72–74, 155, 167

Quebec, 172

ratification procedures, 65, 67, 69, 73, 75, 165
rational choice theory, 36–37, 44, 47, 58, 199, 209n27, 212n94
rationality: assumption, 40, 199; bounded, 40, 104, 111, 139; and collective action problems, 46, 105–106; and complex systems theory, 47; game theory, 42
Real Clear Politics, 16
reciprocity, 43–44, 62, 116, 118
regimes: and agent-based models, 155–169, *156*, *157*; construction, 26, 108; finance, 25, 142–151, 229n36; hegemonic stability theory, 148; international, 59, 144; monetary, 148–149

regression: and agent-based models, 89–90, *91*, 129–130, 165; event-history (hazard) models, *135*; multicollinearity in, 227n69; ordinary least squares (OLS), *130*, *132*
regulation: and common pool resources, 101, 110; and complex adaptive systems, 33; finance, 19, 26, 32–33, 49, 75, 105, 141–146, 149–150, 152, 155, 229n36; and globalization, 224n13; and international regimes, 167; and networks, 168; self, 146; state-based, 2, 153, 169, 194
regulators: airline, 188; banking, 32–33, 138, 142, 144–146, 148–151, 153–156, 167, 169
relationalism, 35
replication: of agent-based models, 48, 54–56; and genetic algorithms, 44; of norms, 44; self, 6
Resnick, Mitchel, 215n149
resources, common pool. *See* common pool resources
resources, natural, 26, 104
risk-weighting formulas. *See* banks: risk-weighting formulas of
robustness: of agent-based models, 50; of networks, 136, 169, 172, 176–177, 189; of social structure, 45, 196
Rodrik, Dani, 149, 229n36
Rosenau, James N., 4, 16, 19, 29, 175, 204n53, 210n50, 224n13
Rousseau, Jean-Jacques, 83
Rudin, Kenneth, 16
rules: in agent-based models, 49, 51, 53–54, 61, 67, 111–112, 117–118, 124–125, 128–129, 131, 134, 139; behavioral, 46–47; and collective action problems, 194; and common pool resources, 106–107, 109, 194; in complex adaptive systems, 7–8, 40–41, 45, 60; and finance, 142–143, 145–150, 155–156, 228n18; and institutions, 62, 104; of selection, 184; transmission of, 44; in two-

level games, 65; and world politics, 197–198. *See also* genetic algorithms
rumor registries, 11
Russian-Georgian War, 5

Safari (web browser), 18
salmon, 107
San Diego, 172
San Salvador. *See* airports: San Salvador
Santa Marta, Colombia. *See* airports: Santa Marta, Colombia
Santiago. *See* airports: Santiago
Santos, F. C., 80, 85, 93
Sarkozy, Nicolas, 142
satisficing, 36, 40. *See also* rationality
Sawyer, R. Keith, 31, 37, 211n83
scale-free networks. *See* network structure: scale free
Schelling, Thomas C., 22, 36, 40, 45, 78
Schmitz, Stefan W., 158
Scholte, Jan Aart, 173, 207n114, 224n13
Schultz, Kenneth A., 73
Schumpeter, Joseph, 20, 22
science: of complexity, 221n83; computer, 200, 214n127; controversies about, 23; goals of, 48; natural, 23, 27; "normal," 200; physical, 27, 33; progress of, 25, 48; reductionism in, 46, 191; social, 27, 46, 199–200; "third way," 50. *See also* computational social science
secessionism, 3, 55
Second Coming, The, 3
securities, 32, 146, 153
Security Council, U.N., 24
segregation model, 45
Seigenthaler, John, 13, 204n63
selection: in agent-based models, 47; community enforcement and, 13; in complex adaptive systems, 11–16, 23; and evolutionary game theory, 43, 81, 90; in genetic algorithms, 50, 66, 67, 90–92, 116, 118, 181, 182–184, 188, 222n45; and innovation, 14; natural, 12, 43, 81, 212n94; fitness proportionate versus pairwise, 86, 90, 182–184, 219n35; and prediction markets, 15–16; self, 14; sexual, 12–13
self-organization. *See* emergence; organization: self
Seoul. *See* airports: Seoul
Sexes, Battle of the. *See* dilemmas: Battle of the Sexes
Shalizi, Cosma Rohilla, 179
Shambaugh, George, 85
Shanghai, 176
Sikkink, Kathryn, 72
Silicon Valley, 195
Simon, Herbert A., 36, 109
simulation: and agent-based models, 50, 52, 78, 207n114; criticisms of, 53–54; and evolutionary game theory, 44; and genetic algorithms, 74; Monte Carlo, 176; purposes, 43, 81, 111, 177–178, 198–199; research design, 82, 180; and science, 48; software, 54; and systems thinking, 52; validity, 55, 87
Singapore, 34
Sklair, Leslie, 39
Skyrms, Brian, 79
slime mold, 11–12, 41, 52
small worlds. *See* network structure: small world
Snidal, Duncan, 72, 80
social network analysis. *See* network theory
socioecological systems, 102, 104. *See also* common pool resources
sociology, 26, 35, 37, 48, 72
software: and agent-based models, 49, 214n127; open-sourced, 18; massive parallelism, 40; Network Workbench Tool v. 1.0, 158; object-oriented programming, 214n127; power grid, 6; research and development, 14; social network analysis, 119, 158. *See also* NetLogo

Soramaki, Kimmo, 157, *158*, 159
Soutchanski, Mikhail, 79
South Pole, 2
space: in agent-based models, 53, 79, 112, 120; network, 49, 77; physical, 49, 77, 79, 138; reconfiguration of, 7, 30; social, 7, 77
Spain, 198
Sparkassen, 152
Spencer, Herbert, 12
Stag Hunt. *See* dilemmas: Stag Hunt
State, U.S. Department of, 17
Stein, Arthur A., 83
Strategy of Conflict, The, 78
strategy: of Al Qaeda, 174; cooperation, 88, 89; deterrent, 34; encoding, 67, 86, 88, 112–116, *114– 115*, 117, *181*, 182, 222n45, 222n48, 225n54, 226n55; evolutionary game theory, 43, 81; evolutionarily stable, 42, 44, 212n94; in genetic algorithms, 50, 67, 90, 92, 116, 119, 182–183, *183*, 188; heterogeneity, 90; and learning, 124; measurement, 88, 90; minimax, 182; mixed, 22, 87, 218n21; tit-for-tat, 43–43, 82, 87–88, 89
Strogatz, Stephen H., 80, 84, 231n75
structuration, 45, 192, 195–196, 198
structure: and agent-based models, 49, 52, 55; biophysical, 110; and computational social science, 55; of governance, 194, 198, 224n13; levels of analysis, 4, 8, 22, 30–31, 45; logical fallacies, 8; network, 3, 6, 9–10, 17, 32, 72, 79–80, 95, 104, 144, 151–154, 157–158, 167, 169, 172–173, 176–179, 191, 199; of production, 173, 194; robustness, 196; social, 42, 44–46, 78–80, 99, 103, 136, 169, 192, 195, 199–200; spatial, 79; world politics, 4, 17, 24, 29, 33, 37–39, 60, 192, 195–196. *See also* agent-structure debate; emergence; network structure
strukturpolitik, 152

sturgeon, 101–102, 104, 107–108, 138
subsidies, 192–193
Supreme Court, U.S., 37
Switzerland, 143, 154
Syria, 95, 193
system dynamics (method), 36, 207n114
systems: agent-based models of, 49–53, 55, 111; biological, 12–13, 41, 103; change, 197–198; decomposability, 19, 109; defined, 8; emergence and, 8; financial, 32–33, 142–147, 154–155, 176, 229n36; global, 2, 4–5, 7–8, 45–47, 102, 148, 195; hierarchical, 18; health reporting, 15; imperfection of, 206n102; information, 5–6, 9, 13, 32, 153, 171, 176; international, 30–31, 35, 45, 60; massively parallel, 17–18, 48; monetary, 149; as networks, 8–10; physical, 41; self-organized, 2; shipping, 177; "system of systems," 2, 32; tightly coupled, 21; transportation, 187–189. *See also* common pool resources; complex adaptive systems; ecosystems

Tahrir Square, 77
Tarullo, Daniel K., 149
technology: agent-based model of, 112–113, *114–115*, 117, 120, *121*, 123–134, *126–127*, *130*, *132–133*, *135*; biofuels, 192; effect on common pool resources, 102–103, 106–107, 110, 137; and globalization, 7, 177, 197; information, 4, 13–14, 16, 32, 171; network effects, 18, 141; networks, 29; positive feedbacks, 103–104
Tegucigalpa, 182
Teitenberg, Tom, 107
terrorism: collective action problems, 139; cyberattacks, 34; economic targets of, 174; globalization and, 175; internet and, 13; learning, 41; networks, 85, 172; optimal terrorist,

34, 172, 182, 188; self-organization of, 10
Texas, 1
text messaging, 4–5
Thailand, 4
theories: Big Bang, 22; constructivism, 31, 37, 40, 44, 47–48; critical, 29, 37; endogenous growth, 22, 34; globalization, 26, 29, 31, 37, 45, 173–175, 197; Gramscian Marxism, 29, 37; hegemonic stability, 148; neoliberal institutionalism, 36–37, 47, 59–60, 97–98; neorealism, 47, 97–98; new economic geography, 22. *See also* complex systems theory; game theory; network theory; rational choice theory
tipping points, 73, 95, 196, 198
tit-for-tat. *See* game theory: tit-for-tat strategy
Tokyo, 172. *See also* airports: Tokyo
topology, 34, 39, 49
Toronto. *See* airports: Toronto
tournament: as mechanism of selection, 67, 90, 91, 94, 96, 182–184, 219n35; Prisoner's Dilemma, 44, 82, 87, 97
trade: balances, 192, 196, 198; Champagne fairs, 13; of endangered species, 102; of illicit goods, 139, 196; liberalization of, 174; as networks, 24, 83, 153, 158, 172–173, 176; in prediction markets, 15–16; rules of, 148–149; in world politics, 47, 145, 173–175, 191, 197, 207n113
traffic: automotive, 11, 21–22, 40–41, 52, 92; between airports, 184, 186–187; small world networks, 176
Tragedy of the Commons, 2, 46, 78, 104–105
transaction costs. *See* economics: transaction costs
transactions, 144–145, 157–159, 167
transnational advocacy groups, 10–11, 29–30, 39, 58–59, 99
transnationalism: actors, 4, 10, 59, 175; in agent-based models, 63–65, 64,

68, 70–72, 71, 75, 168–169; markets, 101, 143; networks, 35, 39, 139, 175; processes, 17, 19; systems, 35; theories, 59–60
Transportation, U.S. Department of, 173, 178
transportation: agent-based model of, 180, 181, 185–186; asset specificity of, 188; air, 172–174, 176–180, 189; costs, 171; networks, 6, 9–10, 25–26, 169, 171–172, 176, 187–189, 191; and terrorism, 174
Troitzsch, Klaus G., 207n114
trust: and common pool resources, 106; and democracy, 72; learning and, 102, 104, 116, 118, 138; norms, 45; and networks, 72
turbulence, 4, 35, 52, 55, 204n53
Twitter, 5, 17
two–level game, 58, 61, 65, 69, 73, 75, 167, 169

Uganda, 4
Ukraine, 3
uncertainty: and common pool resources, 106, 108–110, 136; constructive role of, 23; and game theory, 98, 225n37; and networks, 104; in world politics, 73
United Kingdom, 142, 154
United States: agent-based models of, 155–157, 156, 158, 161, 167, 182, 184–187; agriculture, 192; air transportation network, 172–173, 177–178, 189; armed forces, 18; automotive industry, 172; and Basel negotiations, 143–145, 148, 150, 155–156; biofuel subsidies, 192–193; border with Mexico, 195; financial crisis of 2008, 19, 32–33, 207n113; financial services network, 19, 145, 149, 152, 154, 157–159, 168, 195; Great Pacific Garbage Patch, 1; as hegemon, 149; internet, 34; Iranian protests, 17; narcotics shipments to, 172; power grid, 6, 171, 175;

United States (continued)
presidential elections, 15; and Soviet Union, 41; vulnerability to terrorism, 13, 34, 171, 177
University of Toronto, 6
Upper, Christian, 154, 157, 159
Ushahidi, 5, 11

validity, 48, 51, 53–55, 87, 98, 167, 177
vertices. See nodes
volunteers, 5, 14, 18, 20, 23, 57–58, 76
von Neumann, John, 44
voters: and climate change, 23; social networks, 20; and state preferences, 57–58, 74; unit of analysis, 55, 76

Wales, Jimmy, 13
Walker, R. B. J., 31, 37, 49
Wall Street Journal, The, 16, 141
Waltz, Kenneth N., 7, 29, 35, 192
Washington State, 107
Washington, DC, 5, 6
Washington Post, The, 5, 6, 16

water. See common pool resources: irrigation systems
Watts, Duncan J., 80, 84, 231n75
weights. See links: weights
Wendt, Alexander E., 31, 37, 45, 47, 49
Westphalian state system, 30
Wight, Colin, 45, 49
Wikipedia, 13, 17–18, 23. See also Seigenthaler, John
Wilensky, Uri, 215n149
Wilson, James, 109
win set, 65, 73–74
Wolfe, Nathan, 14
Wood, Duncan, 149
World Health Organization, 6
World Trade Organization, 219n26
World War I, 3
Worms, Andreas, 154, 157, 159

Yeats, William Butler, 3–4
Yemen, 193
Young, H. Peyton, 74
YouTube Smackdown Corps, 13
Yuma, Arizona, 172

www.ingramcontent.com/pod-product-compliance
Ingram Content Group UK Ltd.
Pitfield, Milton Keynes, MK11 3LW, UK
UKHW041928140426
5217IPUK00014B/373